Principal Acronyms

AHMSA	High Ovens Steelworks of Mexico
ASPA	Association of Aviator Pilots
ASSA	Association of Aviation Flight Attendants
CGF	Commission of Finance and Expenditure
CMC	Cananea Mining Company
DDF	Department of the Federal District
DEP	Directorate of Public Enterprises
FINASA	National Sugar Financier
FUMOSA	Monterrey Foundry
GCEP	General Coordination for Environmental Projects
HACIENDA	Ministry of Finance
LGEE	General Law of Ecological Equilibrium and Environmental Protection
MZ	Metropolitan Zone of Mexico City
NAFINSA	National Development Bank
OD	Office of Deregulation
OESA	Office of Economic and Social Analysis

OP	Office of Privatization
OPR	Office of the Presidency
PAN	National Action Party
PEMEX	Mexican Petroleums
PICCA	Comprehensive Program against Air Pollution in the Valley of Mexico
PRD	Party of the Democratic Revolution
PRI	Institutional Revolutionary Party
PRONASOL	National Solidarity Program
SCT	Ministry of Communications and Transportation
SECOFI	Ministry of Commerce and Industrial Promotion
SEDESOL	Ministry of Social Development
SEDUE	Ministry of Urban Development and Ecology
SEMIP	Ministry of Energy, Mines, and Parastatal Industries
SICARTSA	Lázaro Cárdenas-Las Truchas Steelworks
SIDERMEX	Mexican Steelworks
SNTTAM	National Union of Technicians and Workers of Aeronaves de México
SPP	Ministry of Budget and Planning
STMMRM	Mining and Metallurgical Workers of the Mexican Republic
TELMEX	Mexican Telephones

Preface

Toward the end of the twentieth century Mexico, like many developing countries, abandoned statist development policies for more market friendly, "neoliberal" ones. Despite the undeniable progress it achieved through decades of statism, Mexico's economy suffered increasing debilities and periodic crises; moreover, partly as a consequence of its development model, air pollution in the nation's capital assumed frightening proportions. From the mid-1980s onward government leaders sought to change their country's economic trajectory and ameliorate the capital's environmental woes by replacing statism with market economic policies, and employing market-oriented tactics to resolve environmental problems. Mixed results followed: in the economic realm policy makers achieved remarkable success in privatizing public sector firms and deregulating the economy; in the environmental realm, however, they made little headway.

The question this book probes is simple: Why can governments implement reform successfully sometimes, but other times they cannot? Rather than simply explaining "Mexican politics," this book speaks to the broader political dynamics behind the success or failure to implement reforms—first, by assessing new policy initiatives in multiple arenas across presidential administrations in Mexico, then by comparing Mexico's privatization experience to that of Argentina's. Two of its core contentions are that the fate of dramatic reform projects turns on coalition politics both inside and outside the state, and that institutional dynamics strongly affect the prospects of reformers' success. My own thinking on these subjects has evolved considerably over time. This book—culminating ten years of investigation—reflects that personal odyssey.

Financially, this work was supported in part by the National Science Foundation, the Mellon Foundation, the Tinker Foundation, the Fundación Harvard en México, the Center for U.S.-Mexican Studies at the University of California, San Diego, and both Harvard University's Graduate School of Arts and Sciences and Department of Government. At various stages, the Autonomous Technological

Institute of Mexico, the Weatherhead Center for International Affairs at Harvard, the Center for U.S.-Mexican Studies, and Middlebury College all provided institutional and intellectual support.

While this book bears a single author, in many respects it has been a collaborative effort in which I have incurred a number of debts. It is my pleasure to express thanks to those who extended me courtesies, shared their insights, opened doors (physical and intellectual), read drafts, and offered valuable critiques along the way. I deeply appreciate the able research assistance provided by Eduardo Campos, whose good humor, analytic skills, and exceptional connections proved invaluable. Special thanks go to Mary Enríquez Schneider; to David Ronfeldt of the RAND Corporation; to David Kang of Dartmouth College; to Rafael Fernández de Castro, Denise Dresser, Emilio Zebadua, and Blanca Heredia at the Autonomous Technological Institute of Mexico; to Wayne Cornelius, Kevin Middlebrook, Van Whiting, and Eric Van Young of the Center for U.S.-Mexican Studies; and to Michael Kraus of Middlebury College. I offer special thanks to a number of Mexican policy makers and political actors who walked me through the intricacies of their experience in the events this book examines. These individuals, whom I promised anonymity, graciously shared their time and this study would not have been possible without their kind assistance. I hope the final product does justice to the interest they exhibited in this project.

Finally, I am grateful to my professors at Harvard University, and especially to my mentors, Jorge Domínguez, Merilee Grindle, and Peter Hall, of the Weatherhead Center for International Affairs, John F. Kennedy School of Government, and Center for European Studies, respectively. Each has been extraordinarily supportive, constructively critical, and a source of great intellectual stimulation and encouragement.

Part I

Introduction and Theory

Chapter 1

Caught in the Paradigm Shift

During the past few years, the Latin American countries have gone through major economic reforms that have greatly changed the region's economic landscape. What started as an isolated and slow process . . . has become a sweeping movement affecting virtually every country in the region.

—Sebastian Edwards

The 1980s and 1990s saw a paradigm shift sweep the developing world as governments abandoned statist development models for more market-friendly, "neoliberal" ones. In scores of countries the proprietary state and extensive regulation gave way to divestment, deregulation, and other market-oriented reforms. Nowhere did more governments embrace neoliberalism than in Latin America, and among these, none pursued a more extensive, sustained, and in some respects, successful campaign than Mexico.

To greatly oversimplify the regional experience, inaction, muddling, false starts, and policy reversal often characterized much of the reform efforts in Brazil, Ecuador, Argentina, and Venezuela, respectively. But from 1983 onward the Mexican government divested hundreds of state-owned enterprises, deregulated dozens of economic sectors, and transformed the economy from a highly protected to a much more open one. Finally, the Salinas administration (1988-94) accelerated the reforms considerably and expanded the scope of market-oriented policies to include environmental policy reform.

This book investigates the politics of Mexico's policy transformations between 1988 and 1994. Its chief focus is three critical areas of policy change: privatization, deregulation, and environmental policy reform. In each policy realm the government devoted considerable time, energy, and resources to reform. Yet, despite these efforts its record of successful implementation was mixed: while new economic policies were implemented fully, environmental reforms were not.

3

In Mexico and beyond, successful policy reform remains one of the key political issues of our time, for the outcome of these initiatives helps determine "who
gets what." The questions of why some governments can implement reform successfully while others fail, or why the *same* government succeeds in one area—but
not another—are of critical importance and lie at the heart of this study. Chapter 2
outlines the framework used to analyze the politics of policy reform. Chapters 3
through 5 apply this framework to five cases of attempted policy change, cases
that differ both by policy realm and outcome. To help generalize the study's findings beyond the Mexican context, chapter 6 employs the framework to assess divestiture dynamics in Argentina. The conclusion draws out the study's broader
theoretical implications, details some of the major political/social consequences
Mexico's reforms produced, and assesses the continued viability of reform in light
of these changes. The balance of this chapter briefly profiles Mexico's political,
economic, and environmental experience preceding the reforms, reviews the record
of accomplishment and failure, previews the argument to come, and situates the
study within the existing theoretical literature.

Backdrop to Policy Change

The Economy: From Growth to Crisis

As in many developing countries, the Mexican government traditionally took
an active, interventionist role in economic development. Under the guidance of
the Institutional Revolutionary Party (PRI), the government consistently exhibited
strong predilections for statist orientations that characterize "late, late"
industrializers.[1] Vested with exclusive constitutional rights in key economic sectors, the state established development banks, nationalized oil production, and
through planned and unplanned means, became owner of a host of enterprises.[2]
By 1982 the state owned 1,155 enterprises in sectors ranging from steel, aviation,
and mining, to commercial banking and telecommunications.[3] It also had con-
structed a complicated framework to regulate trade, foreign investment, transportation, and other sectors.

Statism changed Mexico's political landscape in important ways. Public enterprises and regulatory frameworks produced a set of beneficiaries whose interests depended on maintaining statist policies. Organized labor grew accustomed to
generous public sector contracts, state ministries acquired interests in complex
regulations and public enterprise operations, and private sector groups derived
protection, subsidies, rents, and other benefits from statist policies. In sum, statism
spawned powerful groups of beneficiaries who would struggle to protect their interests when the neoliberal reform movement threatened to sweep them away.

For decades, however, statism paid handsome development dividends, and from the mid-1950s to the early 1970s Mexico's economy grew, on average, by 6.5 percent per year.[4] By the mid-1970s, though, this "golden era" had passed. The policy paradigm that fostered robust growth had been undermined by mismanagement, debt, technological advances, and evolving international patterns of production, finance, and trade. By 1982 growth was replaced by what became a protracted depression, investment by enormous debt, and development had spawned frightening environmental problems.

The Environmental Crisis

By far, the most vexing environmental problem Mexico faced was air pollution in Mexico City. Here, a unique geography, concentrated industrial base, extraordinary population density, and a motor vehicle fleet numbering in the millions caused pollution levels to soar. By the early 1980s public concern forced environmental issues onto the government's policy agenda. Critics had christened Mexico City one of the world's most polluted urban centers, and air pollution had become the government's number one environmental concern.

In response, the government created a cabinet-level environmental ministry in 1983, and concentrated administrative and enforcement responsibilities at the federal level. The Ecology Ministry adopted a *command and control* strategy to curb air pollution.[5] In general, this involved devising and enforcing emissions norms, mandating "clean" technologies in the energy sector, creating inspection programs for industry and motor vehicles, and either fining industrial polluters or forcing their relocation outside of Mexico City.

For the most part, though, the execution of these responsibilities was spotty and ineffectual, and the policy goals only partially achieved. Pollution levels remained high, fines were levied infrequently, and relocations were rarer still. A major impediment to pollution control was Mexico's deepening economic crisis, which diverted public spending toward debt servicing. As a result, by the mid-1980s both the government's environmental record and its environmental ministry came under severe, sustained public criticism. It was in this context of economic and environmental crisis that Mexico's policies began to change—at first, gradually, and then with increasing speed.

Assessing the Reform Record

The reform movement began cautiously under President Miguel de la Madrid (1982–1988). On the economic front, the administration began to sell, liquidate, or transfer small-scale public enterprises to state governments in 1983, and to rationalize economic regulations.[6] In 1985 the government abandoned statism altogether; in 1986 Mexico finally joined the General Agreement on Tariffs and Trade, and thereafter, the pace of reform accelerated. Under President Carlos Salinas de Gortari (1988-94) the state moved aggressively to privatize large-scale assets and deregulate the economy. Within three years Salinas had purged the government's portfolio of many politically important enterprises and deregulated dozens of economic sectors.

By 1988 the reform movement had transcended economics to include environmental policies as well, especially air pollution. First, the state began to retreat from the centralized approach that marked its early antipollution efforts. A new General Law of Ecological Equilibrium transferred various administrative and enforcement responsibilities from the federal to lower levels of government. The government also adopted the "polluter pays principle" to reduce public outlays for pollution control,[7] and policy reformers began crafting strategies to increase compliance with emissions standards through market-like incentives. The basic objectives behind all these initiatives were to replace an ineffective, centralized program with a decentralized approach and supplement a traditional *command and control* strategy with economic instruments.

Because my primary goal is to explain the politics of neoliberal policy reform, succeeding chapters assess the success or failure to implement new policies in strictly *political* terms. That is to say, "success" is not a question of whether any set of reforms actually accomplished its broader economic or environmental goals. For example, whether divestment really increased efficiency in privatized firms, or deregulation lowered consumer costs, is immaterial to the purpose at hand (although some data suggest this in fact occurred).[8] In political terms, success simply means *implementing* a specific policy such that the government realizes its most fundamental goals as elaborated when that policy is first announced. Thus, a successful divestment initiative is one that announces the privatization of company X, and in the end, actually privatizes company X; or one that announces the deregulation of sector Y, and goes on to fully deregulate that sector, etc.

Doubtless some may find this definition of success somewhat "narrow"; however, reform achievements of this sort are hardly trivial. Governments face extraordinary difficulties advancing aggressive reform campaigns. Any attempt to understand the politics of reform, therefore, must begin with the recognition that the ability to attain success even in these narrow terms constitutes a remarkable accomplishment; hence, the bulk of this study centers on this theme.

That said, in the long term a crucial subtext of political success entails the capacity to implement what the government perceives as "good" policies in "good" ways—i.e., those which kindle broader social acceptance of reform and bolster a reformist government's political legitimacy. Here, patterns of policy implementation assume greater importance. Because policy changes of the magnitude examined here invariably penalize important constituencies, failure to implement reforms in ways that address at least some of the concerns "losers" harbor will draw down a government's political capital and jeopardize prospects for sustaining reform projects over the long run. I will return to these points shortly, and develop their significance more extensively in chapter 2.

A close examination of Mexico's overall reform project supports three principal findings. First, the government's record on economic reforms constitutes clear *political* success. Salinas, like his predecessor, claimed he would divest the state's "nonstrategic" public enterprises and create "a clear system" of economic rules by deregulating the economy.[9] On balance, these goals were met. Between 1982 and 1993 the state divested 942 "nonstrategic" public enterprises, and under Salinas, deregulated nearly fifty different economic sectors.[10] Consequently, today the state's *entrepreneurial reach* is decidedly smaller because of privatization, and thanks to deregulation, its *regulatory reach* is market-conforming, rather than market-shaping or market-resistant. These accomplishments demonstrate the government attained its fundamental goal of economic policy reform.

In the chapters that follow I detail the political dynamics behind the Mexican government's achievements with respect to a select set of reform initiatives. These include the privatization of Mexico's national airlines, steelworks, and second largest copper mine (sixth largest, worldwide), and the deregulation of a critical economic sector, freight transport. I also explain the politics behind the government's failed effort to reform Mexico City's air pollution regime. To produce truly meaningful findings among this small set of cases, I employ a "structured, focused" comparative approach. Following the lead of Alexander George, among other things this entails the careful "selection of *appropriate* cases for controlled comparison."[11] Accordingly, the case studies selected cut across policy arenas (privatization, deregulation and environmental policy) and across presidential administrations; they also vary in terms of implementation outcomes.

In assessing the factors behind successful reform I have found the comparison of environmental and economic reform efforts of significant analytic value, given the parallels exhibited in terms of their scope, motives, substance, and determinants of success. To begin, nowhere outside the economy did Mexican leaders attempt as radical a policy change and for similar reasons—the failure of past policy and the intellectual/practical appeal of a more market-like approach. Moreover, the fact that a good share of Mexico's environmental problems had roots in prior development policies only bolstered the logic of addressing environmental issues via market incentives. Finally, because the same factors which proved critical to outcomes in economic cases were operative in the environmental realm, by assessing the failure to reform environmental policy we subject the study's causal arguments to the "multiple tests" standard required of persuasive social science research.[12]

The second major finding of this study concerns the pattern of implementation, and here, significant variation exists across cases, and within policy arenas. The most salient point is that while reformers met stiff opposition in every case examined, in *some* cases the state employed blunt coercive tactics to implement policy change. For example, to divest the national airlines and copper mine the government busted unions, prosecuted and jailed labor leaders, and even unleashed the military to quash opposition and implement new policy. Yet it did not use these tactics to divest the national steelworks or deregulate the freight transport sector—even though labor and an entrenched trucking cartel vehemently opposed both measures. These dissimilar outcomes represent significant variation in the dependent variable (success) and raise important analytical questions: Why did implementation carry a punitive edge in some reform episodes but not others? Why did the pattern of implementation vary across policy realms?

To answer these questions satisfactorily is no mean feat, because from the outset these variations caution against explaining outcomes based on systemic factors alone (i.e., Mexican authoritarianism, centralized power or presidentialism). The main drawback to such an approach is that these systemic factors hold the capacity for coercion "constant" throughout the reform period, while the actual exercise of state coercion varied. Yet, if systemic factors do not explain implementation outcomes adequately, what does? On this point, existing scholarship on Mexico's reform experience provides little theoretical traction. Most studies of the reforms correctly note the incidence of coercive implementation, but do not address the issue of noncoercive implementation in a systematic, theoretically rigorous manner.[13] To understand the politics of reform fully, we need to explain the implementation patterns, identify conditions that "trigger" the state's coercive power, plus assess the extent to which such tactics *mattered* to the aggregate success of Mexico's reform project.

Succeeding chapters discuss the reasons why the state employed coercion selectively, and the consequences of doing so. In brief, struggles over the distribution of policy costs color all efforts to implement new policy,[14] and in Mexico, the pattern of implementation is strongly influenced by the degree to which reformers compensate losers for the costs of policy change. To cite just one example: when divestment threatens to shrink the size of unionized labor in privatized public firms, generous severance packages or worker training can offset the costs of lost jobs. Such compensation reduces the intensity of labor opposition, and thereby, increases the likelihood of implementing change noncoercively. Not all costs *can* be recompensed, of course. Sometimes, for political, practical, or economic reasons reformers were unwilling to (or simply could not) compensate all cost-bearers to the point of pacification. In these cases, reformers chose to impose the costs of policy change on reform opponents, reaping the public's acclaim in some instances but incurring its wrath in others. As we shall see, more than simply systemic factors, it was the decisions made regarding the "costs" of policy change that influenced implementation patterns most directly. And depending on time and circumstance, coercion either enhanced or tarnished the government's legitimacy, affecting its capacity to advance the reform project accordingly.

The third major finding is that in contrast to its economic achievements, the government largely failed to implement environmental policy reforms. Among the state's principal goals were to decentralize administrative and enforcement responsibilities, and incorporate economic incentives to complement traditional *command and control*. By December 1988 decentralization had been achieved; but for the next five years, the government failed to implement both the "polluter pays principle" and other market-like incentives reformers sought. By mid-1993 these policy makers had thrown in the towel and abandoned any hope of reforming Mexico's environmental regime before the Salinas term expired.

In broad terms, then, Mexico's record of reform is impressive, yet mixed. In the economic policy realm the government implemented its reforms fully; in the environmental policy realm, it did not. In some respects, this outcome is quite surprising. Like its predecessor, the Salinas regime enjoyed enormous presidential power; and even *more* than its predecessor, it was staffed by savvy politicians, dominated by highly skilled technocrats, and publicly committed to environmental improvement. Yet despite these advantages, it made little headway in environmental policy reform. Why?

One possibility might simply be that some policies are *harder* to change or implement than others, and that the complexity of different policy issues accounts for differential outcomes. Indeed, some policy analysts suggest that the success of implementation varies across policy types and issues, depending upon the degree of change required and the degree of consensus involved for any given case.[15]

There is no doubt that degrees of complexity increase as one moves from deregulation to privatization, to environmental policy reforms. Nor is there any question that policy makers must develop increasingly sophisticated approaches to deal with these policy problems. For example, to reform regulatory policies only requires the state to stop doing something it has previously done, but to privatize public enterprises the state must do something *new*—i.e., sell public enterprises rather than create and manage them. This requires greater administrative capacity to assess state assets and draft appropriate sales packages. To reform air pollution policies is more complicated still, because these initiatives seek to remedy problems caused by complex interactions between production, transportation, geography, and demographic factors.

There are plausible reasons, then, to see the complexity of policy problems as a major determinant of successful reform, and the contrast between the government's economic and environmental achievements appears to support such a position. Still, this proposition does not pass close scrutiny because the actual outcomes of the reform initiatives differ markedly from expected results. As will be shown, the divestment of Mexico's national airlines was simpler and less complicated than that of the national copper mine, which in turn, was simpler than selling the national steelworks. But increasing complexity does not explain why *all* these divestment initiatives were implemented successfully, nor why the state employed coercion to implement reforms in *less* complex cases (copper) than more complicated ones (steel). To be sure, the complexity of policy problems tests the state's capacity to implement policy change;[16] but complexity itself cannot fully account for Mexico's mixed record of success.

The Politics of "Successful" Reform: An Overview

Implementing market reforms successfully is no easy task. As Bates and Krueger note, throughout the 1980s and 1990s many governments "made repeated efforts [at reform] with little result."[17] Since even the record of a committed reformer like Mexico is mixed, understanding the reasons behind success or failure has real-world implications. Yet, how should we approach this subject? Which factors most determine success or failure? To begin, we must recognize that policy change—from formulation to implementation—is a political process produced through political dynamics within and outside the state. For the most part, formulation occurs inside the state and culminates in policy adoption. Alternatively, implementation typically involves interaction between state and nonstate actors. At no point, however, is the reform process inherently "easy"; in fact, it often is quite difficult. Politically, it is difficult because policy change affects the interests of multiple actors in government and out; and these actors—whether pro or con reform—will strive to protect and promote their interests.

Understanding these dynamics is the first step toward identifying the major determinants of success or failure. Thus, throughout this book my basic argument rests on two fundamental propositions. First, to *formulate and adopt* comprehensive reform packages requires the development of a cohesive coalition inside the state—a coalition committed to reformist ideas, resistant to bureaucratic challenges, and sufficiently powerful to translate policy ideas into government policy. Second, to *implement reforms successfully,* this coalition must win the support of actors outside the state, specifically among those whose interests the reforms threaten.

Due to the nature of neoliberal reforms—and of politics—neither condition is easy to meet. Inside the government a single reform (like deregulation) can affect operations in multiple agencies; and to complicate matters further, neoliberal agendas typically consist of a policy *package.* This makes cross-agency coordination and support crucial to formulating and adopting such initiatives, yet generating this support is no mean feat. Even in a centralized political system like Mexico's, bureaucracies have their own interests, and often resist new policies that jeopardize them.[18] Only a strong, strategically placed coalition, therefore, can obstruct opponents inside the state and push reforms successfully from formulation to adoption.

Yet, victory within the state is only half the battle; the reforms still must be implemented successfully. A crucial aspect of this process is the coalition's capacity to expand its support base outside the state to include at least some of those most likely to oppose policy change. Typically, these opponents are those who bear the "costs" of policy change (as measured in lost jobs, rents, privileges, benefits, etc.). To the degree the coalition can compensate such "losers" to help defray their costs, opposition declines and the prospects of successful implementation improve accordingly.

Thus, powerful coalitions and cost compensation are critical to successful implementation. In instances where these conditions hold, governments can advance a reform agenda more successfully; where such conditions fail to emerge, they cannot. This book, then, explains the success or failure to implement reform by examining the impact of coalitional politics, and by analyzing the process whereby the costs of reform are offset or recompensed. As we shall see, these dynamics strongly influence the prospects of successful policy change.

Explaining Policy Reform: Contending Perspectives

As the 1980s gave way to the 1990s, the paradigm shift in development policy sparked keen scholarly interest. Political scientists and economists scrambled to explain why some reform campaigns had succeeded while others had not. Their efforts, in turn, spawned a broad body of literature that has advanced our knowledge of policy change in many respects. But the arguments generated to explain policy reform are not altogether consistent, comprehensive, nor entirely convincing. Some lines of argumentation explain the "why" of reform, others the "how"; some focus on policy implementation to the neglect of policy formulation or adoption, while others the reverse. Perhaps their most prominent deficiency, however, is an underdeveloped conception of the linkages between reform stages, i.e., formulation, adoption, and successful implementation. This, I argue, derives from the absence of a fully articulated concept of coalition politics.

Adjustment Arguments

One strain of analysis that emerged early on might be termed the "adjustment arguments."[19] These tightly focused, cross-national studies detail the impact external shocks and pressure had on national development strategies. While they pursue various lines of inquiry, some form of adjustment argument is prominent in each. These accounts have explained a great deal about why governments in developing nations undertook neoliberal reforms. Specifically, they suggest that dramatic shifts in global market forces—especially changing financial flows—created economic and political problems of such magnitude they compelled states to respond through policy innovation. Moreover, the urgency to adjust was compounded by external pressure from international financial institutions.[20]

For Latin America, the basic adjustment argument begins with the international debt crisis of the 1980s. Thanks to overborrowing and the aggressive recycling of petrodollars, the region as a whole owed over $330 billion by 1982 (Mexico's debt was $105 billion). The inability to meet interest payments slowed foreign capital inflows to a crawl. This shutoff in foreign credit, coupled with capital flight, inflation, and oil shocks systematically defunded statist programs. These developments placed Latin governments in an exposed position—prone to domestic instability and vulnerable to pressure from multilateral lending institutions who forcefully advocated a more orthodox policy approach. In Mexico and throughout Latin America, the result was a widespread trend away from statism as governments adjusted into neoliberal programs.[21]

Besides explaining the "why" of neoliberal reforms, one of the most useful contributions of the adjustment literature is its explanation for the general timing of the paradigm shift in developing countries. Where such arguments are less helpful, however, is explaining why—despite intense external pressures—only *some* governments were able to forge and implement reform projects successfully. The critical questions that remain, then, are what determines successful policy formulation and implementation.

Autonomy Arguments

Another strain of analysis took up these issues by suggesting the key factor separating success from failure was the degree of autonomy the state—or key state actors—enjoyed from social and bureaucratic pressures. One of the major contributions state autonomy scholars made to the policy discourse was an understanding that states are more than neutral mediators between contending social forces or mere tools of any one social class. Rather, these scholars claimed states are separate, distinct entities that can pursue their own interests even to the disadvantage of privileged groups or social classes.[22]

This insight influenced subsequent work on the rise of new market policies; because reform engenders strong opposition from some quarters, autonomy appeared crucial if reformers were to achieve their goals.[23] Three strands of argument that emerged from the "generic," state autonomy literature bear directly on the reform process. One explains reform outcomes in reference to systemic power relations, a second concerns the composition and structural position of the policy making elite, and the third centers on the concept of "embedded autonomy."

The first variant of autonomy arguments emphasizes the influence systemic-level factors exert over policy outcomes. Specifically, it is argued that concentrated authority is essential to undertake market reforms in developing countries.[24] Typically, this type of autonomy stems from a political system's basic institutional design. Systems that disperse power play to the strength of reform opponents. They facilitate effective antireform lobbying, create procedural and bureaucratic veto points, and inhibit the rapid, stealthy initiatives some deem crucial to undertake market reforms.[25] Conversely, political systems that concentrate power help "insulate" decision makers from societal pressures, enabling reformers to avoid these traps.

With respect to policy elites, the key factor is the existence of a committed, technocratic "change team," sheltered from societal and bureaucratic pressures, backed by the head of state, and vested with sufficient authority to formulate and execute tough policy choices.[26] Whether it is the "Chicago Boys" of Pinochet's

Chile, Mexico's "Ivy League" group, or the foreign-trained "two-passport Turks" of Turkey, governments that implemented reforms most successfully did so through the work of skilled, competent technocrats who enjoyed strong executive support. The impact of insulated, technocratic "change teams" is well documented. Throughout the developing world (including Mexico), the most successful reform campaigns were those where such groups—aided by strong executive support—led the charge.[27]

The third strand of autonomy arguments centers upon the notion of "embedded autonomy," a hybrid concept developed by sociologist Peter Evans. "Embedded autonomy" is defined first, as policy makers' capacity to formulate policies and adopt them unencumbered by constituent pressures, and second, by the maintenance of external ties that permit reformers to monitor, assess, and shape societal reactions to government initiatives. It is this combination of internal coherence and external connectedness, Evans suggests, that facilitates both the formulation of new policies and their implementation and consolidation.[28]

The recent work on state autonomy has sharpened our understanding of how policy reform actually occurs in developing countries. Autonomy arguments speak directly to the issue of why some governments can advance reforms contrary to the preference of important state and societal actors. Also, the most recent approaches represent an advance over early "generic" state autonomy arguments—which neither help us make accurate predictions (since how much autonomy is required for success is hard to determine a priori), nor explain just how "autonomous states" actually produce and implement reform successfully.

Still, even these refinements are limited in their explanatory power. Pure systemic explanations, for example, overpredict outcomes. Consider the Mexican case, where systemic factors like centralized, top-down decision making and presidentialism concentrate power vertically (at the national level) and horizontally (within the executive).[29] Ceteris paribus, such factors should tip the balance toward reformers; and in fact, some studies of the Salinas reforms confirm a correlation between presidential power and successful policy change.[30] Yet, if systemic factors really are the sine qua non of success, what then explains Mexico's failed efforts at environmental policy reform? A systemic argument cannot account for this outcome, nor explain how reforms that germinate inside autonomous states are successfully implemented thereafter. These are real problems, and they are problems only partly solved by the notion of autonomous "change teams."

Basically, the "change team" concept highlights a fundamental element of state capacity, and is developed most fully by John Waterbury. Composed of highly trained, insulated technocrats, these teams provide governments the technical capacity required to craft coherent reform programs. For Waterbury, this capacity is essential to formulate and advance reforms inside the state (an environment steeped in bureaucratic interests), and is made effective only via strong executive support: "the crucial factor [behind success]," he notes, "is the public backing of the team by the head of state."[31]

Since policy technocrats are almost always political appointees their need for executive support is clear. But to explain the success of change teams this way still leaves two major analytical problems. First, executive backing is far too nebulous a variable to operationalize the change team concept effectively. For one thing it leads too easily to post hoc, tautological analysis (i.e., reforms in country X succeeded or failed because the president did or did not support them); for another, the process by which executives provide reformers enough autonomy to overcome opponents inside the state is underdeveloped. Are these insulated positions the product of new legislation? Of organizational changes? Are team members dependent for autonomy solely on executive initiative, or can they somehow create it themselves?

In response to these questions (and in contrast to Waterbury) this book stresses the role reformers played over that of the executive. Evidence in subsequent chapters will demonstrate that in every case of successful policy reform, it was change team members themselves who orchestrated their own autonomy, either by altering institutional rules and organizational structures to their advantage, or by proposing legal initiatives to accomplish the same. To be sure, the Mexican president signed off on these measures, but he was not their architect. Put differently, the systemic power of the Mexican presidency was a necessary but insufficient cause of reformers' autonomy. To employ the change team concept effectively we also must resolve a second analytical challenge. Even with the president's backing it is not at all clear how (or why) autonomous change teams can implement reforms successfully over societal opposition. On this point, the idea of "embedded autonomy" provides some helpful insights.

According to Evans, once a change team is assembled and supported by the chief executive, it still must have an appropriate "apparatus" to implement new policies successfully, and this means more than providing technocrats an insulated enclave.[32] Rather, it entails substantial state restructuring such that autonomous reformers are bound to societal groups in ways that facilitate "continual negotiation and renegotiation of goals and policies."[33] Such give and take between policy makers and external actors lies at the heart of successful implementation. It is on this basis Evans explains successful industrialization in Japan, South Korea, and Taiwan. Though specifics varied, these governments achieved embedded autonomy—internal bureaucratic cohesion coupled with external linkages—and became prototypes of the developmental state.[34]

Yet Evans is the first to concede that "few states" boast the features that approximate his ideal type of embedded autonomy, and that restructuring a state to fit his model "is a project of decades, if not generations."[35] As we shall see, Mexico's policy transformations occurred much more rapidly. Moreover, the utility of applying a concept designed to explain state expansion (i.e., industrialization) to policy reforms that seek "state shrinkage," is debatable: many of the goals and a great deal of the politics are qualitatively different. The former allows the state to distribute benefits to select groups; the latter requires the state to administer pain.

Still, there is a powerful insight in Evans's position, and one that provides a useful corrective to a purely systemic or "change team" approach. Because these latter two emphasize dynamics inside the state, they speak mainly to issues of policy formulation and adoption. The virtues of Evans's logic, on the other hand, are threefold: (1) its concern with the reform process as a whole—from formulation through implementation, (2) its recognition that implementation occurs, in part, outside the state, and (3) its appreciation that state-societal interaction is crucial to successful implementation. This logic underscores a key element of my argument. Successful implementation is as much political as instrumental, because it requires that actors *affected* by policy change will *accept* (if not support) it. To succeed in these endeavors reformers must build societal support for undesired, "costly" policy change. The question remaining, then, is how?

Coalition Arguments

Arguments that deal most directly with this issue focus on coalition politics and enter the discourse on market reforms at two points. First, prior statist development models typically spawned "classic" ISI (import-substitution industrialization) coalitions, composed of the political elite, state managers, organized labor, large industrialists, and sometimes, the military.[36] Second, because the shift from statism to neoliberalism penalizes ISI constituents, it disrupts these coalitions and threatens successful policy change.[37] To solve this dilemma astute reformers must either construct a pro-reform coalition based on a new set of policy beneficiaries, or alternatively, find some means to retain support from aggrieved parties.[38] In either case the task is to package reforms in ways that generate near-term winners, and the more reformers can accomplish this, the more likely implementation will succeed.

To date, one of the most nuanced accounts of how coalition politics facilitated market reforms is that advanced by Edward Gibson, who explains the success of reform projects in Argentina and Mexico as a function of effective coalitional restructuring.[39] According to Gibson, both the Menem and Salinas administrations recast their country's traditional ISI coalitions to ensure the success of new market policies. They did so by selecting winners and losers from among business and labor circles, then rewarding these new constituents with tangible economic and political benefits. The result was the displacement of old, ISI-dependent coalition members by new members who were internationally competitive (in the case of business), adaptable to flexible labor markets (in the case of unions), and therefore, inclined to support the reformist regimes.

Like Gibson, other scholars have framed their analysis of policy reform, in part, around the coalition dynamics outlined above. Waterbury, for example, argues that as the reform process deepens, almost without exception reformist governments face the prospects of coalitional "dissolution, or at least . . . realignment"; Haggard and Webb contend that coalitions between state reformers, labor, and business are essential to successful reform, while Stephan Haggard and Robert Kaufman assert "no reform can be sustained in the longer run unless it appeals to, or creates, a new coalition of beneficiaries."[40] And Mick Moore specifically employs Gibson's coalitional model to explain Sri Lanka's reform experience.[41]

By focusing on state-societal interaction, coalition analysis captures the fundamental political nature of policy implementation and helps fill the gaps left by autonomy explanations of market reforms. However, as currently employed, coalition analysis demonstrates two major deficiencies with respect to explaining policy reform. First, these arguments emphasize coalition formation between state and nonstate actors. Since implementation involves such interaction, this focus is quite appropriate; however, it downplays or ignores how coalitions inside the state affect the prospects of successful reform. The next chapter spells out why this oversight seriously restricts our ability to explain the reform process. Second, despite the consensus that coalitions *matter* for implementation, the factors that actually confer power on coalitions, that is, which explain why a particular reform coalition might "win," remain sketchy, at best. These limitations present opportunities to advance the study of policy reform, and constitute one of the major tasks of chapter 2.

Finally, it is worth stressing that a study of Mexico's reform experience invariably offers an array of intriguing research possibilities. Crony capitalism and the corruption of Mexico's privatization process (by which the friends of President Salinas enriched themselves), the extent to which centralized, closed-door policy deliberations offset the presumed democratizing tendencies of marketization, the broader political repercussions of reform (e.g., could the ruling party survive the dismantling of Mexico's expansive public sector?), or the post-1994 collapse of the "Mexican Miracle" and Carlos Salinas's subsequent fall from grace, are subjects worthy of entire volumes. Especially given the dramatic events in Mexico since 1994, such topics invite serious investigation. While this work will of necessity touch upon some of these issues, due to space constraints it cannot examine them in depth. Consequently, this book is less about "Mexican politics," per se (what some might term a classic area study), than about the broader political dynamics of successful policy reform. This focus, in turn, requires an analytic approach that parts company somewhat with methods often employed to explain Mexican politics.

Those familiar with the Mexico-centric political and policy analysis literature will recognize commonalties between this work and that body of scholarship. Both note the influence Mexico's centralized political system exerts over the policy process; similarly, both stress the importance of collaboration between state actors in producing policy output. Still, the basic analytic framework advanced in this book (and developed fully in chapter 2) is fundamentally different.

In explaining political and policy dynamics Mexico-centric literature tends to stress (with some notable exceptions) systemic, centralized, presidential authority and the political alliance networks commonly termed *camarillas*. Centralization promotes a closed door, top-down policy making style with opportunities to influence policy output reserved to a select elite.[42] *Camarillas,* meanwhile, are loyalty-based, patron/client political networks that link individuals of different political status, ministries, and levels of government. They are pyramidal structures linked vertically and horizontally to one another which consist of a political benefactor and various clients who seek career advancement. They facilitate information-gathering (an important resource for political aspirants); they advance their memberships up the career ladder en masse, generally in time with the six-year cycle of presidential terms; and they work on the basis of confidence, collaboration, and loyalty. *Camarillas* are ubiquitous in Mexican politics, and the most important *camarilla*—the one to which all significant *camarillas* are linked—is that of the incumbent president.[43]

Some studies have employed centralization and *camarillas* quite profitably to explain both a president's capacity to direct (or redirect) policy, plus the incentives subordinates have to support a president's policy agenda.[44] This approach has advanced our knowledge of Mexican politics considerably. Yet notwithstanding their value, traditional Mexico-centric concepts have limitations too. In terms of explaining the policy outcomes addressed in this book, the limits of pure systemic arguments have already been noted. *Camarillas,* meanwhile, exhibit limitations as well.

To begin, despite the allegiance owed to a patron, *camarilla* members remain self-interested actors, with sometimes quite distinct policy preferences (indeed, diversity is one property that helps make *camarillas* valuable to patrons). Coupled with the competition between members for influence, advancement and favor, this diversity can lead members far afield of the close, collaborative relations characteristic of coalitions at the heart of this study. A classic example occurred in 1986 when an intense policy struggle erupted among key members of President de la Madrid's *camarilla* against the backdrop of external debt, ongoing structural adjustment measures, and the collapse of world oil prices. At issue were the direction of future economic policy and the jostling of position for presidential succession. As Judith Teichman demonstrates, this clash pit Finance Minister Jesus Silva Herzog against Budget Minister Carlos Salinas de Gortari; the former pushed hard for stricter austerity in line with International Monetary Fund (IMF) prescriptions; the latter sought less draconian measures, a tougher negotiating stance toward the IMF, and more external borrowing.[45] In the end, Silva Herzog lost both the policy dispute and his job, while Salinas saw his political fortunes soar to become de la Madrid's heir apparent.

As this incident illustrates, the mere existence and operation of *camarillas* do not automatically ensure close policy collaboration between members (or even policy agreement). This, in turn, cautions against employing *camarillas* as the basic unit of analysis to explain the politics of reform. It further suggests that despite apparent similarities, *camarillas* are not simply "coalitions by another name," nor do they offer equivalent analytic leverage. While *camarillas* shed light on the peculiarities of Mexican politics, research based largely on this concept is unlikely to yield findings of robust comparative value. By contrast, a coalitional framework is less context-bound. This property permits close scrutiny of the determinants of successful reform in Mexico, plus situates Mexico within a broader body of theoretically informed policy literature. The resulting analysis generates findings that capture fully the essence of Mexico's experience, yet are of wider theoretical significance than a more generic area studies approach could provide.

Notes

1. The effects of "late, late" industrialization include partial or complete state ownership of certain productive facilities, and a host of protectionist regulations affecting trade, investment, commerce, production, and distribution. See Albert Hirschman, "The Political Economy of Import-Substituting Industrialization in Latin America," *Quarterly Journal of Economics* 82, no. 1 (February 1968): 1–32.

2. Douglas C. Bennett and Kenneth E. Sharpe, *Transnational Corporations versus the State: The Political Economy of the Mexican Auto Industry* (Princeton, N.J.: Princeton University Press, 1985); see also Oscar Humberto Vera Ferrer, "The Political Economy of Privatization in Mexico," in William Glade, ed., *Privatization of Public Enterprises in Latin America* (San Francisco, Calif.: ICS Press, 1991).

3. *The Divestiture Process in Mexico* (México, D.F.: Secretaría de Hacienda y Crédito Público, 1991).

4. See Robert E. Looney, *Mexico's Economy: A Policy Analysis with Forecasts to 1990* (Boulder, Colo.: Westview, 1978), 15; and Phillip Russell, *Mexico in Transition* (Austin, Tex.: Colorado River Press, 1977), 45.

5. A *command and control* approach involves the promulgation of universal emissions standards and their consistent enforcement via on-site inspections. It does not tap economic forces to encourage compliance with environmental standards.

6. *Reestructuración del sector paraestatal* (México, D.F.: Fondo de Cultura Económica, 1988).

7. The "polluter pays" principle says that those who cause pollution should bear the cost of any measures government takes to reduce it. See *OECD and the Environment* (Paris: OECD, 1986).

8. See Arturo M. Fernández, "Deregulation As a Source of Growth in Mexico," in Rudiger Dornbusch and Sebastian Edwards, eds., *Reform, Recovery, and Growth: Latin America and the Middle East* (Chicago, Ill.: University of Chicago Press, 1995); and Manuel Sánchez et al., "The Privatization Process in Mexico: Five Case Studies," in Manuel Sánchez and Rossana Corona, eds., *Privatization in Latin America* (Washington, D.C.: Inter-American Development Bank, 1993).

9. Carlos Salinas de Gortari, *Reforming the State* (México, D.F.: Presidencia de la República, n.d.), 17; and Carlos Salinas de Gortari, *The Mexico We Want by 1994* (México, D.F.: Presidencia de la República, 1989), 22.

10. Mexico's Constitution defines strategic sectors as the postal service, satellite telecommunications, basic oil and petrochemicals, hydrocarbons, currency, nuclear energy, electricity, and railroads. On the scope of the divestment and deregulation initiatives see Jacques

Rogozinski, *La privatización de empresas paraestatales* (México, D.F.: Fondo de Cultura Económica, 1993); and Nora Lustig, *Mexico: The Remaking of an Economy* (Washington, D.C.: Brookings Institution, 1992).

11. See Alexander L. George, "Case Studies and Theory Development: The Method of Structured, Focused Comparison," in Paul Lauren, ed., *Diplomacy: New Approaches in History, Theory, and Policy* (New York: Free Press, 1979), 55.

12. On the theoretic value of multiple tests see Arthur L. Stinchcombe, *Constructing Social Theories* (Chicago, Ill.: University of Chicago Press, 1968), 18–20.

13. Illustrative of this tendency is Teichman's detailed but largely atheoretical account of Mexico's divestment experience. See Judith A. Teichman, *Privatization and Political Change in Mexico* (Pittsburgh, Penn.: University of Pittsburgh Press, 1995).

14. For discussion of the need to attenuate the distributional costs of reform, see Omotunde E.G. Johnson, "Managing Adjustment Costs, Political Authority, and the Implementation of Adjustment Programs, with Special Reference to African Countries," *World Development* 22, no. 3 (1994).

15. See D. Van Meter and C. Van Horn, "The Policy Implementation Process: a Conceptual Framework," *Administration and Society* 6 (1975).

16. See Theda Skocpol and Kenneth Finegold, "State Capacity and Economic Intervention in the Early New Deal," *Political Science Quarterly* 97 (1983): 256–278.

17. Robert H. Bates and Anne O. Krueger, "Introduction," in Robert H. Bates and Anne O. Krueger, eds., *Political and Economic Interactions in Economic Policy Reform: Evidence from Eight Countries* (Cambridge, Mass.: Blackwell Publishers, 1993), 4.

18. On the nature of bureaucratic politics see Graham T. Allison, *Essence of Decision: Explaining the Cuban Missile Crisis* (Boston, Mass.: Little, Brown, 1971).

19. For example, see Robert R. Kaufman, *The Politics of Debt in Argentina, Brazil, and Mexico: Economic Stabilization in the 1980s* (Berkeley: Institute of International Studies, University of California, Berkeley, 1988); Joan Nelson, ed., *Economic Crisis and Policy Choice: The Politics of Adjustment in the Third World* (Princeton: Princeton University Press, 1990); Joan Nelson, ed., *Fragile Coalitions: The Politics of Economic Adjustment* (New Brunswick, N.J.: Transaction Books, 1989); Stephan Haggard and Robert R. Kaufman, eds., *The Politics of Economic Adjustment: International Constraints, Distributive Conflicts, and the State* (Princeton, N.J.: Princeton University Press, 1992); John Williamson, ed., *The Political Economy of Policy Reform* (Washington, D.C.: Institute for International Economics, 1994); and Bates and Krueger, *Political and Economic Interactions in Economic Policy Reform.*

20. See Barbara Stallings, "International Influence on Economic Policy: Debt, Stabilization and Structural Reform," in Haggard and Kaufman, *The Politics of Economic Adjustment, op. cit.* See also Thomas M. Callaghy, "Toward State Capability and Embedded Liberalism in the Third World: Lessons for Adjustment," in Nelson, *Fragile Coalitions;* and Don Babai, "The World Bank and IMF: Backing the State versus Rolling it Back," in Raymond Vernon, ed., *The Promise of Privatization: A Challenge for U.S. Foreign Policy* (New York: Council on Foreign Relations, 1988).

21. Thomas Biersteker makes this case for neoliberal adjustment in "The 'Triumph' of Liberal Economic Ideas in the Developing World: Policy Convergence and the Bases of Governance in the International Economic Order," in James N. Rosenau and Ernst-Otto Czempiel, eds., *Governance without Government: Order and Change in World Politics* (Cambridge, England: Cambridge University Press, 1992).

22. On state autonomy see Theda Skocpol, "Bringing the State Back In: Strategies of Analysis in Current Research," in Peter Evans, Dietrich Rueschemeyer, and Theda Skocpol, eds., *Bringing the State Back In* (New York: Cambridge University Press, 1985); and Stephen D. Krasner, *Defending the National Interest: Raw Materials Investments and U.S. Foreign Policy* (Princeton, N.J.: Princeton University Press, 1978).

23. See Thomas M. Callaghy, "Lost Between State and Market: The Politics of Economic Adjustment in Ghana, Zambia, and Nigeria," in Nelson, *Economic Crisis and Policy Choice.*

24. For example, see Stephan Haggard and Robert R. Kaufman, *The Political Economy of Democratic Transitions* (Princeton, N.J.: Princeton University Press, 1995), 9; Joan M. Nelson, "Introduction: The Politics of Economic Adjustment in Developing Nations," in Nelson, ed., *Economic Crisis and Policy Choice,* 25; and Jeffrey Sachs, "Life in the Economic Emergency Room," in Williamson, *The Political Economy of Policy Reform.*

25. See, for example, José Piñera, "Chile," in Williamson, *The Political Economy of Policy Reform,* 228. For a general overview of "stealth reform" see Dani Rodrik, "Understanding Economic Policy Reform," *Journal of Economic Literature* 34 (March 1996), especially 31–33.

26. Waterbury coined the term "change team" and has written the most on this subject. See John Waterbury, *Exposed to Innumerable Delusions: Public Enterprise and State Power in Egypt, India, Mexico, and Turkey* (Cambridge, England: Cambridge University Press, 1993); and John Waterbury, "The Heart of the Matter? Public Enterprise and the Adjustment Process," in Haggard and Kaufman, *The Politics of Economic Adjustment.*

27. See especially John Williamson and Stephan Haggard, "The Political Conditions for Economic Reform," in Williamson, *The Political Economy of Policy Reform,* 579; Waterbury, *Exposed to Innumerable Delusions;* and Waterbury, "The Heart of the Matter?" See also Robert H. Bates and Anne O. Krueger, "Generalizations Arising from the Country Studies," in Bates and Krueger, *Political and Economic Interactions in Economic Policy Reform,* 463–464.

28. See Peter Evans, "The State as Problem and Solution: Predation, Embedded Autonomy, and Structural Change," in Haggard and Kaufman, *The Politics of Economic Adjustment.*

29. The most prominent works on Mexico's top-down decision-making style are Susan Kaufman Purcell, *The Mexican Profit-Sharing Decision: Politics in an Authoritarian Regime* (Berkeley, Calif.: University of California Press, 1975); Roderic Ai Camp, *Politics in Mexico,* 2d. edition (New York: Oxford University Press, 1996), 143; and Daniel C. Levy, "Mexico: Sustained Civilian Rule without Democracy," in Larry Diamond, Juan J. Linz, and Seymour Martin Lipset, eds., *Democracy in Developing Countries: Latin America* (Boulder, Colo.: Lynne Rienner, 1989), 471. See also Fernando Henrique Cardoso, "On the Characterization of Authoritarian Regimes in Latin America," in David Collier, ed., *The New Authoritarianism in Latin America* (Princeton, N.J.: Princeton University Press, 1979), 42–43.

30. Miguel Ángel Centeno, *Democracy within Reason: Technocratic Revolution in Mexico* (University Park, Penn.: The Pennsylvania State University Press, 1994); Merilee S. Grindle, *Challenging the State: Crisis and Innovation in Latin America and Africa* (Cambridge: Cambridge University Press, 1996); and Judith A. Teichman, *Privatization and Political Change in Mexico* (Pittsburgh, Penn.: University of Pittsburgh Press, 1995), especially chapter 5.

31. Waterbury, "The Heart of the Matter?" 191.

32. Evans, "The State as Problem and Solution," 178.

33. Peter Evans, *Embedded Autonomy: States and Industrial Transformation* (Princeton, N.J.: Princeton University Press, 1995), 12.

34. Evans, *Embedded Autonomy,* 47–60.

35. Evans, *Embedded Autonomy,* 12. Evans, "The State as Problem and Solution," 181.

36. See Waterbury, *Exposed to Innumerable Delusions;* and Ezra N. Suleiman and John Waterbury, "Introduction: Analyzing Privatization in Industrial and Developing Countries," in Ezra N. Suleiman and John Waterbury, eds., *The Political Economy of Public Sector Reform and Privatization* (Boulder, Colo.: Westview, 1990).

37. For example, see Ziya Önis, "Privatization and the Logic of Coalition Building: A Comparative Analysis of State Divestiture in Turkey and the United Kingdom," *Comparative Political Studies* 24, no. 2 (July 1991); John Waterbury, "The Political Management of Economic Adjustment and Reform," in Nelson, *Fragile Coalitions;* and Stephan Haggard and Robert R. Kaufman, "Institutions and Economic Adjustment," in Haggard and Kaufman, *The Politics of Economic Adjustment.*

38. For representative arguments see Stephan Haggard and Steven B. Webb, "Introduction," in Stephan Haggard and Steven B. Webb, *Voting for Reform: Democracy, Political Liberalization, and Economic Adjustment* (New York: Oxford University Press, 1994); and Joan M. Nelson, "Poverty, Equity, and the Politics of Adjustment," in Haggard and Kaufman, *The Politics of Economic Adjustment.*

39. See Edward L. Gibson, "The Populist Road to Market Reform: Policy and Electoral Coalitions in Mexico and Argentina," *World Politics* 49 (April 1997).

40. See Waterbury, "The Political Management of Economic Adjustment and Reform," 46; Haggard and Webb, *Voting for Reform: Democracy,* 16–25; and Haggard and Kaufman, "Institutions and Economic Adjustment," 8.

41. Mick Moore, "Leading the Left to the Right: Populist Coalitions and Economic Reform," *World Development* 25 (1997).

42. This pattern of policy making has been evident across a range of areas—from social security, education and family planning, to rural development, business-government relations and even environmental policy. For examples, see Guy E. Poitras, "Welfare Bureaucracy and Clientele Politics in Mexico," *Administrative Science Quarterly* 18 (March 1973); Peter Ward, "The Politics of Planning in Mexico," *Third World Planning Review* 8 (August 1986); Guy Benveniste, *Bureaucracy and National Planning: A Sociological Case Study in Mexico* (New York: Praeger, 1970); Terry L. McCoy, "A Paradigmatic Analysis of Mexican Population Policy," in Terry L. McCoy, ed., *The Dynamics of Population Policy in Latin America* (Cambridge, Mass.: Ballinger Publishing Co., 1974); Merilee S. Grindle, *Bureaucrats, Politicians, and Peasants in Mexico: A Case Study in Public Policy* (Berkeley, Calif.: University of California Press, 1977); Susan Kaufman Purcell, "Business-Government Relations in Mexico: The Case of the Sugar Industry," *Comparative Politics* 13 (1981); and Stephen Mumme, C. Richard Bath, and Valerie J. Assetto, "Political Development and Environmental Policy in Mexico," *Latin American Research Review* 23, no. 1 (1988). For counterarguments detailing the influence nonstate actors have exerted over state policy see Sylvia Maxfield, *Governing Capital: International Finance and Mexican Politics* (Ithaca, N.Y.: Cornell University Press, 1990); and Nora Hamilton, *The Limits of State Autonomy: Post-Revolutionary Mexico* (Princeton, N.J.: Princeton University Press, 1982).

43. For a concise portrait of these alliance networks see David Ronfeldt, *Wither Elite*

Cohesion in Mexico: A Comment, P-7509 (Santa Monica, Calif.: RAND Corporation, 1988); Merilee S. Grindle, "Patrons and Clients in the Bureaucracy: Career Networks in Mexico," *Latin American Research Review* 12, no. 1 (1977); and Peter H. Smith, *Labyrinths of Power: Political Recruitment in Twentieth-Century Mexico* (Princeton, N.J.: Princeton University Press, 1979). On the primacy of presidential *camarillas* see Wayne A. Cornelius and Ann L. Craig, "Politics in Mexico," in Gabriel Almond and G. Bingham Powell, eds., *Comparative Politics Today* (Boston, Mass.: Little, Brown, 1988), 446.

44. See for example, Miguel Ángel Centeno, *Democracy within Reason: Technocratic Revolution in Mexico* (University Park, Penn.: The Pennsylvania State University Press, 1994).

45. See Teichman, *Privatization and Political Change in Mexico,* 86–87; see also Blanca Heredia, "Interview: Jesus Silva Herzog," *Journal of International Affairs* 43, no. 2 (Winter 1990).

Chapter 2

Explaining Policy Reform:
Strategies, Institutions, and Coalitions

The revolution in the Mexican economy that had begun during the administration of Miguel de la Madrid exploded in the first three years of the Salinas government.

—Riordan Roett

History surely will record the 1980s and 1990s as a period of profound political significance and policy change in Mexico. In just a few years, the country's leaders completely overturned decades of statist development policies in favor of more market-friendly, "neoliberal" ones. Indeed, by the early 1990s Mexico stood as Latin America's preeminent reformer. The scope, pace, and success of these policy reversals caught many analysts off guard. Yet, how were these achievements realized? And why did a government that amassed such an impressive reform record in economic policy prove unable to replicate its accomplishments in the environmental policy realm? Politics is an integral facet of policy making, and large-scale policy reform is a complex process. Any attempt, therefore, to explain Mexico's reform experience and speak more generally to broader reform dynamics outside the Mexican context requires a considerably nuanced approach.

This chapter develops an analytical framework to explain the politics of policy reform. Subsequent chapters apply that framework to specific economic and environmental neoliberal initiatives. A compelling explanation of successful policy change must do four things. It must capture the inherent difficulties of implementing a neoliberal project, explain how such obstacles are overcome, consider the influence institutions exert on actors' capabilities and prospects for success, and account for dissimilar outcomes (success/failure). I take up these issues below, beginning with the challenges of policy reform.

The Challenge of Policy Reform

Implementing market reforms successfully is no easy task. Assuming states have the administrative and technical capacity to launch reform projects (as did Mexico), policy reform remains a highly political process, and the path to success is strewn with obstacles in and outside the state. Two factors are particularly important in this respect: one is the notion of "policy feedback"; the other is a related concept I call the "reformer's dilemma."

Policy Feedback

In broad terms "policy feedback" refers to the impact past policy has on current politics. More precisely, it is the notion that prior "policy choices have political consequences."[1] These consequences, in turn, matter when governments attempt market reforms, primarily because they transform the political context in which new policy is made. As Judith May and Aaron Wildavsky observed some years back, "past policy becomes an important (and sometimes the most important) part of the environment to which future policies must adapt."[2] Among the many political consequences of policy feedback, those most likely to complicate the reform process are the tendency of feedback to: (1) create strong political interests anchored in prior policy, (2) provide significant incentives to protect those interests, and (3) promote policy "lock in" effects that can encourage governments to forego alternative policy options.

With respect to political interests and incentives, policy feedback can hinder the shift from statist to market economic policies in ways quite straightforward. As statism expands government bureaucracy, the public sector, and regulatory frameworks, it spawns beneficiaries with strong motivations to preserve or extend existing policies. Often, the development of political interests is particularly acute in organized labor, state ministries and public sector firms, and the private sector, each of which derives specific benefits from statist policies. Once created, these interests—or policy legacies—"feed back" into current politics in ways that greatly complicate the reform process. Unions balk at divestments that threaten public sector contracts, state ministries resist measures that threaten their bureaucratic responsibilities and prestige, state managers "foot drag" efforts to divest their firms, business protests the elimination of subsidies and protectionism, etc. In each case the basic issue is the same: statism creates its own constituents who are penalized by market reforms. This, in turn, provokes intense opposition to policy change, and a host of studies on market reforms have alluded to these dynamics.[3]

Past policy can further hinder reform by creating conditions that tend to lock in particular policy trajectories. In an important study on the retrenchment of the welfare state, Paul Pierson identified several factors whose convergence promotes lock-in effects. In general, lock in is more likely when past policies (1) are highly interdependent, (2) create dense economic or social networks, (3) prompt actors to make significant sunk costs, (4) encourage the adoption of prevailing technology standards, and (5) involve extended periods of state intervention.

To illustrate how lock in can impede the shift from statism to neoliberalism, consider two policy sets typical of state-led, import-substitution economics—protectionism and economic regulations, and public enterprises and labor policy. Both policy sets are highly interdependent: by default, effective protectionism *requires* substantial regulation of imports and prices, and public enterprise sectors typically are highly unionized. Both policy sets also penetrate society deeply and link state organs, economic sectors, and social groups in complex ways. This process creates dense economic and social networks, whose constituents (the private sector, labor, and state bureaucracies) often become defenders of the status quo. Protectionist policies in particular encourage private and public sector industries to invest heavily in noncompetitive technologies, which in protected economies become the prevailing standards of production. Because these long-term commitments represent significant sunk costs, the longer the state promotes such policies, the more disruptive policy change will be, and the greater the disincentives to adopt policy reforms.

Environmental policies can spawn similar characteristics. *Command and control* strategies normally mandate that industry adopt specific technologies to curtail emissions, and require environmental agencies to invest heavily in inspection and monitoring schemes. To the extent industry complies and environmental agencies shoulder their responsibilities (both varied greatly in Mexico), the private and public sector incur substantial sunk costs—not just in the *command and control* environmental regime, but in long-term investment decisions and bureaucratic operations too. As a result, multiple incentives emerge that "protect" status quo policies from easy alteration.

In sum, policy feedback dynamics can exert strong counter reform pressures that constrain even highly committed reformist governments. Indeed, Pierson asserts that during the 1980s such factors were pivotal in preventing large-scale welfare reform in the United States and Britain, despite Reagan and Thatcher's repeated attacks against the welfare state.[4] It should be clear that my own argument owes a debt to Pierson's work. However, it differs from Pierson's thoughts as well. Pierson viewed feedback as the major impediment to policy change, no doubt because his study focused on reform efforts within pluralist political systems. In this context, feedback gave interest groups strong incentives to contest reform, and the "institutional rules" that govern pluralist politics facilitated and legitimized social input on public policy.

By contrast, my research shows feedback played an important, but more qualified role in Mexico. To be sure, feedback complicated Mexico's reform process, but if any set of policies should have proved hard to reverse, it was precisely those encompassed by state-led development—most of which exhibit many lock-in qualities. Yet it was in this realm where the government made the most significant strides toward reform.

As we shall see, this occurred, first, because the rules of Mexico's political system militate strongly against autonomous interest group influence, and so limit the ability of societal actors to contest policy change effectively. It also occurred, however, because reformers countered the influence of policy feedback inside the state by forging strong pro-reform coalitions that manipulated institutional variables to their advantage, marginalized reform opponents from policy decisions, and at times, minimized the costs that policy "losers" incurred. One key distinction, then, between my approach and Pierson's, is that for Pierson, feedback is an *implicit* dependent variable affected primarily by past policy choices.[5] The argument here takes no issue with this position, but does stress that the intensity of feedback will also vary depending on the broader political context and reformers' political agility.

That the challenges of policy feedback can be met successfully, however, is not to minimize the obstacles it erects to successful reform. Because these obstacles generally reflect the "costs" some actors incur when policies change, they also highlight a familiar problem I call the "reformer's dilemma." Conceptually, the reformer's dilemma can be distinguished from policy feedback. The latter generates broad macroeffects that transform the overall political landscape—creating reform impediments and vested interests in the policy status quo. The former reflects a microlevel quandary of political choice that reformers face as opponents contest the "costs" imposed by policy change.

The Reformer's Dilemma

Most reformers believe their agenda, if implemented, will distribute widespread benefits throughout society in the long term. In the short term, however, they recognize it imposes penalties on concentrated groups of "losers." The most prominent problem reformers face advancing their programs, then, is opposition from the beneficiaries of current policy. Such opposition is no mystery, nor is the identity of likely opponents.

The sharp distinction between neoliberal and statist models means the negative impact of new policy falls heavily on predictable groups. As we have seen, privatization and deregulation strike directly at: (1) unions with privileged enclaves in the public sector, (2) government ministries that administer public enterprises or regulate public services, (3) state managers who direct public enterprises, and (4) private sector actors who derive rents and other benefits from statist policies.

Because these cost-bearers comprise concentrated groups, collective action against reform becomes easier to mobilize and the potential to derail reform projects grows.[6] Herein rests the reformer's dilemma; as Joan Nelson observes, "losers know who they will be,"[7] and each group has strong incentives to contest reform.

Again, these incentives stem from the "costs" generated by major policy shifts. The more significant the shift, the higher some actors' costs are likely to be and the greater their incentives to join the opposition. In this way, "new policies create a new politics," as E. E. Schattschneider wrote,[8] but unfortunately for reform advocates, the new political context can be decidedly hostile to change. To advance their agendas successfully, reformers must devise some means to overcome the problem of policy costs.

Overcoming the Reformer's Dilemma

In tackling the reformer's dilemma, policy makers face two basic options. They can seek to minimize opposition by solving the problem of policy "costs," or if able, they can simply impose the costs over the opposition. Option one requires strategies of compensation, persuasion, and division; option two requires strategies of coercion. In most cases reformers find option one preferable because it offers the greatest political protection. But as I detail in later chapters Mexican policy makers sometimes chose option two when they deemed it necessary. Table 2.1 outlines the relationship between these strategies and policy reform.

Table 2.1   **Strategies to Solve the Reformer's Dilemma**

Strategy	Potential Effects on Policy Reform
Minimizing strategies:	
Compensation	reduces intensity of opposition; facilitates policy formulation and implementation
Persuasion	helps shape beliefs regarding economic interests; encourages "losers" to count on, rather than discount future payoffs
Division	exploits cleavages among reform opponents; reduces potential of widespread antireform mobilization
Imposition strategy:	
Coercion	eliminates immediate opponents to change; enhances credibility of reform program; chilling effect preempts additional opposition

Minimizing Strategies: Compensation, Persuasion, and Division

From a political standpoint, perhaps the most appealing way to diffuse opposition is to compensate policy "losers" for the costs they bear. A compensated actor might still find policy change painful, but is less likely to perceive it as fatal, and has less incentive to oppose change "unto the end." Compensation can take the form of direct side-payments to affected actors; for example, workers laid off through privatization might be offered generous severance packages. Compensation also can be indirect, such as complementary policies that offer some form of acceptable relief—job training, or income maintenance schemes like public works and social investment funds, etc.[9]

For policy losers inside the state, both real and symbolic compensation might be provided. Ministerial responsibilities lost due to divestment and deregulation can be partially offset by new tasks that conform to a market-oriented, "downsized" state: expanding and improving the national infrastructure, devising transparent regulations for privatized firms, etc. Conceivably, budget hikes could accompany these new tasks. In addition, "golden parachutes" might be furnished to state managers whose firms are divested. In some cases, reformers might even permit bureaucratic losers to claim credit for reforms they originally opposed. In the hothouse of interagency competition, even such largely symbolic compensation as "credit claiming" can increase an institution's prestige and bring political gains despite concrete losses. As Kenneth Dam observed, sometimes *who* decides an issue is "more important than *what* is decided,"[10] and the recognition received as a "participant" can outweigh the negative effects of the decision itself. Though at first blush paradoxical, this dynamic is quite analogous to traditional bandwagoning, and stems from similar motivations—namely, the primacy placed on being inside the winner's circle.

Besides buying off opponents with compensation, at times it is also possible to minimize opposition through persuasion and playing upon the uncertainty over reform outcomes. Because neoliberal agendas typically consist of policy packages (deregulation, privatization, trade liberalization, etc.) the true effects of multiple policy shifts are hard to gauge *ex ante*. Not only are "economists who advocate changes in macroeconomic policies unable to determine their precise impact on specific interests . . . [but] persons subject to reforms remain uncertain" too.[11] Granted, as Nelson reminds us, some "losers" have a fairly clear idea of their fate under reform policies, but other potential losers will remain uncertain.[12] Such uncertainty provides reformers a chance to shape people's beliefs of where their economic interests lie. Skillful reformers might even persuade opponents that proposed reforms will bring their own rewards.

To succeed, however, persuasion tactics require that policy makers posit plausible constructs of future outcomes, possess well-honed negotiating and political skills, and provide reassurance that an altered policy environment will still meet the needs of those affected by reforms. On this point, reform arguments given a certain "spin" can prove quite useful: efficiency gains from deregulation bring lower consumer prices, and thus higher sales; market incentives can reduce pollution emissions more cost effectively; the private sector—freed from government intervention—will power economic growth and job creation; eliminating barriers to entry generates new investment and profit opportunities in overregulated economic sectors, etc. To the extent such arguments mold people's beliefs regarding their economic interests, they can raise expectations of the future—persuading some groups *not* to discount future payoffs, and thereby converting opponents of change into stakeholders in the reform project itself.

Finally, reformers might reduce the intensity of opposition by trying to divide the opponents' camp. Astute reformers will look for cleavages to exploit among potential losers. When organized labor balks at divestment, for example, policy makers might structure reforms so the "costs" of change fall unequally among union locals, thus reducing the potential for unified, widespread antireform mobilization. As shown in chapter 3 Mexican reformers employed this very strategy to splinter labor's opposition to the divestment of the national airline, Aeroméxico.

Similarly, reformers might exploit natural distinctions among heterogeneous, yet potentially cohesive groups. For instance, regulatory reforms can be structured to "balance" the benefit asymmetries generated in some overregulated markets. By highlighting the potential income opportunities of deregulation, reformers can exploit the resentment felt by those who derive modest rents against those whose rents—protected and guaranteed by existing regulations—are more extensive. In chapter 4 I detail how Mexico's deregulators used this tactic to divide a powerful freight cartel, convert some truckers from opponents to supporters of deregulation, and transform the entire freight transport sector.

The basic goal of these strategies is to transform opponents of change into stakeholders in the reform program, if not active advocates of it. While such a carrot-and-stick approach does not solve the problem of policy costs writ large, it may still vent enough pressure to preclude broad antireform mobilization among potential losers. Moreover, to the extent minimizing strategies (especially compensation) win converts among erstwhile opponents, they bolster social acceptance of the reform project, and hence, its credibility. On the whole, governments that pursue perceived "good policies" in "good ways" are less likely to see their programs imperiled by declining legitimacy than those who do not.

Imposition Strategies: Coercion

Where minimizing strategies seek to solve the problem of policy costs, imposition strategies do not. Rather, they impose the costs of change on recalcitrant cost-bearers, generally through hardball politics. These strategies are highly coercive and entail *punishing* reform opponents through union busting or prosecution, etc. Consequently, when reformers adopt this tactic the costs imposed transcend those normally associated with a given reform (i.e., lost rents, jobs, or privileges).

Besides eliminating the immediate opponents to policy change, imposition strategies can advance reform in other ways too. Such tactics send signals regarding the state's commitment to policy change and its willingness to employ coercion against those blocking the way. These signals, in turn, resonate among diverse groups and can affect the economic/political climate in ways conducive to reform. On the one hand, the stronger the government's commitment to reform seems, the greater the reform program's credibility appears to investors, ever seeking more certain investment climates. On the other, by dramatizing the risks—particularly the *additional* costs—of resisting new policy, the chilling effect of imposition strategies can preempt opposition and encourage potential losers to be more accommodating.

Caveats

Minimizing and imposition strategies can be useful political tactics to advance a reform agenda. However, neither guarantees success and both are limited in their applicability. Compensation has a number of practical drawbacks, beginning with the drain on state revenues. Both direct side-payments and indirect forms of compensation are costly and most governments that embrace neoliberalism are highly sensitive to the bottom line. Compensation may also require new institutions and infrastructure to administer compensatory programs—an expansion of the state that cuts against most neoliberals' ideological preference for smaller government. Finally, compensation strategies are not always feasible. On the one hand, they may require allocating state resources that are not under reformers' control; on the other, the compensation offered may not satisfy opponents.

Persuasion strategies, meanwhile, have their own set of limitations. First and foremost, they require a high degree of political acuity and negotiating skill on the part of policy reformers—commodities often in scarce supply among many technically trained policy personnel.[13] These strategies also are more policy specific than compensation. For example, it is easier to persuade some affected actors that reforms will enhance their economic interests when the reforms themselves serve to expand the economic pie (as with deregulation). But it is far more challenging to do so when the reforms in fact shrink the pie and promise no plausible future payoff (as with jobs lost due to divestment). Finally, the fact that persuasion strategies ask losers to embrace risk taking and to count on, rather than discount the future, narrows their potential range of applicability.

Imposition strategies have clear limitations too. To begin, the capacity to coerce and punish opponents turns in large part on the broader political environment. Thus, imposition tactics are less viable in robust democratic systems than in those like Mexico's where centralized power and authoritarian practices prevailed. Yet even within a "favorable" political climate, the exercise of coercion expends a government's political capital, and if used repeatedly or against sympathetic targets, coercive tactics can tarnish a regime's legitimacy. As chapter 3 explains, the Salinas government discovered this the hard way when it employed highly coercive tactics against the mineworkers union to privatize the Cananea copper mine. Not only did the union *not* buckle in the face of state power (in this case, a literal military siege of the mine's facilities), but the public backlash that followed helped force the government to abandon its strict hard-line stance. In the end, divestment occurred, but only after a chastened government provided miners some unanticipated compensation.

As later chapters will show, policy makers must choose their targets carefully when contemplating imposition strategies. They also must consider both the timing and frequency of such moves. Whereas well-timed, judiciously applied crackdowns on "corrupt" unions or monopolists can reap public acclaim (and help safeguard a reform program), a series of highly coercive actions at the beginning of a reform campaign can deplete a government's popular support and provoke a political backlash that threatens the remainder of the project. For reformers, therefore, prudence is a virtue, because the more governments rely on imposition strategies, the more vulnerable the reforms may be to backlash-induced delays or reversal.

The strategies above constitute a menu of options that policy makers can use— singularly or in combination—to address the effects of policy feedback and the reformer's dilemma. Still, simply identifying these options is not to say successful reform is easy, nor is it a surrogate for understanding the larger political dynamics that influence the probabilities of success. What determines reformers' capacity to pursue these tactics successfully? What broader constraints work against them? The next two sections explore these issues. They explain how institutions influence the politics of policy making, and why coalition politics are fundamental to reformers' success or failure.

The Institutional Context

Policy makers that seek to implement market reforms have their work cut out for them. Tackling the effects of policy feedback and solving the reformer's dilemma are only part of the challenge. They also must accomplish these tasks in the context of institutions and institutional relationships—both of which affect actors' capacities, constrain political action, and influence the outcome of political struggles. By institutions, I refer to formal and informal patterns of governance, decision rules, standard operating procedures, and ministerial mandates. By institutional relationships, I mean the arrangements based on institutions that constrain state actors, and structure their relations with others in and outside the state. To appreciate the broader dynamics that influence the probabilities of success we must take institutions *seriously*—particularly their capacity to structure political interaction in ways that limit what some actors can do, and enable others to do things they otherwise could not. The renewed focus on institutional analysis by political scientists reflects the growing recognition that institutional variables are politically consequential.[14]

From the rational choice school, for example, Kenneth Shepsle found the outcomes of U.S. congressional politics systematically followed the preferences of well-placed legislators "upon whom institutional structure and procedure conferred disproportionate agenda power."[15] From the positive theory of institutions school, Terry Moe explained politics as efforts to structure institutions in ways that protect incumbents' interests, and foreclose future threats from those with opposing interests. Incumbents, he says, will "fashion structures to insulate their favored agencies and programs" from future meddling, going so far as to write rules that "specify in excruciating detail, precisely what the agency is to do and how it is to do it, leaving as little as possible . . . for future authorities to exercise control over."[16] In comparative politics, meanwhile, historical institutionalists have used institutional variables to explain political outcomes in welfare policy (Weir, Orloff, and Skocpol), economic policy (Hall), and tax policy (Steinmo); still others have explained how institutions—by creating distinct arenas of contestation and veto points—produced dissimilar health policy outcomes in Europe (Immergut).[17]

With respect to market reforms the influence institutions exert on the reform process should not be minimized. Reform initiatives typically generate struggles over the policy agenda and policy content, and in these struggles patterns of governance matter. Where power resides in a political system, who wields it and whose interests are represented have a direct impact on the policy-making process. These factors, in turn, are determined by institutional rules that establish distinct patterns of decision making and representation, and thereby, condition the relative influence actors can exert in the policy process.

Besides power and representation, the type and extent of contestation a political system allows over public policy matters too. Rules that govern contestation determine the *legitimacy* of the contestants as well as the arenas where contestation occurs; such rules privilege some actors over others, providing greater or fewer opportunities to influence policy outcomes. Similarly, the decision rules and standard operating procedures within the polity or bureaucracy bear directly on the process of policy reform. Both specify who can participate in the decision-making process and how collective choices are reached when legitimate participants disagree. These institutions also pattern specific bureaucratic practices, and affect the distribution of resources (like information gathering and dissemination) as well as their *value*. Moreover, they structure the decision-making process in ways that provide some actors more leverage over the policy agenda.

Finally, ministerial mandates—which to my mind, serve interest-shaping, role-defining, and power-conferring functions—influence policy making too. Rooted in legal statutes, they assign state actors specific responsibilities and public constituents, delineate those who can make authoritative decisions from those who

Table 2.2   Mexico's "Classic Model": Institutional Arrangements and Policy Making

Patterns of Governance	Pattern Linkages and Effects on Policy Making
Concentrated power	
vertical concentration at federal level; horizontal concentration within the executive	subordinates state actors and ruling party to executive authority; supports top-down decision making
PRI electoral monopoly and lack of influence over political decision making	reinforces top-down decision making
Representation	
limited pluralism	prioritizes social control over interest representation
PRI corporatist structures	restricts autonomous interest group formation and lobbying; requires groups to interact with state via the party on terms the government established
congressional subordination to executive	strips Congress of representative functions and influence in legislative process; occludes access points for public lobbying over policy issues
Contestation	
public electoral arena	confers no particular policy mandate
public policy arena	limits contestation to policy implementation; reduces intensity of policy feedback
private elite bureaucratic arena	allows contestation of policy content and formulation

cannot, and structure interagency interaction by creating superior/subordinate positions inside the bureaucracy with respect to policy issues. Again, in the contest
over the policy agenda these patterns advantage some actors over others.

In sum, institutions and institutional relationships are politically consequential. As a result, institutional dynamics influence both the type of struggles that
ensue over policy change and the likelihood of certain political outcomes. Below I
discuss a few of the more prominent institutional variables in Mexican politics—
patterns of governance, representation, and contestation—and explain their general significance to the policy-making process. These variables and their effects on
policy making are previewed in table 2.2. Subsequent chapters elaborate more
fully upon other institutional variables (decision rules, standard operating procedures, and ministerial mandates) and the influence they exert over the process of
policy reform.

Patterns of Governance and Representation

Although the 1980s and 1990s brought significant political change to Mexico,
the basic contours of what might be termed the country's "classic" political model
remained. Indeed, even in 1994—well into the reform era—scholars noted that
"major aspects of Mexican politics . . . still reflect[ed]" those of the postrevolutionary
classic model.[18] The discussion below, then, is confined to the general framework
that characterized Mexican politics for much of the twentieth century.

In terms of patterns of governance, the Mexican state of the classic era was
unique. Its formal institutions concentrated power vertically at the federal level,
and horizontally inside the executive branch.[19] Mexicans referred to this phenomenon as *presidencialismo*—a political reality in sharp contrast with the federalist
framework of the national constitution. For much of the twentieth century
presidencialismo's centralizing tendencies were evident. The executive (not Congress) dominated the legislative agenda.[20] The executive also could issue decrees
that carried the force of law; and only the president, not semiautonomous agencies, could authorize regulations interpreting congressional legislation. This
pattern of governance privileged the executive over other state actors, restricted
the opportunity for those outside the executive to influence policy, and supported
a logic conducive to top-down policy making.

Concentrated power emerged in Mexico's party system as well, where the
Institutional Revolutionary Party, or PRI, long held sway. Formed in the ashes of
postrevolutionary power struggles, the PRI became the state's chief pillar of social
support. As Stephen Morris notes, the party machinery "reached into the factory,
the peasant community, the neighborhoods, the schools, and the bureaucratic offices."[21] The PRI incorporated Mexico's major social sectors; its flexible ideology

spanned the political spectrum; and for decades, it effectively monopolized the "political space," leaving weak opposition parties at the margins.

Under Mexico's informal political rules the PRI became the "official" party, by which a symbiotic relationship evolved between the party and the state. The regime provided the PRI financial support, fashioned electoral laws to ensure its hegemony, and supported the party's various social groups. The PRI, in turn, mobilized electoral campaigns and provided the president a rubber-stamp majority in Congress. Like the Congress, however, the PRI remained subordinate to the president. It never controlled political decision making,[22] nor even the selection of its own presidential candidate (traditionally, outgoing presidents handpicked their own successors). Despite its ubiquity, therefore, the party reinforced—rather than challenged—patterns of top-down decision-making.

Centralized power also influenced the type and extent of political representation in Mexico, basically by depriving Congress of its representative functions. By controlling the legislative agenda presidents left Congress little influence over legislative output and marginalized representatives from the lawmaking process. The net effect of congressional subordination was twofold: it transformed the legislature into a ratifying—not decision-making—body, and shut down crucial access points where interest groups might otherwise influence policy decisions. Stripped of its representative functions Congress ceded this role to the PRI, whose corporatist structures forged a "limited pluralist" system that prioritized social control *over* interest representation.[23]

Mexican corporatism arranged society into vertically structured organizations composed of legally recognized functional groups. In this vein, the PRI's corporatist structures encompassed three crucial social sectors: labor, the peasantry, and the popular sector, or middle classes. The party, in turn, "represented" each sector through a peak organization containing hundreds of smaller groups.[24] Unlike pluralist systems, Mexican corporatism did not facilitate open competition between organized interests nor restrict the state to being a neutral mediator between competing social groups. Instead of competing to influence public servants (and thereby public policy), interest groups dealt with them directly, through the ruling party's peak organizations, and *on terms the government itself established.*

These terms, or rules, were straightforward. State sanction provided these groups political protection, a legal monopoly to represent their constituents, and guaranteed access to decision makers; in exchange, corporatist leaders accepted limits on their members' behavior and demands. The result, notes Roger Hansen, was a pattern of "upward-flowing obligations and loyalties" on the part of corporatist leaders rather than downward-oriented responsibilities to group constituents.[25] The net effect of these inducements and constraints was to restrict vigorous political representation, more than promote it,[26] and combined with centralized executive power, this influenced the scope, type, and substance of political contestation in Mexico.

Patterns of Contestation

Under Mexico's informal political rules contestation occurred in two distinct realms. One was public, the other private. In the open, public sphere electoral competition occurred at regularly scheduled intervals, and historically, PRI candidates prevailed handily in these contests. Yet these victories—sometimes a function of genuine popularity, sometimes of fraud, irregularities, and procedural chicanery—cannot be viewed as credible contests over public policy.

First, for more than sixty years the PRI was the only viable partisan game in town. Besides limiting voters' electoral choice, the party's hegemony, and lack of influence over policy, constrained voters' capacity to influence policy content via the ballot. Outgoing presidents selected their own successor whose candidacy was tantamount to election; and as explained below, once in power, incumbents often decided public policy with only passing nods to the public will. Consequently, elections seldom functioned as true referendums on public policies, and election results conferred on presidents no particular policy mandate.[27]

Second, even when elections did offer real choice, the PRI's status as Mexico's de facto "government party" encouraged voters *not* to cast ballots solely on personal policy preferences. Instead, the longtime government-PRI nexus forced voters to consider the *country's* future absent the PRI. Perhaps the best example of this was the 1988 presidential election where a viable opposition candidate challenged the PRI and its market reforms. Despite the clear policy choice this provided, survey data revealed only a weak relationship between support for the anti-reform candidate and opposition to specific reform measures like privatization.[28] Most Mexicans simply did not vote for or against reform, but rather, based their votes on more national concerns over the prospects of social peace and economic performance, and their support/disapproval of the Mexican president. Consequently, note Domínguez and McCann, in 1988, presidential candidates drew support from "people who held diverse views on the central issues of the day," and even in this crucial election, "attitudes on policy issues hardly mattered."[29]

That elections typically did not provide vehicles to contest public policy, however, is not to suggest the absence of policy-relevant public contestation under Mexico's classic political model. Where public contestation did bear on policy issues were the struggles over policy implementation. Such matters as who would bear the costs of increased social security taxes (employers, employees, or the state), or who would gain from subsidized credit (large or small farmers) are two examples where the public was expected, and permitted, to influence how prior policy decisions were implemented.

But it is important to emphasize that public contestation was confined strictly to policy *implementation* (not policy content),[30] and it is in this respect we see the effects of *presidencialismo* and corporatism most clearly. On the one hand, centralized power helped crowd issues of policy content and formulation into the executive domain, where decision making was reserved to a small elite; on the other, corporatist restrictions on social mobilization simply reinforced this trend. In-depth case studies of major public policies in Mexico underscore how limited an impact public contestation had on the content of policy decisions. With respect to rural development policies, for example, Merilee Grindle found that "demand-making behavior of citizens and parties in support of policy alternatives play[ed] a very insignificant part in the development or approval of government plans."[31] In a similar fashion, David Mares discovered "little evidence that organized labor, business, or peasants" directly influenced the government's 1980 decision not to join the GATT.[32]

Limits on public contestation gave Mexican decision makers great latitude over policy decisions, but not an entirely free hand. Parallel to (and largely hidden from) the public domain, more vigorous contestation occurred within a private, elite political sphere. Here, struggles ensued within the upper bureaucratic echelons over issues of policy content and formulation, as well as for political position and influence. In terms of policy making, these contests were the more important, for it was here—within a closed, opaque arena—that state policy was made and policy content decided, and neither the public, the Congress, nor the ruling party were central actors in this process.

To summarize the discussion, Mexico's traditional patterns of governance strongly influenced the policy-making process. It could hardly be otherwise. Centralization reserved power for the few, corporatism insulated decision makers in a layer of autonomy by demobilizing societal actors, and contestation over policy-content was confined to select elites. The result was a strong top-down decision-making pattern characterized by closed, elite deliberations, and marginalized, relatively ineffective demand making among organized interests.

Two implications for the study of Mexico's policy reforms arise from these observations. First, it is reasonable to view successful reform as a two-stage process, whose first stage—policy formulation and adoption—occurs amidst contestation inside the state. Because Mexico's patterns of governance restricted policy discussions to political elites, it is crucial to understand how institutional variables influenced reformers' probabilities of success in this realm. Second, understanding why reformers might have prevailed here is only half the story. New policies must still be implemented and with the public encouraged to contest implementation, interaction between reformers and nonstate actors assumes more prominence. It is at this point of the process that most scholars stress the importance of coalition politics. In the following section I briefly review their arguments and suggest ways to extend the explanatory power of coalition analysis.

Coalition Politics, Organizational Strength, and Policy Reform

Coalitions

A coalition is an alliance of actors joined together to advance a shared interest. Most analysts stress three main factors behind their development: actors coalesce to pursue shared goals; they base their decisions on calculations that the payoffs from joint action exceed the costs; and typically, they join forces with those who exhibit minimal conflict of interest over policy preferences.[33] Although most political analyses of market transitions view coalitions as important to successful reform, they generally undervalue the role coalition politics actually play in the reform process.

Throughout the economic transitions literature scholars have underscored the importance of coalitions to the implementation and consolidation of reforms. Their chief contention is that coalitions between state reformers, business, and/or labor are required to build social consensus around new policies, provide reformist governments the support they need to govern effectively, and thereby help ensure the policies themselves are durable.[34] Representative of this perspective is Haggard and Webb, who, based on eight case studies of developing countries conclude that in the long term, the successful implementation of reform measures "must be seen as a process of coalition-building."[35]

This position on coalitions provides some important insights into the politics of successful reform, but not without serious opportunity costs. As I mentioned in chapter 1, by focusing solely upon policy consolidation or implementation, it downplays the role of coalitions during the earlier process of policy formulation, and thus, overlooks the importance of reform coalitions *inside* the state. In contrast, the argument here considers coalitions integral to both stages of the reform process, and this perspective extends coalition analysis considerably. Specifically, it suggests that some of the most important coalitions are those within the state— between different groups or ministries—and that scholars seeking to understand the reform process should not confine themselves solely to issues of state-societal coalitions and policy consolidation. To the contrary, a full understanding of the politics of policy reform requires we consider coalition dynamics "upstream" at the point of policy formulation, and closely examine the role coalition politics play inside the state.

Coalitions inside the state are crucial to successful reform, first and foremost, because policy making itself is a collective process. Under "ordinary" conditions, i.e., no fundamental reform, individual actors—whether presidents or finance ministers—cannot superintend the entire policy-making process. Indeed, issues of policy formulation, interagency coordination, and administration all require joint action, and this holds true even for decidedly top-down political systems like Mexico's.

Under *extraordinary* conditions of fundamental policy change, the need for joint action becomes more acute.

Because neoliberal reforms typically consist of policy packages (deregulation, privatization, etc.) they affect the interests of multiple agencies, and to advance these initiatives successfully requires close interagency coordination. Also, as we have seen, these reform measures are fundamentally opposed to past modes of bureaucratic operations. Rather than promote consensus, their introduction can provoke subtle (or sharp) opposition, "bureaucratic politics," foot-dragging, etc., and intense struggles over the policy agenda. Moreover, policy makers work within a web of institutional constraints. These institutional variables give some actors more influence than others, but need not automatically privilege reformers over reform opponents. Finally, successful reform is a highly political process that requires political muscle, not just technical expertise. Stated bluntly, dramatic policy change will not come simply because individual reformers believe it is needed; they also must have the power to promote their ideas, control the agenda, and ensure their policy preferences become state policy.

Against these odds, unified (as opposed to isolated) efforts are more likely to advance preferred policy outcomes at both stages of the reform process. Coalitions can engage in reform efforts more efficiently because these aggregations reduce the transaction costs involved in gathering and processing policy-relevant information.[36] Cohesive reform coalitions also can prevail inside the state more easily because they enlarge the pool of resources (administrative, intellectual, informational, financial, political, etc.) needed to formulate policy, coordinate joint action, and manipulate institutional variables to their advantage. Even after reformers achieve victory inside the state, however, coalition politics remain crucial to whether new policy is implemented successfully or not. As Haggard and Webb remind us, successful implementation requires reformers to expand their coalition membership outside the state and facilitate implementation via the compensation or imposition strategies previously discussed.

In critical ways, then, coalitions are a central part of successful reform, and in terms of coalitions inside the state, their value in this process has been under studied and underappreciated. But this point raises important analytical issues: What exactly are the determinants of a "winning" reform coalition? And how might we assess its potential to succeed?

A natural response to these questions is to view winning coalitions in terms of their power, and hypothesize that in struggles over policy reform, "strong" coalitions—i.e., those with the most power resources—will prevail. But this approach is unsatisfactory. For one thing, because "power" is multifaceted, defining and measuring it accurately is a tricky enterprise,[37] and standard conceptions of power as the capacity to secure outcomes (*A*'s ability to change *B*'s behavior, the ability to pursue and achieve goals, etc.) encourage post hoc explanations. For another, the factors that confer power on actors and could, therefore, help predict outcomes are legion (legal authority, information, agenda control, status, financial and administrative capacity, etc.). They also are closely interdependent, and thus difficult to untangle.

Finally, pure power arguments simply are too mechanistic because they explain political outcomes in Weberian "capacity-outcome" terms. For Weber, power was "the capacity of an individual to realize his will, even against the opposition of others."[38] Weber's position notwithstanding, even actors with substantial power resources are not predestined to triumph over weaker opponents (recall the Vietnam War). This point cannot be overstated. Struggles over policy change are just that—*real struggles*—and in these conflicts power itself is more relative than absolute. Political outcomes depend as much upon each protagonists' moves and countermoves, as on any initial power endowment one side enjoys. Thus, while the distribution of power might make some outcomes more probable than others, each outcome is produced in the course of the struggle itself.[39]

I will come back to these points a bit later. For now, I simply wish to note that due to these concerns—and because my primary focus is coalitions within the state—it is useful to assess a coalition's potential for success in terms of its *organizational strength*. This concept draws heavily upon the work of organizational and "New Institutionalist" theorists, and encompasses a coalition's organizational position within the bureaucracy, its capacity for institutional innovation, and the policy ideas reformers embrace (see table 2.3).

Organizational Strength

Organizational Position

Where coalition members are located within the bureaucracy is an important facet of organizational strength. Organizational theorists have long understood that those who occupy hierarchically superior positions in a bureaucracy generally exercise greater influence than their subordinates.[40] This leverage—often the product of legal authority vested in higher rank—empowers those in high posts to take authoritative actions and compels subordinates to submit. In this case, the domain of leverage provided is largely *vertical,* and thus, confined mostly to actors housed in the same agency. Besides providing vertical domains of influence, certain organizational positions confer *lateral* leverage as well, especially when they permit the control of resources on which others depend. As Aldrich and Mindlin note, "If A cannot do without the resources mediated by B and is unable to obtain them elsewhere, A becomes dependent on B. Conversely, B acquires power over A."[41]

Real-world situations support this proposition. In a study of industrial enterprises, Perrow showed the power a company's salesmen exerted over its production unit, by virtue of the latter's dependence on the markets the former provided.[42] In Mexico's reform experience a very similar dynamic emerged. As I detail in chapter 3, some ministries that controlled Mexico's public enterprises were able to thwart early

Table 2.3   **Attributes and Effects of Organizational Strength**

Attributes	Effects
Organizational position	
vertical leverage	empowers top-down authoritative actions
lateral leverage	creates structural dependency and leverage over others of equal rank
network centrality	influences reintegration of agency workflows; facilitates acquisition/control of resources; creates bureaucratic "veto points"
Capacity for institutional innovation	
rule-changing behavior	alters organizational position; enhances resource base, agenda access, and ability to contest alternative policy proposals
instrument-creating behavior	displaces conflict over reform initiatives; provides reformers greater autonomy
strategizing behavior	ensures future stream of preferred outcomes via most efficient expenditure of resources
Policy ideas	
cohesive policy paradigm	promotes problem definition and policy solutions; facilitates uncertainty-coping and agenda control; bolsters coalitional cohesion and autonomy
political property rights	links policy-making structure to policy ideas; provides exclusive jurisdiction over a policy realm; deflates opposition and elicits deferential compliance

privatization efforts. They did so by restricting the flow of information about corporate operations that reformers—of equal bureaucratic standing—required to assess these firms and fashion appropriate sales packages. In these cases, lateral domains of influence emerged due to each actor's organizational location and the way the integration of workflow patterns structured their relationship.[43]

These examples illustrate how organizational positioning can affect an actor's influence inside the bureaucracy. But the role bureaucratic location plays in *organizational strength* is even more complex. State bureaucracies consist of a matrix of entities. They can, in fact, be viewed as multicomponent *systems* whose work is segmented vertically and horizontally by ministry, division, and department. The division of labor assigns each subunit its own tasks, and the output of these workflows is then reintegrated as policy via patterned interactions between agencies. Actors located at critical points of intersection within the bureaucratic matrix, therefore, occupy strategic organizational space (or what organizational theorists call "network centrality").[44] It is on this basis that organizational positioning can provide coalition members significant *organizational strength*.

Nestled within a strategic niche, such actors obtain more leverage over the policy-making process. They are better positioned to acquire and control information and other resources, can influence the reintegration of agency workflows, and in some cases, even transform their positions into effective bureaucratic "veto points." The chapters that follow are filled with examples in which actors enjoyed (or carved out) such niches within Mexico's bureaucracy, and employed these tactics to advance their particular policy goals. That some—but not all—of these enclaves were located at high bureaucratic ranks, affirms the proposition that network centrality and organizational position can provide coalition members a powerful tool to affect the course of policy change.

Institutional Innovation

A second facet of *organizational strength* resides in a coalition's capacity for institutional innovation. As I suggested earlier, successful reformers can pursue several political strategies to solve the reformer's dilemma and policy feedback problems. Coalitions able to compensate "losers," coerce or punish opponents, or persuade them to become stakeholders in the reform process are more likely to advance policy formulation inside the state, and implement policy successfully thereafter. In part, these abilities are the product of the coalition's initial resource base and organizational position, plus its members' political skills. Because the latter can be enhanced only through the experience and learning aptitudes of individual reformers, it is often a "static" property. In contrast, the former two factors are more dynamic and can be bolstered significantly by the coalition's capacity for institutional innovation.

By institutional innovation I mean the ability to manipulate institutional variables to one's advantage. Successful coalitions exercise this capacity by engaging in one of the following: (1) rule- and procedure-changing behavior, (2) instrument-creating behavior, and (3) strategizing behavior.

Earlier I noted that institutions have profound political consequences because they limit what some actors can do, and enable others to do things they otherwise could not. Changing the rules of these institutions, therefore, can prove extremely effective in advancing a policy preference.[45] Of particular importance are the institutional rules and procedures that structure or govern representation, contestation, decision-making processes, interagency relations, patterns of information gathering, processing, and dissemination, and legal jurisdiction over a policy domain.

For coalitions seeking greater leverage over the policy process, the payoffs from these efforts can be considerable. Effective institutional innovation can increase reformers' access to (and control over) the policy agenda, and their capacity to contest alternative policy proposals. It can provide reformers a new set of resources (plus increase the value of existing ones) and forge effective veto points inside the bureaucracy. Rule changes also can shift the legal jurisdiction of a policy from one state actor to another—providing reformers a new legal or ministerial mandate to effect policy change, and bolstering their autonomy from political pressures in the process. Most important, by changing the rules and procedures that structure decision making and interagency relations, coalition members can alter their organizational position inside the bureaucracy, achieve network centrality, and thereby acquire enormous leverage over the policy process.

A second way innovative coalitions might augment their *organizational strength* is to engage in "instrument-creating behavior," by which I mean the creation of new bureaucratic entities whose sole purpose is to advance a particular policy. The contentious nature of policy reform makes the capacity to create such agencies crucial for reasons both political and practical.

In political terms, the transition from statist to neoliberal policies challenges longtime bureaucratic interests. As Brian Levy observed, this confronts bureaucracies with a sometimes irresistible temptation *not* to engage in "actions that had hitherto been part of their organizational function."[46] Housing key decision makers in an insulated policy unit, therefore, removes reform discussions from a highly politicized arena, and helps provide the autonomy reformers need to make tough policy decisions absent countervailing pressures.[47]

In practical terms the challenge is one of putting "new wine into old skins," because it is extremely difficult to redesign existing agencies to perform new tasks. On the one hand, entrenched procedures and bureaucratic routines act as counterweights against policy change; on the other, they provide opportunities for bureaucrats to reinterpret reform objectives to suit existing modes of operation.[48]

The literature on policy reform is filled with examples of instrument-creating behavior of various stripes. In some cases governments have created ad hoc or task force-like entities composed of economic ministries and the central bank; Bolivia, Honduras, and Peru all pursued this route.[49] In other cases, like Argentina and Turkey, governments combined ministerial portfolios to streamline decision making and consolidate control over the policy process.[50] The basic goal of instrument creation, of course, is to centralize decision making authority and remove policy decisions from the crossfire of political conflict. This tactic rests on the principle of conflict-displacement and the politics of structural choice. Writing in another context several decades back, Schattschneider clearly articulated the principle of conflict-displacement:

> All politics deals with the displacement of conflicts . . . [because the] conse-quences of conflict are so important that it is inconceivable that any regime could survive without making an attempt to shape the system. . . . All forms of political organization have a bias in favor of the exploitation of some kinds of conflict and the suppression of others. . . . Some issues are organized *into* politics while others are organized *out*[51] [emphasis mine].

By restructuring state bureaucracies reformers can minimize conflict over policy deliberations, if not completely "organize it out" of the policy process. So important is the displacement principle—so frequently is it manifest as instrument creation in episodes of policy change—that some scholars deem it indispensable to successful reform. As Nelson notes, "In almost all cases of vigorous and sus-tained reform, political leaders concentrated authority for economic management in 'change teams' *and protected those teams from political pressures both from outside and from within the government itself*" (emphasis mine).[52]

Besides conflict-displacement, instrument-creating behavior also is closely related to the politics of structural choice—a recent and more policy-relevant con-cept advanced by Terry Moe. In explaining why some bureaucracies take the struc-tural form they do, Moe pointed to the following:

> Structural choices [about bureaucratic agencies] have important consequences for the content and direction of policy, and political actors know it. When they make choices about structure, they are implicitly making choices about policy. A politically powerful group . . . can use its power more productively by selecting the right types of bureaucrats and designing a structure that affords them reason-able autonomy.[53]

That conflict-displacement and the politics of structural choice bear power-fully on the reform process seems persuasive, yet few scholars have linked these concepts explicitly in ways that draw forth their full explanatory potential. Espe-cially for analysts of neoliberal transitions the key "blind spot" has been a notice-able omission of coalitions. At least implicitly, Moe envisions coalitions as a po-tential vehicle of instrument creation (actually he employs a "dominant" coalition example mainly as a heuristic to clarify certain theoretical points).[54] Students of market reforms, however, have been slow to incorporate this insight into their own analysis. Instead, they have focused exclusively on government leaders (i.e., presi-dents) as catalysts behind instrument creation and virtually ignored coalitions al-together.[55]

One factor that distinguishes this study from prior research on the reform process is that the concept of *organizational strength* explicitly affords coalition members a prominent role in instrument creation. The virtue of this approach is twofold. On the one hand, unlike presidentialist accounts which obscure rather than clarify the individual agency of various state actors, it brings to light the multiple interests at work inside the state, both pro-reform and antireform. On the other, it explains how individual reformers or reform coalitions can augment their leverage over the policy process by enhancing their organizational positions. The result is a closer, more systematic treatment of reform dynamics than presidentialist explanations can provide.

This shift of emphasis is not to say that presidential backing is unimportant, or not required to create new bureaucratic instruments. It simply suggests a full account is more complex. A close examination of Mexico's reform record will show that coalition constituents were as important as the chief executive in creating new agencies and displacing conflict over policy deliberations, if not more so. In fact, the most successful reform episodes were those where coalition members seized the initiative to create new policy instruments and *then* gained the president's support for these measures. This tactic proved to be a major factor in their victories inside the state.

Although coalitions can boost their organizational strength considerably through institutional innovation, in the process they also incur costs that tax their resource base. Time, energy, political capital, administrative capacities, and technical expertise are all valuable resources. How coalitions expend these resources in pursuit of their goals (more efficiently, or less so) can enhance or weaken their organizational strength, and thereby affect the probabilities of successful policy change. Sagacious reformers, therefore, will try to maximize the efficiency of resource expenditures required to change the institutional rules or create new policy instruments. In doing so they engage in what I call strategizing behavior.

Strategizing behavior is a highly valuable form of institutional innovation. It complements—but is distinct from—both rule-changing or instrument-creating behavior, and it is what separates truly astute reformers from less adept ones. When actors pursue institutional innovation they face two basic options. Rule changes and new policy instruments can be made such that they capture short-term benefits; alternatively, they can be arranged to ensure a future flow of preferred outcomes.[56] The latter is the essence of strategizing behavior, and it is what "successful" coalitions are particularly adept at doing.

In real-world politics strategizing behavior assumes various forms across various policy realms. Governments seeking to reduce the welfare state might forego trying to cut welfare benefits directly (due to political costs), and instead simply change the tax code to make it harder to raise revenues for future social spending. Actors wanting to reduce regulation might defer a case-by-case reform approach (due to time costs), but rather seek legislation requiring *all* regulations, present and future, pass a cost-benefit analysis threshold or be deleted. In the case of neoliberal policies, reformers can save time and energy by restructuring decision rules to restrict specific policy discussions (of say, divestment) to economic ministry personnel, and exclude ministries that traditionally supervised public enterprise operations.

Because strategizing behavior ensures preferred outcomes in the long run most efficiently, it can maximize the payoffs of institutional innovation. The more coalitions pursue this tactic, the greater their *organizational strength* will likely be over the long term, and the higher their probabilities of success.

Policy Ideas and Paradigms

Finally, *organizational strength* can develop from the policy ideas coalition members advance. Students of comparative public policy suggest the more closely some ideas "fit" the contemporary policy issues leaders face, the greater political prominence they assume.[57] Studies also indicate a cohesive set of ideas—or policy paradigm—provides greater political value in policy contests.

Not all ideas constitute a policy paradigm, of course. In general, those that do provide interpretations of reality, delimit the possibilities of action, and model the problems and solutions found in that reality. In short, a policy paradigm constitutes a framework of ideas and standards that guides decision making on policy issues. This framework, Peter Hall suggests, "specifies not only the goals of policy and the kinds of instruments that can be used to attain them, but also the very nature of the problems they are meant to be addressing. Like a *Gestalt,* this framework is embedded in the very terminology through which policymakers communicate about their work."[58]

Cohesive policy paradigms provide reformers a powerful resource on four fronts, beginning with the ability to diagnose or define a policy problem and offer plausible (often proven) policy solutions. "The course of conflicts," Robert Alford suggests, "may be partially understood by reference to the ability of groups to establish their definition of the situation as the appropriate one."[59] For reformers, this capacity is particularly useful because problem definition is integral to agenda setting, political conflict, and policy outcomes: how an issue is defined can determine its agenda status as well as its possible policy solution.[60]

Mexico's reform experience illustrates these dynamics nicely. Where statist development spawned a bloated public sector with subsidy-dependent public enterprises (the problem), privatization promised to shrink the state and pad the balance sheets at the Treasury (the solution); where statism erected complicated inefficient regulatory regimes, deregulation promised to cure resource misallocation and improve efficiency, etc. That such policies already had been tried and "proven" elsewhere enhanced their appeal, and against these types of policy arguments reform opponents faced an uphill battle. In part, this occurred because policy paradigms—like neoliberalism—come with their own lexicon, which William Riker observed, helps structure decision making in ways that tilt outcomes one way or another.[61] As later chapters demonstrate, in contests over market reforms those fluent in neoliberalism were greatly advantaged over their opponents. The inability to defend status quo policy in terms of neoliberalism's central tenets (efficiency and rationality) strengthened reformers' control of the policy agenda, and reinforced their positions inside policy circles.

A second way ideas enhance *organizational strength* is by helping reformers meet the challenge of uncertainty, one of the central concerns faced by leaders of any large organization (or government). A number of studies on organizational dynamics call attention to uncertainty, and demonstrate how actors that excel in "uncertainty-coping" gain power and influence within the organization.[62] The same logic applies to governments and policy reformers. As I have explained, the reform process is shrouded in uncertainty. Because of incomplete information, it is hard for decision makers to gauge the effects of policy change *ex ante,* or the unintended consequences of interlinkages between policy subsets. Those best able to cope with uncertainty gain leverage in policy discussions, and it is here the cause-and-effect, prescriptive properties of coherent policy paradigms play a role.

Besides uncertainty-coping, cohesive policy paradigms can increase the degree of autonomy policy makers enjoy vis-à-vis countervailing forces. This was shown in Peter Hall's insightful work on British economic policy. Here, Hall discovered that during the Thatcher government, policy makers who pushed the central ideas of monetarism were better positioned to resist pressure from old-line Keynesians. His argument mirrors the discussion above: unlike Keynesianism, which failed to anticipate stagflation and whose prescriptions seemed only to aggravate it, monetarism appeared to identify the problems bedeviling the British economy and provide intellectually justified and politically practical solutions. Despite the backlash Thatcherism unleashed in some quarters, the monetarists prevailed. On this basis, Hall concluded that in general, policy makers are "in a stronger position to resist pressure . . . when they are armed with a coherent policy paradigm. . . . Conversely, when such a paradigm is absent or disintegrating policymakers may be much more vulnerable to outside pressure, as the 1974-79 Labour government was once the Keynesian paradigm began to collapse."[63]

Finally, in some cases cohesive policy paradigms help reformers obtain what might be called "political property rights" over a given policy realm or problem.[64] Like their generic counterparts, "political" rights provide their holders almost exclusive jurisdiction over a policy issue and exclude "outsiders" from the same. The development of such situations has important implications for the policy agenda and policy output; and in the struggles inherent in policy making, these can prove pivotal. In one of the classic studies of American social security policy, Derthick demonstrated the dominance a relatively small group of actors wielded over this important policy realm.[65] In this case just a handful of individuals—mainly from the House of Representatives, Social Security Administration, and organized labor—controlled the government's policy agenda to the exclusion of others.

To secure political property rights coalitions must forge a close, intimate connection between their institutional environment and policy ideas. Specifically, they must erect an institutional policy-making structure that limits access to the policy process, and associates that structure with a cohesive set of ideas (or paradigm).[66] This entails institutional innovation, but leads to an outcome qualitatively different from some other aspects of *organizational strength*. Like organizational position, political property rights invest their holders with legitimacy to take authoritative action; in turn, this legitimacy confers influence that lowers the potential for opposition inside the state. But there is an important distinction between the influence born of political property rights and the "vertical leverage" of organizational position. In the latter, authority rests mainly on legal statute or ministerial mandates. In the former, it also is a function of *psychological deference* characteristic of Weberian legitimacy—a legitimacy based not on incumbency alone, but on the perceived policy expertise of the incumbents. The result, note Elder and Cobb, gives those who acquire such legitimacy an almost unquestioned "presumptive right" to monopolize policy in the realm of their presumed expertise.[67]

Secure political property rights can enhance a coalition's *organizational strength* considerably. On the one hand, cohesive policy ideas combined with effective institutional innovation reinforce its position inside the state; on the other, they pigeonhole reform opponents between forces whose constraints are mutually reinforcing. The trick, though, remains to associate the coalition's policy ideas with institutional arrangements that limit access to the policy process, and to convince others of the superiority of those ideas. As we shall see, not all reform advocates demonstrated this capacity, and not all reform opponents lacked it.

Caveats

Organizational position, the capacity for institutional innovation, and a cohesive set of policy ideas are crucial to a reform coalition's *organizational strength*. This, in turn, is critical to its success. It is important to note, however, that like power, *organizational strength* alone does not predetermine political outcomes. The concept's true utility is that it situates analysis in the proper institutional/bureaucratic setting. This allows us to examine which factors confer power inside the bureaucracy, and thereby assess a coalition's potential to achieve its goals inside the state. The ability to prevail, though, remains conditioned by institutional variables, the means coalitions employ, how they employ them, and how others react to such moves.[68]

Conclusion

Implementing market reforms successfully is inherently problematic. Policy feedback, the reformer's dilemma, and institutional constraints erect enormous obstacles to reform inside the state and out. But while these factors complicate the reform process they need not derail it. Institutional arrangements and rules can be changed, losers compensated, and costs imposed. A central argument of this chapter is that in isolation, reform advocates will accomplish little, but in concert their prospects improve handsomely. This book, then, puts coalitions at the center of analysis and suggests they play a pivotal role throughout the entire reform process. The argument shares some common ground with theorists who stress autonomy, "change teams," and coalitions; but it remains conscious of these perspectives' limitations and applies coalition analysis more broadly than before.

If coalition politics are as critical as I contend, this argument has important implications for how we should study the *politics* of policy reform—in Mexico and beyond. To begin, Mexico itself is a relatively "hard" case in which to apply coalition analysis. Concentrated power, a subordinate Congress, hegemonic party, limited pluralism, and top-down decision making all tend to militate against using coalitions as a principal unit of analysis. Yet if coalitions prove determinate in a relatively hard case like Mexico, coalition analysis will likely prove useful in more pluralist, decentralized contexts as well. However, the dynamics of *reform* coalitions will deviate from those associated with more "generic" coalition politics. The principal factors behind the development of political coalitions—shared goals, minimal conflict over policy preferences (i.e., shared ideology), and cost-benefit calculations—remain important. But in the context of neoliberal reform, the latter especially will affect reform coalitions in unique ways.

In terms of "costs," political scientists have stressed how various decision, opportunity, and transaction costs influence actors' decisions to join a coalition. Adrian and Press, for example, cite eight types of costs that potential members must weigh against the expected payoffs of joint action (information, time, and persuasion costs, etc.).[69] The ratio of costs to anticipated benefits affects the development and composition of the coalition, and these scholars demonstrate this principle on a range of explicitly *political* coalitions. By contrast, "costs" take on new meanings for reform coalitions and affect their development in different ways: instead of opportunity and transaction costs, potential participants will be more concerned over the costs of reform itself.

This occurs because the shift from statist to market policies creates winners and losers inside the government, and generates substantial costs for actors that administered statist programs. Such costs produce a certain logic that affects a reform coalition's formation and composition. On the one hand, actors who must internalize these costs are unlikely to initiate reform efforts themselves; on the other, actors able to externalize these costs are more likely to advocate and embrace them. Consequently, when reform coalitions develop, the founding members will likely be those who can externalize the costs of policy change to others.[70] On this basis, we should expect reform coalitions to spring from state economic ministries (Treasury, Budget and Planning, etc.) rather than agencies that supervised public enterprises or regulated the protected market. Similarly, we should expect environmental reforms to germinate outside those agencies responsible for Mexico's *command and control* regime. Evidence in the following chapters affirms these propositions.

By selecting coalitions as a principal unit of analysis the conditions of successful reform become clear. Policy feedback and the reformer's dilemma stand between reformers and success, and at both stages of the reform process (formulation and implementation) coalition politics will prove crucial. As subsequent chapters illustrate, only where reformers forged coalitions endowed with *organizational strength* did they overcome obstacles inside the state; and only by expanding their membership outside the state were they able to implement reforms successfully.

Notes

1. See Paul Pierson, "When Effect Becomes Cause: Policy Feedback and Political Change," *World Politics* 45 (July 1993): 597.

2. Judith V. May and Aaron Wildavsky, eds., *The Policy Cycle* (Beverly Hills, Calif.: Sage, 1978), 13.

3. For example, Naím has written extensively on these issues with respect to Venezuela's reform initiatives under Carlos Andrés Pérez; Teichman and Córdobo chronicle the same with respect to Mexico; and Urrutia, Petrazzini, Grosse, and Corrales detail setbacks to privatization programs in Colombia and Argentina respectively. See Moisés Naím, *Paper Tigers and Minotaurs: The Politics of Venezuela's Economic Reforms* (Washington, D.C.: Carnegie Endowment for International Peace, 1993); Judith Teichman, *Privatization and Political Change in Mexico* (Pittsburgh: University of Pittsburgh Press, 1995); José Córdoba, "Mexico," in John Williamson, ed., *The Political Economy of Policy Reform* (Washington, D.C.: Institute for International Economics, 1994); Miguel Urrutia, "Colombia," in Williamson, *The Political Economy of Policy Reform;* Ben Petrazzini, "Telephone Privatization in a Hurry: Argentina," in Ravi Ramamurti, ed., *Privatizing Monopolies: Lessons from the Telecommunications and Transport Sectors in Latin America* (Baltimore: Johns Hopkins University Press, 1996); Robert Grosse, "A Privatization Nightmare: Aerolíneas Argentinas," in Ramamurti, *Privatizing Monopolies;* and Javier Corrales, "Do Economic Crises Contribute to Economic Reform? Argentina and Venezuela in the 1990s," *Political Science Quarterly* 112, no. 4 (1997-98).

4. Paul Pierson, *Dismantling the Welfare State? Reagan, Thatcher, and the Politics of Retrenchment* (Cambridge: Cambridge University Press, 1994), 5.

5. Granted, the thrust of Pierson's argument is that feedback is explicitly an independent variable which affects subsequent political outcomes. My point, while subtle, is that feedback also is an *implicit dependent* variable.

6. Olson's work established the general proposition that concentrated interests have stronger motivations to pursue collective action than less concentrated ones. See Mancur Olson, *The Logic of Collective Action: Public Goods and the Theory of Groups* (Cambridge, Mass.: Harvard University Press, 1965). For applications of this principle to market reforms see Steve H. Hanke and Stephen J. K. Walter, "Privatization and Public Choice: Lessons for the LDCs," in Dennis J. Gayle and Jonathan N. Goodrich, eds., *Privatization and Deregulation in Global Perspective* (Westport, Conn.: Quorum Books, 1990); Nicolas Van de Walle, "Privatization in Developing Countries: A Review of the Issues," *World Development* 17, no. 5 (1989); and William Glade, "Toward Effective Privatization Strategies," in William Glade, ed., *Privatization of Public Enterprises in Latin America* (San

Francisco: ICS Press, 1991), 120.

7. Joan Nelson, "The Politics of Economic Transformation: Is Third World Experience Relevant to Eastern Europe?" *World Politics* 45 (April 1993): 434.

8. E. E. Schattschneider, *Politics, Pressures, and the Tariff* (New York: Prentice-Hall, 1935), 288.

9. For discussion of these issues see Carol Graham, *Safety Nets, Politics, and the Poor: Transitions to Market Economies* (Washington, D.C.: Brookings Institution, 1993).

10. Kenneth W. Dam, *The Rules of the Game* (Chicago: University of Chicago Press, 1982), 4.

11. Robert H. Bates and Anne O. Krueger, eds., "Generalizations Arising from the Country Studies," in Robert H. Bates and Anne O. Krueger, *Political and Economic Interactions in Economic Policy Reform: Evidence from Eight Countries* (Cambridge, Mass.: Blackwell, 1993), 456.

12. See Raquel Fernández and Dani Rodrik, "Resistance to Reform: Status Quo Bias in the Presence of Individual-Specific Uncertainty," *American Economic Review* 81, no. 5 (1991).

13. In contrast, a few scholars have focused attention on a smaller group of policy makers who excel at politics as well as economics, and are in fact political creatures. As Domínguez observes, "technopols" (as he calls them) make reforms "acceptable" by fashioning policies "guided by their political analysis [and acting] in ways that are unfamiliar to many professional economists." The atypical embrace of the *political* situates these decision makers in the real world of policy reform (as opposed to an economics textbook scenario). From this vantage point they seek to persuade skeptics to accept market policies via plausible constructs of future outcomes. Jorge I. Domínguez, "Technopols: Ideas and Leaders in Freeing Politics and Markets in Latin America in the 1990s," in Jorge I. Domínguez, ed., *Technopols: Freeing Politics and Markets in Latin America in the 1990s* (University Park, Penn.: Pennsylvania State University Press, 1997), 4.

14. A variety of perspectives comprise the body of "New Institutionalist" literature. See, for example, Stephen Skowronek, *Building a New American State: The Expansion of National Administrative Capacities, 1877–1920* (New York: Cambridge University Press, 1982); Peter A. Hall, *Governing the Economy: The Politics of State Intervention in Britain and France* (New York: Oxford University Press, 1986); Sven Steinmo, Kathleen Thelen, and Frank Longstreth, eds., *Structuring Politics: Historical Institutionalism in Comparative Analysis* (New York: Cambridge University Press, 1992); James G. March and Johan P. Olsen, *Rediscovering Institutions: The Organizational Basis of Politics* (New York: Free Press, 1989); and Douglass C. North, *Institutions, Institutional Change, and Economic Performance* (New York: Cambridge University Press, 1990).

15. Kenneth A. Shepsle, "Studying Institutions: Some Lessons from the Rational Choice Approach," *Journal of Theoretical Politics* 1, no. 2 (1989): 137.

16. Terry M. Moe, "Political Institutions: The Neglected Side of the Story," *Journal of Law, Economics, and Organization* 6 (1990): 228.

17. See Margaret Weir, Ann Shola Orloff, and Theda Skocpol, "Introduction: Understanding American Social Politics," in Margaret Weir, Ann Shola Orloff, and Theda Skocpol, eds., *The Politics of Social Policy in the United States* (Princeton, N.J.: Princeton University Press, 1988); Hall, *Governing the Economy;* Sven Steinmo, "Political Institutions and Tax Policy in the United States, Sweden, and Britain," *World Politics* 41 (July 1989): 502; and Ellen M. Immergut, "The Rules of the Game: The Logic of Health Policy-Making in

Switzerland, and Sweden," in Steinmo, Thelen, and Longstreth, *Structuring Politics*.

18. Maria Lorena Cook, Kevin J. Middlebrook, and Juan Molinar Horcasitas, "The Politics of Economic Restructuring in Mexico: Actors, Sequencing, and Coalition Change," in Maria Lorena Cook, Kevin J. Middlebrook, and Juan Molinar Horcasitas, eds., *The Politics of Economic Restructuring: State-Society Relations and Regime Change in Mexico* (La Jolla, Calif.: Center for U.S.-Mexican Studies, University of California, San Diego, 1994), 7.

19. For example, see Pablo González Casanova, *Democracy in Mexico* (London: Oxford University Press, 1970); and John J. Baily, *Governing Mexico: The Statecraft of Crisis Management* (New York: St. Martin's Press, 1988). For an excellent general discussion of Mexican presidentialism see Jeffrey Weldon, "The Political Sources of Presidencialismo in Mexico," in Scott Mainwaring and Matthew Soberg Shugart, eds., *Presidentialism and Democracy in Latin America* (New York: Cambridge University Press, 1997).

20. Through 1993 roughly 90 percent of all bills emerged from the executive, not Congress; and bills sent to Congress by the executive took precedence over those originating in Congress itself. See Roderic Ai Camp, *Politics in Mexico* (New York: Oxford University Press, 1993), 136; and Howard F. Cline, *Mexico: Revolution to Evolution, 1940-1960* (New York: Oxford University Press, 1963), 143.

21. Stephen D. Morris, *Political Reformism in Mexico: An Overview of Contemporary Mexican Politics* (Boulder, Colo.: Lynne Rienner, 1995), 18.

22. See Dale Story, *The Mexican Ruling Party: Stability and Authority* (Stanford: Hoover Institution, 1986), 131-132.

23. On Mexico's "limited pluralism" see John F. H. Purcell and Susan Kaufman Purcell, "Mexican Business and Public Policy," in James M. Malloy, ed., *Authoritarianism and Corporatism in Latin America* (Pittsburgh: University of Pittsburgh Press, 1977), 94.

24. The PRI's peak organizations include the Confederation of Workers of Mexico (labor), the National Peasant Confederation (campesinos), and the National Confederation of Popular Organizations (middle-class professionals and state employees). On corporatism in general, see Guillermo O'Donnell, "Corporatism and the Question of the State," in Malloy, *Authoritarianism in Latin America;* and Philippe C. Schmitter, "Still the Century of Corporatism?" in Fredrick B. Pike and Thomas Stritch, eds., *The New Corporatism: Social-Political Structures in the Iberian World* (Notre Dame, Ind.: University of Notre Dame Press, 1974). On Mexican corporatism see Rose Spalding, "The Mexican Variant of Corporatism," *Comparative Political Studies* 14 (July 1981); and Evelyn P. Stevens, "Mexico's PRI: The Institutionalization of Corporatism?" in Malloy, *Authoritarianism in Latin America*.

25. Roger D. Hansen, *The Politics of Mexican Development* (Baltimore: Johns Hopkins University Press, 1971), 113.

26. Ruth Berins Collier and David Collier, "Inducements versus Constraints: Disaggregating Corporatism," *American Political Science Review* 73 (December 1979).

27. Roderic Ai Camp, *Politics in Mexico, 2d ed.* (New York: Oxford University Press, 1996), 170.

28. Based on survey data of the 1988 and 1991 national elections Domínguez and McCann found that Mexicans did not use the ballot to express their policy preference. Indeed, economic policy concerns "had no direct impact on voter choice" in either election. See Jorge I. Domínguez and James A. McCann, "Shaping Mexico's Electoral Arena: The Construction of Partisan Cleavages in the 1988 and 1991 National Elections," *American Political Science Review* 89, no. 1 (March 1995): 41.

29. Jorge I. Domínguez and James A. McCann, *Democratizing Mexico: Public Opinion and Electoral Choices* (Baltimore: Johns Hopkins University Press, 1996), 113.

30. This is as true for labor and peasants as it is for business. Smith notes that policy disputes between the private sector and the state "often centered on the implementation of existing law, rather than on the formulation of new laws." See Peter H. Smith, "Does Mexico Have a Power Elite?" in José Luis Reyna and Richard S. Weinert, eds., *Authoritarianism in Mexico* (Philadelphia: Institute for the Study of Human Issues, 1977), 142.

31. See Merilee S. Grindle, *Bureaucrats, Politicians, and Peasants in Mexico: A Case Study in Public Policy* (Berkeley: University of California Press, 1977), 109.

32. David Mares, "Explaining Choice of Development Strategies: Suggestions from Mexico, 1970-1982," *International Organization* 39 (Autumn 1985): 685.

33. On coalition formation and payoff see William H. Riker, *The Theory of Political Coalitions* (New Haven, Conn.: Yale University Press, 1962), and Jerome M. Chertkoff, "Sociopsychological Theories and Research on Coalition Formation," in Sven Groennings, E. W. Kelley, and Michael Leiserson, eds., *The Study of Coalition Behavior: Theoretical Perspectives and Cases from Four Continents* (New York: Holt, Rinehart and Winston, 1970). On coalition formation and cost calculations see Charles R. Adrian and Charles Press, "Decision Costs in Coalition Formation," *American Political Science Review* 62 (1968). For discussion of coalition formation and policy preference see William A. Gamson, "A Theory of Coalition Formation," *American Sociological Review* 26 (1961). On coalition formation and minimal conflict of interest see Robert Axelrod, "Conflict of Interest, an Axiomatic Approach," *Journal of Conflict Resolution* 11 (1967).

34. For example, see G. John Ikenberry, "The International Spread of Privatization Policies: Inducements, Learning, and 'Policy Bandwagoning,'" in Ezra N. Suleiman and John Waterbury, eds., *The Political Economy of Public Sector Reform and Privatization* (Boulder, Colo.: Westview, 1990), 94-95. See also John Waterbury, "The Political Management of Economic Adjustment and Reform," in Joan M. Nelson, ed., *Fragile Coalitions: The Politics of Economic Adjustment* (Washington, D.C.: Overseas Development Council, 1989); and Stephan Haggard and Joan Nelson, "Panel Discussion," in John Williamson, ed., *The Political Economy of Policy Reform* (Washington, D.C.: Institute for International Economics, 1994), 468, 473.

35. Stephan Haggard and Steven Webb, "Introduction," in Stephan Haggard and Steven Webb, *Voting for Reform: Democracy, Political Liberalization, and Economic Adjustment* (New York: Oxford University Press, 1994), 16.

36. The classic work on transaction costs and organizational efficiency is found in Ronald H. Coase, "The Nature of the Firm," *Económica* 4 N.S. (1937); and Herbert A. Simon, *Administrative Behavior,* 2d ed. (New York: Free Press, 1957).

37. Robert Dahl, "Power," in David L. Sills, ed., *International Encyclopedia of the Social Sciences,* vol. 12 (New York: MacMillan and Free Press, 1968).

38. Max Weber, *Economy and Society,* vol. 1 (New York: Bedminster Press, 1968), 127.

39. For discussion of these points see Barry Hindess, "Power, Interests, and the Outcomes of Struggles," *Sociology* 16 (November 1982).

40. See, for example, Peter M. Blau and Richard A. Schoenherr, *The Structure of Organizations* (New York: Basic Books, 1971); and D. J. Hickson et al., "A Strategic Contingencies Theory of Interorganizational Power," *Administrative Science Quarterly* 15 (1971).

41. Howard E. Aldrich and Sergio Mindlin, "Uncertainty and Dependence: Two Per-

spectives on the Environment," in Lucien Karpik, ed., *Organization and Environment: Theory, Issues, and Reality* (London: Sage, 1978), 156.

42. Charles Perrow, "Departmental Power and Perspective in Industrial Firms," in Mayer Zald, ed., *Power in Organizations* (Nashville, Tenn.: Vanderbilt University Press, 1972).

43. On relations of "structural dependency," see Richard M. Emerson, "Social Exchange Theory," in Alex Inkeles, James Coleman, and Neil Smelser, eds., *Annual Review of Sociology* 2 (Palo Alto, Calif.: Annual Reviews, 1976); and Jeffery Pfeffer and Gerald R. Salancik, *The External Control of Organizations* (New York: Harper and Row, 1978).

44. For example, see Noel M. Tichy and Charles Fombrun, "Network Analysis in Organizational Settings," *Human Relations* 32, no. 11 (1979).

45. For a related discussion, see Giandomenico Majone, *Evidence, Argument and Persuasion in the Policy Process* (New Haven, Conn.: Yale University Press, 1989), especially 97-98.

46. See Brian Levy, "The Design and Sequencing of Trade and Investment Policy Reform," *World Bank PRE Working Paper Series* 419 (May 1990), 25.

47. Nelson, "The Politics of Economic Transformation," 440. The logic of this approach is based on "delegated authority," and is not limited to the politics of market reforms in developing countries. Government decision makers often create new entities to which they delegate responsibility for a specific policy realm, especially when the politics surrounding that policy are particularly contentious. Examples in the United States would be the bipartisan "base closing" and "social security" commissions.

48. Benjamin L. Crosby, "Policy Implementation: The Organizational Challenge," *World Development* 24 (1996).

49. See Lawrence Cooley et al., "Evaluation of UDAPE and the Policy Reform Project," Final Report, Implementing Policy Change Project (Washington, D.C.: U.S. Agency for International Development, May 1991); Benjamin L. Crosby, "Honduras' UDAPE: A Case Study," Implementing Policy Change Project (Washington, D.C.: U.S. Agency for International Development, 1996); and Silvio De Franco and Rafael Díaz, "PAPI Project Implementation Review," Final Report, Implementing Policy Change Project (Washington, D.C.: U.S. Agency for International Development, November 1994).

50. On Argentina, see Javier Corrales, "Why Argentines Followed Cavallo," in Domínguez, *Technopols,* 64; on Turkey, see Yavuz Canevi, "Turkey," in Williamson, *The Political Economy of Policy Reform,* 185.

51. E. E. Schattschneider, *The Semisovereign People: A Realist's View of Democracy in America* (Hinsdale, Ill.: Dryden Press, 1960), 68-69.

52. Nelson, "The Politics of Economic Transformation," 436.

53. Terry M. Moe, "The Politics of Bureaucratic Structure," in John E. Chubb and Paul E. Peterson, eds., *Can the Government Govern?* (Washington, D.C.: Brookings Institution, 1989), 268, 273.

54. Ibid., 270.

55. For representative examples, see Haggard and Kaufman, *The Political Economy of Democratic Transitions,* 9; Haggard and Kaufman, "Introduction," in Haggard and Kaufman, *The Politics of Economic Adjustment* (Princeton, N.J.: Princeton University Press, 1992), 23.

56. Strategizing behavior is completely analogous to the theory of capital put forth by Austrian economist Eugen von Böm-Bawerk, who believed "roundabout" production methods were more efficient than direct ones (why catch one fish at a time using your hands when you can catch a whole school by expending resources on constructing a net). Thus,

Böm-Bawerk argued: "That roundabout methods [of production] lead to greater results than direct methods is one of the most important and fundamental propositions in the whole theory of production." Quoted in Mark Blaug, *Economic Theory in Retrospect,* 3d ed. (Cambridge: Cambridge University Press, 1979), 526.

57. As Hall observed, "the persuasiveness of economic ideas depends, in part at least, on the way those ideas relate to the economic and political problems of the day." Peter A. Hall, "Conclusion: The Politics of Keynesian Ideas," in Peter A. Hall, ed., *The Political Power of Economic Ideas: Keynesianism across Nations* (Princeton, N.J.: Princeton University Press, 1989), 369.

58. Peter A. Hall, "Policy Paradigms, Social Learning, and the State: The Case of Economic Policymaking in Britain," *Comparative Politics* 25 (April 1993): 279.

59. Robert Alford, *Bureaucracy and Participation: Political Cultures in Four Wisconsin Cities* (Chicago: Rand McNally, 1969), 31.

60. To quote Elder and Cobb, "To define a situation as a policy problem is to imply its solution and to delimit its solution possibilities." Charles D. Elder and Roger W. Cobb, "Agenda-Building and the Politics of Aging," *Policy Studies Journal* 13, no. 1 (September 1984): 123.

61. See William H. Riker, *The Art of Political Manipulation* (New Haven, Conn.: Yale University Press, 1986).

62. On the influence conferred by uncertainty-coping see the classic study by James D. Thompson, *Organizations in Action* (New York: McGraw-Hill, 1967). For a succinct yet thorough literature review on this topic see Hickson et al., "A Strategic Contingencies' Theory of Intraorganizational Power."

63. Hall, "Policy Paradigms," 290-291.

64. My discussion here builds upon Gusfield's notion of "problem ownership"—a concept well established in the political science and policy analysis literature. See Joseph Gusfield, *The Culture of Public Problems: Drinking-Driving and the Symbolic Order* (Chicago: University of Chicago Press, 1981), 10-11. See also the discussion of "policy monopolies" in Frank R. Baumgartner and Bryan D. Jones, *Agendas and Instability in American Politics* (Chicago: University of Chicago Press, 1993).

65. Martha Derthick, *Policymaking for Social Security* (Washington, D.C.: Brookings, 1979).

66. Baumgartner and Jones, *Agendas and Instability,* 7.

67. Elder and Cobb, "Agenda-Building and the Politics of Aging," 120.

68. The absence of predetermined outcomes is a central feature of political dynamics. As Przeworski writes, "[t]he capacity of particular groups to realize their interests is shaped by the specific institutional arrangements of a given system . . . [but] outcomes of conflicts are not uniquely determined." Similarly, Krasner suggests that political outcomes depend in large part on how actors "play the game" and interact; even should actors *change* the institutions that structure politics, they are not automatically guaranteed preferred outcomes. See Adam Przeworski, "Some Problems in the Study of the Transition to Democracy," in Guillermo O'Donnell, Philip C. Schmitter, and Laurence Whitehead, eds., *Transitions from Authoritarian Rule: Comparative Perspectives* (Baltimore: Johns Hopkins University Press, 1988), 58; and Steven Krasner, "Sovereignty: An Institutional Perspective," in James A. Caporaso, ed., *The Elusive State: International and Comparative Perspectives* (Newbury Park, Calif.: Sage, 1989), 88.

69. Adrian and Press, "Decision Costs in Coalition Formation."

70. An example would be when bureaucracy "A" initiates a reform that curtails the responsibilities of "B," or imposes costs on "B's" non-state constituents; here, the reform initiator has effectively externalized the costs to others.

Part II

Case Studies

Chapter 3

Privatizing Aeroméxico, Cananea, and Sicartsa

If a country is really committed to its people, why then should its government retain an airline and use billions of dollars [to] modernize its fleet when only two percent of its population has ever used the service and at the same time demands better public services?

—Pedro Aspe

This chapter examines efforts to privatize operations in what the Mexican government traditionally considered "priority" economic sectors: aviation, mining, and steelmaking. To ensure analytical breadth, it contrasts the experience of the de la Madrid and Salinas administrations. While divestiture became a cornerstone of Mexico's neoliberal project, not all state actors supported the initiatives; outside the state, most unionized labor was decidedly opposed. The increasing complexity of divestiture initiatives also challenged reformers as they moved from aviation to mining to steel. Each new divestment seemed to require more sophisticated measures to evaluate and "package" corporate assets, administer sales, and respond to broader market constraints (table 3.1). Nevertheless, between 1988 and 1991 the government successfully privatized its national airline, Aeroméxico, the Cananea copper mine, and the gigantic Sicartsa steelworks. Because divestment brought reformers into direct conflict with powerful vested interests, these achievements are particularly significant.

The patterns of policy implementation, however, differed markedly across cases. In some instances like aviation, reformers implemented new policy via highly coercive tactics (union busting, prosecutions); in others like steel, they did not. In the case of copper even massive coercion (military force and union busting) proved an ineffective means to implement controversial new policy. What explains the dissimilar patterns of policy implementation? How did reformers overcome the

59

Table 3.1   Dimensions of Policy Complexity

Complexity Factor	Aeroméxico	Cananea	Sicartsa
Packaging/Asset Evaluation	in-house evaluation	in-house evaluation	in-house and external evaluation
New Administrative Unit	no	no	yes
Buyers' Pool	ample	shrinking	limited
Broader Market Conditions	favorable	favorable	unfavorable
Legal Framework	no change	no change	major changes

impediments of feedback and the dilemma produced by policy "costs"? A persuasive explanation must account for both the outcomes (success) and the variance of implementation patterns.[1]

In tackling these questions this chapter stresses the role that coalition politics, organizational strength, and policy "costs" played in the reform process. Where reform coalitions coalesced early on inside the state (Aeroméxico and Sicartsa), reformers formulated and adopted divestment plans swiftly. They drew upon their organizational strength to marginalize opponents, and bolstered their positions inside the state through effective institutional innovation. Where coalitions developed later in the process (Cananea), divestiture initiatives absent cross-agency coordination met setbacks, and proceeded more slowly. In all cases, however, the pattern of policy implementation hinged upon how central political actors calculated and responded to the costs of policy change. Minimizing strategies (i.e., division, persuasion, compensation) helped reformers mollify resistance, incorporate potential and erstwhile opponents into their coalitions, and implement new policy noncoercively. Alternatively, imposition strategies—made feasible via Mexico's authoritarian political system—carried a more punitive edge.

Close scrutiny of Mexico's experience provides clear evidence that arguments for successful reform based on policy complexity, technocratic "change teams," or centralized power cannot fully explain why reformers prevailed in the struggles over policy change. Nor can they account for the variance in patterns of policy implementation. "Embedded autonomy" (again, internal coherence among reformers combined with their external connectedness to societal actors) played an important role during the phase of policy implementation. But ultimately, the interests arrayed against reform—manifestations of policy feedback and the reformer's dilemma—plus the institutional context in which reformers operated made coalition politics and organizational strength crucial to success.

The Challenges to Widespread Divestiture

Public sector growth is a hallmark of statist development models.[2] In Mexico the expansion of public enterprise also reflected nationalist/sovereignty aspirations, constitutional mandates,[3] and a practical response to various concrete objectives: serving the public interest, job creation, advancing social goals, bolstering industrial output, and providing subsidized services and production inputs like energy and credit, etc. Consequently, as revealed in figure 3.1, between 1930 and 1982 the Mexican government created or acquired well over 1,100 public enterprises (PEs) across a host of economic sectors.[4] Many became highly inefficient, ran yearly deficits, and were kept afloat through state subsidies.

Some analysts credit these problems primarily to the multiple distortions produced by overregulation—a common ancillary to large public sector operations. In a comprehensive World Bank study of Latin America's market reforms, for example, Sebastian Edwards notes:

> In almost every country, the growth of the state-owned enterprise sector was accompanied by the development of massive regulatory legislation. . . . Entry into and exit from certain industries were tightly controlled, the price and quantity of goods produced were regulated, and . . . labor relations became more rigid. The combination of a very large state-owned enterprise sector and massive regulations generally resulted in a lethargic public sector. . . . By the mid-1980s, in most countries, state-owned enterprises were incurring major losses that imposed a heavy burden on public finances, fueled the inflationary process, and resulted in very poor provision of services.[5]

But while important, overregulation was simply one facet of the dilemmas that bedeviled many PEs in Mexico. A good deal of their economic problems stemmed from a set of constraints built into public sector operations that systematically undermined efficiency and profitability.

One major constraint from which others flowed was the perversion of the principal-agent relationship—an arrangement whereby "one party (the agent) acts on behalf of another (the principal)" to maximize the latter's welfare.[6] For public corporations the principal-agent relationship casts the general public as principal and the PE as its agent; when perverted, politicians supersede the "public" as principals and companies and corporate directors remain agents subject to their bidding.

In firms like Aeroméxico, this perversion injected politics directly into corporate decision making, adversely affecting its route structure and profit potential. To boost their popularity some Mexican presidents ordered the carrier to extend service to new, low-demand regions.[7] State governors too, used the government's airline for their own agendas and petitioned the Transportation Ministry to service marginal localities for "development" purposes. Eventually, such political tinker-

Figure 3.1   Mexico's Expanding Public Sector, 1930–1982

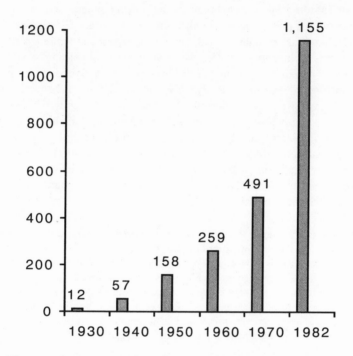

Source: *El proceso de enajenación de entidades paraestatales* (México, D.F.: Secretaría de Hacienda y Crédito Público, 1992).

ing saddled Aeroméxico with many unprofitable routes (*rutas políticas*), and gave rise to a tradition of literal "free riding" whereby free air travel was extended to (and expected by) well-connected politicians. As several high officials recall these times, flights filled with "nonpaying bureaucrats" were not uncommon.[8]

The perversion of the principal-agent relationship helped tilt incentive structures away from prudent financial management in other ways too. It left directors few incentives to watch the bottom line and made public managers increasingly risk averse. As "agents," directors had a unique political relationship with their principals: they understood a manager's tenure was subject more to his political performance (i.e., maintaining "normal" business operations, providing political perks) than the firm's economic well-being,[9] and could count on routine subsidies to cover corporate red ink. In terms of risk-aversion, managers tended to avoid actions that might reflect poorly on the government, especially when dealing with organized labor. The constant weighing of management decisions against the political costs of labor unrest opened the door to dramatic union conquests: within three decades Aeroméxico's unions ranked among the highest paid, best compensated workers in the country;[10] unions in other public sector firms, meanwhile, racked up similar victories.

As Edwards observed, regulations also placed constraints on public sector performance. In the case of steel, the Commerce Ministry fixed the price of steel products to ensure downstream industries affordable inputs. These price caps—always lower than actual steelmaking costs—burdened public steel firms with chronic deficits and to maintain their operations the state compensated for lost revenues with subsidies. By the 1980s steel subsidies averaged between $75 and $100 million per year,[11] and a "survival by subsidy" mentality prevailed among firms like Sicartsa. In the aviation sector, meanwhile, a similar story unfolded. For decades the Transportation Ministry kept ticket prices well below market value or even international fares for similar distances. As late as 1989 one-way fares for a 200-mile trip were over $100 cheaper in Mexico than the United States, and almost *$300* cheaper than a comparable 300-mile flight.[12] Again, subsidies made up for revenue shortfalls.

Still other constraints derived from pro-labor policies and the Federal Labor Law. The former facilitated overmanning by inflating the number of job categories in collective contracts;[13] the latter encouraged redundancy through obligatory—and significant—severance payments to discharged workers.[14] While these policies reflected the social welfare function many Mexican public enterprises were expected to fulfill,[15] they also helped bloat corporate payrolls and undermine efficiency. Moreover, once rigid job classifications were inserted into a contract clause, union locals acquired vested interests in maintaining it. Much of the conflict that later erupted over restructuring and divesting public enterprises would center on reformers' efforts to eliminate overmanning (and the subsidies that sustained it) and union efforts to preserve the practice. It is worth stressing, however, that while neoliberal reformers routinely viewed labor as the chief source of corporate inefficiency, the evidence does not wholly support this position. To be sure, such "labor problems" were real; but they constituted merely one of many factors working against PE profitability.

Still, the effect that regulations and pro-labor legislation/policies had on public corporate finances was systematic and pernicious. On the one hand, price controls limited firms' revenue potential; on the other, labor policies and the federal labor code helped boost labor costs. The upshot was the paradox of a *near-monopoly* (Aeroméxico) or protected firm (Sicartsa) unable to turn a profit in Mexico's protected market; throughout the public sector cash flow problems, low productivity, and labor redundancy became the norm.

For reformers, Mexico's problem-plagued public sector offered both rationales and opportunities to seek dramatic policy change. But even so, success would not come easy. Whether in aviation, mining, or steel, divestiture efforts confronted intense opposition from vested interests, and often reformers discovered their institutional environment was more a constraint than a benefit.

Vested Interests

The public sector's dramatic expansion created a dense network of vested interests inside the state where careers, institutional prestige, and budget allocations were linked closely to public sector operations. Bureaucratic agencies like the ministries of Transportation or Energy, Mines, and Parastatals (SEMIP) defended their corporations aggressively. During the early years of the de la Madrid administration, for example, SEMIP—a bureaucratic heavyweight whose corporations were a dominant force in industrial sectors—staved off divestment plans by restructuring its firms to increase their productivity.[16] As privatization gained momentum in the mid-1980s, some ministry personnel changed tactics and resisted divestment by withholding data needed to prepare companies for sale.[17] Though passive, such resistance proved highly effective and had important political consequences; it forced reformers to forge coalitions inside the bureaucracy and devise means to isolate protectors of the status quo.

Outside the state, public sector expansion spawned important status quo constituencies as well. Past policies helped organized labor establish privileged enclaves in public enterprises and rack up impressive victories at the negotiating table. Eventually, contracts held by Mexican airline, mining, and steel workers became so generous that reformers believed revising them "downward" was critical to promoting privatization. The costs of these measures (lost jobs, benefits) made unions unlikely prospects for membership in reform coalitions; but for reformers, expanding their constituency outside the state to include at least some "losers" was crucial to policy implementation and governability. In various ways, then, the vested interests born of statism produced lock-in effects that raised the political costs of privatization considerably; the reformer's dilemma only complicated matters. Overcoming these obstacles hinged upon reformers' organizational strength and coalitional expansion.

The Institutional Environment

Privatizing public enterprises is an administratively intense process involving asset evaluation and sales preparation, buyer selection, bid appraisal, sales negotiation, and authorization for closure, etc.[18] Each stage is complex, with responsibilities often spread across actors and agencies. Norms and procedures that govern the divestment process form an important part of what I have called the institutional context: by advantaging some actors over others and enhancing or eroding the value of actors' resources, decision rules and procedures can have profound affects on political outcomes.

Like vested interests, the broad institutional context inside Mexico's bureaucracy also worked against reformers. In fact, during divestment's early years (through the late 1980s), patterns of decision making actually favored privatization opponents. Most important were the norms or decision criteria used to determine which PEs would be divested and the standard operating procedures that structured the divestment process.

Under the de la Madrid government each ministry responsible for a public enterprise (the sector ministry) could nominate a firm as a divestment candidate, based on one of five criteria. Divestment was justified if a PE: (1) duplicated the activities of another, (2) failed to achieve its original goals, (3) had fulfilled its original mandate, (4) suffered serious financial or technical liabilities, or (5) was engaged in neither strategic nor priority activities.[19] Once a ministry selected a candidate the nomination passed through layers of bureaucracy before reaching the president's desk. Upon the president's approval, the National Credit Society (NCS) administered the sale, after which, the company finally passed from the ministry's control to its new private owners. To evaluate and prepare a public enterprise for auction the NCS relied on company managers to provide detailed financial information like profit-loss statements, productivity rates, assets and liabilities, etc.[20]

These institutional arrangements affected the scope, pace, and success of divestment significantly. With five divestment criteria, ministries enjoyed broad discretion to select a divestment candidate; state managers retained control over (and could manipulate) vital corporate information; and PEs remained under a sector ministry's jurisdiction until a sale was concluded. In short, policy procedures structured decision making in ways that made reformers dependent on potential opponents and placed the onus to privatize on those least likely to favor large-scale asset transfers.

Not surprisingly, throughout the 1980s few ministries offered to sell their "crown jewels," but instead used their discretion to nominate firms that were the least attractive to potential buyers.[21] PE managers foot-dragged divestment too, by exploiting the "bottom up" information flows policy procedures established. In some cases they could forestall a divestment for years simply by providing partial or faulty corporate information.[22] In others, they engineered the sale of corporate lemons—firms whose material assets did not match the sales prospectus, had substantial undisclosed debts, or operated in gross violation of environmental statutes.[23] Litigating purchase disputes after the fact or renegotiating the terms of sale taxed reformers' energies, slowing the divestment process even more.

Despite the obstacles (and many setbacks) the de la Madrid administration successfully privatized hundreds of firms, and under Salinas the successes multiplied. One of the principal reasons was that after 1989 reformers altered the institutional context of privatization policy radically. They made crucial changes in candidate selection criteria, policy procedures, and administrative structures. Ministries lost much of their discretionary power, as did managers their monopoly of corporate information, and reformers gained complete control over the divestment process.

Divestment under de la Madrid: Aeroméxico Airline

Thanks to the fiscal policies of President José López Portillo (1976-82) and an uncooperative international economy, Miguel de la Madrid assumed the presidential sash amidst a severe economic crisis.[24] The continuation of that crisis—characterized by enormous debt, near insolvency, negative growth rates, and a shutoff in foreign credit—required drastic measures. But corrective efforts notwithstanding, economic deterioration escalated sharply in 1985–1986.[25] Inside the state the crisis forced key policy makers into what Nelson Polsby termed "search behavior"—driving them to question the future of Mexico's statist development model, hotly debate policy options, and rethink what the government's "proper" role in the economy should be.[26]

Since divesting money-losing public enterprises provided one source of relief, privatization became a viable strategy, but not necessarily an easy path to take. For one thing, Mexico's ruling party had long championed public sector operations, and some PEs were renowned as symbols of nationalism and sovereignty (e.g., the oil monopoly Petroleos Mexicanos and Cananea). Moreover, the administration's five-year National Development Plan gave the state a central role in economic development and President de la Madrid was reluctant to abandon it.[27] In fact, in line with Mexico's historic development trajectory his initial inclination was to retain (but improve) statism despite the crisis. But as the president explained, the severity of Mexico's plight impelled a fundamental reorientation: "My earlier experience in government taught me that the state was interventionist, but I saw through practical experience the limits of intervention. Governing is a learning process. You enter office with a set of policy ideas, but as conditions change you learn to refine or alter them to meet the situation."[28]

With respect to divestment, therefore, Mexico's reform program began gradually with small firms, but gained momentum as the government acquired experience selling PEs. By late decade the administration had graduated to larger firms like Aeroméxico.

Aviation: History and Market Structure

Mexico's commercial aviation sector developed around two trunk airlines established in 1921 and 1934 respectively: Mexicana and Aeroméxico.[29] In 1929 the U.S. carrier Pan American acquired all shares of Mexicana, and in 1940, purchased 40 percent of Aeroméxico. Foreign capital and aeronautical expertise were a boon to Mexico's fledgling aviation sector and the domestic market quickly developed into a duopoly largely under foreign control.

Invariably, this situation bred a system of noncompetition whereby trunk airlines carved out market niches, but generally shared the market more than they

competed for market share. Mexicana came to dominate the country's northeast-
ern market (especially regions close to the U.S. border) while Aeroméxico concentrated on the tourist areas along the Pacific coast. By the 1980s the trunk lines
had captured over 96 percent of the domestic market[30]—their positions sustained,
in part, by air transport regulations. Through route concessions the Ministry of
Transportation tightly regulated Mexico's domestic market and awarded concessions in ways that restricted competition and protected the established carriers'
sunk costs.[31] This, plus fixed airfares, sheltered the trunk lines from domestic competitors, preempted the outbreak of price wars between them, and sustained the
duopoly for decades. During the same time span the carriers' ownership profile
changed considerably.

With the shift to import substitution during World War II, the Mexican government actively promoted domestic growth. To reserve the fruits of growth for
Mexican nationals it pursued a policy of *mexicanization* that limited foreign ownership in various sectors, generally to 49 percent. A 1947 presidential decree extended *mexicanization* to aviation. Pan American resisted *mexicanization* for years,
but finally sold its Aeroméxico shares to Mexican nationals in 1957. Ten years
later it sold off Mexicana. Despite the change of ownership Aeroméxico's fortunes
failed to improve; by 1959 the company was headed toward bankruptcy. To save
the carrier, the government purchased all the company's stock and transformed
Aeroméxico into a public enterprise.[32]

But as a public carrier Aeroméxico performed no better economically than
under private ownership. Between 1959 and 1988 it was a consistent money loser
with liabilities exceeding revenues every year save three (1979–1981). Despite
repeated corrective attempts, profits remained elusive, the labor force continued to
grow, and expenses outpaced income such that by the 1980s, annual subsidies to
Aeroméxico averaged 15 percent of total revenues.[33] The airline's grim profit statements mirrored its performance record: flights were routinely late, service extremely
poor,[34] and in the late 1980s Aeroméxico ranked seventeenth among eighteen Latin
American carriers (barely nudging out Cuba's Cubana Airlines for last place).[35] To
reformers, Aeroméxico had become a privatization "poster boy"—the quintessen-
tial example of an inefficient, subsidy-dependent PE that cried out for divestment.

Table 3.2 displays the correlation between Aeroméxico's expanding payroll
and declining productivity. Here, productivity is measured in standard terms of
employment and output ratios—i.e., the number of revenue passenger-kilometers
(or RPKs) flown divided by the number of employees. Two points are particularly
noteworthy. First, between 1983 and 1987 company finances deteriorated sharply:
while subsidies averaged about 15 percent of total revenues the company hired
more than 1,000 new workers. Second, between 1985 and 1987 the number of RPKs
per worker fell nearly 10.5 percent, yet the company hired still *more* workers.

Table 3.2   Aeroméxico: Financial and Productivity Indicators,
                 1981–1988

Year	Subsidy in millions of constant pesos (and as % of yearly revenues)	# of passengers carried	# of employees at year's end	Thousands of RPKs performed (per 1,000 workers)
1981	—	5,539	10,532	6,658 (705)
1982	368 (1.91)	5,497	10,301	6,190 (594)
1983	6,215 (12.83)	5,982	10,624	7,363 (704)
1984	11,150 (14.95)	6,195	10,957	8,048 (746)
1985	21,250 (17.77)	6,644	11,062	8,298 (754)
1986	35,001 (14.22)	6,053	11,366	7,766 (693)
1987	95,600 (14.94)	5,803	11,644	7,832 (681)
1988	—	3,153	7,015*	4,101 (585)
1989	—	4,349	4,683	5,462 (1,294)

Source: Derived from Pankaj Tandon, *Welfare Consequences of Selling Public Enterprises:
Case Studies from Chile, Malaysia, Mexico and the U.K. Mexico: Aeroméxico, Mexicana*
(Washington, D.C.: The World Bank, 1992), figures 17-1, 17-7, 17-8, and 17-26.
* 1988 figures based on *average* number of workers before bankruptcy.

Coalition Politics and Policy Reform

By 1987 Aeroméxico had caught the eye of budget watchers in the de la Madrid
administration. Chronically in debt and subsidy dependent (projected subsidies
for 1988 approached U.S. $100 million), they viewed the carrier as a dysfunc-
tional labor receptacle and a source of endless headache. As to solutions, however,
opinions were divided: some officials favored restructuring and retaining
Aeroméxico in the government portfolio; others, especially among economic circles,
believed divestment a wiser course.

The Ministry of Communications and Transportation (SCT) was no fan of
divestment. Instead, it favored a restructuring scheme drafted by the airline's then-
vice president of finance, Rogelio Gasca Neri. Released in early 1987, it called for
major changes in the company's finances, compensation, route structure, and labor contracts, including worker flexibility and substantial layoffs. These measures,
Transportation hoped, would stave off divestment by increasing Aeroméxico's cash

flow. The restructuring plan won the support of President Miguel de la Madrid as well, who announced the administration's policy in his fifth State of the Nation report. "We shall proceed with the restructuring of the national commercial aviation companies," the president said, because "their service leaves much to be desired, their efficiency indices are very low and they continually require important government subsidies."[36]

With the president's backing and Gasca Neri's promotion to general director that June, management implemented many reforms; but efforts to shrink the work-force and amend collective contracts went nowhere. The unions refused to negotiate contract givebacks and rejected attempts to increase labor flexibility. This opposition convinced some reformers that simple restructuring was inadequate: even if reforms did improve Aeroméxico's short-term cash flow, labor costs inevitably would undermine its economic performance in the long run. Better to divest the airline, they believed, than be forced to mount yet another rescue attempt down the line.

The chief architects of Aeroméxico's divestment were members of the Spending and Finance Commission (*Comisión Gasto-Financiamiento,* or CGF), an interministerial body established in 1985 to manage macroeconomic policy (debt, spending, and public sector operations).[37] Composed of the ministers and subministers of Mexico's chief technocratic bureaucracies (Finance, Budget and Planning) and the director of the central bank, the commission's responsibilities, influence, and membership quickly expanded.[38] As minister of budget in the de la Madrid government, Carlos Salinas sat on the CGF and was intimately involved in de la Madrid's divestment project. In 1986 the CGF was empowered to review all divestment proposals and pass the most promising candidates to the president for his approval. Thrust into the thick of the privatization process, the commission eventually was "converted into a virtual arm of the president's economic cabinet."[39] With few exceptions (Cananea would be a notable one) its members became a leading force behind public sector downsizing.

That the drive to privatize Aeroméxico should sprout from this body rather than the carrier's sector ministry, the SCT, is not surprising. Like most "change teams" the CGF worked with relative autonomy and full presidential backing. Moreover, its members were highly trained technocrats whose focus on fiscal austerity predisposed them to consider the macroeconomic effects of public sector operations and view privatization in terms of its stabilizing benefits.[40] Accordingly, they generally embraced a unified policy solution to public sector problems: any parastatal that required subsidies, was unprofitable or "nonstrategic," should be divested. In the case of Aeroméxico, the fact that commissioners had little to lose and much to gain from privatization enhanced this predisposition. A successful divestment would strip Transportation of its national airlines, but also help stanch the hemorrhage at Treasury and balance the books at Budget and Planning. In short, divestment advocates shared key attributes characteristic of reform coalitions—a common policy preference for market reforms and the capacity to externalize the costs of selling state assets. This, plus prior collaboration on stabilization measures, provided the raw material from which they built a powerful, pro-privatization reform coalition.

To succeed, reformers needed to control the policy agenda, neutralize the opposition anticipated from Aeroméxico's sector ministry, management, and labor unions, and if possible, bring some of the potential opponents into the reform coalition. These were tall tasks. Under existing policy procedures even controlling the policy agenda was problematic. Sector ministries enjoyed broad discretion to nominate a divestment candidate; the *Comisión Gasto-Financiamiento* could only approve divestment proposals, not initiate them; and Transportation was under no obligation to send Aeroméxico to the auction block. With decision-making rules stacked against them, privatizers "encouraged" the agency to divest through powers inherent in their organizational positions inside the state. The encouragement came in the form of a 50 billion peso rescission of Aeroméxico's 1987 subsidy appropriation, coauthorized by the Treasury and Ministry of Budget and Planning.[41] This heightened the airline's financial plight considerably and placed extraordinary pressure on Transportation. Under duress the agency reluctantly joined the reformers and nominated Aeroméxico for divestment.

Contrary to expectations, winning the support of Aeroméxico's general director, Rogelio Gasca Neri, proved remarkably simple. The former vice president of finance well understood Aeroméxico's economic plight and bleak prospects: absent dramatic contract changes or a substantial (and unlikely) subsidy spike, the airline was doomed; the government would either liquidate the carrier as it had other failing PEs,[42] or divest it. Of the two, Gasca Neri believed divestment best served the company's interests and he actively supported reformers' plans to facilitate it.

With divestment now official state policy and management on board, the reformers turned to organized labor. From their perspective, a quick sale seemed unlikely without significant contract modifications: overmanning, rigid job categories, and many benefits would all have to go to entice potential buyers. The unions, of course, saw things differently. Not surprisingly, contract negotiations fared poorly. The Association of Aviator Pilots (ASPA), the Association of Aviation Flight Attendants (ASSA), and the groundworkers union—the National Union of Technicians and Workers of Aeronaves de México (SNTTAM)—were decidedly cool toward proposed revisions. To break this impasse the coalition pursued two tactics. Initially, reformers tried to extract union concessions by dramatizing Aeroméxico's financial plight. Ultimately, this approach would fail to break labor intransigence. The second track, however, which mixed minimizing and imposition strategies, would prove more successful.

To gain more leverage at the bargaining table Director Gasca Neri turned to Pedro Aspe, minister of budget (and president of the CGF). At Gasca Neri's behest, Aspe authored a letter stipulating that Aeroméxico would receive *no* subsidies the next fiscal year (1988). This new bargaining chip, the director hoped, would finally bring labor around. During contract talks that September, management made its case: Aeroméxico's revenue/expense ratio (1 to 1.25 pesos)[43] and projected deficit ($100 million) required dramatic reductions in routes, fleet size, labor force, and contract benefits. Brandishing the government's letter respecting subsidy cutoffs, Gasca Neri framed the issues in terms of mutual survival. "This is what we've got to do to make the company viable," he explained; "some of these things will hurt your unions but they're necessary for the good of both the company and the unions in the long run."[44]

Labor leaders, however, remained unimpressed. In public the SNTTAM attacked management's modernization program as contrary to standard principles of labor-management dialogue. In private, union leaders were less diplomatic. In blunt terms they told the director: "Your job as president [of Aeroméxico] is not to make these kinds of [contract] changes, but to go to the government and get the money we need to operate. That's your job."[45] They further maintained that any talk of Aeroméxico going bankrupt was simply that—talk. "We've seen a lot of general directors come and a lot of them go," they told Gasca Neri; "you're no different. They all talked about bankruptcy but we are still here."[46]

Union Busting and Bankruptcy: Implementation via Coercion

Throughout the fall the unions held firm, and by year's end the reformers' patience was gone. Abandoning simple negotiations they determined to split the united labor front by minimizing the costs of divestment for Aeroméxico's pilots—whose particular skills made them indispensable—and imposing the costs of change on remaining syndicates. In early January 1988, coalition members summoned leaders of the pilots' union to a private meeting where they explained that Aeroméxico would be thoroughly restructured then sold to the private sector.[47] Conceding these measures would cost the unions plenty, the reformers offered ASPA 35 percent of the newly privatized carrier in exchange for its support. This compensation package fell short of the pilots' preference,[48] but promised enough carrots to win ASPA's allegiance. ASPA's switch from opponent to stakeholder in the divestment process left ASSA and the SNTTAM isolated; and for these holdouts the reformers would provide not carrots, but a stick.

Through careful interagency coordination coalition members worked to precipitate a labor strike that would force Aeroméxico's bankruptcy. This tactic would break the unions, annul their contracts, and eliminate redundancy in one fell swoop. Thereafter, a new company could be formed, less generous contracts signed, and a more attractive Aeroméxico sent to the auction block.

Reformers moved quickly to operationalize this plan. On January 20, the administration announced a new austerity plan that promised large-scale changes in commercial aeronautics: "the two national airlines (Aeroméxico and Mexicana)," the administration explained, "will be thoroughly restructured in aspects of their operations, routes, and itineraries."[49] A week later (January 28) management unveiled the plan's specifics.[50] It called for more fleet reductions, route eliminations, and canceled aircraft orders—measures which threatened at least 2,000 positions in the groundworkers union alone. The *Comisión Gasto-Financiamiento*'s newest members (the Labor Ministry and comptroller general) then upped the pressure. The former refused to support union efforts to avert the restructuring;[51] the latter released an official communiqué (March 2) which expressed the need for still more cuts. Noting an 11 percent jump in Aeroméxico's workforce since 1981, the letter identified labor costs as one area where more should be done, and reaffirmed the government's intent to withhold additional subsidies in 1988.[52] These developments quickly alarmed the groundworkers who saw the steady march toward reform as a direct assault on job security.[53]

With the first phase of restructuring slated to begin on April 13 (the retirement of thirteen aircraft), the SNTTAM tried to block this move by voting to strike Aeroméxico on April 12 (the Federal Labor Law prohibits asset liquidations during a legally recognized strike).[54] Inadvertently, the syndicate stepped into the reformers' trap and from the very beginning the strike proved a disaster. An hour after the walkout began, company officials petitioned the Federal Conciliation and Arbitration Board to declare the strike *inexistente* (legally unrecognized); for lack of a quorum during the strike vote, the board agreed. With its revenues cut off and fixed expense payments due, the government quickly declared Aeroméxico bankrupt (*en quiebra*), terminated its labor contracts, fired its workers en masse, and crushed the groundworkers union.[55]

In the wake of Aeroméxico's belly flop the administration portrayed the bankruptcy as in the public interest. As President de la Madrid explained, Mexico could no longer afford "the luxury of. . . . inefficient and deficitary companies that represent a burden for society."[56] In light of Aeroméxico's poor reputation many Mexicans agreed, and the government's decisive actions met broad public acclaim.[57]

Nevertheless, the *quiebra* stunned the SNTTAM and ASSA. The SNTTAM, in particular, believed the government had baited it to strike just to precipitate the insolvency, and there is more than paranoia behind this suspicion.[58] Normally, a strike at either national airline would trigger a *requisa*—a temporary state takeover of corporate facilities that would force strikers back to work and preserve existing labor contracts.[59] In fact, only five months before the de la Madrid administration had used this very device to end a pilots' strike at Mexicana Airline.[60] But with Aeroméxico, the goal was to *eliminate* union contracts, not preserve them; bankruptcy provided a foolproof way to achieve this.

With labor issues settled and Aeroméxico in receivership, restructuring proceeded rapidly. Assets were liquidated, fired employees indemnified, and a limited number of workers signed short-term *individual* (as opposed to collective) contracts to ensure provisional air service. Five months after the walkout the carrier's trustee unveiled the "new" Aeroméxico (Aerovías de México, S.A. de C.V.), owned jointly (65/35 percent) by the trustee and ASPA respectively.[61] This company signed new, less generous (and more flexible) collective contracts with ASPA, ASSA, and the "Independencia" union that replaced the defunct SNTTAM.[62] When Aeroméxico finally went private in September 1988, Dictum S.A. de C.V.—a joint venture between the Commerce Bank and private investors—acquired 75 percent of the equity, while the pilots retained 25 percent.

In privatizing Aeroméxico the Mexican government cut its financial liabilities substantially, realized a "savings" in future subsidies and fleet upgrades, and expanded the tax base. But unlike other divestments, the federal government received no net revenues from the transaction. The carrier's liabilities exceeded its selling price by nearly $15 million, and after discharging its financial obligations out of that purchase price, nothing remained to transfer back to Treasury.

The absence of significant and more visible short-term economic gains heightened the bankruptcy's political symbolism. Reformers intended the *quiebra* to send a strong, unambiguous message to other public sector unions: the government was intent on divesting unproductive parastatals and was prepared to impose enormous costs on those who stood in the way; how labor responded to the costs of reform would condition the pattern policy implementation would take.

Throughout public sector labor circles the fate of Aeroméxico's unions loomed large. Save for the pilots, labor's defeat was total. ASSA and the SNTTAM absorbed all the costs of restructuring (wage and benefit cuts, layoffs, reduction of job categories, expanded responsibilities, etc.), plus the additional costs incurred when the state decapitated the leadership of ASSA and the SNTTAM, prosecuted and jailed their ex-presidents for corruption and tax evasion, and dissolved the groundworkers union.[63] Reformers, on the other hand, achieved remarkable success. Despite initial obstacles they managed to control the policy agenda, protect it from bureaucratic opposition, and keep the terms of debate focused on neoliberal precepts like efficiency and financial viability. Thereafter, they skillfully divided union opposition, boxed in the SNTTAM, then sprang the bankruptcy trap. In the process they notched another victory against the proprietary state.

One of the principal lessons reformers apparently learned from Aeroméxico was the utility of bankruptcy as a device to impose the costs of reform on recalcitrants. As future finance minister, Pedro Aspe later explained: "sometimes one bankruptcy is worth many sales [because] bankruptcies constitute a clear signal to society that the government. . . . is committed to doing whatever is necessary to permanently correct the economic disequilibria."[64] The record suggests, however, that reformers learned this lesson too well. When the Salinas government tried the same strategy to divest the giant Cananea copper mine in 1989, similar tactics failed to yield similar results. The political fiasco that followed ultimately taught reformers the limits of pure coercive power and the bankruptcy ploy.

Divestment under Salinas: Cananea and Sicartsa

Even more than its predecessor, the Salinas administration was determined to shrink the public sector. While the de la Madrid government divested over 460 companies, very few had been industrial enterprises or as high profile as Aeroméxico. In tackling such firms as Cananea and Sicartsa the Salinas team expanded the scope of divestment, took aim at some of the largest, most politically important PEs in the government's portfolio, and went on to establish an impressive record on privatization.

As with Aeroméxico, reformers encountered resistance to privatization inside the state and out, yet ultimately they prevailed. These similarities aside, however, struggles to divest these companies posed challenges fundamentally different than Aeroméxico in terms of the obstacles and opportunities for reform. Coordinated reform efforts developed much later with Cananea than Sicartsa; institutional variables were more favorable toward reform in the latter; and some cost-bearers demonstrated surprising political skill and resilience. Although labor responded predictably to the costs of policy change (i.e., resistance), since each firm employed only a *single* union local (as opposed to Aeroméxico's multiple syndicates), fragmenting the opposition was a non-starter. Consequently, strategies that brought reformers success in the past proved ineffective and patterns of policy implementation changed accordingly.

Privatizing Cananea

The Compañía Minera de Cananea (CMC) is Mexico's second most productive copper mine. Located in the city of Cananea in the northern state of Sonora, it is the municipality's largest employer.[65] Rich in historical symbolism, Cananea ranks among the top ten copper mines worldwide, and its production (5 percent of annual global copper extraction)[66] provided Mexico an important source of foreign exchange. Under Miguel de la Madrid the government twice tried (and failed) to divest Cananea. With the corporation "in play," the Salinas administration inherited a troubled situation, then confounded it through missteps before bringing the sale to fruition.

History and Development
Cananea marked the birth of modern commercial mining in 1899, when the American entrepreneur, William C. Greene, founded the Cananea Consolidated Copper Company, or 4C's.[67] In June 1906, Mexican workers struck Cananea over a wage dispute. After shooting erupted (and many had died) Greene called on the Sonoran governor, Rafael Izábal, to help quell the strike. The governor complied and a troupe of Mexican rural police, backed up by a contingent of Arizona Rangers moved in to restore order.

Accounts differ greatly over what actually transpired, but by the time the uprising was put down about thirty Mexican workers and six U.S. citizens were dead.[68] In the process, Cananea gained nationwide notoriety as a hallmark of "foreign exploitation." Although the workers' uprising often is described as a "revolutionary" act and precursor to the fall of dictator Porfirio Díaz, history disputes this interpretation.[69] Nevertheless, the potent mix of gringos, seeming capitalist exploitation, and worker solidarity ensured Cananea a special place in popular folklore, and after the strike, it was emblazoned on the national psyche as the birthplace of the Mexican labor movement.

Mining operations in Cananea evolved under conditions of extreme geographical, social, and political isolation. Nestled in the inhospitable Sonoran sierras and bordered by a foreign country to the north, the region is virtually cut off from surrounding localities in Sonora and the Mexican interior (Cananea is 155 miles from the state capital of Hermosillo). This isolation created a unique sociopolitical environment with long-term consequences. Absent alternative employment opportunities or effective links to the interior, the mine became the community's lifeline in almost every sense of the word and a symbiotic, functionalist relationship evolved between the company and local population: the city provided the workers, the mine depended on local labor and worked to maintain/reproduce the labor force, and the city depended on the mine. These circumstances encouraged the company to assume responsibilities more typical of political authorities including social welfare, education, and public works, etc. Eventually, corporate provision of social services (housing, water, sewage, gas, electricity, educational facilities, and so forth) formed part of labor's contract benefits—an arrangement that continued into the 1980s.[70]

In 1917 the U.S. firm Anaconda Copper acquired William Greene's 4C's, and for the next fifty-four years Cananea operated as an American subsidiary. Under pressure to *mexicanize* its holdings, Anaconda sold off 51 percent of Cananea in 1971 to a group of Mexican investors headed by Nacional Financiera (NAFINSA), Mexico's chief development bank.[71] In 1977 Anaconda itself was acquired by Atlantic Richfield, which *mexicanized* its remaining Cananea shares in 1981. By 1988 the Mexican government owned 99.8 percent of Cananea stock—three-quarters of which was controlled by Nacional Financiera and a special NAFINSA trust fund, with the remaining equity held by Mexico's Mining Promotion Commission.[72]

Public ownership notwithstanding, Cananea evolved into a highly atypical state-owned enterprise. Isolated from central authorities in Mexico City and controlled by a semiautonomous development bank, it operated in an institutional context distinct from most other public sector firms.[73] Unlike other parastatals it never came under the supervision of a federal ministry (the most logical choice would have been the Ministry of Energy, Mines, and Parastatals), reported its financial activities only to NAFINSA, not the ministries of Budget and Planning (SPP) or Finance, and was never placed "on budget" at SPP. Moreover, unlike Aeroméxico, political meddling was minimal at Cananea. Its majority owner—

Nacional Financiera—met with CMC's director once a quarter, but seldom intervened in company operations; management, meanwhile, relished and protected its own independence.[74]

These factors provided Cananea a great deal of autonomy (out of sight, out of mind) and allowed it to function more like a private than a public enterprise.[75] Equally important, they placed Cananea outside the normal divestment procedures supervised by the *Comisión Gasto-Financiamiento*. Consequently, instead of close interagency coordination, early efforts to divest Cananea engendered bureaucratic power struggles that helped stall reform until a coalition finally emerged.

In 1982 Cananea launched an ambitious, billion dollar program to modernize operations and increase output.[76] Initiated at the dawn of Mexico's debt crisis amidst sharp cuts in public spending,[77] this project was the largest, most expensive public investment program ever undertaken during the de la Madrid administration. It typified the entrepreneurial initiative that distinguished Cananea from its peers: with federal assistance out of the question the company unilaterally secured a series of external loans which NAFINSA agreed to underwrite and administer.[78]

Unfortunately, the expansion program coincided with a steady drop in copper prices on the world market. Between 1980 and 1982 world copper prices fell from about $1 per pound to $0.75, and bottomed out at about $0.65 per pound in 1986.[79] Coupled with currency devaluations and CMC's conversion of long-term liabilities to short-term debt, the bear copper market took its toll. The result was a cash flow problem that crippled the timely repayment of loans NAFINSA had underwritten. Throughout the 1980s corporate debt accumulated (reaching $652 million in 1989),[80] with Nacional Financiera legally responsible for it all.

For NAFINSA the most expedient solution was to divest Cananea and recoup its loans from the purchase price. This move fit the administration's divestment program and Cananea's unusual status meant NAFINSA could take the action unilaterally. The bank's governing board first considered selling Cananea in 1986, but delayed a formal call for bids until January 1988. By this time the expansion program was complete (CMC's output had quadrupled over 1982 levels from 3 to 14,000 tons per month),[81] market conditions were more favorable (copper prices had rebounded to $1.20 per pound), and Cananea itself was a more attractive buy. Despite the favorable conditions, however, repeated efforts to divest the firm fell flat.

To cover CMC's outstanding debts NAFINSA set the company's reference price at U.S. $850 million, and on January 13, 1988, it called for bids. This first round of competition drew a winning bid ($910 million) from Grupo Protexa, an industrial manufacturing conglomerate. The sale was significant both in terms of its magnitude and pareto optimality. Under the terms of sale Protexa would acquire all CMC assets, retain the firm's CEO and upper management, and accept CMC's existing labor contract without prior modifications (these last points were particularly important, since the lack of appreciable "costs" to management or labor precluded opposition from these quarters). Announced with great fanfare in April, the sale quickly bogged down in interbureaucratic tussles.

The *Comisión Gasto-Financiamiento,* in particular, questioned the price and pace of the sale: did the winning bid reflect Cananea's true value or was it a bargain basement price?[82] Cut out of this particular divestment, CGF members like the ministries of Budget and Planning, Finance, and the comptroller general chafed at NAFINSA's unilateralism and demanded the entire sales package be reviewed. Almost overnight the sale that seemed a "done deal" as one participant recalls, grew increasingly doubtful as the commission combed through Cananea's books and reworked NAFINSA's calculations.[83] These developments helped unsettle Protexa's external creditors, and on May 27 the sale collapsed when the First National Bank of Chicago withdrew its pledge to help fund the purchase.[84]

With relations tense between the CGF and NAFINSA, a second round of competition ensued in September. The bids submitted this time, however, fell well below Cananea's new reference price ($910 million) and were rejected as "economically insufficient;" on November 8, NAFINSA declared the competition void.[85] This second failure marked the end of unilateral divestment efforts. With three weeks before Carlos Salinas assumed the presidency and NAFINSA itself facing a leadership change (Juan José Páramo would replace Ernesto Marcos), privatization plans were shelved until after the transfer of power.

Coalition Politics and Policy Reform

Divesting Cananea was a priority from the outset of the Salinas administration. Past failures raised questions regarding the government's overall commitment to economic reforms and its ability to implement them. Moreover, since the government first sent Cananea to the auction block in January 1988, the company had postponed reinvestments in replacement parts and upkeep. Consequently, the value of CMC assets had declined along with its sales appeal. Unlike Aeroméxico, opposition to divestment inside the state was limited: Cananea had no sector ministry jealous to preserve its PE status, and Nacional Financiera had strong financial incentives to privatize the firm. In this context a reform coalition quickly emerged to steer Cananea into the private sector. As majority owner, NAFINSA would still spearhead the divestment drive. But under new leadership, it would work in concert with the CGF; interagency cooperation became the norm.

Nevertheless, a successful divestment was no sure thing. To compensate for the declining value of its physical assets NAFINSA had to lower Cananea's reference price and hope to entice buyers by boosting productivity through dramatic cuts in labor costs. The bank was uncertain, however, of management's ability or willingness to put the squeeze on labor: the company already paid generous wages and benefits, plus helped finance the community's local hospital, public library, primary and postsecondary schools, and basic infrastructure. To management these costs were necessitated by Cananea's isolation and dependence on local workers; to reformers they appeared excessive and inefficient. Beginning in January 1989, therefore, NAFINSA increasingly intervened in corporate affairs, exercising the vertical leverage afforded by its organizational position. Management—long accustomed to autonomy—resisted. By February the bank had ousted Cananea's CEO, and by March, taken complete control of the board of directors.[86]

With the purge complete reformers turned their attention to labor, and not surprisingly, labor/management relations deteriorated sharply. Management pressured the union to increase efficiency, and workers countered by decreasing output; the two-month work slowdown that ensued between April and May cost the company (management claimed) $15 million.[87] This skirmish set the tone for highly combative (and ultimately futile) contract talks in June with local #65 of the Mining and Metallurgical Workers of the Mexican Republic.[88]

The Salinas administration approached the labor showdown in textbook neoliberal form and no doubt with Aeroméxico in mind. From their perspective, Cananea's labor contract (like those at Aeroméxico) was generous to a fault and "economically irrational." By the late 1980s average wages at CMC were 3.5 times greater than other unionized workers in Mexico, and the contract's rigid division of labor (400 distinct job categories) seemed to impede flexibility, encourage overmanning, and undermine efficiency. Moreover, it gave labor veto power over subcontracting and equipment modernization, required promotions based solely on seniority, and set work standards according to "custom"—which in Cananea meant no work on Sundays, holidays, or "saints' days."[89] Since the union had negotiated many of these provisions precisely to maximize job security, they became the principal point of contention during contract talks.

But while contract disputes were similar in both cases, the broader context was not. Unlike Aeroméxico, local #65's contract benefits had never hinged on CMC's state ownership or routine subsidization. Aeroméxico's unions had squeezed concessions from a highly subsidized, long-term PE whose soft budget constraints and political imperatives gave management powerful incentives to accommodate labor demands. Local #65, by contrast, secured its benefits via "hand-to-hand" conflict with Anaconda Copper.[90] In fact, the syndicate won its most generous contract provisions—customary no-work days, health and educational facilities, and community services—as early as the 1940s, well before Cananea's nationalization.

The scope, content, and broader political significance of labor's contract stemmed directly from Cananea's extreme isolation and the mutual dependence it produced between corporation, community, and syndicate. The failure to appreciate this led reformers to greatly overestimate their capacity to deal with local #65 as expeditiously as Aeroméxico's unions. To understand why, consider the contrasts between Cananea's workforce demographics and those of Mexico's other major copper producer—Mexicana de Cobre (table 3.3).[91]

In 1988 *over 80 percent* of CMC's workforce hailed from Cananea itself; by contrast, the vast majority of Mexicana workers were younger, had less experience and seniority, and originated outside the mine's immediate vicinity of Nacozari,

Table 3.3   **Labor Demographics, 1988:**
Cananea vs. Mexicana de Cobre

Labor Force	Company	
Demographics	Cananea (%)	Mexicana de Cobre (%)
worker age (yrs.)		
15-24	21.2	41.1
25-34	37.1	37.4
35-44	23.2	12.6
45-54	11.3	5.9
over 55	7.2	3.1
seniority (yrs.)		
less than 1	9.3	29.4
1-3	21.1	15.5
3-6	16.9	18.0
6-12	26.0	24.8
more than 12	26.7	2.3
place of origin		
Cananea, Son.	80.0	5.7
Nacozari, Son.		
other	20.0	94.3

Source: Derived from Oscar Contreras and Miguel Ángel Ramírez, "Novedades de la postguerra: fin del auge exportador y repliegue hacia el mercado interno," in José Carlos Ramírez, ed., *La nueva industrialización en Sonora: El caso de los sectores de alta tecnología* (Hermosillo, Sonora, México: El Colegio de Sonora, 1988), 292-294.

Sonora. These distinctions are striking and their implications enormous. Since the nineteenth century Cananea's insularity, rich mining culture, and capacity to reproduce its own labor force from one generation to the next literally transformed the community and its people. The very process that reproduced the labor force created strong sociocultural ties that fused miners' personal interests with those of the community; these workers, in turn, passed a community-linked (and often militant) mining culture down from cohort to cohort. The sheer volume of workers emanating from Cananea enhanced the influence these shared values had on labor/management and company/community relations, such that local #65 evolved into more than a simple union. Over time, it was "converted into the mouthpiece and conduit of the local population's political, economic and social demands."[92]

For reformers, equating Cananea with Aeroméxico would prove a big mistake. The union's deep roots in the local community and practice of delivering

concrete benefits to city residents established a natural set of constituents and political allies. These would rally to defend both the miners' interests, and by extension, their own. Moreover, as the reputed birthplace of Mexico's labor movement,
Cananea was a lodestone that tugged at nationalist heartstrings across the republic.
It offered an enormous reservoir of political symbolism which might be leveraged
to protect miners' interests. By overlooking these factors reformers entered contract talks that June under a profound misimpression, then pursued an imposition
strategy unlikely to yield gains in the Cananea context.

Almost immediately the two sides deadlocked over management's proposals
to eliminate redundancy, increase workforce flexibility, and raise productivity via
mechanization and third party subcontracting.[93] Rejecting these proposals, labor
called for hikes in wages, benefits, and the number of justified absences.[94] For the
syndicate privatization per se was not the problem, but rather the costly contract
changes management deemed essential to secure it. As Napoleon Gómez Sada, the
mineworkers' national president, later explained, "as long as our jobs and contract
were preserved we didn't care who owned the company."[95]

As the talks dragged on chances for quick agreement grew more remote. To
protect their contract labor leaders began circulating strike petitions; reformers,
meanwhile, feared even a partial concession might jeopardize divestment plans.
By late summer reformers apparently determined to break the stalemate—not by
minimizing the costs the syndicate faced, but by imposing them on local #65 through
bankruptcy. This tactic offered two advantages. On the one hand, it would allow
the state to effect mass firings and rewrite the collective contract expeditiously. On
the other, with the old contract void, the state could evade the heavy severance
payments the old agreement required, and instead, indemnify discharged workers
with the bare minimum stipulated by the Federal Labor Law—a difference of 83
billion pesos.[96]

Divestment proponents calculated they could execute this strategy in three
steps: (1) take the miners' baseline contract demands (which NAFINSA calculated
as a 330 percent hike in total wages and benefits) at face value, (2) use CMC's
inability to meet these demands as evidence of corporate insolvency, and (3) use
the bankruptcy to break the syndicate and preempt the strike—set for August 28—
with a stunning display of force. Confident of orchestrating "another Aeroméxico,"
the reformers sprang the bankruptcy trap.

Union Busting and Bankruptcy:
The "Boomerang" of Coercive Implementation

On Sunday morning, August 20, 4,000 troops descended on Cananea, seized
CMC facilities, and evicted workers from the company compound.[97] While army
helicopters dropped leaflets explaining CMC's insolvency, the government declared that Cananea was bankrupt, the labor contract void, and that workers would

be liquidated according to the provisions of the Federal Labor Law. Local residents christened August 20 *el Domingo verde* (green Sunday), in reference to the 1906 confrontation with the American, William Greene.

Insisting they took these actions for reasons "strictly financial," reformers blamed the bankruptcy squarely on labor. A NAFINSA press release claimed the union was "the principal problem" behind the company's inefficiency and high production costs;[98] management insisted the syndicate's contract was a prescription for "inefficiency," its demands impossible to meet, and the only recourse had been bankruptcy;[99] meanwhile, the Labor Ministry (the CGF's sole nontechnocratic, noneconomic member) asserted that factors "strictly financial" had determined CMC's fate.[100] Five days after the army seized CMC, President Salinas declared the firm's insolvency "irreversible"; the Financiera Nacional Azucarera (FINASA) would serve as trustee.

Reformers expected that Cananea's bankruptcy—like Aeroméxico's—would meet broad public acclaim, quickly resolve the labor problem, and facilitate the company's divestment. Instead, it precipitated a firestorm of condemnation nationwide,[101] revealed local #65 to be a surprisingly potent opponent, and cast divestment plans in doubt. Overnight, city residents made common cause with the syndicate. In solidarity with workers the Cananean Feminine Solidarity Front sprang into action to confront central authorities. It supplied picketing miners with foodstuffs and functioned as the union's direct-action political wing. More sheltered from repression due to its gender, the front blocked city streets, occupied the Ministry of Finance building, and kept officials from dispensing severance payments to fired miners.[102]

Beyond Cananea, the union quickly forged important alliances with Sonorans of various stripes. The University of Sonora at Hermosillo provided miners office space, legal counsel, and accounting services to fight the bankruptcy in federal court. Regional unions backed local #65. The archbishop of Sonora, Carlos Quintero, cloaked the workers' struggle with the church's own moral authority. Quintero led a protest march through downtown Cananea, absolved the miners of any responsibility in the company's demise, and demanded the immediate withdrawal of military forces. Even the state governor, Rodolfo Félix Valdés (a PRI member), offered the miners cautious, qualified support: he pronounced the bankruptcy "a disgrace," appropriated 6 billion pesos to maintain Cananea's streets and infrastructure, and shipped 3,500 baskets of basic foodstuffs to the suddenly unemployed.[103]

At the national level, Cananea's historic symbolism and the government's seeming overkill elicited a groundswell of support. Across Mexico public opinion sided with labor. Efforts to confine the bankruptcy to economic issues proved futile, and critics pointed out legal inconsistencies surrounding the *quiebra* with devastating effectiveness.[104] To cite just one example, the company's own balance sheet refuted the insolvency claim: in 1988 CMC's net profit was almost $75 million (year-end figures for 1989 were unavailable at the time), productivity had risen dramatically over 1987 levels, and the corporation was current on all debt payments when the bankruptcy occurred.[105] Administration critics used such discrepancies to excoriate the government and claimed its actions could "not withstand even minor analysis."[106]

The bankruptcy's political aspects quickly overshadowed the state's "strictly economic" arguments. As the *Economist* observed, "The real issue" behind the bankruptcy and military occupation "was the government's wish to prune Cananea's payroll and increase its productivity, so making the company a more attractive prospect for potential private investors."[107] While the state endured a withering barrage of public criticism, labor leaders petitioned the court to declare the bankruptcy illegal on procedural grounds. When this failed, they still refused to capitulate; the union agreed to discuss job liquidations but only in terms of the now-defunct collective contract, not the letter of the Federal Labor Law.

As the conflict dragged on, the coalition gradually realized the enormity of its miscalculations. It had completely misread public reaction and underestimated labor's resilience, stumbled over its own sophistries, and failed to appreciate how CMC's dependence on local labor gave the union a tactical advantage. Only now did reformers fully appreciate that to reopen CMC (and eventually sell it) required the active cooperation of Cananeans; and that to secure this cooperation reformers had to moderate their hard-line, reach an accommodation with labor, and offer miners some unplanned compensation for the costs of policy change.

On September 11, President Salinas extended the first olive branch to labor during a public address in Puebla. Conceding the affair had been poorly managed,[108] he insisted the government had no wish to "punish" labor. He pledged to reopen the mine as soon as possible, provide employment for laid-off workers, and offered local #65 a 25 percent equity stake in the newly privatized firm.

These concessions cracked the reformers' initial hard-line, but failed to compensate for the one cost labor deemed completely unacceptable—the abrogation of its contract. FINASA still determined to liquidate workers according to the labor code (not the contract) and reopen Cananea with a completely new labor agreement. The syndicate, however, refused to discuss liquidations in any context other than the contract, and the community displayed complete solidarity with the miners' demands.[109] This left the state but two options to move the divestment process ahead: either stay the course and try to break community solidarity—and labor—via attrition, or concede to the syndicate and provide severance pay according to the labor contract. In short order, however, the bankruptcy had generated such severe economic dislocations that the first option became moot.

Each week miners pumped more than 900 million pesos into the local economy and with the mine's shutdown, Cananea's local economy nose-dived. In the first week alone, sales dropped 75 percent, and by the middle of the second week the state Chamber of Commerce reported a 90 percent falloff.[110] These multiplier effects generated strong incentives to reopen the mine quickly and expedite its privatization. Convinced that a successful divestment hinged on a reconciliation with workers and city residents, President Salinas countermanded FINASA's rective and ordered the workers be compensated according to their contract. W this last concession secured, labor and FINASA hammered out the details of cc tract revisions, reaching final agreement on October 11.

The settlement modified eighteen clauses in the original collective contrac and was approved by union rank and file on October 19.[111] Cananea resumed operations on November 7, 1988; bidding reopened the following June, and on August 27, 1989, the government finally sold CMC to Grupo Minera México for $475 million.[112]

Cananea proved to be an important, but qualified victory for Mexico's reformers and local #65 as well. The transaction shrank the size of Mexico's public sector, expanded the government's tax base, and evidenced the state's continued commitment to policy reform. The syndicate, meanwhile, managed to avoid the fate of Aeroméxico's groundworkers, but its victory remained a partial one. After divestment, Cananea's new owner refused to honor the equity structure Salinas had promised miners back in September (25 percent), and in the end, local #65 acquired only 3.9 percent of company stock.[113]

The struggle over Cananea would have long-term consequences for the Salinas divestment campaign. It marked the second time in less than two years that a major PE had gone bust prior to privatization, and taught both government and labor important, if distinct, lessons. These lessons redefined their approach toward divestiture, and ultimately helped pave the way for a broader (and in some sense, less disruptive) transition to a smaller public sector. The bankruptcy's political fallout taught reformers the limits of the bankruptcy device. The government had expended a sizable chunk of political capital pursuing a hard-line stance, only to see divestment delayed and be forced to compensate mineworkers to effect a sale. While the administration would privatize other large PEs with entrenched unions (i.e., steel, telecommunications, fertilizers), hereafter no firm was bankrupted to effect its divestment. Labor, on the other hand, learned that when it came to privatization, even the threat of a strike placed workers on thin ice. After Cananea, public sector unions reluctantly but increasingly elected to negotiate workforce reductions and contract revisions,[114] and often the government met them halfway. When reformers determined to divest the public steelworks, therefore, they pushed hard for labor concessions, but ultimately pursued a minimizing—rather than imposition—strategy to ensure the policy's implementation.

Privatizing Sicartsa Steelworks

The Siderúrgica Lázaro Cárdenas-Las Truchas, or Sicartsa, is Mexico's second largest integrated steelworks. Located in the Pacific coast city of Lázaro Cárdenas, in the state of Michoacán, its two divisions (Sicartsa I and Sicartsa II) employed different technologies and served distinct market niches.[115] Along with

li-
th
l.
)nterrey (FUMOSA) and Altos Hornos de México (AHMSA),
                    Mexico's public steel conglomerate, Sidermex. In the 1980s these
                    d for 65 percent of Mexico's total steel production (see table 3.4).

        itorical Developments
        ercial interest in the Las Truchas ore deposits dates back to 1907 when
        ?orfirio Díaz awarded a mineral concession to the U.S. firm Bethlehem
        / the next forty years Bethlehem failed to exercise those rights, preferring
        ae Las Truchas deposits as a strategic reserve for its U.S. operations. Even-
        .his strategy raised the ire of Mexican leaders, and in 1948 President Miguel
        an (1946-52) canceled Bethlehem's concession. Due to private sector oppo-
        .1, interbureaucratic struggles, and alternative development schemes backed
        powerful ex-politicians, it took another two decades before Sicartsa was for-
        .lly incorporated in 1969.[116]

Table 3.4   Public vs. Private Steel Production:
Capacity and Domestic Market Share, 1986–1989

Firm	Location	Yearly capacity (thousands of metric tons)	Output (thousands of metric tons)				% of 1989 domestic output
			1986	1987	1988	1989	
AHMSA	Monclova, Coahuila	3,000	2,868	3,086	3,083	2,862	44
Sicartsa	Lázaro Cárdenas, Michoacán	3,200	1,192	1,190	1,131	1,336	21
FUMOSA[1]	Monterrey, Nuevo Leon	1,000	254	—	—	—	—
Private Sector	2,770	1,815	2,147	2,250	2,280	39

Source: Derived from Orlando Martino, Jerome Machamer, and Ivette Torres, *The Mineral Economy of Mexico* (Washington, D.C.: United States Department of the Interior, Bureau of Mines, 1992), 71.
[1]FUMOSA was closed in May 1986.

In contrast to Aeroméxico and Cananea, the state owned Sicartsa from the beginning. During Mexico's oil boom the government borrowed extensively to finance construction of Sicartsa I (1973); production runs commenced three years later. Sicartsa II was commissioned in 1980, again funded by external loans, and began operations in 1989. Both projects were problem plagued from the start: inefficient, cash strapped, and increasingly in debt. Besides the traditional burdens of price controls and overmanning, Sicartsa also suffered under a complicated bureaucratic framework that systematically undermined its profitability. By the turn of the decade the company—as well as Sidermex itself—had fallen into the crosshairs of Mexico's policy reformers.

As a cornerstone of the statist model, the government pumped billions of dollars into public steel firms to promote industrialization, regional development, and job creation. Significant state intervention accompanied the growth of this priority sector, creating a labyrinthine organizational structure and operating procedures far from optimal. Decision making was both centralized *and* dispersed; managers "managed," but did not *decide;* and company products were distributed in ways that isolated steelmakers from their market and undermined corporate profitability.

Three separate ministries played direct roles in formulating corporate policies: the Ministry of Energy, Mines, and Parastatals (SEMIP), the Ministry of Commerce (SECOFI), and the Ministry of Budget and Planning, or SPP. SEMIP functioned as the corporations' sector ministry; it appointed the firms' board of directors,[117] served as liaison between the steelworks and economic ministries, and analyzed economic data relevant to the steel sector. It also developed policy recommendations for domestic prices, quotas, and trade restrictions. *The power to*

Figure 3.2   The Institutional Structure of Sidermex, 1985

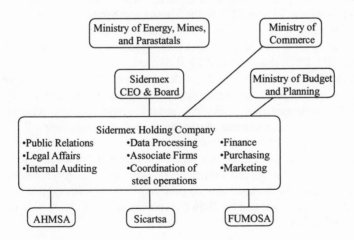

set policy in these areas, however, rested with the Ministry of Commerce, which could approve, modify, or reject any recommendation SEMIP proposed. The Ministry of Budget and Planning, meanwhile, approved the steel firms' yearly budgets. In theory, it helped coordinate the companies' investment programs; in practice, SPP often intervened in the nitty-gritty of operational decisions, especially those relating to corporate expenditures.

This framework (expressed in figure 3.2) bred patterns of inefficiency. It diffused control of corporate operations among three separate ministries, yet centralized decision-making authority *outside* the companies themselves; it placed the entire corporate superstructure under the supervision of committees in Mexico City, far from actual plant operations; and it required managers to obtain prior approval not just for major purchases, but even some routine transactions. Inevitably, this reduced the firms' overall flexibility: decisions that should have been made "on site" at Lázaro Cárdenas, were made instead by bureaucrats in the capital, or on occasion rescinded by SPP. The upshot was a slow, awkward decision-making arrangement that kept managers from seizing market opportunities.[118]

Compounding these problems were those generated by a highly centralized product distribution network. Government-owned commercial enterprises (*comerceladores*) purchased steel products at controlled prices direct from the factory, then sold them at a 30 to 50 percent markup to various outlets throughout the country. These outlets, in turn, resold the products to downstream industries. This practice isolated plant managers from downstream consumers and hindered normal feedback mechanisms that might tip management to new product preferences in the market. *Comerceladores,* meanwhile, held legal monopolies that made some of their directors rich, but offered few incentives to provide clients consistent service, and fewer still to improve their service. Over time, limited product selection and poor service led consumers to abandon the public steel firms in favor of smaller, private ones.

At least from management's perspective, Sicartsa also encountered its share of "labor problems." Local #271 of the Mining and Metallurgical Workers of the Mexican Republic (the same union that represented Cananea's workers) fought hard to win steelworkers higher wages and benefits; despite Mexico's economic crisis, in 1983, 1985, and again in 1987, it succeeded. In terms of low revenues and productivity, however, Sicartsa's real problem was not high wages, but contract provisions that encouraged overmanning through numerous job categories, a rigid division of labor, subcontracting prohibitions, and union veto over new technologies.

When coupled with its other constraints these factors took their toll. Throughout the 1980s Sicartsa faced continual financial crises. Between 1981 and 1985 its total factor productivity (i.e., output, labor, and capital) declined 25.4 percent per year.[119] Despite significant restructuring at mid-decade its ledgers consistently ran red: annual subsidies averaged over 25 percent of total revenues (table 3.5); operating deficits ballooned; and by 1986 the combined debt of its two divisions totaled $1.143 billion.[120]

Table 3.5   Sicartsa's Economic Indicators: Transfers vs. Internal Revenue Income; Deficit/Surplus Ratios, 1982–1989

Year	Transfers (as % of total income)	Internal Resources (as % of total income)	Deficit (in billions of pesos)
1982	23.0	44.0	-10.5
1983	16.0	41.0	-26.6
1984	22.3	48.0	-32.9
1985	21.6	27.6	-95.7
1986	28.5	41.7	-79.9
1987	25.4	42.5	-278.8
1988	30.7	38.8	-403.7
1989	36.2	50.7	-143.6

Source: Carlos Salinas de Gortari, *Segundo informe de Gobierno,* Anexo; and Carlos Salinas de Gortari, *Quinto Informe de Gobierno,* Anexo (México, D.F.: Presidencia de la República, 1990, 1993).

These liabilities made Sicartsa—and Sidermex—obvious targets for reform. But again, opinions were divided inside the state. In general, the *Comisión Gasto-Financiamiento* hoped to rationalize public steel sector operations, improve productivity, and make the firms self-financing (some commissioners favored simple divestment). Given the companies' economic straits the Energy Ministry could hardly oppose the merits of restructuring, but some officials were disquieted by the direction it might take: closer toward the market and divestment, and further away from ministerial oversight.

As a compromise, the CGF engineered significant sector-wide reforms beginning in 1986 through a *convenio de rehabilitación* (rehabilitation accord). This legal instrument promised neither a total free market nor traditional statist solution. It did not, for example, mandate divestment. It did, however, force the Sidermex conglomerate to decentralize its decision making and product distribution networks, take steps toward financial self-sufficiency, and bolster productivity by rationalizing the workforce (i.e., eliminate overmanning, induce flexibility).[121] To ease the adjustments, increase revenues, and facilitate technological upgrades, the government phased out price and trade restrictions and assumed a sizable portion of corporate debt.

In the end, the restructuring boosted output and partially stabilized Sidermex finances, but the improvements were distributed unevenly across each firm. By

1989 Sicartsa's situation had grown worse: a $14.8 million operating deficit remained after interest payments, the firm still required hundreds of millions of dollars to complete plant modernizations, and the federal government was poised to assume another $1.4 billion of corporate debt the following year. To reformers in the newly elected Salinas government divesting Sicartsa became a high priority.

Coalition Politics and Policy Reform

From the outset the Salinas administration proved fertile ground for the type of coalition politics conducive to successful divestment. To begin, the government inherited an effective, insulated structure to coordinate interagency actions (the CGF). It also established a strong intellectual climate where neoliberal precepts like rationality and economic efficiency formed the basis for policy discourse regarding public sector operations.[122] Moreover, in staffing his administration Salinas placed highly skilled technocrats in key economic posts—Pedro Aspe at Finance, Jaime Serra at Commerce, Ernesto Zedillo at Budget and Planning. Each held an Ivy League economics doctorate, shared common policy ideas of economic rationality, and formed the backbone of the *Comisión Gasto-Financiamiento*. For these technocrats more public spending on Sicartsa was hardly a priority. To the contrary, efficiency, fiscal discipline, and a smaller public sector topped their wish list.

Just days into the new administration Salinas met with the general directors of the major state-owned enterprises to outline the administration's public sector policy. With the exception of such strategic areas as oil, electricity, and railroads, etc., most public enterprises would be sold or liquidated. Nor would the state subsidize upgrades to modernize a PE and increase its sales appeal: every public enterprise that required subsidies would be sold or closed.[123] Toward these ends Salinas stressed he would sideline those who refused to be team players, and notes Merilee Grindle, "indicated that those on the bandwagon—the winners—would be those who identified themselves unequivocally with 'modernization.'"[124]

Despite these marching orders an agenda this ambitious could not easily be carried out under the existing privatization policy framework. To recap: these procedures gave ministries wide discretion to nominate divestment candidates based on one of five criteria; the nomination then passed from the sector ministry to the *Comisión Gasto-Financiamiento,* the Budget Ministry, and Finance, then to the president. Upon approval, the National Credit Society administered the sale, relying on company managers to provide the financial data required to evaluate the firm. Once a sale was consummated the PE passed from the ministry's control to its new owners (see figure 3.3). As noted earlier, these procedures made reformers dependent on those least likely to favor significant divestiture and provided potential opponents the resources and organizational position to affect policy outcomes (e.g., information, discretion, and lateral leverage, respectively).

Figure 3.3   The Policy-Making Structure of Privatization, pre-1990

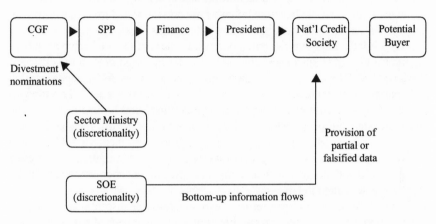

Procedural Process

Institutional Innovation

To safeguard its reform program the administration quickly took steps to rewrite the rules of privatization, making crucial changes in candidate selection criteria, policy procedures, and administrative structures. First, the president narrowed the parameters of state proprietorship solely to those entities mandated by the Constitution.[125] This reduced the divestment criteria from five categories to one and abolished the ministerial discretion that bedeviled divestiture in the past. Other measures to enhance reformers' organizational position inside the state soon followed.

The crucial moves came from the new finance minister and CGF president, Pedro Aspe. Well acquainted with the problems of discretionality and bottom-up information flows, Aspe established new procedures to govern the privatization process, the most important being *resectorization*. Under resectorization, once the *Comisión Gasto-Financiamiento* and president had signed off on a particular divestment proposal, the company was transferred from its traditional ministry and "resectored" to Aspe's ministry, Finance (Hacienda). In the process, Hacienda gained sole legal jurisdiction over the enterprise, complete access to its financial information and the finance minister became its chief executive officer with authority to hire managers amenable to privatization or fire corporate footdraggers.

To complement resectorization Aspe lobbied the president to create a new institutional subunit of full-time privatization specialists inside Hacienda. One advantage of the restructuring was pragmatic: with a specialized unit Aspe could handpick talented analysts and centralize their work directly under his supervision. This would facilitate the sale of large, complicated firms like banks, the steel-works, and telephone company without diverting Hacienda from its primary financial responsibilities. A second set of advantages was political: the presidential decree required to create a separate unit inside Finance would provide privatizers a firm legal mandate, shelter from bureaucratic pressures, and in conjunction with his position on the CGF, establish Aspe's authority as Mexico's chief privatizer.

By 1990 the lobbying campaign bore fruit. The result was a decree establishing the *Unidad de Desincorporación de Entidades Paraestatales,* or the Office of Privatization (OP)—a separate, autonomous operation inside Hacienda, staffed by economists, accountants, attorneys, and public policy analysts.[126] This innovation created an institutional structure that streamlined and limited access to the entire divestment process. Along with resectorization, it greatly enhanced the reformers' organizational strength to the point of providing them virtual "political property rights" over public sector operations. As outlined in figure 3.4, the result was more efficient procedures with a higher degree of technocratic control, and a program better suited to large-scale divestments like Sicartsa.

The twelve months it took reformers to transform the institutional context of privatization established the legal and institutional framework of a powerful pro-divestment coalition. In the long run these innovations paid off handsomely and were crucial to reformers' success. More than facilitating simply a short-term victory for a single privatization initiative like Sicartsa, they positioned reformers to realize a stream of future victories in subsequent divestment struggles.

With new procedures in place the administration laid plans to divest Sicartsa. By this time resistance inside the state was minimal. Past policy failure (i.e., restructuring) and the prevailing neoliberal orientations of the Salinas inner court had raised the costs of maintaining the status quo. These factors facilitated collaboration between reformers and potential policy "losers."

For its part, SEMIP realized that under the new divestment criteria Sicartsa's

Figure 3.4   The Policy-Making Structure of Privatization, post-1990

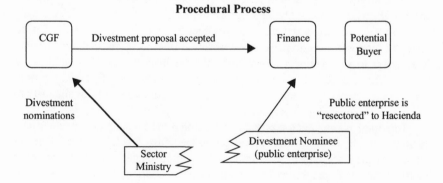

continued subsidy requirements (25 percent of total revenues) automatically qualified it for divestment, and with no viable policy alternative, opposing divestment
was politically untenable. In March 1990 the ministry implicitly joined the reformers by nominating Sicartsa's divestment.[127] Similar dynamics helped bring
management into the reformers' camp. On the one hand, the new policy procedures provided little leverage to stall privatization; on the other, opposition—co-
vert or otherwise—risked any chance of a postdivestment "golden parachute" into
the Mexican bureaucracy (a traditional sanctuary for well-connected, out-of-work
officials).[128] Consequently, as the divestment initiative advanced Sicartsa's general manager, Gabriel Magallón, led the charge to pare back union benefits and
rewrite the collective contract.

Coalitional expansion inside the state improved the prospects of a successful
divestment, but privatizing Sicartsa was still more challenging than any prior initiatives: legal, constitutional, and environmental issues erected significant barriers
to potential buyers.[129] There were "packaging" problems too. The corporation's
two separate divisions were actually two distinct steelworks, each with its own
facilities and problems. Evaluating the firm's assets, liabilities, and market potential, plus resolving the issues above proved so taxing that the Office of Privatization
hired foreign consultants to lighten the burden. Finally, the international market
for steel firms was simply suboptimal in 1990: excess capacity already had forced
steel plants in industrialized countries to undergo painful restructuring, and the
simultaneous auctions of state-owned steelworks in Argentina and Brazil made for
a buyer's market.[130] Consequently, the trial balloons officials floated abroad of
Sicartsa's potential sale garnered little enthusiasm.[131]

Despite unfavorable circumstances the administration pressed forward, and
in September 1990, it resectored Sicartsa from SEMIP to the Ministry of Finance.[132]
Pedro Aspe became the firm's new CEO and the entire sales process fell under his
supervision—coordinated through the Office of Privatization. To simplify its tasks,
plus provide potential buyers smaller, more affordable sales packages, the OP split
Sicartsa into two distinct corporations (Sicartsa I and II).[133] But even these inducements, reformers reasoned, might fail to attract buyers without significant contract
modifications to reduce labor costs. As one OP official intimately involved in the
process explained: "No one would have bought [the steel firms] in the state they
were in."[134] To encourage concessions at upcoming contract talks, therefore, the
CGF borrowed a page from the Aeroméxico playbook and zeroed out Sicartsa's
1991 subsidies to dramatize the firm's financial plight.[135]

Contract negotiations began in May 1991, and to steelworkers management's
proposals seemed severe. The costs in terms of jobs (1,700 positions) and job
security (subcontracting and a substantial reduction in job categories) were enormous, yet mindful of Cananea's fate, a strike seemed untenable. Stopping just
short of this, workers voted overwhelmingly to reject management's offer in September and a season of political brinkmanship followed that threatened to repeat
the Cananea experience.[136]

Local #271 shrugged off appeals to accept management's offer, and instead sent a delegation to Mexico City to negotiate directly with the company's new CEO, Pedro Aspe. This time the state played hardball. Instead of receiving the delegates, the finance minister insisted there was "nothing to negotiate"; dramatic cuts were essential to keep Sicartsa solvent. Returning empty-handed to Michoacán, the local's delegates tried to call the government's bluff: "We have made our decision," union leaders proclaimed, now "the government will decide if the company closes or not."[137] All signs now pointed toward bankruptcy—an outcome neither camp preferred.

Lessons Learned: Implementation via Compensation

For the state, bankruptcy posed two critical problems. First, plant operations would cease—perhaps for months—until Sicartsa could be reopened with a new contract. In the meantime, routine maintenance would stop and equipment depreciate at the very time officials needed a high appraisal value to attract investors. Second, reformers feared "another Cananea," on whose bankruptcy the government squandered enormous political capital and crippled the local economy, only to be forced into an abrupt about-face. Already agitated over a bankruptcy's potential multiplier effect,[138] Michoacán's private sector implored policy makers to consider regional issues parallel to their privatization goals. In the end, prudence trumped hubris and reformers cobbled together a compensation package to offset the impact of any layoffs.

Under this plan the syndicate still found the costs of management's proposal onerous: scores of job categories would be erased, third-party subcontracting permitted, and 1,700 jobs eliminated. But the remaining workers would receive a 12 percent pay raise, and the state would compensate those discharged with a generous severance package. To sweeten the pot further, the federal government vowed to chip in a set of side payments: the National Solidarity Program and Nacional Financiera promised to funnel $26 million to Lázaro Cárdenas to provide more jobs, job training, and additional public services.[139]

The reformers' final position put labor on the spot. Brinkmanship had not altered the government's fundamental position on layoffs or contract revisions, and if Sicartsa went bust, local #271—like Aeroméxico's groundworkers—would be crushed. This calculus moved the syndicate to reevaluate its position. Jobs and the collective contract remained its primary interests, but further resistance or a strike held little promise of securing them. Reluctantly, local #271 came to terms with management, and with the labor issues resolved the divestment proceeded rapidly. The Finance Ministry opened the bidding process on October 14, 1991. On November 22 it awarded Sicartsa I to a Mexican conglomerate, Grupo Villacero, for $170 million; Sicartsa II went to the Indian firm Caribbean ISPAT, for $220 million.

Along with the sale of its sister firms in the Sidermex holding company, Sicartsa's divestment put the state "out of business" with respect to steel production. For reformers it marked another step toward reducing the scope and size of government proprietorship. For steelworkers the outcome was better than it could have been, but less than they hoped. Nevertheless, when weighed against the potential additional costs of resistance (union deregistration, legal prosecutions), it probably represented the best settlement possible under difficult circumstances.

Explaining Outcomes

Despite obstacles and setbacks, between 1988 and 1991 Mexico established an impressive privatization record as reformers brought radical change to what were traditionally "priority" economic sectors. After Cananea and Sicartsa, other significant divestments followed, including the national telephone company, Telmex, FERTIMEX (fertilizers), and eighteen commercial banks. In hindsight the reformers' achievements may appear to have been easy, but divestment analysts saw few reasons a priori to expect this outcome. Indeed, as late as 1990 such clear thinkers as Dennis Gayle and Jonathan Goodrich concluded that with few exceptions, large-scale privatization programs were "essentially an advanced industrial country phenomenon."[140] Explaining why Mexico confounded such expectations is challenging. Indeed, standard views on the politics of reform cannot easily account for these accomplishments, nor the varied pattern of policy implementation.

One line of argument would suggest the outcomes were a function of a given initiative's relative complexity; that is, the more complicated the reform attempted, the less likely reformers would succeed. This position, however, provides little traction. To be sure, divestment initiatives did grow increasingly complex as reformers moved from Aeroméxico to Cananea to Sicartsa. But degrees of complexity do not explain why reformers succeeded in all instances, nor why they chose to implement reforms coercively in less complicated ones.

A second possibility is that successful outcomes were the product of an effective, committed, and insulated "change team." Given the reformers' technocratic background, degree of autonomy, and strong presidential support, this seems plausible. It assumes, however, that simply having the capacity to make sound policies ensures their successful implementation. And as Cananea demonstrates, when institutional arrangements impede or discourage collaboration even skilled technocrats can work at cross-purposes to the detriment of their overall objectives. Also, autonomy can cut both ways. At least in part, NAFINSA's initial failure to divest Cananea was a product of the conflict its relative autonomy created with the CGF. Finally, this approach says little about why change teams could *implement* reforms successfully or why the implementation patterns they chose varied so greatly.

A third perspective might stress the role of Mexico's centralized political system. On the one hand, centralization and corporatist arrangements reduced the intensity of feedback problems by limiting nonstate actors' capacity to oppose reform through congressional lobbying. On the other hand, certeris parabis, concentrated power should expedite decision making and render opposition inside the state relatively impotent. But this approach too falls short. Mexican *presidencialismo* can certainly minimize disruptive bureaucratic policy disputes and lead policy along the executive's preferred path. But it does not preclude their outbreak entirely. As Aeroméxico and Cananea attest, even when the executive's preferences were clear the institutional context played a major role in reformers' ability to control the agenda and translate those preferences into policy outcomes. In addition, while presidential power provides some purchase on why the state *could* employ coercion, it offers no compelling explanation for why the state periodically implemented reform with such a heavy hand. Given the limitations of many standard arguments, does a coalitional approach fare any better? The evidence strongly suggests it does.

Because policy making is intrinsically a collective process it encompasses multiple actors who often hold competing interests. As the case studies illustrate, the capacity to press those interests to the point it affects policy outcomes is strongly influenced by the degree of joint action between actors, the organizational position they occupy inside the state, their aggregate organizational strength, and the institutional arrangements that structure political interaction in the policy arena.

In the case of Aeroméxico the preexistence of a protocoalition (the *Comisión Gasto-Financiamiento*) facilitated the carrier's divestment. Not only did commission members occupy influential bureaucratic posts, but working relationships already were established, as were divisions of labor within the commission itself. These factors helped minimize the time, opportunity, information, and transaction costs, etc., required to formulate and execute the initiative. Similar dynamics held with respect to Sicartsa. With Cananea, by contrast, the absence of these factors inhibited early collaboration between NAFINSA and the CGF; this opened the door for reformers to work at cross-purposes, duplicate functions, fuel institutional jealousies, and ultimately delay reform.

The fact that formulation and adoption of new policy proceeded swifter and more smoothly in instances where reform coalitions emerged early on than where they did not (Aeroméxico and Sicartsa vs. Cananea), provides prima facie support for a coalitional approach. The evidence grows stronger still when we consider the crucial role coalition dynamics played throughout the reform process (from formulation and adoption through implementation). In contests over the policy agenda coalition partners used their organizational position to advance their policy preference. The Treasury and Ministry of Budget and Planning "turned" Transportation, prompting the agency's capitulation to divestment by withholding Aeroméxico's subsidies; Nacional Financiera exploited its vertical leverage over Cananea to ensure the company's management was on the reform team, and thereafter, both parties worked to privatize the firm; and the *Comisión Gasto-Financiamiento* compelled Sicartsa (and Sidermex) to comply with the market-friendly terms of the 1986 *convenio de rehabilitación.* In each case these measures helped reformers secure agenda control, offset opposition, and expand the coalition inside the state. Throughout the second phase of the reform process (implementation) "embedded autonomy" helped coalition members advance their goals during pitched battles over the distribution of costs. By engaging nonstate actors through several channels (i.e., management-labor negotiations, ministerial-labor interaction) reform teams could monitor workers' response to reform initiatives and alter their own positions (or not) accordingly—persuading, cajoling, coercing, or compensating opponents to advance policy change.

As divestment initiatives grew larger and more complicated, the opportunity for setbacks multiplied. However, the CGF's transformation from a body that monitored macroeconomic policy into a coalition dedicated to privatization helped minimize reversals, as did Salinas's redefinition of divestment criteria. Even more decisive, however, was the added leverage reformers gained over privatization policy through effective institutional innovation. Here, the rule-changing, instrument-creating, and strategizing behaviors outlined in chapter 2 proved politically consequential.

"Resectorization" and the Office of Privatization went a long way toward centralizing authority, streamlining divestment procedures, and marginalizing bureaucratic foot-draggers. Equally important, they bolstered the coalition's organizational strength to the point that reformers—led by Pedro Aspe—could claim "political property rights" over public sector downsizing. Although privatization remained a hotly debated topic in some quarters of society, overt challenges to the policy inside the state virtually ceased. In the internal struggles over policy agendas and content, these developments tipped the balance decidedly toward reform proponents. They were crucial to advancing Sicartsa's divestment and positioned reformers to realize many more victories down the line.

In terms of implementation patterns the assaults against organized labor were, of course, designed to advance reform by punishing precisely those syndicates which displayed the most independence from co-opted national leaders (Cananea), and/or the greatest hostility to policy change (Aeroméxico). Reformers could employ these tactics largely due to the centralized power inherent in Mexico's authoritarian system. However, coercive tactics also reflected a broader political agenda than simply battering antireform labor elements into submission. Given the growing dissonance aggressive market policies sparked between the traditional PRI-labor alliance, Salinas sought to create a "new unionism" more amenable to labor flexibility and supportive of reform by favoring those willing to support his project and disfavoring (sometimes quite coercively) those which were not.[141] Toward these ends Salinas replaced recalcitrant union leaders with more accommodating ones, and worked to link those unions willing to compromise closer to the presidency, if not the ruling party (among these were unions representing the telephone, streetcar, electrical, and financial services workers, plus pilots and flight attendants).

That said, the government's coercive tactics were not simply a function of "power politics," but also of a unique cost-benefit calculus played out in the quest to achieve neoliberal goals. Just as a variety of costs (institutional losses, jobs, contract benefits, etc.) helped condition opponents' response to reform, the calculations reformers made regarding their own cost profile affected their choice of implementation strategies. In each case examined the belief that overmanning or unduly generous contracts lowered a corporation's sales appeal led reformers to push substantial contract givebacks. This sparked opposition from labor unions who viewed their benefits as partial compensation for the ravages of Mexico's economic crisis. Efforts to address that opposition formed one dimension of the reformers' cost profile. The other emerged from subtle interactions between the transaction and opportunity costs inherent in each case.

Each divestment initiative occasioned various transaction costs; these affected the likelihood of a sale and the margin of benefits it might produce. For example, should a firm's labor force and collective contract be restructured prior to auction? Was it financially more cost effective to mollify opposition (and hence, expand the coalition) by providing unions compensation? Could the state absorb the political fallout born of a controversial *quiebra?* How reformers addressed these issues bore directly on potential outcomes. The choices they made carried opportunity costs and reflected their assessment of a given union's "strategic value" to the preferred outcome.

That assessment, in turn, was filtered through the neoliberal paradigm which viewed production factors like labor as relatively mobile. On this basis, reformers concluded some unions were of greater strategic value than others. Thus, Aeroméxico's pilots—whose skills were essential and in short supply—were invited into the reformers' camp, while the carrier's groundworkers and flight attendants were not. The reformers made a similar (but erroneous) judgment call with respect to Cananea. Failing to appreciate the obstacles to labor mobility at Cananea (and the company's utter dependence on local labor), they underestimated the mineworkers' strategic value and pursued an ineffective coercive strategy. The collateral costs CMC's bankruptcy generated on the political front—and throughout the local economy—informed decisions regarding Sicartsa. Accordingly, in this case reformers determined it was more cost effective to compensate steelworkers and the local community rather than risk another *quiebra.* In short, while coalition politics were critical to successful policy reform, it was the cost calculations actors made, not simply the government's power or political agenda, that influenced implementation patterns.

Finally, the changing pattern of implementation across divestment cases speaks to that aspect of political success described in chapter 1, namely, the capacity to advance perceived "good" policies in "good" ways (i.e., those which address at least some of the concerns that preoccupy policy losers, and thus, encourage broader social support). As detailed in chapter 7, efforts to implement divestiture via sheer hardball politics damaged the government's historic alliance with organized labor, in particular, the rank and file. That the Salinas administration moderated its implementation strategies after Cananea reflects its growing appreciation of these factors. Providing compensation, plus working to revise labor contracts—rather than simply abrogate them—helped temper labor opposition, strengthen the administration's governing capacity, and safeguard the divestiture program's overall credibility.

Complementing such moderation, the administration also sought to broaden support for divestment among the general population. The key here was the National Solidarity Program (PRONASOL) which channeled billions of dollars in social spending to grassroots projects, often in regions where the PRI ran poorly in 1988. Through a permanent public relations campaign the Salinas government saturated print and electronic media with PRONASOL advertisements, and linked PRONASOL spending squarely to privatization revenues. By associating the provision of mass benefits with a cornerstone of Mexico's new development model, the administration deflected criticism it was unconcerned with the social strains privatization occasioned, while cultivating popular support. The result was high political dividends for the president, his party, and program. After its near debacle in 1988, the PRI rebounded in 1991 midterm elections to retain the Congress and expand its partisan majority, and as Davis and Coleman discovered, it was among those groups with access to PRONASOL benefits where "the PRI made its greatest gains."[142] Accordingly, as electoral victory bolstered the government's political capital, the political climate surrounding divestiture grew more secure.

Mexico entered the 1980s with a bloated, economically distressed and inefficient public sector, largely sustained by external borrowing. By 1982 the public sector represented nearly one-fifth of Mexico's total economic output and consumed, through subsidies, about 12.7 percent of GDP.[143] Although the 1982 debt crisis signaled the need to change policy direction, given the vested interests past policies had created, few anticipated the success or magnitude of the policy response.

The de la Madrid and Salinas administrations managed to achieve significant public sector reform, in part, because centralized political power reduced the intensity of various feedback problems, generally astute minimizing/imposition strategies helped policy makers surmount the reformer's dilemma, and PRONASOL helped cultivate popular support. Nevertheless, these factors did not preordain successful reform. The central lesson Mexico's divestment experience teaches is that reformers who band together, maximize their organizational position within the state, and enhance their leverage through effective institutional innovation are well situated to prevail. As chapter 4 demonstrates with respect to regulatory reform, under these conditions the prospects for success are bright.

Notes

1. For a fairly detailed, if largely atheoretical description of Mexican divestiture, see Judith A. Teichman, *Privatization and Political Change in Mexico* (Pittsburgh, Penn.: Pittsburgh University Press, 1995).

2. This does not to imply that state-owned enterprises are confined to statist models. Many countries that eschewed inward-oriented development also developed large public sectors (e.g., Britain, France).

3. Villarreal, for example, suggests public sector expansion reflected the state's "permanent constitutional objective" to promote social and economic development. René Villarreal, *Mitos y realidades de la empresa pública. ¿Racionalización o privatización?* (México, D.F.: Editorial Diana, 1991), 57.

4. See also Pedro Aspe, *Economic Transformation the Mexican Way* (Cambridge, Mass.: MIT Press, 1993), 181.

5. Sebastian Edwards, *Crisis and Reform in Latin America: From Despair to Hope* (New York: Oxford University Press, 1995), 175.

6. Yair Aharoni, "State-Owned Enterprise: An Agent without a Principal," in Leroy P. Jones, ed., *Public Enterprise in Less-Developed Countries* (New York: Cambridge University Press, 1982), 68.

7. This practice began when Aeroméxico served as the official airline of Mexican presidents (1959 to the late 1970s). See Manuel Camposeco, "Aeroméxico: el gatopardismo de la modernidad," in Esthela Gutiérrez, ed., *Reconversión industrial y lucha sindical* (Caracas, Venezuela: Fundación Friedrich Ebert-México, Editorial Nueva Sociedad, 1989), 154, 156; and author's interviews, Mexico City, July 6 and 14, 1993.

8. Author's interviews. Mexico City, July 6 and 22, 1993.

9. At Aeroméxico, for example, when one director tried to restrict "political" air travel and reduce labor costs in the 1980s, he wound up in early "retirement." Author's interview. Mexico City, July 6, 1993.

10. See Lorenzo Martíntez Vargas, "La línea aérea que fué para abajo: Aeroméxico," *Novedades,* May 5, 1988, 25. See also Camposeco, "Aeroméxico: el gatopardismo de la modernidad," 159.

11. Subsidy figures are derived from an unpublished World Bank assessment.

12. For example, in 1989 one-way airfares between Mexico City and Acapulco (approximately 200 miles) were U.S. $70, while fares between New York City and Boston (200 miles) were $178; fares between Mexico City and Guadalajara (approximately 300 miles) were $78 while tickets for the New York City-Buffalo route, or the Chicago-Nashville route (both approximately 300 miles) were $238 and $371 respectively. See Pankaj Tandon, *Welfare Consequences of Selling Public Enterprises, Case Studies from Chile, Malaysia, Mexico and the U.K., Mexico: Aeroméxico, Mexicana* (hereafter referred to as *Mexico: Aeroméxico, Mexicana*), vol. 2 (Washington, D.C.: The World Bank, 1992), figure 17–30.

13. Beginning in the 1960s the government adopted a new labor policy to achieve full employment. The basic strategy was to divide available work among a growing labor pool by encouraging a rigid division of labor in collective contracts; the unions, of course, happily fell in line with the new policy. In the steel sector the metalworkers union negotiated contracts that restricted workers' horizontal mobility through rigid job classifications. La-

bor redundancy multiplied as mechanics who could perform multiple tasks (equipment repair, welding, metal cutting, etc.) were limited to *one,* and three new workers were hired instead. Similar practices developed in mining and aviation, and with predictable results: at Cananea the mineworkers' contract eventually contained 400 different job classifications; at Aeroméxico the groundworkers' contract topped 270.

14. Mexico's 1931 Federal Labor Law required that any worker dismissed "unfairly" receive adequate compensation. A "fair" discharge was one where a firm could prove a specific employee somehow damaged the company's interests. All other dismissals—whether based on falling demand, low productivity, or redundancy—were forbidden. Companies that discharged workers for these reasons were required to make compensatory severance payments. The standard severance package equaled three months' salary, plus twenty days' pay for each year worked. Workers with at least ten years' seniority received an additional twelve days' salary, and anyone displaced by new technology was entitled to the payments above, plus an extra four months' salary. For a worker with ten or more years' seniority, the average severance package equaled about a year's salary.

15. The social welfare function of Mexican public enterprises stemmed directly from constitutional mandates obliging the state to promote the general good. Article 3 of the 1917 Constitution outlines a broad political project charged to the Mexican state. Its chief goal is to promote a "way of life" to which all Mexicans are entitled, based on constant economic improvement. Historically, Mexican governments have interpreted this article as justification of public sector operations.

16. See "La Semip ante la LII Legislatura," *Cuaderno de Divulgación* 24 (México, D.F.: Secretaría de Energía, Minas e Industria Paraestatales, 1984), 12–18.

17. According to the Finance Ministry's Office of Privatization, SEMIP officials often used this tactic to keep large public enterprises under their jurisdiction. Former president Miguel de la Madrid also conceded that while ministerial leaders cooperated with his privatization program, passive resistance from mid-level officials was a problem. Author's interviews. Mexico City, July 14 and 21, 1992; June 28, 1992.

18. For discussion see Pierre Guislain, *The Privatization Challenge: A Strategic, Legal, and Institutional Analysis of International Experience* (Washington, D.C.: The World Bank, 1997), 167–168; see also Charles Vuylsteke, *Techniques of Privatization of State-Owned Enterprises,* vol. 1, *Methods and Implementation* (Washington, D.C.: The World Bank, 1988).

19. The 1917 Constitution reserved "strategic" economic sectors solely for the state. These include coining money, printing currency, postal services, satellite communications, oil, hydrocarbons and petrochemicals, and railroads. The Constitution also permits government participation in state-defined "priority" sectors like steel, mining, and aviation.

20. See *Reestructuración del sector paraestatal* (México, D.F.: Fondo de Cultura Económica, 1988).

21. According to the Office of Privatization, the Ministry of Energy, Mines, and Parastatals often used this tactic to keep large public enterprises under its jurisdiction. Not all ministries were reluctant to part with large assets, however. For example, the Ministry of Tourism was one of the first agencies to propose the sale of its El Presidente and National hotel chains. Author's interview. Mexico City, July 21, 1992. See also "Privatizaciones: Un Camino de Regreso," *Época* (November 18, 1991).

22. Author's interview. Mexico City, July 21, 1992.

23. Author's interviews. Mexico City, July 29, 1993.

24. From 1976 to 1982 public spending averaged 36 percent of GDP annually, with much of it designed to increase output, raise living standards, and create jobs in the public

sector including such PEs as Sicartsa, Diesel Nacional, Renault de México, PEMEX (oil), the Federal Electricity Commission, and the Mexican Food System. The government financed this spending spree by borrowing against its oil reserves; consequently, between 1977 and 1982 Mexico's external debt jumped from $32.3 to $92.4 billion. On public sector spending see Benito Rey Romayo, *La ofensiva empresarial contra la intervención del estado*, Anexo Informativo (México, D.F.: Siglo Veintiuno Editores, 1984); on debt, see Carlos Bázdresch and Santiago Levy, "Populism and Economic Policy in Mexico, 1970-1982," in Rudiger Dornbusch and Sebastian Edwards, eds., *The Macroeconomics of Populism in Latin America* (Chicago: University of Chicago Press, 1991), table 8.1, 232–233.

25. Wayne A. Cornelius, "The Political Economy of Mexico under de la Madrid: The Crisis Deepens, 1985-1986," *Research Report Series* 43 (La Jolla, Calif.: Center for U.S.-Mexican Studies, University of California, San Diego, 1986).

26. For detailed discussion of Mexico's policy debate see José Córdoba, "Mexico," in John Williamson, ed., *The Political Economy of Policy Reform* (Washington, D.C.: Institute for International Economics, 1994). On "search behavior" see Nelson Polsby, *Political Innovation in America: The Politics of Policy Initiation* (New Haven, Conn.: Yale University Press, 1984), 168.

27. For example, the plan stressed the government's public enterprises could strengthen Mexico's "mixed economy," facilitate provision of social goods and services, and offset the market's tendencies to foster inequality. See *Plan Nacional de Desarrollo 1983-1988* (México, D.F.: Secretaría de Programación y Presupuesto, 1983), 6.3.3.1-6.3.3.5.

28. Author's interview. Mexico City, June 28, 1993.

29. These carriers were officially known as Compañia Mexicana de Transportación Aéra (Mexicana) and Aeronaves de México (Aeroméxico). See R. E. G. Davies, *Airlines of Latin America since 1919* (Washington, D.C.: Smithsonian Institution Press, 1984). This section draws heavily from chapters 1 and 2 of Davies's work.

30. In the international market (mainly flights to the United States) a similar pattern of noncompetition ensued: Aeroméxico catered to the eastern U.S. states, Mexicana served those in the West. Together they accounted for 55 percent of all U.S.-bound flights originating in Mexico. See *Estudio del esquema rector del sistema nacional del transporte aéroa* (México, D.F.: Aconsa Consultores, S.A. de C.V., September 30, 1990), 31; Tandon, *Welfare Consequences of Selling Public Enterprises*, 8; and *Privatization in Latin America: New Competitive Opportunities and Challenges* (New York: Business International Corporation, 1990), 55.

31. Although the ministry awarded a number of concessions to new entrants, it also denied new *concesionarios* landing rights at points already serviced by Aeroméxico or Mexicana.

32. See César Vázquez, *La reconversión industrial en la aviación comercial* (México, D.F.: Universidad Autónomo Metropolitano, Xtapalapa, 1992), 104. Mexicana remained a privately held corporation until its nationalization in 1982.

33. See Tandon, *Mexico: Aeroméxico, Mexicana*, 2.

34. In field interviews numerous informants—government officials, ex-government officials, ex-airline employees, and informants not connected with Aeroméxico at all—repeatedly made these observations. Author's interviews. See also Luis Pazos, "Las Ensañanzas de Aeroméxico," *Novedades*, January 2, 1991, 15.

35. See Robert W. Moorman, "Privatization in Mexico Revisited," *Air Transport World* 28, no. 12 (1991).

36. See Miguel de la Madrid, *Quinto informe de gobierno* (México, D.F.: Presidencia de

la República, 1987), 96.

37. *Reestructuración del sector paraestatal*, 65–66.

38. Later members included the ministries of Labor, Commerce and Social Development, and the comptroller general.

39. Author's interview. Mexico City, July 23, 1993.

40. Disciplining public spending was the most important norm of the commission's work. As one high-level official explained, "fiscal austerity" was "the byword of each and every member" of the CGF. Author's interview. Mexico City, July 23, 1993.

41. *Las razones y las obras, gobierno de Miguel de la Madrid: Crónica del sexenio 1982-1988*, vol. 6 (México, D.F.: Presidencia de la República, Fondo de Cultura Económica, 1988), 469.

42. Most notably the steelworks Fundidora de Monterrey, which the government bankrupted and closed in 1986.

43. Vázquez, *La reconversión industrial en la aviación comercial*, 71; Pilar Vázquez Rubio, "El plan de mejoramiento del servicio en Aeroméxico," *El Cotidiano* 21 (January-February 1988): 75.

44. Author's interview. Mexico City, July 22, 1993.

45. Author's interview. Mexico City, July 22, 1993.

46. Author's interview. Mexico City, July 22, 1993.

47. Although the ministers of Transportation and Labor attended the meeting, Budget Minister (and CGF president) Pedro Aspe took the lead. He labeled Aeroméxico's economic performance "shameful," and likened its consumption of subsidies to pouring water down a sewer. See Camposeco, "Aeroméxico: el gatopardismo de la modernidad," 165.

48. ASPA initially proposed that the union itself buy all of Aeroméxico's shares, or at least acquire 51 percent. Government officials rejected both proposals: the terms of the agreement were set and the pilots could either take it or leave it.

49. Salvador Corro, "En diciembre Aeroméxico aún era viable; en enero se decidió ponerla en picada," *Proceso* 599 (April 25, 1988): 26.

50. See especially Corro, "En diciembre Aeroméxico aún era viable"; *Las razones y las obras*, 466–468; "Aeroméxico Bankruptcy Unprecedented for State Airline," *Airfinance Journal*, no. 91 (June 1988): 36; and William A. Orme, Jr., "Strike-Ridden Aeroméxico Files for Bankruptcy," *Journal of Commerce* (April 19, 1988): 5B.

51. See Corro, "En diciembre Aeroméxico aún era viable," 27.

52. Ibid., 26.

53. *Las obras y las razones*, 467; and Ana María Conesa R., and Eduardo Larrañaga S., "Aeroméxico: El derecho de huelga en quiebra," *El Cotidiano* 25 (September-October 1988): 66.

54. Orme, "Strike-Ridden Aeroméxico."

55. The termination of its contract stripped the SNTTAM of all juridical rights and essentially *de*-registered the syndicate as a legal union.

56. Miguel de la Madrid, quoted in *Expansión*, May 11, 1988, 112.

57. Almost anyone who had flown Aeroméxico knew of the carrier's shortcomings—delayed or canceled departures, chronically late arrivals, lost luggage, etc. Those with no personal experience (the vast majority of Mexicans) readily accepted the government's contention that "privileged" groups (labor) had abused their positions to extract personal benefits from the nation's airline, deliver poor service in return, then shift the costs of inefficiency onto the public.

58. In private, some government officials described the bankruptcy as an "impeccable strategy" to break the union and facilitate divestment. See Orme, "Strike-Ridden Aeromexico."

59. The state's power of *requisa* is based on Article 112 of the General Law of Routes and Communication. It permits a federal takeover of public service entities (airlines, railroads, ground and maritime transport, and the telephone system, etc.) during international conflicts, grave public disorders, immediate danger to internal security, or imminent danger to the national economy. For discussion see the essays in Eduardo Larrañaga, Ana María Conesa, Manuel Reyna, and Paco Ignacio Taibo, eds., *El derecho laboral en México: Realidad y encubrimiento* (México: Universidad Autónoma Metropolitana, Azcapotzalco, 1991).

60. See Eduardo Larrañaga and Héctor Mercado, "Requisa e inexistencia de huelga en la CMA," *El Cotodiano* 21 (January-February 1988).

61. The National Bank of Public Works (BANOBRAS) served as Aeroméxico's trustee.

62. For different reasons the pilots and flight attendants unions were not liquidated. ASPA had signed a contract with the interim airline and would be a share holder in the coming private firm; ASSA escaped liquidation because it maintained its contract with Mexicana Airline. The groundworkers union on the other hand (SNTTAM) was dissolved and replaced by a new syndicate called the National Union of Service Workers of Similar Airlines and Connections "Independence." On specific contract changes see Vázquez, "La aviación: una reconversión en los aires," 85.

63. Author's interview. Mexico City, July 22, 1993. See also Vázquez, "La aviación: una reconversión en los aires," 85.

64. Aspe, *Economic Transformation the Mexican Way,* 203.

65. See Oscar Contreras and Miguel Ángel Ramírez, "Novedades de la postguerra: fin del auge exportador y repliegue hacia el mercado interno," in José Carlos Ramírez, ed., *La nueva industrialización de Sonora: El caso de los sectores de alta tecnología* (Hermosillo, Sonora, México: El Colegio de Sonora, 1988), 293.

66. These figures are from Orlando Martino, Jerome Machamer, and Ivette Torres, *The Mineral Economy of Mexico* (Washington, D.C.: United States Department of the Interior, Bureau of Mines, 1992), 65; Manuel Sánchez, Rossana Corona, Otoniel Ochoa, Luis Fernando Herrera, Arturo Olvera, and Ernesto Sepúlveda, "The Privatization Process in Mexico: Five Case Studies," in Manuel Sánchez and Rossana Corona, eds., *Privatization in Latin America* (Washington, D.C.: Inter-American Development Bank, 1993),116; and *Mercado de Valores* 13 (July 1, 1988): 14.

67. The founding of Cananea—and the wider exploits of William Greene—are chronicled in C. L. Sonnichsen, *Colonel Greene and the Copper Skyrocket* (Tucson, Ariz.: University of Arizona Press, 1974).

68. Most of the actual gunfire seemed to take place between miners and company officials, not the miners and Arizona Rangers. The U.S. "soldiers" actually were volunteers from Bisbee, Arizona, not a regular attachment of the state militia; they were deputized and put under the direct control of the Cananean sheriff. According to some accounts the American militia put down the workers' rebellion with high loss of life; others insist that before the Americans could actually wade into the fray, Mexican *rurales* had arrived, took control of the situation, and the Americans returned to Arizona without firing a shot. See the various references in Sonnichsen, *Colonel Greene and the Copper Skyrocket,* 199-201.

69. Mexican historian Ruiz Harrel, for example, attributes the uprising to political, xenophobic, and labor factors internal to Cananea's operations, not to revolutionary sentiments directed toward President Díaz. See Rafael Ruiz Harrel, *Historia general de México,*

vol. 2 (México, D.F.: El Colegio de México, 1976), 988.

70. See *Compañía Minera de Cananea: Reinicio de operaciones, relaciones con la comunidad, prestaciones especiales,* Internal Report (México, D.F.: Financiera Nacional Azucarera, n.d.), 9; and Sánchez et al., "The Privatization Process in Mexico," 116–117.

71. See Juan Luis Sariego, Luis Reygadas, Miguel Ángel Gómez, and Javier Farrera, *El Estado y la minería mexicana: Política, trabajo y sociedad durante el siglo XX* (México, D.F.: Fondo de Cultura Económica, 1988), 254. For a broad discussion of the rationales and impact of *mexicanization* on the mining sector see Theodore B. Borek, "Evaluating a Developing Institution: Mexicanization of Mining," *Arizona Law Review* 13, no. 3 (1971).

72. The actual equity holdings were as follows: NAFINSA = 75.1 percent (43.1 percent of which was held by the bank's trust fund); the Mining Promotion Commission = 24.7 percent; and private investors = 0.2 percent. Sánchez et al., "The Privatization Process in Mexico," 121.

73. Cananea was never listed in the official *Biographical Dictionary of the Mexican Government,* which catalogues all state-owned enterprises according to the ministries which administer them. Ironically, it *was* listed in *Expansión*'s prestigious catalogue of Mexico's 100 most important corporations along with other private sector giants. See "Los 100 director generales de las empresas más importantes de México," *Expansión,* June 8, 1988, 60–81.

74. Management consciously tried to avoid the attention of central authorities. It chose not to establish a public relations department, rarely issued news briefs, and seldom accepted calls from bureaucrats in Mexico City. Author's interview. Mexico City, July 14, 1993.

75. See John Waterbury, *Exposed to Innumerable Delusions: Public Enterprise and State Power in Egypt, India, Mexico, and Turkey* (New York: Cambridge University Press, 1993), 127-128.

76. This project included a complete upgrade of the mine's open pit, eight new mills, an oxygen plant to improve efficiency of the copper smelter, and new environmental technologies to curb toxic airborne emissions. Management projected the improvements would boost CMC's output by 40,000 tons per year. For discussion see Stephen P. Mumme, "The Cananea Copper Controversy: Lessons for Environmental Diplomacy," *Journal of Inter-American Economic Affairs* 38, no. 1 (Summer 1984).

77. Mexico's economic crisis forced the de la Madrid administration to cut public spending over 17 percent under the Immediate Program for Economic Readjustment. See Aspe, *Economic Transformation the Mexican Way,* 15.

78. External funding sources included the International Finance Corporation, U.S. Export-Import Bank, the Japanese Export-Import Bank, and the Banco Exterior de España. See Mumme, "The Cananea Copper Controversy. "

79. See Manuel Sánchez, Rossana Corona, Otoniel Ochoa, Luis Fernando Herrera, Arturo Olvera, and Ernesto Sepúlveda, *El proceso de privatización en México: Un estudio de casos* (México, D.F.: Centro de Analisis e Investigación Económica, 1992), 113.

80. CMC owed $568 million to Nacional Financiera, $67 million to American Express, and roughly $17 million more to suppliers and the Treasury. See Richard Johns, "Mexico Declares Cananea Copper Mines Bankrupt," *Financial Times,* August 22, 1989, 4.

81. "Transferencia de Empresas con Participación Accionaria de Nacional Financiera," *Mercado de Valores* 3 (February 1988): 11; and Márquez and Serrano, "Minera de Cananea Pasará al Sector Privado."

82. See Ricardo Vázquez, "Incertidumbre Financiera Sobre la Venta de Minera Cananea,"

El Financiero, May 17, 1988, 30. Author's interview, Mexico City, July 14, 1993.

83. Author's interview. Mexico City, July 14, 1993.

84. Perhaps drawing on the CGF's own uncertainty regarding asset evaluations, First National claimed that NAFINSA had overvalued Cananea. It also cited Protexa's undisclosed financial weaknesses to justify its decision. See William A. Orme, Jr., "Mexicans Cancel Plan for Copper Mine Sale," *Journal of Commerce* (June 24, 1988), 1A.

85. Patricia Paredes, "Rechazó NAFINSA las dos ofertas sobre Cananea," *El Universal,* November 8, 1988, 22.

86. Initially, NAFINSA's new director general, Juan Páramo, tried to replace CMC vice presidents with political appointees, but since these positions already were filled by persons duly elected by the board, his efforts went nowhere. Páramo then urged his candidates be appointed as special "advisers" to the CEO, but the company president refused. In February 1989, NAFINSA ousted CMC's president, Emilio Ocampo (whom the board had just reelected in January), installed its own director of industrial promotion and trusts in his stead (Luis Alberto Pérez Aceves), bought up a majority of recently issued stock, fired fifteen board members, and seized control of the board. Author's interview, Mexico City, July 14, 1993. See also Sánchez et al., *Privatization in Latin America,* 122.

87. See Salvador Corro, "Todo mundo sabía que la corrupción conducía a Cananea al desastre," *Proceso* 670 (September 4, 1989): 18; see also Carlos Acosta, "Hasta marzo, la empresa decía que Cananea era ejemplar; en cinco meses se volvió un desastre," *Proceso* 669 (August 28, 1989): 6.

88. Formed in 1934, the Mining and Metallurgical Workers of the Mexican Republic (STMMRM) encompasses mineral, ferrous, and nonferrous mineworkers, and boasts 200,000 members nationwide. See Kevin J. Middlebrook, "State-Labor Relations in Mexico: The Changing Economic and Political Context," in Kevin J. Middlebrook, ed., *Unions, Workers, and the State in Mexico* (La Jolla, Calif.: Center for U.S.-Mexican Studies, University of California, San Diego, 1991), 8.

89. On Cananea's contract provisions see Oscar F. Contreras Montellan, *La Minería en Sonora: Modernización industrial y fuerza de trabajo* (Hermosillo, Sonora, México: El Colegio de Sonora, 1986), 38; and Theres García, "La Milicia de Cananea, Ayer fue Declarada en Quiebra; los Bienes Bajo Custodio Militar," *El Financiero,* August 21, 1989, 3.

90. Oscar F. Contreras and Miguel Ángel Ramírez Sánchez, "Mercado de Trabajo y Relaciones Laborales en Cananea: La Disputa en Torno a la Flexibilidad," *Trabajo: Sociedad, Tecnología y Cultura* 8 (1992): 15, n. 2.

91. In 1989 Mexicana's giant La Caridad copper mine contributed 55 percent of Mexico's total copper production. Martino Machamer and Torres, *The Mineral Economy of Mexico,* 63.

92. Jorge Luis Ibarra M., José Luis Moreno V., and Leopoldo Santos R., "Cananea: Resistencias regionales a la política de modernización," *Revista de El Colegio de Sonora* 2 (1990): 137.

93. See Contreras and Ramírez, "Novedades de la postguerra," 9; José Luis Moreno, "Efectos laborales de la política de modernización en Cananea," in Felipe Mora and Victor Manuel Reynosa, eds., *Modernización legislación laboral en el noreste de México* (Hermosillo, Sonora, México: El Colegio de Sonora, 1990); Ibarra M., Moreno V., and Santos R., "Cananea: Resistencias regionales"; and Sánchez et al., "The Privatization Process in Mexico," 126.

94. Sánchez et al., "The Privatization Process in Mexico," 125.

95. Author's interview. Mexico City, July 13, 1993.

96. While the Labor Law sets the *minimum* legal standards required to indemnify discharged workers, union contracts often set much higher criteria for indemnification. Under the STMMRM's contract Cananea's bankruptcy trustee would have to pay 100 billion pesos in severance payments to discharged workers, while under the Federal Labor Law those payments would equal only 17 billion pesos. Ibarra M., Moreno V., and Santos R., "Cananea: Resistencias regionales," 142, n. 16.

97. See "Salinas Strikes before the Miners Can," *Business Week*, September 4, 1989, 50; and especially Fernando Ortega Pizarro, "Los soldados, para anunciar que Cananea había sido declarada en quiebra," *Proceso* 669 (August 28, 1989).

98. Acosta, "Hasta marzo, la empresa decía que Cananea era ejemplar," 8.

99. See Salvador Corro, "Los mineros de Cananea: de los golpes a los apachos verbales," *Proceso* 679 (November 6, 1989): 19, and the public communiqué released by CMC on August 21, 1989.

100. "La STyPS Agilizará los Trámites de Liquidación Conforme a la Ley," *El Financiero*, August 23, 1989, 25.

101. Criticism was harsh, and came from virtually all sides: the left, the church, the state government of Sonora, opposition parties, and to an extent, from within the PRI itself. Some critics denounced the state for settling labor disputes via military force; others drew parallels between the 1989 and 1906 "occupation" by U.S. forces. Only the private sector (the Employers' Confederation of the Mexican Republic) applauded the *quiebra*, yet even the business community declared that the military should withdraw. See Ibarra M. et al., 149; and Ortega Pizarro, "Los soldados," 8.

102. Corro, "Los mineros de Cananea," 20.

103. Governor Valdés was given no prior notice of the impending bankruptcy or military occupation.

104. Typical of these critiques was a series of articles by the noted Mexican legal scholar Néstor de Buen, who elucidated a number of legal irregularities in *La Jornada*, August 23 and September 27, 1989.

105. Between 1987 and 1988 CMC's production jumped from 37,068 to 70,279 metric tons. In addition, after servicing its loans, Cananea's 1988 net profit was U.S. $74.7 million—a fourfold increase over 1987. See Martin, Machamer, and Torres, *The Mineral Economy of Mexico*, 66; Johns, "Mexico Declares Cananea Copper Mines Bankrupt," Richard Johns, "Privatisation Programme to Release Untapped Potential," *Financial Times*, October 12, 1989, 7; and Theres García and Martín Hernández, "Minera de Cananea, en lo Financiero, no Estaba en Quiebra," *El Financiero*, August 22, 1989, 22.

106. Cuauhtémoc Cárdenas, quoted in Acosta, "Hasta marzo, la empresa decía que Cananea era ejemplar," 12.

107. "Mexico," *Economist Intelligence Unit, Country Report*, no. 4 (1989): 7.

108. "Mexico: Privatization, Deregulation, and Liberalization," *Privatization in Latin America: New Competitive Opportunities and Challenges* (New York: Business International Corp., 1990), 65.

109. For example, four days after the president's peace offering Cananeans celebrated Mexico's national independence day (September 15), and in an extraordinary display of unity, support, and nationalism, the celebrants shunned the traditional independence day site (the municipal palace) in favor of the mineworkers' union headquarters. See Moreno, "Efectos laborales de la política de modernización en Cananea," 281.

110. Reported in *El Sonorense,* August 24 and September 6, 1989.

111. Among the most important provisions were the discharge of 719 workers, the reduction of job categories from 400 to 6, round-the-clock production shifts, promotions based on merit, not seniority, subcontracting permitted by union consent, a 33 percent wage hike, and CMC's continued responsibility to subsidize local community infrastructure. See *Acuerdos para fijar las condiciones en que habrán de reanudarse las labores en la Compañía Minera de Cananea* (México, D.F.: Secretaría del Trabajo y Previsión Social, 1989).

112. Because Grupo Minera México is the parent firm of Mexicana de Cobre, its acquisition of Cananea brought 90 percent of Mexico's total copper production under the control of that corporation's largest shareholder—Jorge Larrea. On the acquisition of CMC, see Juan Antonio Zuñiga M., "Obtuvo Mexicana de Cobre la adjudicación de Minera de Cananea," *La Jornada,* August 28, 1990, 17, and "Cananea Is Finally Awarded to Mining Magnate Larrea," *Latin American Weekly Report* (September 20, 1990); on Jorge Larrea's virtual copper monopoly see "Compañía Minera de Cananea: ¿Cobre por Libre?, *Expansión* (November 21, 1990); and Carlos Acosta and Ramón A. Sallard, "Corruptelas y maniobras convirtieron a Jorge Larrea en magnate mundial del cobre," *Proceso* 723 (September 10, 1990).

113. See Sánchez et al., *El proceso de privatización en México,* 113.

114. One prominent example was the divestment of the phone monopoly, Teléfonos de México (Telmex), which the Salinas government privatized in December 1990 with the full backing of the Union of Telephone Workers of the Mexican Republic (STRM). Instead of opposing the deal, the STRM supported it and negotiated new labor/management relations to facilitate it. In 1989, for example, the union negotiated contract revisions to help promote Telmex's technological modernization, reduce the number of job categories (from 585 to 41), and introduce greater flexibility into workforce patterns; however, the agreement also preserved a number of contract clauses and prohibited worker layoffs. One of the chief reasons for this outcome were the "lessons of Cananea" the STRM had begun to assimilate. As STRM president Francisco Hernández Juárez explained, negotiating the privatization of Telmex directly with the state at least gave labor a voice in its own future and preserved a measure of union interests. This, he believed, was far preferable to awakening one morning only to learn "the company has already been closed, declared bankrupt, or already sold, and we are liquidated." See Salvador Corro, "Al contrario de Cananea, en Teléfonos el sindicato ni las manos metio," *Proceso* 673 (September 25, 1989): 9. See also Enrique de la Garza Toledo, "¿Quién ganó en Telmex?" *El Cotidiano* 32 (1989).

115. Sicartsa I produces non-flat steel (bars, reinforcing bars, coiled wire rods) using coke ovens, a blast furnace, basic oxygen converters, and a rod and bar mill for continuous casting. Sicartsa II manufactures steel slab and plate using the more advanced direct reduction process, four electric ovens, two ladle furnaces, three continuous casters, and a fully modern plate mill. See Banca Serfin, Banca Mercantil del Norte, and S.G. Warburg & Co., Inc., *Sidermex: Sidermex, S.A. de C.V., Private and Confidential Executive Summary* (company prospectus, on file at the Office of Privatization, Ministry of Public Credit and Finance, Mexico City, n.d.); see also William T. Hogan, *Global Steel in the 1990s* (Lexington, Mass.: Lexington Books, 1991), 93.

116. The obstacles to the Las Truchas project are discussed at length in Ranier Godau Schücking, *Estado y acero: Historia política de Las Truchas* (México, D.F.: El Colegio de México, 1982). The alternative site for a new steel mill at Manzanillo was the personal pet project of former president Miguel Alemán. For a complete discussion of Sicartsa's found-

ing see Hector Fernández Moreno, "Origen y desarrollo del complejo de Siderúrgica Lázaro Cárdenas-Las Truchas," *Comercio Exterior* 25 (October 1975); and *Sicartsa, Crisol de México* (Lázaro Cárdenas, Michoacán, México: Siderúrgica Lázaro Cárdenas-Las Truchas, S.A., 1986).

117. Although SEMIP held sway over the companies' board, it did not select the firms' CEOs. The Mexican president approved the candidates for general director and the companies' board then ratified this choice through elections.

118. The Budget Ministry, for example, based its spending decisions on the five-year National Development Plan (PND), not market signals. Produced during the first year of a new administration, the PND identifies the basic issues, sectors, or themes the administration will prioritize. On this basis, Budget and Planning treated Sidermex expenditures the same way it did those for other development projects (i.e., schools, hospitals). To maximize efficiency, however, required careful attention to market fluctuations, unexpected opportunities and cash flow, etc., and too often management and SPP held different perspectives on corporate operations. Thus, an expenditure could either be a necessity or budget buster depending on one's vantage point. A former Sidermex board member explained how frustrating this practice could be: "If a private firm needs a warehouse it rents a facility based on what it considers to be a fair price. The PE on the other hand, finds a suitable facility at a reasonable price, but then must go to SPP for approval. The SPP then rejects the deal because the price is 'too high' and the process starts all over again." Author's interview. Mexico City, July 26, 1993.

119. See Alenka Guzmán Chávez, "Siderúrgica Lázaro Cárdenas-Las Truchas, 1977-1988," *El Cotidiano* 38 (November-December 1990).

120. On Sidermex debt, see René Villarreal, "Industrial Restructuring of the Public Steel Industry: The Mexican Case," *Public Enterprise* 10, no. 3 (September–December 1990): 265.

121. The Sidermex *convenio* was one of eight such accords the *Comisión Gasto-Financiamiento* created to effect structural adjustment in Mexico's public sector. Others targeted the railroads (Ferronales), the Federal Electricity Commission, the basic foods corporation (CONASUPO), a second food production firm (Albamex), the Institute of Mexican Television (Imevision), and two state-owned paper companies (Fapatux and Mexpape). See *Reestructuración del sector paraestatal,* 100–104. See also Guillermo Becker Arreola, "El fortalecimiento de la industria siderúrgica paraestatal," in *Sidermex: Ciclo 'Rectoría del Estado'* (México, D.F.: Instituto de Estudios Políticos, Económicos y Sociales, 1987), 55.

122. The intellectual environment under Salinas was decidedly neoliberal. For example, the president's 1989 National Development Plan argued that PEs "should be subjected to criteria of profitability and should be governed according to the competition that the market imposes for their best operation and highest social utility." In 1990 the administration promulgated new regulations to govern parastatal activities that again stressed rationality, austerity, and economic efficiency. See *Plan Nacional de Desarrollo 1989-1994* (Secretaría de Programación y Presupuesto, 1989), 5.3.9; and *Diario Oficial,* January 26, 1990.

123. Author's interview. Mexico City, July 15, 1993.

124. Merilee S. Grindle, *Challenging the State: Crisis and Innovation in Latin America and Africa* (New York: Cambridge University Press, 1996), 92-93.

125. Again, these operations included coining money, printing currency, postal services, satellite communications, oil, hydrocarbons and petrochemicals, and railroads.

126. See *Reglamento interior de la Secretaría de Hacienda y Crédito Público,* Chapter

12, Article 144 (México, D.F.: Secretaría de Hacienda y Crédito Público, 1990).

127. See J. Antonio Zúñiga M., "Anunció la SPP la venta de Altos Hornos de México y Sicartsa a la IP," *La Jornada,* March 8, 1990, 19; Noé Cruz Serrano, "El Gobierno, Fuera de la Industria Siderúrgica; las Paraestatales AHMSA y Sicartsa, en Venta," *El Financiero,* March 8, 1990, 3; and "El Gobierno Federal Desincorpora las Empresas AHMSA y Sicartsa," *El Mercado de Valores* 6 (March 15, 1990): 23-25.

128. For discussions of Mexico's bureaucratic "safety net" see John Waterbury, "The Political Context of Public Sector Reform and Privatization in Egypt, India, Mexico, and Turkey," in Ezra N. Suleiman and John Waterbury, eds., *The Political Economy of Public Sector Reform and Privatization* (Boulder, Colo.: Westview Press, 1990), 303; and Peter H. Smith, *Labyrinths of Power: Political Recruitment in Twentieth-Century Mexico* (Princeton, N.J.: Princeton University Press, 1979), 149.

129. For example, while Sicartsa and its deepwater port sit on the Pacific coast, the Constitution prohibits foreign ownership of coastal property and by legal statute all Mexican ports must be state owned. Circumventing these obstacles to encourage bids by foreign investors required creative solutions. In the end, the government created trusts through which foreigners might "own" the plant and property, and persuaded the Transportation Ministry to establish port concessions that could assure private investors access to Sicartsa's port. The environmental concerns centered on Sicartsa's compliance with emissions standards and investors' fears the plant would be closed or fined heavily immediately following a purchase. In this case reformers hired an outside consultant (the British firm McLellan) which recommended Sicartsa acquire new antipollution equipment and follow a five-year "green plan" to ensure compliance. The Office of Privatization incorporated the plan into its sales package, making its acceptance by buyers a condition of sale.

130. See Alejandro Castillo, "La Difícil Desincorporación de SIDERMEX," *Expansión,* August 15, 1990, 90. See also *Privatization in Latin America: New Competitive Opportunities and Challenges* (New York: Business International Corporation, 1990), 106; "The 1991 Directory to Privatization in Latin America," in *Privatization in Latin America, a Latin Finance Supplement* (March 1991): 42; and "La privatización siderúrgica, mas compleja de lo que se cree," *La Jornada,* October 21, 1991, 42.

131. Both Finance Minister Pedro Aspe and Sidermex President Guillermo Becker broached the sale of Sidermex corporations with European, U.S., and Japanese steel executives. In each case the reply was the same: "thanks, but no thanks." Author's interview, Mexico City, July 9, 1993.

132. See "Pedro Aspe asume la presidencia de Sidermex," *Novedades,* September 7, 1990, F1; and Marco A. Mares, "Aspe sustituye a Hiriart como presidente del Consejo de Administración de Sidermex," *Uno Mas Uno,* September 7, 1990, 19.

133. These were called Sicartsa (Sicartsa I) and Sibalsas (Sicartsa II).

134. So said Aaron Tornell, the Office of Privatization official who supervised the Sidermex (and Sicartsa) divestments. Quoted in Damien Fraser, "Mexico Prepares for Toughest Privatization," *Financial Times,* November 6, 1991, 32.

135. "Sidermex, fuera del presupuesto," *La Jornada,* December 4, 1990, 2.

136. For more information on these negotiations see "'Entre la Espada y la Pared,' los Mineros Decidirán en Asamblea el Rumbo a Seguir. La Presunta Quiebra Técnica de Sicartsa, en el Aire," *Voz de Michoacán,* September 6, 1991, 1C; Benito Ortíz, "Sicartsa A la Quiebra: Obreros Dijeron No!" *El Diario Lázaro Cárdenas,* September 2, 1991, 1; and Cortés Ramírez, "La Producción en Sicartsa Avanza de Acuerdo a lo Previsto."

137. "Obreros: Es Responsabilidad del Gobierno el Cierre de Sicartsa," *Voz de Michoacán,*

September 7, 1991, 1C.

138. Uncertainty regarding Sicartsa's future produced widespread apprehension in Lázaro Cárdenas's private sector, particularly within the Confederation of Mexican Employers. See "Preocupación en el Sector Patronal por la Posible Quiebra Técnica de Sicartsa," *Voz de Michoacán,* August 31, 1991, 5C; and "Al ya receso económico denotado el cierre o venta de Sicartsa, tensa la inquietud," *El Quijote,* August 27, 1991, 1.

139. Side-payments included community passenger train service, a local television station, and new commercial establishments such as a supermarket and shopping complex. The National Solidarity Program's contribution was the Costa de Michoacán project created in January 1992 to fund industrial and commercial development, new infrastructure, and various urban/municipal renewal projects. See John Bailey and Jennifer Boone, "National Solidarity: A Summary of Program Elements," appendix, in Wayne A. Cornelius, Ann L. Craig, and Jonathan Fox, eds., *Transforming State-Society Relations in Mexico: The National Solidarity Strategy* (La Jolla, Calif.: Center for U.S.-Mexican Studies, University of California, San Diego, 1994); and Jesús Cantú, "Solidaridad, además de electorero, se manejó en Michoacán coercitivamente," *Proceso* 819 (July 13, 1992).

140. Dennis J. Gayle and Jonathan N. Goodrich, eds., *Privatization and Deregulation in Global Perspective* (Westport, Conn.: Quorum Books, 1990), 12.

141. See James G. Samstad and Ruth Berins Collier, "Mexican Labor and Structural Reform under Salinas: New Unionism or Old Stalemate?" in Riordan Roett, ed., *The Challenge of Institutional Reform in Mexico* (Boulder, Colo.: Lynne Rienner, 1995), 20. See also Edward L. Gibson, "The Populist Road to Market Reform: Policy and Electoral Coalitions in Mexico and Argentina," *World Politics* 49 (April 1997).

142. Charles L. Davis and Kenneth M. Coleman, "Neoliberal Economic Policies and the Potential for Electoral Change in Mexico," *Mexican Studies/Estudios Mexicanos* 10 (Summer 1994): 362.

143. Marko Voljc and Joost Draaisma, "Privatization and Economic Stabilization in Mexico," *Columbia Journal of World Business* 28, no. 1 (March 1993); and Pedro Aspe, *Economic Transformation the Mexican Way,* 220.

Chapter 4

Deregulating Freight Transport

Our economy was feudal, medieval, in the sense that it was deliberately
designed to favor groups at the tip of the social pyramid.
— Arturo M. Fernández

In December 1988 the Salinas administration launched an ambitious campaign of economic deregulation as part of its broader program to modernize the economy. The general goal was to replace Mexico's complicated regulatory regimes with simpler, less pervasive and more transparent ones. Policy makers deemed these measures an essential complement to liberalized trade and divestment policies, and critical to achieving internationally competitive business operations. Spearheaded by the Ministry of Commerce, the campaign was nothing short of a frontal assault on decades of regulatory practices.

Because many of these reforms targeted areas directly under other ministries' jurisdiction, successful deregulation was a daunting task. Notwithstanding this, the reformers were extraordinarily successful: by 1993 the administration had deregulated nearly fifty sectors including foreign investment, banking, insurance, packaging, aviation, petrochemicals, and mining.[1] One of the most prominent—and indeed, strategically important—sectors deregulated was freight transport. It was the first target of reform, and success in this realm paved the way for many others.

Yet success did not come easy. The reform movement germinated inside the executive branch, pushed by a small group of neoliberal technocrats. Their policy prescriptions conformed to the president's general modernization agenda and enjoyed the commerce minister's unequivocal support; yet resistance to change inside the state proved so potent it stopped the initial reform movement in its tracks. Outside the state, meanwhile, a powerful freight cartel and longtime PRI ally strongly opposed the initiative. But within six months the tables had turned: opposition declined even among freight haulers, reformers prevailed, and in June 1989 implemented sector-wide deregulation that completely dismantled the old cartel.

That reformers managed to implement such radical change noncoercively is as striking as the speed with which they accomplished it.

This achievement is partly explained by the difficulties of marshaling effective opposition inside Mexico's centralized political system. As bit players in the policy process, Congress and the PRI offered opponents little leverage to affect the policy outcome.[2] But the fact that status quo protectors managed to fend off the reformers' initial assault—despite Salinas's backing—and that a substantial portion of the cartel came to support reform as well, strongly suggests systemic factors tell only part of the story.

More important was that after their initial defeat, reformers managed to change the balance of power inside the bureaucracy. They enlisted new allies to help press their agenda and created new mechanisms and procedures to insulate and control the policy process. Finally, deregulators also found ways to offset the costs incurred by potential policy losers and exploit cleavages among cartel members. In short, more than the constraints opponents faced in a centralized political system, it was the reformers' organizational strength, capacity for institutional innovation, and adept use of minimizing strategies that proved critical to success.

Mexico's Policy-Making Process
and Transport Regulatory Regime

Governments typically adopt economic regulations to offset the social welfare losses produced by "market failures": imperfect information, negative externalities, monopoly, and oligopoly, etc.[3] To address these concerns, regulations govern the degree of competitive behavior among firms, the market structures they operate in, and at times, such variables as prices, service levels, product quality, and so forth. In the Mexican context "market failure" also included deep foreign penetration and/or perceived exploitation—factors produced by the policies of Mexico's longtime dictator, Porfirio Díaz, and which ultimately helped spark the Mexican revolution.[4] Consequently, Mexico's postrevolutionary government began to regulate economic activities early on. The state became proprietor of all natural resources and guarantor of public services like commercial transport. Private interests could exploit these resources and profit from public service provision, but only on a concession basis pursuant to the public good.

With the shift to import-substitution at mid-decade, the government assumed new development responsibilities and its regulatory reach expanded accordingly. Two features of the institutional framework that governed regulatory policy making would complicate later reform efforts. First, Mexico's legislation granted executive bureaucracies—not autonomous agencies or commissions—the broad statutory authority to promulgate regulations. This practice permitted all ministries to regulate operations relative to their sectoral jurisdiction (commerce, communications, etc.). Second, the law required the Mexican president to sign each regulation before it acquired the force of law. This obliged ministries to propose new regulations directly to the Office of the Presidency where legal scholars reviewed the proposals prior to receiving the president's signature.

These procedures (expressed in figure 4.1) formed the institutional context of regulatory policy making. They clearly delineated each ministry's responsibilities and established their legal equality before the president with respect to regulatory functions. One outgrowth of this arrangement was a tendency to promote an incoherent aggregate body of regulations. Before 1989 there was no institutional mechanism to handle a situation where the regulations of ministry X ran counter to the policy/program goals of ministry Y, etc., mainly because the Office of the Presidency lacked the staff to orchestrate a more coherent regulatory regime.[5] Consequently, as statism expanded, Mexico's regulations grew administratively complex, economically inefficient, and/or conflictual. Freight transport regulations were no exception.

Figure 4.1   The Institutional Context of Regulatory Policy Making, pre-1989

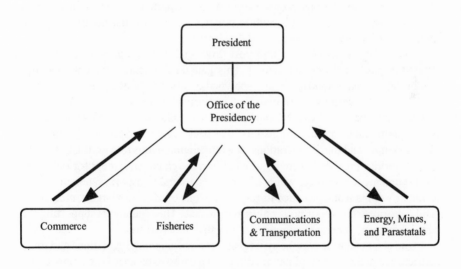

Regulations interpreted and implemented by various ministries.

ministry regulatory
proposals to the Office
of the Presidency

regulations approved
by the Office of the
Presidency

For decades Mexico's commercial transport sector was governed by a web of complicated regulations based on legislation dating back to 1931.[6] In place of market forces, this regime relied on government directives to regulate freight transport—an approach by no means unique to Mexico.[7] The Ministry of Communications and Transportation (SCT) tightly regulated shipping fees and awarded concessions that authorized commercial transport along one of eleven route corridors.[8] Each concession stipulated the type of service firms could offer (and the type of cargo permitted on each route), the number of trucks they could use, and the technical specifications required for each vehicle. The law also allowed large concession holders to control regional freight centers that supervised cargo loading/unloading, coordinated contracting services, and assigned cargo loads to truckers. At many centers the general practice was to assign freight loads on a roll-call basis (first come, first served). Each load required an official certificate issued by SCT personnel operating out of these centers.[9]

Under a system of controlled freight assignments and fixed prices truckers could not compete for customers and users could not select the carrier of their choice. These restraints on competition opened the door to rent-seeking, corruption, and the emergence of oligopolistic "commercial coalitions."[10] Eventually, these oligopolies formed a powerful (but legal) freight cartel that controlled the entire transportation sector.[11] While transport regulations sustained the cartel's basic structures (i.e., concessions, protected routes, route committees, and regional freight centers), Mexico's import-substitution policies and corporatist traditions helped maintain its internal cohesion.

Throughout the statist era transport flows and earnings grew parallel to the expanding protected internal market. This generated a relative revenue balance among large *concesionarios,*[12] and spawned a community of interests intent on perpetuating the cartel system. In time, the transport sector took on organizational characteristics patterned after Mexico's corporatist traditions. The National Chamber of Transport and Communications served as peak organization for freight haulers, plus passenger and tourist operations (it would maintain this role until 1989).[13] By law, all service providers were required to join the chamber. Except for railroads, this arrangement placed the whole of Mexico's ground transport system under the chamber's domain and provided its president—one of Mexico's largest, most powerful *transportistas*—enormous political influence. The regulations supporting the cartel, however, generated a number of negative externalities.

One clear example was the synergism between shipping regulations and route restrictions. In the context of natural directional cargo imbalances (i.e., more cargo to haul at point A than point B), fixed routes and prohibitions against transporting third-party cargo bred underutilized capacity. In many cases they produced empty back-hauls: one study released by the Transportation Ministry, for example, showed that at any one time 50 percent of the trucks in circulation throughout the country carried no freight at all; eventually, the average annual costs of underutilized capacity topped $426 million.[14]

Another source of inefficiency stemmed from regulations that prescribed appropriate service levels (i.e., delivery deadlines, incidents of lost or damaged merchandise). On the whole, they offered truckers few incentives to improve service and shifted the costs of inefficiency to transport users. To cite just one example, truckers enjoyed generous transit times for hauls of 200 kilometers along paved highways: a full day to load, another to unload, and a full day to transport goods. Penalties for noncompliance were lenient. Truckers one to five days late lost only 5 percent of the official tariff; those who missed the deadline by five to ten days lost 15 percent, and truckers more than ten days late forfeited 30 percent.

Moreover, the progressivity of these penalties was deceptive. A shipper who took eight days to deliver a haul of 200 kilometers or less (say, from Mexico City to Tepoztlán) lost only 5 percent of his fee; the user, meanwhile, got stuck with 95 percent of the bill. Similarly, users bore a disproportionate share of the costs to ensure safe cargo deliveries. Under the law truckers could only be held liable for 800 pesos per ton of damaged or lost goods (about U.S. 31¢ in 1989). These arrangements did nothing to reduce the incidence of lost or damaged merchandise or increase the proportion of timely deliveries.[15] They did, however, force many large industries to adapt through policies that sapped their efficiency. To ensure safe deliveries some companies purchased their own fleet of rigs (which legally could only carry the firm's products, and hence, were saddled with empty back-hauls); others, meanwhile, expended capital accruing "just in case" inventories as substitutes for nonexistent "just in time" deliveries.

Finally, the entire concession system constituted an absolute barrier to entry. To gain a concession applicants, first had to petition the Transportation Ministry and provide evidence that unfulfilled demand warranted a new concession. The SCT retained formal authority to grant concessions, but in practice it deferred judgment to route committees formed of established concession holders and SCT personnel. Often, the committees determined demand was insufficient to warrant a new concession. But when the demand *was* there, committees typically awarded the concession to an established *transportista*—i.e., a cartel associate. The rejection of applicants became so routine that between 1979 and 1989 not a single new applicant received a concession despite the flood of imports unleashed by Mexico's 1986 accession to the GATT.[16] Shut out of the legitimate transport market, many small shippers moved underground, creating a fleet of "pirate" truckers that numbered in the tens of thousands.

The cartel's hammerlock on freight sector operations positioned its members to extract substantial rents. By limiting concession awards route committees forced small truckers to affiliate with large *concesionarios* to operate legally. The price tag for this privilege ranged from 10 to 25 percent of their gross earnings,[17] and not surprisingly the cartel's leading fifteen families captured the lion's share of the rents. One government study concluded that on average each family "obtained monopoly rents of approximately $30 million annually, besides the earnings inherent in [freight] service."[18] Rent-seekers outside the cartel found ways to share the booty, too, particularly a small slice of SCT personnel. Much of this activity occurred at the regional freight centers where bills of lading were counterfeited, or sometimes certified for a *fee,* instead of for free. Rent-seeking also occurred in the route committees where ministerial personnel exchanged negative votes on concession awards for kickbacks. In short, the old regulatory regime was great for some, but decidedly less so for society as a whole. Service was inconsistent and unreliable, the security of goods shipped uncertain, and all told, the cartel generated aggregate social costs that approached $500 million in hidden subsidies.[19]

Yet, despite such deficiencies the old system did provide certain benefits. For years it served the government's broader economic and political goals. It helped integrate the Mexican market (albeit inefficiently), and created a cozy, symbiotic relationship between the freight cartel and Mexico's ruling party. During election campaigns, for example, powerful *concesionarios* helped mobilize rural voters on behalf of PRI candidates, providing trucks and buses to transport *campesinos* to campaign rallies and the polls. In return, *transportistas* received political protection from serious regulatory reform, and in effect, "paid" for this protection with the two things the party needed most—votes and transportation resources. The nexus between the PRI and freight cartel was a classic example of the quid pro quo arrangements George Stigler argued would spring up between private beneficiaries of government regulation and the party that controlled the state apparatus.[20] It also was one of the major reasons the old system endured. By 1989, however, Mexico's technocratic leadership determined to dismantle it. Three factors motivated this disposition.

First, deregulation resonated with the reformers' preference for market principles, and indeed, was an integral component of the neoliberal reform package. Second, the political value of the PRI-cartel axis had declined considerably. On the one hand, dramatic rural-to-urban migration had eroded some of the premium formerly attached to rural voters (between 1950 and 1990 the proportion of Mexico's population that lived in villages of less than 2,500 dropped from 57 to 29 percent).[21] On the other hand, the administration already had a substitute to garner rural votes in the National Solidarity Program, PRONASOL.[22] Third, the sheer magnitude of efficiency costs under the old system threatened economic recovery. Since trucks carried over 80 percent of all goods (and consumed 90 percent of all the energy used in transportation),[23] the less efficient the sector, reformers reasoned, the more drag it exerted on the economy as a whole. Pragmatically, it made little sense to push policies like divestment and ask the private sector to generate growth in a system riddled with inefficiencies. But in tackling the freight sector reformers had their work cut out for them. They expected opposition from truckers with protected routes, and from the transport sector's longtime regulator, the SCT. Still, when resistance came they were unprepared.

Deregulation Aborted:
The Imperative of Organizational Strength

The Ministry of Commerce (SECOFI) launched its deregulation drive in December 1988. The project was originally designed as a *program*, not unlike many others run by Commerce.[24] Commerce Minister Jaime Serra recruited a leading economist, Arturo Fernández, to oversee the enterprise, and Fernández in turn recruited his own staff of technocrats—each personally approved by Serra.[25] With unanimity of purpose, an assembled change team, and strong presidential support, the prospects for success appeared bright. But early hopes that deregulation might "hit the ground running" would go unrealized.

First, the specifics of what deregulation might actually entail were unclear. For one thing, Salinas's National Development Plan (in which regulatory reform would figure prominently) was still months away,[26] and even Commerce found the idea of *de*-regulation out of step with some of its traditional responsibilities. As late as January 1989, for example, more than 500 SECOFI personnel were still involved in approving the import of foreign technologies on a case-by-case basis;[27] consequently, establishing the program's legitimacy inside the ministry itself was a challenge. As one official intimately involved in the deregulation campaign explained: "At first we had to prove ourselves—that we were credible, not "crazy"—and that what we did was credible. In order to be taken seriously we had to convince people inside and outside of SECOFI of our importance and our work's importance."[28]

The main problems, however, lay in the institutional context that governed regulatory policy making. Because legislation and policy procedures distributed regulatory authority across state ministries according to their sectoral jurisdiction, they afforded deregulators little real leverage over the policy agenda. Consequently, on their maiden assignment the reformers floundered badly.

The debacle occurred during the first meeting between Fernández and Transport officials, when SECOFI proposed reducing barriers to entry into the freight sector to increase competition, cut costs, and eliminate inefficiencies. Whatever the proposal's merits, the SCT would have no part. Ministry officials openly scoffed at the proposal, labeled it "crazy," and explained that as far as the SCT was concerned, existing regulations would remain in force.[29] Case closed. For SECOFI, this rebuff underscored the constraining influence of the broader institutional environment. Since the SCT clearly retained legal authority to regulate transport, it was under no obligation to adopt reformers' proposals (nor for that matter would any other ministry be). Absent radical changes in the institutional context, therefore, reformers faced an uphill battle over freight transport, and most likely, many more defeats down the line.

This realization moved Fernández to reflect seriously upon his program's basic (and currently ambiguous) objectives, and how best to accomplish them. Ultimately, he concluded the main goal was not merely to simplify the administration of regulations, but rather eliminate the broad, structural conditions that produced administrative complexity in the first place. Since this would require deep penetration of other ministries' operations, the entire venture was fraught with potential setbacks. To succeed, the project had to be completely reorganized and transformed from a simple "program" into a separate division inside SECOFI. Moreover, this new division would need to be insulated from bureaucratic opponents and vested with sufficient legal authority and political clout to prevail in inter-bureaucratic policy disputes. All these changes, in turn, required new legislation and this could only occur with the president's assent.

Institutional Innovation and Coalition Building

In late December Fernández made his case for restructuring to Commerce Minister Serra, and in January 1989, Serra pitched the proposal to President Salinas. The result was a presidential decree promulgated in February 1989, which established the *Entidad de Desregulación Económica*, or the Office of Deregulation (OD).[30] The decree gave the OD a clear, single-theme mandate: to analyze the operations of *any* economic sector and propose its deregulation directly to the president and his economic cabinet. This mandate put teeth into SECOFI's initiatives but did not alter the fundamental balance of power in regulatory affairs. That is, it gave SECOFI legal standing to initiate regulatory reform, but no means to ensure its proposals took precedence over those of other legitimate actors (i.e., the ministries). To augment their political clout reformers needed powerful friends to support their initiatives and a greater capacity to control the policy agenda itself.

SECOFI worked swiftly to achieve these goals. Through back channels Fernández forged an alliance with the Office of the Presidency (OPR). This agency coordinated the work of specialized presidential cabinets (economics, social, agrarian), safeguarded the administration's policy agenda, and held de jure review authority over all regulatory initiatives. Its director, José Córdoba Montoya, also functioned as Salinas's chief of staff. Like most of the president's inner camp, Córdoba bore the credentials of the technocrat, i.e., advanced economics training at a prestigious foreign institution (Stanford University) and service within the Mexican technocracy.[31] Moreover, as chief of staff he wielded enormous power over policy and careers.[32]

Together, the offices of Deregulation and the Presidency produced a coalition especially well suited to advance regulatory reform. Like its privatization counterparts, the founding members were united by shared policy preferences and uniquely positioned to externalize the costs of policy change. As we shall see, under SECOFI's proposal the clear loser inside the state would be the SCT; in fact, complete deregulation would cost the agency plenty (i.e., lost institutional prestige, budget allocations, personnel, and rent-seeking opportunities). For reformers, meanwhile, the situation was reversed. On the one hand, if the coalition succeeded it would bolster the OD's credibility considerably and brighten prospects of achieving regulatory reform in other sectors. On the other hand, it would help the OPR safeguard the linchpin connecting all aspects of Salinas's economic modernization program—from trade and competitiveness, to privatization and investment. In short, coalition members had much to gain and little to lose by pushing reform; the only scenario in which they stood to lose big was if their efforts to deregulate *failed.*

The alliance between deregulators and the Presidency proved an enormous boon to reformers. Working in concert the two camps quietly (and informally) altered the regulatory policy-making procedures to their advantage. Legally, the procedures remained unchanged: each ministry retained the right to formulate new regulations and submit them to the Presidency for review. Now, however, the OPR forwarded all non-SECOFI proposals to the Office of Deregulation where reformers subjected them to rigorous cost-benefit analysis. These subtle changes in the institutional context proved enormously consequential. They transformed the OD from a weak, ineffective actor into the hub through which ministerial regulatory workflows passed. From this vantage point it could veto any regulatory proposals submitted by other ministries (figure 4.2), and modify, approve, or reject virtually all changes in Mexico's regulatory regime. These modifications—combined with

Figure 4.2   The Structure of a Bureaucratic Veto

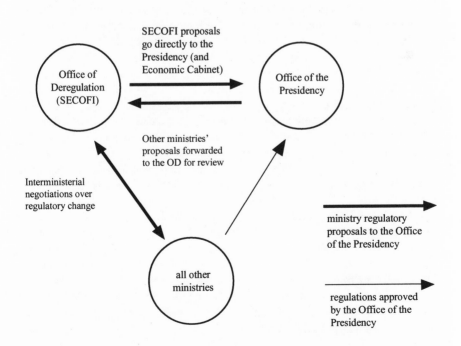

its own authority to initiate regulatory reform—represented a substantial net gain in organizational strength.

Coalition Politics and Policy Reform

Emboldened by these innovations, reformers took up the task of deregulation with renewed vigor. To begin, the Office of Deregulation researched the freight sector extensively. Its analysts canvassed service providers and users to learn first-hand how the system functioned; they videotaped operations at regional freight centers to document inefficient and corrupt practices; they poured over deregulation case studies from other countries; and through cost-benefit analysis they determined that maintaining the cartel siphoned roughly a half billion dollars in hidden subsidies out of the Mexican economy each year.

Armed with these data the OD drafted a proposal to increase efficiency and lower transport costs by eliminating the concession system, protected routes, and fixed tariffs, plus the anticompetitive aspects of the regional freight centers. With the commerce minister's approval, it submitted these recommendations to the president and his economic cabinet, and once approved, Salinas instructed the OD to begin negotiations with Transportation pursuant to restructuring its fundamental regulatory approach.

A great deal would ride on these discussions. Even with the president's backing Transportation officials could still weaken the reforms' effectiveness simply by "misinterpreting" their intent or applying their own standards to concepts like efficiency and productivity. The reformers hoped to avoid these problems by explaining the reforms' purpose and correct interpretation to SCT officials face to face. Their ultimate goal, however, was to expand their coalition by persuading the agency to embrace the full gamut of proposals. But this was easier said than done. From Transportation's perspective the proposal's costs were excessive; they seemed a direct attack on longtime institutional prerogatives, and if implemented, might force the elimination of entire departments inside the ministry. In subsequent negotiations, therefore, Transportation went to the mat to protect its interests. It vigorously stressed the political/pragmatic obstacles to SECOFI's proposal, and tried to preempt comprehensive change by sponsoring a more modest, incremental reform initiative.

Leading the charge was the SCT's Operations Division, which sketched in broad strokes the dangers it believed deregulation posed. Essentially, Operations argued that complete deregulation was impossible. Freeing truckers to concentrate only on routes with large markets would deprive other regions of freight service; eliminating the freight centers' service contracting operations would create disorder between providers and users; finally, forcing truckers to compete for what had once been "their" routes would spark violence, disrupt service, and spawn even more violence in the broader society.

Transportation did not put all its eggs in one basket, however. It also tried to seize the agenda by proffering its own "reform" initiative. Its alternative proposal would reconstitute the route committees to permit SECOFI input on awarding new transport concessions. Under this scheme deregulation experts would join the SCT and established *transportistas* to determine the optimum number of *concesionarios*. A major drawback of this arrangement, of course (or better, the agency's hope), was that numerically, it would stack the deck against reformers two to one, perpetuate barriers to entry, and perhaps "capture" the reformers as well. These tactics helped delay the march of regulatory reform, but ultimately did not derail it, and throughout the negotiations the deregulators countered each argument point by point.

First, it was not the case that truckers served remote areas because the law required them to. They served these areas because they were profitable and would remain so under deregulation; the possibilities of service deprivation were marginal. Second, eliminating service contracting at the freight centers would free users to contract service directly and force truckers to improve service to attract clients; the result would be greater efficiency, not chaos. With respect to social violence, SECOFI took this threat quite seriously and promised to address the problem through parallel negotiations with the freight cartel. As for the SCT's "preemptive reform" attempts, coalition partners ensured these efforts went nowhere. The SCT submitted its proposal to the Office of the Presidency, which simply shuttled it back to the Office of Deregulation for review, and ultimately, rejection.[33]

After weeks of intense negotiations Operations eventually threw in the towel and embraced SECOFI's initiative. A number of factors lay behind this "conversion." First, the deregulators' counterarguments were plausible; in fact, SECOFI officials were so persuasive (and annoyingly persistent) that among some quarters at the SCT, grudging respect displaced hostility as the basis for interagency negotiations. Second, officials realized that bucking the winds of change in an administration so clearly committed to it was simply to court unnecessary political risks. Third, the reformers had done their homework well. By grounding their analysis on precepts like economic rationality, efficiency, and productivity, they set the terms of policy debate squarely on neoliberal theory (a terrain unfamiliar to Transportation and one the agency found difficult to traverse). Combined with videotapes of cartel operations, this played to the reformers' advantage. The fact was, the freight sector *was* inefficient, and corruption and low productivity were rampant. Lacking any viable alternative, the SCT found it hard to defend the status quo and impossible to refute the taped evidence.

Equally important, however, was the compensation reformers offered to help Transportation offset its institutional losses: in exchange for supporting the initiative the SCT, not SECOFI, could take full credit for deregulation. To be sure, the exchange was one of symbolic institutional prestige for the loss of tangible institutional responsibilities. But by claiming credit for a reform measure it initially opposed, Transportation could vault into the vanguard as the first agency to implement an important aspect of the Salinas modernization program.[34] In the end, this proved enough to help bring this faction of opponents into the reformers' camp.

Yet, no sooner did Operations drop its objections than did the SCT's Legal Division pose new ones, and here, the opposition was on much firmer footing. Federal legislation clearly supported the cartel's structure and operating procedures.[35] Until Congress repealed or modified the law, the SCT officials argued, any move to eliminate fixed routes and tariffs stood on dubious legal footing. This point was particularly problematic. The 1988 elections had cost the PRI its commanding majority in Congress. Out of 500 seats in the lower house the party held a bare majority of 260; however, a two-thirds majority would be needed to change the law with dispatch, and the opportunity to recapture a majority in mid-term elections was thirty months away. With opponents still challenging the legitimacy of Salinas's controversial election victory, attempts to alter a fundamental law of the land could easily bog down in partisan politics.

These political realities drove reformers to focus solely on changing transport regulations instead of altering the transportation law. The question then became how far could deregulation go without actually touching the law itself. The strategy finally adopted was to *redefine* the spirit of the law without abrogating it: trucking routes, therefore, were redefined as "all federal highways," and tariffs were redefined as "ceiling prices." This tactic satisfied legal requirements, took the wind out of SCT protestations, and ultimately brought the Legal Division on board. Transport deregulation became official government policy and all major government actors embraced it.

In forging this consensus, reformers hurdled a major obstacle to deregulation and won an important victory inside the state. To secure the ultimate prize, however, they had to address the thorny issue of implementation. On this point, both the economy's overall dependence on freight transport and the opposition anticipated from truckers required a delicate approach. The costs deregulation posed to *concesionarios* (i.e., the loss of guaranteed revenues, protected routes, and opportunities to rent-seek) virtually ensured their opposition, and in the freight cartel, reformers faced a formidable and potentially cohesive opponent. From the outset, therefore, they dismissed any thoughts of an imposition strategy. Coercion could easily provoke violent resistance and policy makers could ill afford prolonged service disruptions or violence along the nation's highways. The most reasonable path to success, they believed, was to expand the coalition somehow, and convert freight haulers from opponents to stakeholders in the reform process.

This would be no small feat. Many powerful *transportistas* saw little to recommend deregulation at all. Why compete, they reasoned, for a route that *legally* was already theirs? Why forego the benefits of guaranteed revenues for the potential rewards of a system subject to market vagaries? More than self-interest lay behind this resistance to change; the inability to peer beyond the horizon and determine with confidence the outcomes of deregulation made many truckers risk-averse. This uncertainty—coupled with the initiative's obvious costs—led transport leaders to dig in their heels. Still, the reformers retained some advantages. The SCT's capitulation had cost truckers an important ally inside the state and left few viable means to exercise influence over policy outcomes. Moreover, uncertainty cut both ways: the more reformers underscored the unappreciated benefits of deregulation, the more likely they could raise truckers' expectations of future payoffs. To the extent this helped mold beliefs regarding economic interests, reformers stood a good chance of converting at least some *transportistas* into stakeholders in the reform process.

Despite the loss of their SCT ally, cartel leaders stood ready to contest the proposed policy shift. Initially, the president of the National Chamber of Transport and Communication (the cartel's informal leader) hoped to water down SECOFI's reforms by co-opting the deregulators. Accordingly, exotic trips, vacations, and even opportunities to enjoy an "enhanced social life" were all dangled before OD personnel.[36] When these carrots failed to elicit a positive response, the leadership threatened a harder line: if SECOFI insisted on pushing regulatory change, truckers would blockade Mexico City and deprive the capital of food and supplies until the government caved in.

Since freight haulers' capacity to make good on this threat was beyond question, the negotiations proceeded under the specter of social violence. But reformers soon caught a major break. As the talks progressed they discovered the cartel suffered two potential vulnerabilities that might prove susceptible to exploitation. One was economic, the other political. On the economic front, Mexico's increasingly liberalized trade regime had opened a fault line between cartel associates.[37] Traditionally, high trade barriers had kept imports low; this produced a relative revenue balance among cartel associates that helped keep jealousies and resentments in check. After liberalization, the demand for imports surged; freight runs between the United States and the Mexican interior grew more frequent, and routes that served the U.S. border became much more lucrative.[38] This bred dissension among truckers confined by law to internal routes.

On the political front, a prolonged power struggle had festered inside the cartel's organizational home, the National Chamber of Transportation. For years a group of disaffected associates had tried to unseat the chamber's longtime president and promote leadership rotation. By and large their efforts floundered: the president's political connections and ability to protect truckers from regulatory reform won him reelection time and again. These repeated defeats left insurgents frustrated and bitter, and the fact that some of the disgruntled were shackled to internal routes only heightened their resentment.

Quick to capitalize on these latent economic and political cleavages, reformers downplayed talks with the chamber president and opened up a direct dialogue with insurgent leaders. Their basic argument stressed three points: (1) trade liberalization was a fact of life and imports would continue to pour into Mexico; (2) tight regulation allowed only a few to benefit from this windfall; but

(3) deregulation promised all truckers a chance to compete for a share of the growing economic pie. These arguments appealed powerfully to disaffected truckers who increasingly saw deregulation as the key to their economic and political objectives. To the extent deregulation made the need for traditional political protection moot, it also could erode the president's electoral appeal and provide access to border routes in one fell swoop. On this basis the insurgents tentatively accepted SECOFI's reform agenda but pressed the government for still more tangible compensation.

Throughout the 1980s the combination of economic crisis and vehicle import restrictions had hindered fleet upgrades and road maintenance. Consequently, roughly 50 percent of Mexico's trucks had become technically obsolete (see table 4.1), and a large backlog of highway maintenance and expansion projects had been deferred. The administration's urgency to achieve freight deregulation plus its disinclination toward coercion positioned insurgents to extract concessions on

Table 4.1   Mexico's Aging Freight Carrier Fleet: Model Year and
Cumulative Model of Vehicles as a Percentage of Fleet*

Model Year	1988 Vehicles	1988 Cum. %	1989 Vehicles	1989 Cum. %	1990 Vehicles	1990 Cum. %	1988–90 % change
1975	10,837	43.2%	10,694	39.1%	13,001	33.9%	20%
1976	10,462	50.0%	10,285	45.4%	12,597	39.5%	20%
1977	5,938	53.9%	6,773	49.5%	9,101	43.6%	53%
1978	7,696	58.9%	8,570	54.7%	12,319	49.1%	60%
1979	10,715	65.9%	11,548	61.8%	16,138	56.4%	51%
1980	18,128	77.7%	19,090	73.4%	25,769	67.9%	42%
1981	17,194	88.9%	18,209	84.6%	24,132	78.7%	40%
1982	6,739	93.3%	7,958	89.4%	11,336	83.8%	68%
1983	2,073	94.7%	2,924	91.2%	5,003	86.1%	141%
1984	2,044	96.0%	2,907	92.9%	5,019	88.3%	146%
1985	2,784	97.8%	3,851	95.3%	6,192	91.1%	122%
1986	1,583	98.8%	2,671	96.9%	4,902	93.3%	210%
1987	1,062	99.5%	2,197	98.2%	4,054	95.1%	282%
1988	713	100.0%	1,857	99.4%	3,954	96.9%	455%
1989			1,020	100.0%	4,051	98.7%	
1990					2,864	100.0%	

Source: Derived from *Estadísticas Básicas del Autotransporte Federal* (México, D. F.: Secretaría de Comunicaciones y Transportes, 1991).

* Underlined figures represent the standard, twelve-year obsolescence point for commercial trucks.

these issues. In the end, the two camps came to terms. SECOFI would lift import restrictions on modern trucks and tractors, and liberalize other regulations to promote their domestic production; the Finance Ministry would provide special credit lines to help truckers purchase new rigs; and the SCT vowed to undertake a large, nationwide highway construction/maintenance project. The insurgents' defection effectively split the cartel's internal unity, severely weakened its ability to carry out the threatened blockade, and left the chamber president isolated and in retreat.

Table 4.2   Transport Regulations:
Contrasts between Old and New Regimes

Basic Features of Old Regime	Basic Features of New Regime
freight hauls restricted to specific routes, legally available solely to concession holders	concessions abolished; routine approval for new applicants within fourteen to forty-five days; all federal highways constitute a single "route"
route committees authorized new concessions	route committees eliminated; truckers need only prove their nationality, vehicle ownership, and insurance to obtain a SCT permit
loading/unloading restrictions; one-way hauls encouraged	loading/unloading restrictions eliminated; one-way haul requirements deleted
obligatory use of regional freight centers	optional use of regional freight centers
roll-call system of cargo assignments; users could not select carrier of choice	services contracted directly between users and providers
official tariffs set by SCT	freight charges determined by market
underground fleet of trucking "pirates"	legalization of trucking "pirates"

Sources: Derived from *Programa para el autotransporte federal de carga* (México, D.F.: Secretaría de Comunicaciones y Transportes, May 1989); *Review of Trade and Investment Liberalization Measures by Mexico and Prospects for Future United States-Mexican Relation, Investigation* No. 332–282, U.S.I.T.C. Publication 2275 (Washington, D.C.: United States International Trade Commission, 1991), 502–503; and Gabriel Martínez and Guillermo Fárber, eds., *Desregulación económica (1989–1993): Una visión de la modernización de México* (México, D.F.: Fondo de la Cultura Económica, 1994), appendix.

On July 6, 1989, the principal parties formalized the accord and signed the Covenant for the Modernization of Freight Transportation (*Convenio de Concertación para la Modernización del Autotransporte Federal de Carga*).[39] The *Convenio* officially implemented the new regulatory regime. It eliminated barriers to entry and fixed tariffs, plus the noncompetitive aspects of regional freight centers (table 4.2). The covenant also spelled out the tangible compensation truckers acquired in exchange for their support.[40]

Explaining the Reformers' Success

Mexico's reformers viewed the freight transport case as one of the signature successes of the Salinas reform project. In just six months transport deregulation went from apparent defeat to full implementation. Despite strong initial objections the interests arrayed against change eventually proved unable (the SCT) and unwilling (most truckers) to impede this process. Considering the obstacles reformers faced, this outcome is striking. But why exactly did reformers prevail?

One possible explanation is systemic; that is, the influence of Mexico's powerful chief executive ensured a favorable outcome. In some sense, of course, this is true: on the one hand, presidential leadership set the tone and content of administration policy and Salinas strongly supported deregulation efforts; on the other hand political centralism kept opponents from blocking reform through either the Congress or ruling party. But a pure systemic explanation is unsatisfying. For one thing it suggests the state was a monolithic actor with uniform interests throughout—a notion that flies in the face of empirical reality. It also obscures the means by which policy conflicts inside the government were resolved such that a single output became state policy. As we have seen, the individual agency of reform advocates was crucial in this respect. Most important, though, the fact that deregulators required new allies and legal/institutional fortification to advance a program the president *preferred* demonstrates the importance of factors beyond the systemic level.

The evidence in this chapter strongly supports the position that coalition politics, institutional innovation, and astute minimizing strategies on the part of reformers were critical to their success. The reform coalition linked two small elite policy groups inside the Presidency and Office of Deregulation. That both agencies fell under executive control, however, does not bolster a pure presidentialist explanation. Although the OD and OPR were clearly the president's agents, so was the SCT, and as students of bureaucratic politics remind us, agencies have their own agendas in addition to the president's.[41] In this case, those of coalition members coincided with Salinas's; Transportation's did not. Absent a strong, proreform coalition this interest divergence within the bureaucracy—combined with regulatory policy-making procedures that favored the status quo—dimmed prospects of any significant regulatory change.

For reasons easily understood, change was unlikely to come from the SCT. The fact that it already *had* the authority to reform transport regulations but chose not to, provides prima facie evidence of this. Nor did its inaction reflect ignorance of the problems traditional regulations created (the agency's own in-house studies showed that 50 percent of the trucks circulating the highways carried no freight at all, thanks to regulations that encouraged one-way hauls).[42] The SCT strongly preferred the status quo, and as we have seen, worked hard to maintain it. One high ministry official candidly explained that of all the parties involved, the Ministry of Transportation was "least interested" in deregulation: "If things had been left to themselves the SCT would *never* have changed the regulatory framework of the freight sector. It was necessary to have an external force and the president's backing in order to deregulate trucking" (emphasis mine).[43]

SECOFI's deregulators provided that external force. But without political allies or dramatic changes in the institutional context they stood little chance of success. Creating the Office of Deregulation was a good first step: it secured reformers a legal mandate to propose reforms and afforded shelter from countervailing pressures. But without allies, even an insulated "change team" was unlikely to prevail. Under existing policy procedures, at best an OD-SCT matchup would produce gridlock. In conjunction with the presidency, however, it became possible to change the institutional environment decidedly to reformers' advantage. As a result, the Office of Deregulation acquired the capacity to pass judgment on virtually all regulatory issues. This altered its organizational position inside the state dramatically. Concentrating regulatory authority inside an autonomous policy unit transformed the office into the nexus through which all ministerial regulatory initiatives passed—a near perfect example of the "network centrality" detailed in chapter 2. This, combined with their analytic rigor and mastery of neoliberal precepts, positioned deregulators to claim "political property rights" over the regulatory policy arena. After cutting their teeth on freight transport, reformers tackled a host of other sectors—aviation, mining, petrochemicals, etc.—and seemed to move from victory to victory.

One of the principal reasons for this outcome is that after a marathon effort with trucking, reformers determined to pursue their objectives, in part, through what I have called strategizing behavior. This entailed advancing reforms in ways that minimized the resource expenditures required (time, energy, political capital, administrative capacities, and technical expertise), and ensured a stream of preferred policy outcomes in the future. The new regulatory policy procedures achieved in 1989 (i.e., the OD's bureaucratic veto) typified this behavior and prefigured its dramatic extension two years later. Throughout 1991 OD personnel worked to devise some means of achieving reforms more efficiently than the case-by-case, hand-to-hand combat pattern begun with freight transport. Toward year's end, they submitted a comprehensive proposal to Salinas's economic cabinet. Among its most significant provisions were requirements that federal ministries subject their existing regulations (and all future regulatory proposals) to cost-benefit analysis.[44] The goal here was to establish uniform procedures and "rational" standards to govern the promulgation of future regulations and the maintenance of current ones.

Not surprisingly, SECOFI's proposal met stiff bureaucratic resistance. While reformers claimed they sought to simplify and improve the quality of regulations— not eliminate them—often their bureaucratic counterparts failed to grasp the distinction. Many equated SECOFI's penchant for regulatory "reform" with a retreat from regulatory responsibility. Small wonder. After decades of state intervention some agencies could barely *conceive* of "their" sectors functioning smoothly absent an extensive, activist ministerial posture.[45]

Nevertheless, in January 1992 President Salinas issued a decree which formalized SECOFI's proposal.[46] Under the new Federal Law of Norms and Measures, state ministries had eighteen months to catalogue their regulations, analyze them, and forward this data to the OD for review. Thereafter, any regulation whose costs exceeded its benefits (or which a ministry had not assessed on this basis) would be deleted. As with earlier innovations, the new rules helped bolster reformers' organizational strength. They reduced SECOFI's workload considerably without diminishing its authority or influence, and left the OD's alliance with the presidency intact. Instances of successful regulatory reform—already impressive— multiplied thereafter.

In the 1980s many analysts encouraged economically challenged states to liberalize their economies, abandon interventionist practices, and establish clearer, easily applied rules to govern economic transactions, raise efficiency, and heighten competition. Under Salinas, Mexico took up this challenge. When the administration came to power in 1988 it vowed to rewrite Mexico's regulatory frameworks as part of a broader campaign of economic modernization. By and large, it delivered. However, as chapter 5 illustrates, a similar commitment with respect to environmental policy proved far more difficult to fulfill.

Notes

1. Gabriel Martínez and Guillermo Fárber, eds., *Desregulación económica (1989-1993): Una visión de la modernización de México* (México, D.F.: Fondo de la Cultura Económica, 1994): appendix; and Arturo M. Fernández, "Reformas al Marco Regulatorio de la Actividad Económica," *Opción,* no. 53 (December 1991).

2. For a variety of reasons the PRI was riven with divisions and lacked the muscle, capacity, and singularity of purpose to challenge reform. For discussion see Denise Dresser, "Embellishment, Empowerment, or Euthanasia of the PRI? Neoliberalism and Party Reform in Mexico," in Maria Lorena Cook, Kevin J. Middlebrook, and Juan Molinar Horcasitas, eds., *The Politics of Economic Restructuring: State-Society Relations and Regime Change in Mexico* (La Jolla, Calif.: Center for U.S.-Mexican Studies, University of California, San Diego, 1994). For analysis of the party and legislature's historic exclusion from policy-making, see Dale Story, *The Mexican Ruling Party: Stability and Authority* (Stanford, Ca-

lif.: Hoover Institution, 1986), 131–132; and Roderic A. Camp, *Politics in Mexico* (New York: Oxford University Press, 1993).

3. Stephen Breyer, *Regulation and Its Reform* (Cambridge, Mass.: Harvard University Press, 1982).

4. Under Díaz's thirty-year reign (known as the *Porfiriato*), the government encouraged large inflows of foreign investment to the extent foreigners acquired substantial equity in the agriculture, real estate, mining, railroad, banking, and other sectors. See Roger D. Hansen, *The Politics of Mexican Development* (Baltimore: Johns Hopkins University Press, 1971); see also, Daniel Cosio Villegas, ed., *Historia moderna de México: La vida económica* (México, D.F.: Editorial Hermes, 1965).

5. National economic policies fall under the domain of executive economic ministries. Thus, while the presidency's Legal Division is staffed by seasoned jurisprudence scholars, its Economic Division is composed mostly of young economists-in-training.

6. The legal bedrock was the 1931 General Law of Routes and Communication (amended in 1940), and the accompanying regulations contained in the Regulation Chapter of Truck Exploitation. See *Ley y códigos de México* (México, D.F.: Porrua, 1983).

7. As Kahn observed, most governments adopt such an approach to public goods, services, or utilities. See Alfred E. Kahn, *The Economics of Regulation: Principles and Institutions* (New York: Wiley, 1970).

8. This section draws heavily on the author's interviews and the following publications: Oscar de Buen and Juan Pablo Antún, "Reglamentación y prácticas comunes del transporte de carga en México," *Comercio Exterior* 39, no. 5 (May 1989); *Texas-Mexico Multimodal Transportation*, A Report by the Policy Research Project on Texas/Northern Mexico Infrastructure and Free Trade (Austin, Tex.: Lyndon B. Johnson School of Public Affairs, University of Texas at Austin, 1993); Oscar Armando Rico Galeana, *Regulación y desregulación del servicio de autotransporte de carga* (Querétero, México: Instituto Mexicano del Transporte, 1992); *Texas-Mexico Transborder Transportation System: Regulatory and Infrastructure Obstacles to Free Trade* (Austin, Tex: Lyndon B. Johnson School of Public Affairs, University of Texas at Austin, 1991); Alejandro Díaz Landero, "An Economic Appraisal of the Deregulation Process in the Mexican Transport Market," *Journal of Transportation Research Forum* 31, no. 1 (1990); Arturo Fernández, "Trucking Deregulation in Mexico," in José Carbajo, ed., *Regulatory Reform in Transport: Some Recent Experiences* (Washington, D.C.: The World Bank, 1993); and Martínez and Fárber, *Desregulación económica (1989-1993)*, 15–46.

9. Federal police inspected these documents while truckers were enroute; penalties for noncompliance ranged from monetary fines to the seizure of the vehicle. Since certification was only available at the freight centers, it was virtually impossible for truckers to operate legally without affiliating with one. The net effect was to bind truckers to the centers and consolidate the centers' control over freight flows.

10. Enrique R. Dávila C., "La reglamentación del autotransporte de carga en México," in Francisco Gil Díaz and Arturo M. Fernández, eds., *El efecto de la regulación en algunos sectores de la economía mexicana* (México, D.F.: Fondo de Cultura Económica, 1991), 123.

11. Author's interview. Mexico City, June 18, 1993. See also *Review of Trade and Investment Liberalization Measures by Mexico and Prospects for Future United States-Mexican Relation*, Investigation No. 332-282, U.S.I.T.C. Publication 2275 (Washington, D.C.: United States International Trade Commission, 1991), 3-3; and *Mexico: Industrial Policy and Regulation*, chapter 6.

12. Government studies claim the majority of monopoly rents extracted under the old system were divided mainly among the cartel's fifteen leading families. Martínez and Fárber, *Desregulación económica,* 18.

13. The transportation chamber was similar to other commercial and industrial chambers in Mexico that organize sectoral actors into corporatist configurations.

14. See Agustín Rodríguez Trejo, "La Desregulación Eleva la Productividad Nacional: Fernández; Gran Pérdida en Transporte," *Excelsior,* June 8, 1990, 1F; and Martínez and Fárber, *Desregulación económica (1989-1993),* 17.

15. Alvaro Dávila, *El sistema de transporte de carga de México ante el Tratado de Libre Comercio,* Monograph (México, D.F.: Instituto Tecnológico Autónomo de México, n.d.).

16. For discussion see Díaz Landero, "An Economic Appraisal of the Deregulation Process in the Mexican Transport Market," 104.

17. Dávila's figures provide the low end of the rent scale and Fernández's the high. See Dávila, *El sistema de transporte de carga,* 11; and Fernández, "Trucking Deregulation in Mexico," 101.

18. Martínez and Fárber, *Desregulación Económica,* 18.

19. See Trejo, "La Desregulación Eleva la Productividad Nacional."

20. George J. Stigler, "The Theory of Economic Regulation," *Bell Journal of Economics and Management Science* 2, no. 1 (Spring 1971).

21. Wayne A. Cornelius, *Mexican Politics in Transition: The Breakdown of a One-Party-Dominant Regime* (La Jolla, Calif.: Center for U.S.-Mexican Studies, University of California, San Diego, 1996), 63.

22. PRONASOL (the National Solidarity Program) was the signature program of Salinas's domestic policy. It funneled billions of dollars ($1.7 billion in 1992 alone) toward grassroots antipoverty programs, education, social services, and infrastructure projects. As Semo explains, the Salinas government used PRONASOL in pork-barrel fashion to channel spending in regions where the PRI ran poorly in 1988, and some claim it was a major factor behind the PRI's electoral resurgence in 1991. See Ilán Semo, "The Mexican Political Pretransition in Comparative Perspective," in Gerardo Otero, ed., *Neoliberalism Revisited: Economic Restructuring and Mexico's Political Future* (Boulder, Colo.: Westview, 1996), 122. For broader treatment of the National Solidarity Program see Wayne A. Cornelius, Ann L. Craig, and Jonathan Fox, eds., *Transforming State-Society Relations in Mexico: The National Solidarity Strategy* (La Jolla, Calif.: Center for U.S.-Mexican Studies, University of California, San Diego, 1994).

23. See *Review of Trade and Investment Liberalization Measures,* 3-2; and Díaz Landero, "An Economic Appraisal of the Deregulation Process in the Mexican Transport Market," 102.

24. This project was known as the Program of Economic Deregulation.

25. Fernández held an economics Ph.D. from Chicago State University and had served as director of economics at the prestigious Autonomous Technological Institute of Mexico, one of the country's premier technocratic private institutions. His staff included economists, policy analysts, and attorneys, some of whom held advanced degrees from Harvard's Kennedy School of Government.

26. When Salinas unveiled the National Development Plan in May 1989, he singled out deregulation as one of the administration's key priorities. Carlos Salinas de Gortari, *The Mexico We Want by 1994* (México, D.F.: Presidencia de la República, 1989), 13. See also Paula L. Green, "Mexican President Stresses Need for Deregulation," *Journal of Commerce,* November 2, 1989, 3A.

27. Author's interview. Mexico City, August 3, 1992.

28. Author's interview. Mexico City. July 2, 1992.

29. Author's interview. Mexico City, August 3, 1992.

30. See "Reglamento para la Secretaría de Comercio y Fomento Industrial para revisar los reglamentos de actividades económicas nacional," *Diario Oficial,* February 5, 1989.

31. From 1982 to 1983, and again from 1985 to 1987, Córdoba was director of economic and social policy at the Ministry of Budget and Planning.

32. The British *Economist* saw Córdoba as "the equivalent of a super-Chief-of-Staff. . . . responsible for the most significant policy decisions made by the administration;" the Mexican journal *Proceso* noted that every cabinet official was "directly subordinate to José Córdoba Montoya"; other high officials explained Córdoba's power was such that if he recommended the president fire a state minister, that minister's career was effectively over. It was on Córdoba's recommendation, for example, that Salinas removed the minister of fisheries, María de los Angeles Morena, for resisting the deregulation of the fishing sector, and sent her into exile as a PRI regional delegate. *The Economist Intelligence Unit, Business International,* First Quarter (1991): 4; Carlos Acosta and Carlos Puig, "En la oscuridad, a la sombra de Salinas, José Córdoba acumuló un poder inédito; ahora se hunde en el desprestigio, el vituperio y las sospechas," *Proceso* 961 (April 3, 1995): 11; and author's interview, Mexico City, July 2, 1992.

33. The Office of the Presidency took pains to conceal its "tilt" toward SECOFI and did not involve itself directly in these interagency negotiations. Its main function was that of a conduit: it received the SCT's counterproposals according to the law, then recirculated them to the OD for review.

34. Of course, the SCT realized there was always the possibility (or better, the hope) that reform would stall in the parallel OD-cartel negotiations. Should this occur Transportation could reap the benefits of "supporting" the Salinas economic agenda with no appreciable change in the status quo.

35. The General Law of Routes and Communication spoke specifically of routes and tariffs—key structural features that supported the cartel's operations.

36. Besides travel opportunities, the cartel offered reformers access to members of the opposite sex. Author's interview. Mexico City, July 2, 1992.

37. The government liberalized trade in stages. In 1985 it abandoned import-substitution for export-led growth; in 1986 Mexico finally joined the General Agreement on Tariffs and Trade; and in 1987 it signed a bilateral tariff, trade, and investment agreement with the United States. Accordingly, the percentage of imports subject to quotas fell from 83 to less than 28 percent between 1985 and 1988, and the weighted tariff level dropped from 16.4 to 13.1 percent. By December 1988 the maximum tariff had been slashed to 20 percent from a high of 100 percent six years before, and the number of products subject to quantitative restrictions had fallen from 1,200 to 325. See Pedro Aspe, *Economic Transformation the Mexican Way* (Cambridge, Mass: MIT Press, 1993), 156-157.

38. Between 1986 to 1991 the level of imports into Mexico tripled. See Fernández, "Trucking Deregulation in Mexico," 105.

39. The signing took place at the presidential residence of Los Pinos with President Salinas officiating. Signatories included the ministers of Transportation and Commerce, and the leaders of the National Chamber of Transport and Communication. See *Convenio de concertación para la modernización del autotransporte federal de carga* (México, D.F.: Secretaría de Comunicaciones y Transportes, 1989); and *Desregulación del transporte* (México, D.F.: Secretaría de Comunicaciones y Transportes, n.d.).

40. Beginning in 1990 liberalization allowed producers of light and medium-sized trucks to supplement production with imports; specialized truck and tractor imports were permitted in 1991; and in 1992, imports of heavy trucks (over 16,000 lbs.) were allowed. The intent of these changes was to close the technology and production gap between Mexican and foreign truck makers that grew out of import barriers and local content standards. In addition, approximately U.S. $6.5 billion would be used to construct 5,000 km. of new four-lane toll highways, widen two-lane highways to four lanes, rebuild the federal trunk network, and repair and maintain rural and feeder roads. See *Review of Trade and Investment Liberalization,* 3–4; *The Mexican Agenda,* 13th ed. (México, D.F.: Presidencia de la República, July 1992), 119–120; and Gustavo Patiño, "Evolución y Perspectivas del Transporte en México," speech delivered at the Second Binational Transportation Conference, "United States-Mexico Transport '92," Acapulco, March 1992.

41. On bureaucratic politics see Graham T. Allison, *Essence of Decision: Explaining the Cuban Missile Crisis* (Boston: Little, Brown, 1971).

42. See Trejo, "La Desregulación Eleva la Productividad Nacional."

43. Author's interview. Mexico City, July 28, 1993.

44. Some of the proposal's other provisions included: (1) a call for ministries to formulate new regulations through national consultation committees composed of representatives from producer and consumer groups, scientific institutions, and ministerial personnel; (2) a ninety-day period in which committees would publish their recommendations, field any public concerns, and publish their response to those concerns; and (3) the creation of nongovernmental bodies to develop and determine product norms. This function—traditionally carried out by SECOFI—would now be done by nongovernmental entities similar to the U.S. Underwriters' Laboratory. SECOFI would merely ensure the product standards and norms developed did not impede competition or create barriers to entry and monopolies.

45. There was more than bureaucratic inertia behind agencies' antireform attitudes. As Wilson observed, "any organization, and *a fortiori* any public organization, develops a genuine belief in the rightness of its mission that is expressed as a commitment to regulation as a process." See James Q. Wilson, "The Rise of the Bureaucratic State," in Nathan Glazer and Irving Kristol, eds., *The American Commonwealth* (New York: Basic Books, 1976), 98.

46. See "Decreto que reforma la Ley Federal de Metrología y Normalización," *Diario Oficial,* January 7, 1992.

Chapter 5

The Challenge of Environmental Policy Reform

Today, Mexico City is one of the worst environmentally polluted urban areas in the world.

—Carlos Salinas de Gortari

Although economic issues dominated Mexico's policy agenda through the early 1990s they did not monopolize it. Policy makers also faced a number of environmental challenges across the country including deforestation, erosion, and soil/water contamination. None, however, was more visible, embarrassing, and seemingly intractable than air pollution in Mexico City. Government antipollution initiatives date back to the early 1970s. The story of these efforts is complex,[1] but the basic result was fourfold: (1) the adoption of technically oriented *command and control* measures to combat air pollution by enforcing universal emission standards; (2) the creation of a cabinet-level environmental ministry; (3) the concentration of regulatory and enforcement authority at the apex of the political system—the federal government; and (4) the failure of these efforts to arrest (let alone reduce) air pollution in the capital.

In response to public outcries,[2] international embarrassment, and obvious policy failure, policy makers changed course. Beginning in 1988 the government took steps to reform Mexico's environmental policy regime. The result was an upsurge in public spending to fight air pollution and a spate of initiatives designed to decentralize the policy structure and supplement strict *command and control* strategies with economic instruments. Among these were proposals to replace Mexico City's aging car fleet by encouraging the purchase of new, less polluting vehicles through attractive market incentives, apply the "polluter pays principle" to force energy and gasoline consumers to internalize pollution clean-up costs, subject the environmental policy regime to cost-benefit analysis, and harmonize

133

Mexico's environmental policies with its new market reforms.

But in sharp contrast to the government's impressive economic reform record, few of these initiatives were ever adopted as state policy, and virtually none were implemented. Despite the regime's concentrated political power and technocratic expertise, five years of effort yielded meager results. By 1993 the *command and control* paradigm remained substantially unmodified, and reformers conceded the Salinas administration would leave office with little change in the environmental regime.[3] Given the government's significant economic achievements this result is puzzling.

The basic explanation for this outcome rests in the absence of powerful coalitions to advance policy reform inside the state, the capacity status quo proponents displayed to control the policy agenda through effective institutional innovation, and reformers' inability to compensate powerful, potential policy "losers." By and large, reform advocates worked in isolation and an institutional context which favored the status quo. The lack of interagency coordination severely hindered reform efforts and state actors balked at internalizing the costs of policy change. Finally, in contrast to the economic policy struggles, it was status quo proponents—not reformers—who seized the moment to change policy procedures, create new policy subunits, and thereby gain extraordinary leverage over policy outcomes.

The evidence in this chapter strongly supports these propositions. The first section profiles the air pollution problem in Mexico City, the institutional context of environmental policy making, and the centralized, *command and control* paradigm that characterized early antipollution efforts. The second details two reform waves that sought—but failed—to modify the dominant paradigm. The final section contrasts the record of accomplishments and failure in economic and environmental policy with reference to key analytical variables outlined in chapter 2.

Air Pollution in Mexico City: A Brief Overview

Air pollution in "Mexico City" really afflicts two distinct, but interconnected regions. One is Mexico City proper (or the Federal District); the other is the seventeen cities in the state of Mexico that comprise the greater Metropolitan Zone (MZ). In the late 1980s the MZ accounted for more than 40 percent of Mexico's total industrial output. It contained roughly 35,000 manufacturing and service industries, sustained a population of nearly 19 million people, and boasted a vehicle fleet (cars, taxis, trucks, buses) of 2.5 million. By virtue of its shared political borders, industrial base, and transportation system, residents of the Metropolitan Zone have a common environmental destiny and each locality generates negative environmental externalities that affect the other.

By all accounts the capital's air pollution problem is severe. By 1989 over 4.3 million tons of emissions darkened the city's skyscape annually. Composed of suspended particles, toxic gases, hydrocarbons, and heavy metals, this brownish haze sickened city residents and alarmed health officials. Besides these visible contaminants, the "invisible" (but no less dangerous) threat of ozone pollution registered higher in Mexico City than anywhere else in the world.[4] Some analysts view the region's pollution woes as a direct function of centralized growth. As Richard Nuccio of the Inter-American Dialogue observed:

> The outcome of a policy of centralized growth, Mexico City has become the place in which the majority of the natural and artificial sources of contamination are concentrated . . . [including]: emissions from factories, workshops, thermo-electric plants, refineries, petrochemical plants, cement and fertilizer plants, iron and steel foundries, and a large quantity of industrial and domestic incinerators; and millions of internal combustion vehicles.[5]

The root causes of deteriorating air quality, however, are a bit more complex. They stem from dynamic interactions between industrial, demographic, transport, and geographic factors, which in part reflect the impact of Mexico's political centralization and statist development model.

By the late nineteenth century Mexico City claimed the lion's share of investment in the country due to its population size, larger consumer market and labor force, and superior infrastructure.[6] The shift to import-substitution plus the postrevolutionary centralization of political/administrative authority accelerated this trend. Despite ISI's business-retarding tendencies (layers of bureaucracy and regulations), political centralization lowered the transaction costs of starting or expanding a business in the capital. As the locus of financial and political power, Mexico City was where bargains were struck, official approval and support obtained, permits and licenses issued, and regulations promulgated and (re)interpreted. Close proximity to state bureaucracies and politicians eased deal making and helped entrepreneurs cut through the red tape, while key aspects of ISI—energy, credit and input subsidies, tax breaks, joint ventures between the state and private sector, etc.—provided investors powerful inducements to locate in the capital.

These incentives induced rapid industrialization, job creation, and a corresponding upswing in rural-to-city migration. Between 1930 and 1975, the number of industrial enterprises in Mexico City jumped from 3,180 to 34,543, and between 1940 and 1970, over 6.5 million people left rural areas to find work in the capital.[7] By the late 1980s nearly 25 percent of Mexico's total population lived within the Metropolitan Zone and the 35,000 manufacturing and service industries there spanned the gamut of economic activity—from auto, steel, and thermoelectric plants, to oil refineries, paper mills, and cement factories.[8] Although industry flourished under Mexico's statist model, the subsidies, protectionism, and lax competition that fueled expansion left private firms (and public enterprises) little incentive to economize or develop efficient patterns of production and resource use.

Not surprisingly, as the region's industrial base grew so did the quantity of vehicles required to transport workers and products (see table 5.1). In just twenty

Table 5.1   Comparative Spatial Distribution of Industry and Population in the Federal District and State of Mexico, 1960–1980

Year	Location	Number of firms	Number of persons employed	Capital investment (current pesos)	Gross production (current pesos)	Number of vehicles
1960	Fed. Dist.	23,577	332,305	15,989,530	21,050,091	248,038
	St. of Mex.	1,047	74,700	5,759,269	4,487,335	—
1970	Fed. Dist.	29,436	491,264	43,671,195	67,978,692	717,672
	St. of Mex.	3,732	181,200	23,305,161	30,401,633	—
1975	Fed. Dist.	29,654	492,007	55,283,322	139,551,177	—
	St. of Mex.	4,750	211,202	39,883,053	73,632,065	—
1980	Fed. Dist.	28,637	637,382	197,861,511	491,931,791	1,869,808
	St. of Mex.	9,855	421,800	168,951,710	308,689,565	—
				Rate of population growth		
1960–1970	Fed. Dist.			3.4		
	St. of Mex.			12.2		
1970–1980	Fed. Dist.			2.2		
	St. of Mex.			8.3		

Sources: Gustavo Garza, "Distribución de la industria en la Ciudad de México (1960-1980)," in *Atlas de la Ciudad de México* (México, D.F.: Departamento del Distrito Federal, El Colegio de México, 1986); rate of population growth: *Population Growth and Policies in Mega-Cities: Mexico City* (New York: United Nations, 1991), 3; number of vehicles: Emilio Ocampo, "Atmospheric Pollution from Transport Sources in Mexico City," in *Applying Economic Instruments to Environmental Policies in OECD and Dynamic Nonmember Economies* (Paris: OECD, 1994), 235.

years (1960 to 1980) the number of private autos spiked over 650 percent (some studies suggest as much as 1,700 percent), and by the 1980s the vehicle fleet was expanding by 10 percent annually with a majority of these cars well over ten years old (mandatory catalytic converters would not come until 1992).[9] Consequently, motor vehicles—not industry—produce roughly 80 percent of airborne contaminants in a region whose high altitude and mountainous perimeter facilitate ozone formation and "pollution trapping" thermal inversions.[10]

Environmental Policy Making: The Institutional Context

Between 1971 and 1988 Mexico's environmental policy making was governed by federal legislation that centralized authority and increasingly emphasized the technical aspects of pollution control. Both the 1971 Federal Law for the Prevention and Control of Environmental Pollution and its 1982 replacement, the Federal Law of Environmental Protection, concentrated enforcement authority at the federal level: the former inside the Ministry of Health, the latter within the newly created Ministry of Urban Development and Ecology (SEDUE).[11] Like transportation legislation, the implementation of federal environmental law was subject to regulations issued by the responsible ministry. Thus, for most of the 1980s SEDUE—the nation's lead environmental agency—held jurisdiction over most environmental matters throughout the republic, and led the fight against air pollution in Mexico City (local city agencies played only a minor role).[12]

Two aspects of the broad institutional context surrounding environmental policy warrant attention. To begin, SEDUE's mandate and "lead agency" status masked a more complex policy-making environment. State entities whose activities were themselves polluting—or whose cooperation was needed to implement environmental measures—could not be excluded from policy deliberations and the norms governing interagency relations stressed consultation over hierarchy. This forced SEDUE to contend with powerful actors like the state oil and electricity monopolies (Pemex and the Federal Electricity Commission, or CFE) or the Commerce Ministry, but provided little muscle to compel support for its efforts.

This arrangement complicated the policy-making process considerably. For example, in a matchup between SEDUE and these bureaucratic heavyweights the former's initiatives did not automatically trump the latter's. Thus, plans to lower emissions via cleaner fuel mixtures or converting thermoelectric plants to LP gas could not be accomplished by fiat; rather, they entailed laborious negotiations with Pemex and the CFE. Similarly, a mandate that industry acquire "green technologies" (generally through imports) could be stymied by import restrictions administered by the Commerce Ministry. Absent direct presidential intervention, the broader institutional context made an aggressive, comprehensive antipollution program difficult to achieve under the best circumstances. To enhance interagency coordination, environmental policy makers looked for ways to obtain greater leverage inside the bureaucracy. As we shall see, once they achieved it, reformers would face even greater obstacles effecting meaningful policy change.

In the long term, patterns of centralized authority worked against effective pollution control too. By privileging the federal government they deprived state and municipal governments in the MZ of the legal means to combat pollution, hindered development of environmental management expertise at local levels, and stretched thin the federal government's own resources. When the debt crisis struck in 1982, the federal government's profound economic straits revealed the vulnerabilities of this approach. Grappling with economic collapse, the de la Madrid administration slashed government spending to comply with an International Monetary Fund austerity program. This diverted funds from environmental (and other) programs, toward servicing Mexico's external debt. Caught in the economic crunch, SEDUE's fortunes plummeted as budget cutbacks ravished its resources and systematically weakened its institutional capacity. To cite several prominent examples:

- between 1985 and 1988 the agency's budget fell from $263 million to $125 million, effectively defunding two of six divisions in SEDUE's Subsecretariat of Ecology;
- acute fiscal constraints deprived SEDUE of the most basic analytical tools required to operate effectively; as late as 1986 the ministry lacked even a *single* microcomputer to simulate air and pollution dispersion patterns;[13]
- between 1986 and 1989 budget cuts cost SEDUE more than 35 percent of its functioning vehicles and 20 percent of its telephones;[14]
- budget restrictions also decimated the ministry's staff—shrinking its personnel roster from 5,000 to 2,500 by 1988, with turnover particularly high among those with technical expertise;[15]
- consequently, throughout the 1980s the ministry could field only ten inspectors to cover the 35,000 industries and commercial establishments in Mexico City, and failed to develop a single regulation to implement the 1982 federal environmental law (which for all practical purposes rendered the legislation "a dead letter").[16]

Hobbled by an increasingly skeletal crew and little real regulatory punch, SEDUE failed to sanction polluters aggressively.[17] As its institutional capacity waned the agency almost fell into denial regarding the magnitude of the pollution problem, and by minimizing its severity, exposed itself to public ridicule.[18] From 1986 onward, ozone pollution soared to levels previously unrecorded in Mexico (or elsewhere); in 1987 hundreds of birds literally fell dead from the skies, and thereafter, Mexico City's environmental problems seemed to gallop out of control.[19] To many, the government's environmental campaign seemed too little, too late.

The *Command and Control* Paradigm

Yet if Mexico's record of environmental clean up seemed meager, its belated recognition of pollution problems was hardly an anomaly. In most countries environmental degradation engendered serious, sustained political attention only in the late 1960s. As the links and trade-offs between economic growth and pollution grew clearer—and public concern mounted—governments in advanced industrial countries began regulating emission levels to moderate their negative effects. Such regulation forms the backbone of a *command and control* strategy, an approach that governments in developing countries like Mexico would later emulate.

Command and control seeks to stem pollution through universal emissions standards enforced via "source" inspections (production plants, commercial establishments, vehicles, etc.). Typically, governments establish preferred ambient standards and specify the technology a plant must use (or a vehicle contain) to achieve these goals. Successful *command and control* requires highly trained technicians, plus effective administration, monitoring, and enforcement by government. Where these conditions hold a *command and control* strategy can be quite effective; in fact, it is the most common form of environmental policy adopted by governments worldwide.[20]

Throughout the difficult years of the 1980s Mexican policy makers battled air pollution in the Metropolitan Zone largely through a series of stopgap, *command and control* measures, based in part on international experience.[21] Some initiatives brought concrete, if limited results (e.g., lower atmospheric lead levels); others, like temporary plant closings, proved useful in periods of "environmental crises." By decade's turn, these measures were formalized into the *Comprehensive Program Against Air Pollution* (Comprehensive Program, or PICCA).

The Comprehensive Program

An explicitly *command and control* project, the PICCA drew upon studies SEDUE conducted in 1987 and 1988, and outlined a five-point strategy to curb air pollution in the Valley of Mexico.[22] Its major objectives were to reduce levels of (1) ozone, by decreasing the emission of hydrocarbons and nitrous oxide, (2) suspended particulates, by lowering emissions of sulfur and nitrous oxides, (3) lead, by decreasing its content in gasoline, and (4) carbon monoxide emitted from motor vehicles. Funded largely on external credit, the program's price tag totaled $4.6 billion.[24]

To achieve its goals the PICCA targeted emissions from the industrial, transport, and energy sectors, called for beefed up inspection and enforcement measures, cleaner fuels, and the compulsory installation of catalytic converters in new autos. Most measures would be phased in within two to six years. To cut auto emissions further and relieve traffic congestion, authorities later grafted an ancillary "no driving day" program (*Hoy no Circula*) into the PICCA which limited the number of cars in circulation one day per week.[24] Program advocates claimed that full implementation would reduce emission levels on a host of contaminants including nitrous oxides (5.36 percent), hydrocarbons (26.05 percent), sulfur dioxide (79.4 percent), suspended particles (55.2 percent), carbon monoxide (36.1 percent), and lead (40.5 percent).[25]

Although not officially unveiled until 1990, the PICCA's early development also coincided (roughly) with new environmental legislation. In 1988 the de la Madrid administration scrapped the 1982 environmental law and replaced it with the General Law of Ecological Equilibrium (LGEE).[26] This legislation ended the federal government's role as the sole environmental enforcement authority: it obligated local governments to participate with federal initiatives, directed state governments to formulate environmental programs specific to their needs, and transferred important enforcement functions from the federal to the state and municipal levels.

With respect to air pollution in the Metropolitan Zone the LGEE established a new division of labor between SEDUE, the Mexico City government (Department of the Federal District, or DDF), and the state of Mexico. SEDUE would administer an air monitoring system, inspect and enforce fixed-source emissions from *industry,* develop regulations to control air pollution in the capital, and issue technical standards (e.g., emissions standards) to implement the law. The DDF gained jurisdiction over emissions from *commercial* enterprises, private autos, and various public transportation services in Mexico City. The state of Mexico, meanwhile, would enforce emission standards for all fixed and mobile pollution sources within its territory (save for industry, which remained SEDUE's responsibility). From this point on, direct control over the execution of Mexico City's antipollution campaign passed from SEDUE to the DDF.

As the locus of authority shifted, the institutional context of pollution policy and the principal political actors changed too. Accordingly, between 1989 and 1991 efforts to advance (and reform) the PICCA played out inside the Department of the Federal District—a special unit created in 1928 to administer the seat of the federal government. Throughout the Salinas era the Federal District was governed by a presidentially appointed *Regente,* or mayor, and an elected General Assembly with limited authority.[27] The structure of power in the city government mirrored arrangements at the federal level. In terms of sheer power, the mayor's office dwarfed the General Assembly, and the absence of direct elections provided ample (but not total) decision-making autonomy. Unaccountable to the citizens electorally, the *Regente* served at the president's pleasure and sat on the president's cabinet.

With respect to the capital's pollution problem, Salinas sent a clear message. During his 1988 inaugural address he personally directed newly appointed Mayor Manuel Camacho Solís to bring pollution under control. "I am giving precise, urgent and strict instructions to the mayor of the federal district," the president said, "to start working immediately, with effective actions and encouraging community participation, in the fight against pollution."[28] This highly symbolic deputation vested Camacho with a political authority over the city's environmental matters even above that conferred by the 1988 General Law.

A close friend of the president's, Camacho had served as minister of urban development and ecology from 1986 to 1988 and ran Salinas's 1988 presidential campaign. Camacho also harbored presidential ambitions, and if his tenure at City Hall garnered approbation he stood a good chance of being anointed by Salinas as the PRI's 1994 presidential candidate. Of course, many variables could affect this decision, but one key to the prize would be how Camacho handled Mexico City's uphill battle against pollution. With much riding on the DDF's environmental campaign, Camacho placed his hopes in the Comprehensive Program.

Although Camacho's new prominence sparked institutional rivalries between SEDUE and the city government, there was little disagreement over the Comprehensive Program's fundamental *command and control* approach. On the one hand, the PICCA was based on studies conducted under SEDUE's auspices; on the other hand, the ministry's top environmental officials (engineers, biologists, scientists, physicists) naturally favored technical solutions.

Not all policy makers embraced the PICCA, however. For one thing the program contained no explicit timetable for full implementation (how, then, would officials know when to measure its failure or success?). Nor would it address ozone pollution sufficiently; even under the rosiest scenario, the output of ozone's chief elements—nitrous oxides and hydrocarbons—would remain high. A third issue concerned the program's long-term efficacy and financial costs: government studies showed the PICCA would cut aggregate emissions only during its first six years; thereafter, pollution would grow in tandem with the city's population and vehicle fleet. The magnitude of emission levels recorded that year (see table 5.2) gave fiscal conservatives strong incentives to see the multibillion dollar PICCA as little more than a financial black hole. Getting the PICCA past the president's economic cabinet (where not a single member initially supported it) was a tough sell, made possible only because of the program's apparent scientific rigor and because doing *something* seemed preferable to nothing.[29]

Finally, while some observers criticized the PICCA's specifics and financial expense, others took issue with its broader *command and control* approach. The chief concern was that although they could be effective, pure *command and control* projects were far from cost-efficient. Besides obvious financial costs, they imposed substantial, hidden transaction costs including those required to obtain information on potential polluters, enforce compliance, and litigate violations, as well as the costs borne by polluters required to adopt expensive (and sometimes inappropriate) technologies.[30]

This line of criticism—first voiced by Mexican academics and some environmental activists—echoed that expressed in environmental policy literature which claimed that economic incentives, combined with *command and control,* offered a more efficient pollution-abatement strategy.[31] Such arguments helped inform later

Table 5.2   **Polluting Emissions in the Metropolitan Zone, 1989**
(percentage totals by contaminant and source)

Sector	SO$_2$	NOx	HC	CO	PST	Total
Energy (oil & electricity)	35.5	17.5	5.5	1.8	1.1	4.0
Industry & services	42.7	18.5	7.0	0.5	2.8	4.4
Transport (excluding subway)	21.7	75.4	52.6	96.7	2.1	76.6
Natural processes (erosion, fires, etc.)	0.1	0.5	34.9	0.9	94.0	14.9
Totals (ton/year)	205,725	177,339	572,101	2,950,627	450,599	4,356,391

Source: Derived from *Informe de la Situación General en Materia de Equilibrio Ecológico y Protección al Ambiente, 1989-1990* (México, D.F.: Comisión Nacional de Ecología, 1991), 71.

challenges to the prevailing paradigm by those outside environmental policy circles, particularly among Mexico's economic reformers.

Although economic officials were hardly environmental experts, they intuitively grasped the more subtle linkages between environmental deterioration and economics. Two lines of economic logic eventually brought these environmental novices into the policy debate. First, because natural resources are held in common, users exploit them without internalizing the true costs of their actions; instead, they shift the costs of pollution and abatement to society as a whole. To compensate, reformers reasoned, environmental policy should mimic market incentives to minimize environmentally damaging practices. Second, economic dynamics not directly linked to natural resource use could also produce profound, negative environmental externalities. Since policies that encouraged resource misallocation and inefficiency contributed to waste and pollution, Mexico's pollution woes seemed due, in part, to its statist tradition—protectionism, tax distortions, subsidies and inefficient public enterprise operations, etc. If market reforms in general proved a tonic for Mexico's ailing economy, further refinements might aid environmental recovery. These notions, underdeveloped as they were, formed the intellectual raw material economic reformers would carry into environmental policy discussions. Theodore Panayotou's insights on the synergy between ambient quality and economics captured their general mind-set perfectly:

> The prevailing configuration of markets and policies leaves many resources outside the domain of markets, unowned, unpriced and unaccounted for and more often than not, it subsidizes their excessive use and destruction. . . . This results in an incentive structure that induces people to maximise their profits not by being efficient and innovative but by appropriating other peoples' resources and shifting their own costs onto others. . . . The overall objective of policy reform is to reestablish the link between resource scarcity and resource prices that has been severed by a constellation of subsidies, perverse incentives . . . and unaccounted environmental externalities.[32]

The Reform Waves

With opinions divided over the PICCA, attempts to modify it soon followed. But unlike their economic counterparts these endeavors were more a series of disjointed efforts than well-coordinated campaigns between like-minded coalition partners. One reform wave emerged from inside the Mexico City bureaucracy, the other from powerful federal ministries. Both sought to reduce the reliance on *command and control* by introducing economic incentives into the PICCA. The struggles they sparked over the policy agenda were less intense than the conflicts over economic policy, but the struggles themselves (and the stakes) were no less real. As with divestment and deregulation, environmental reform proposals carried costs that status quo adherents found hard to offset; ultimately, few would be adopted as state policy and none were ever implemented.

Struggles within the Department of the Federal District

After assuming power in 1988, Mayor Manuel Camacho reorganized the city's environmental bureaucracy into four administrative units: the General Direction of Ecologic Planning, the General Direction of Pollution Prevention and Control, the General Coordination for Urban Restructuring and Ecological Protection, and the General Coordination for Environmental Projects. Camacho selected (some claim "co-opted") one-time environmental activists to head the two former units, and appointed political protégés to direct the latter.[33] These agencies—whose functions centered on policy analysis, antipollution projects, urban renewal, and financial procurement, respectively—ranked coequals on the bureaucratic flow-chart and operated under policy procedures quite similar to those which governed Mexico's old regulatory policy process (discussed in chapter 4). Each unit formulated its own policy initiatives and submitted them directly to the mayor for approval.

The highly competitive political culture at City Hall left little incentive for interagency collaboration. From the outset political ambition, institutional jealousies, and personality conflicts divided the DDF's environmental agencies, and out of these struggles the General Coordination for Environmental Projects (GCEP) emerged predominant. Led by Fernando Menéndez Garza—a former SEDUE official, Camacho loyalist, and one of the mayor's closest political subordinates— the GCEP was initially an *Asesoría Financiera* (financial consultancy). Its original task was to obtain credit from international lenders to help finance the city's environmental projects. Since Mexico relied on external moneys to fund a good share of its antipollution initiatives (including the PICCA), the General Coordination became the liaison between the city government and donors like the World Bank, Japan, and the U.S. Agency for International Development. The agency soon extended its responsibilities, however, beyond acquiring the financing for environmental projects to actually planning and executing them.

Almost immediately Menéndez began to exploit his political ties to Camacho and the leverage his agency's financial procurement function afforded. As external credit poured into Mexico's antipollution program the GCEP retained ample portions to contract international consultants and expand its pool of skilled technicians.[34] It hired a battery of professionals—chemical and industrial engineers, computer scientists, biologists—whose natural affinity for technical solutions precluded an economic approach to pollution abatement. Its competitors, meanwhile, strapped to their annual city budget allocations, saw their own agencies' resources dwindle in comparison.[35] Through enhanced analytic capabilities and the capacity to self-finance its operations the General Coordination bolstered its organizational position significantly and gained a decided advantage over its peers. The more dependent the city's antipollution campaign grew upon the GCEP's financial and analytic operations, the more influence the agency acquired in DDF environmental policy circles, and the deeper the city's commitment to technical solutions became.

The upshot was dramatic. Without any formal change in the policy procedures at City Hall, the General Coordination became the sole voice on the DDF's antipollution programs, accountable only to the mayor himself.[36] From late 1989 onward it assumed direct control over the city's day-to-day environmental matters (including those related to the PICCA), and with the mayor's support, informally altered the policy-making procedures in ways enormously consequential. The crucial change echoed that which had fortified the Office of Deregulation (discussed in chapter 4): all policy proposals submitted to the mayor's office, whether originating inside city agencies or without, were routed through the General Coordination for review. This informal arrangement (essentially a defacto veto) changed the bureaucratic balance of power significantly and placed would-be reformers on decidedly unfavorable terrain; in the end they would find the obstacles to success nearly impossible to surmount.

Early in the new administration Camacho's director of pollution prevention and control, Ramón Ojeda Mestre, took aim at the single largest source of toxic emissions—motor vehicles. His agency proposed the gradual replacement of Mexico City's aging car fleet with new vehicles equipped with antipollution technology.[37] The plan called for a municipal ordinance requiring all cars registered in the city to have catalytic converters, a substantial discount and trade-in program on new car purchases, and a government buyback/destruction program to take older, polluting vehicles out of circulation. Though this proposal retained a prominent role for government action (which reflected Ojeda Mestre's legal training as an attorney), it also displayed an economic logic the PICCA lacked. By mixing *command and control* with economic incentives, proponents believed the initiative would upgrade the auto fleet, help lower emissions, plus create a new car "market" of sufficient volume to compensate auto dealers for smaller profit margins.

The second initiative was a more frontal assault against *command and control,* and came from the DDF's General Direction of Ecologic Planning. Its chief architect, Gabriel Quadri de la Torre (M.A. economics, University of Texas), sought to introduce "the polluter pays principle" into the Comprehensive Program.[38] In a sophisticated document this agency urged the DDF "to abandon the policy based exclusively on norms and regulations that prevails today, and demonstrates serious limitations and inefficiencies," so that "economic incentives [could play] a crucial role in remodeling energy consumption."[39] Moreover, it argued for an end to fuel subsidies and new energy taxes to force industry, motorists, and transport sectors to internalize the costs of abatement efforts. Tax revenues would help finance the city's antipollution measures, plus reduce the bureaucracy and overhead needed to administer them.

To be sure, translating these novel proposals into policy would be no small feat. At a minimum it required close attention to issues of financing, cross-agency coordination and a fundamental shift in the prevailing *command and control* paradigm. Both initiatives underscored the potential of economic incentives to advance environmental goals; neither, however, passed muster with the city's "environmental czar," Fernando Menéndez. Much of the resistance stemmed from the costs policy change entailed—particularly institutional prestige and political advancement—and the difficulty of defraying them.[40] For one thing the GCEP was intimately linked to the Comprehensive Program and whatever their merits, the counterproposals would cast aspersions on the agency's crown jewel. For another, to embrace either the auto reconversion or anti-fuel subsidy plans (especially *after* they had crossed the mayor's desk) might diminish Menéndez in Camacho's eyes, and weaken the General Coordination's preeminence in environmental policy.

Equally important, the reforms carried significant financial/political costs for Menéndez's mentor, Manuel Camacho, and the greater city government. To transform Mexico City's auto fleet the DDF would have to shoulder the expenses of the buyback phase, and with millions of cars in circulation this would cost a fortune. Moreover, Camacho had gone out on a limb to sell the $4.6 billion Comprehensive Program to Salinas's economic cabinet. Given his presidential ambitions, to backtrack now might be to court political suicide, and the transaction costs of backpedaling would be steep. With no authority over fuel prices, subsidies, or auto production standards (i.e., catalytic converters), Camacho would have to use his political capital to secure the cooperation of other agencies (e.g., Commerce), and he preferred to cash these chips in, instead, on promoting the PICCA.

Under these circumstances reformers faced an uphill battle. With policy-making procedures stacked against them they could propose policy modifications but not ensure their adoption. Accordingly, they dutifully passed their proposals up the pipeline only to have them funneled back to the General Coordination for review. The outcome was no surprise. Both the auto fleet reconversion and energy antisubsidy plans languished inside the Department of the Federal District, and by the end of 1990 the insurgency had been put down: the reformers either had resigned in frustration or had been effectively demoted.[41]

Reform Pressures outside the Department of the Federal District

As the first reform wave ebbed inside City Hall, a second emerged outside the Department of the Federal District. The Ministry of Finance (Hacienda)—and later, a new Ministry of Social Development—took another stab at blending *command and control* with economic incentives. Like its predecessor this reform wave lacked the dynamic coalition politics, effective institutional innovation, and cost-compensating measures that proved crucial to successful economic reforms. And once again, it would fail.

Although the president's economic cabinet had reluctantly backed the PICCA, some officials remained sensitive to its multibillion dollar price tag. Increasing the country's debt burden to fund the program had not gone down well at the Treasury, and notwithstanding that Mexico's national ecology program called for abatement via the "polluter pays principle,"[42] the PICCA did nothing to address pollution's various economic dimensions. Moreover, some aspects of the program showed early signs of backfiring. A prominent example was the no-driving day (*Hoy no Circula*) that restricted autos in circulation one day per week. After a brief period of declining pollution levels and improved traffic flows, some officials saw trouble on the horizon: in 1990 auto dealers sold 156,000 new cars in Mexico City, yet *330,000* vehicles were actually registered that year (the spike in car registrations paralleled rising fuel consumption patterns). This suggested city residents were circumventing the driving restrictions by buying a second (older and often, more polluting) car, and raised doubts over the wisdom of spending $2 million annually to enforce the program.[43]

But existing policy procedures left budget watchers at Hacienda little influence over how the Mexico City government or SEDUE ran the PICCA. This changed in 1990, however, when SEDUE requested World Bank financing to expand its inspection and enforcement operations and improve its analytic capabilities. Since Finance would have to administer the loan, the Ecology Ministry's request opened a window of opportunity to press the agency for policy change. Exploiting its position inside the state, Finance agreed to administer the loan provided that SEDUE join it and the Budget Ministry on a joint task force to reformulate important aspects of environmental policy.[44]

The proposal's scope was enormous. To ensure the most bang for the buck the task force would subject SEDUE's entire environmental program (including the PICCA) to cost-benefit analysis. This would provide a strict accounting of government income and spending on pollution abatement, mapped to the functions assigned to federal, state, and local governments (which was critical to ensure cost efficiency). The task force also would work to harmonize Mexico's environmental policies and new market reforms, develop economic instruments to achieve environmental goals, and devise means to make the government's antipollution program self-financing (i.e., apply the polluter pays principle).[45] These objectives dovetailed nicely with the World Bank's new "green" philosophy and quickly won Bank support.[46] The project also promised to give economic reformers real leverage over Mexico's environmental regime: it would force SEDUE to cede some jurisdiction over policy formulation, and perhaps even influence the DDF via the back door by revealing the Comprehensive Program's economic inefficiencies.

These same features, of course, made the initiative a tough sell. With institutional prestige and political careers tied to the PICCA, exposing the program's potential weaknesses could hardly be less attractive to SEDUE. Eventually the cash-strapped ministry acquiesced, yet even this small step toward reform would be short-lived: once Bank funding was secured in December 1991, the Salinas administration abolished the Ministry of Ecology the next year and transferred its responsibilities to a new Ministry of Social Development (SEDESOL).[47] The new agency refused to honor its predecessor's commitment and the project collapsed.[48] Ironically, officials inside this same agency would spearhead the last environmental reform campaign of the Salinas era. They mounted their campaign, however, in the wake of significant institutional changes engineered by *command and control* proponents, innovations that left reformers little leverage over the policy agenda. This, plus the costs of reform, would prove formidable obstacles to success.

The story of SEDESOL—its creation, capacity to scuttle Hacienda's project, unlikely transformation into a reform proponent, and ultimate failure to advance reform—is complex. It can be understood, however, largely in terms of three factors: partisan politics, the dynamics of presidential succession, and the Office of Deregulation's cost-benefit requirement discussed in chapter 4. With respect to partisan politics the central issue was the continued viability of the National Solidarity Program (PRONASOL)—the signature domestic program of the Salinas presidency and the core of the *Salinista* political economy. A gigantic pork barrel project, PRONASOL was designed to soothe the economic wounds opened by Mexico's neoliberal transformation and bolster the regime's political support in the process.[49] It funneled billions of dollars ($1.7 billion in 1992 alone) toward grassroots antipoverty programs, education, social services, and infrastructure projects; it targeted the spending in regions where the PRI ran poorly in 1988, and some claim it was a major factor behind the PRI's electoral resurgence in 1991.[50]

Until 1992 Salinas ran PRONASOL directly out of the Office of the Presidency. To give the program a firmer institutional home, ensure its continuation beyond his administration, and build a partisan "edge" for the PRI into the state bureaucracy itself, Salinas intended SEDESOL to administer it.[51] In part, this strategic role in partisan politics gave SEDESOL the clout to derail Hacienda's task force project. Another factor, however, was the role the new ministry played in the issue of presidential succession—a theme which grew more prominent as the Salinas administration entered its fourth year.

As per Mexico's unwritten political rules, Salinas expected to select his own successor and the post-Salinas era appeared to require a leader with strong economic *and* political skills. The next president not only had to safeguard Mexico's recent economic reforms and complete the PRI's political resuscitation, but also had to heal the wounds opened by six years of austerity under de la Madrid and the rapid economic changes unleashed by Salinas himself. The pool of pre-candidates, however, was limited; only Manuel Camacho (mayor of Mexico City), Pedro Aspe (Finance), and Ernesto Zedillo (Education, formerly of Budget and Planning) were of presidential timber,[52] and each had weaknesses as well as strengths. Some feared Camacho's zest for the *political* would compromise Mexico's economic reforms; Aspe, meanwhile, could be too technocratic and unwilling to compromise when needed; finally, Zedillo lacked political acumen and a substantive network of political alliances.

To increase the number of *presidenciables* and provide a platform suitable for a presidential bid, Salinas invited Luis Donaldo Colosio to direct the new Social Development Ministry,[53] and tailored SEDESOL to serve this purpose. As minister of social development, Colosio (president of the PRI, ex-senator from Sonora, economics Ph.D. from the University of Pennsylvania) joined the president's economic cabinet and immediately ranked among the contenders.[54] But to remain a contender he had to demonstrate a record of accomplishment untarnished by environmental "incompetence" and economic skill at least equal to his potential competitors. One big problem, of course, was the "baggage" SEDESOL inherited from its predecessor, SEDUE—an agency whose tattered credibility extended to its top officials.[55] The word "ecology," therefore, was dropped from the ministry's name and its environmental functions were split between two new semiautonomous agencies under SEDESOL's domain (the attorney general for environmental protection and the National Ecology Institute).[56]

These cosmetic changes helped disassociate SEDESOL from SEDUE, but to compete with the technocratic, economic ministries would take more substantive innovations. For one thing, Hacienda's influence had grown enormously due to bureaucratic reshuffling: in January 1992 President Salinas abolished the Ministry of Budget and Planning and transferred its budgetary functions to Finance. For another, the relationship between the Social Development and Finance Ministries was inherently conflictual. Not only did SEDESOL disburse vast sums of money (nearly $2 billion via PRONASOL in 1992 alone), but its approach to policy was fundamentally different: where SEDESOL privileged politics (again, PRONASOL) over policy, Finance emphasized *policy* first (privatization, fiscal restraint), then worried about the politics of implementing it. Equally important, SEDESOL's environmental regulations had to meet stiff cost-benefit standards engineered by the Office of Deregulation, and failure here would degrade its standing in the technocracy. Without first class analytic abilities, therefore, SEDESOL stood little chance of holding its own with the technocrats, fulfilling the cost-benefit mandate, or distinguishing its director from other *presidenciables*.

In October 1992 Colosio addressed these concerns by creating the Office of Economic and Social Analysis (OESA)—a highly technocratic policy subunit inside the social development ministry. Designed primarily as a support staff for the social development minister, OESA was similar to its economic counterparts (the Offices of Deregulation and Privatization), yet fundamentally different: the latter enjoyed firm legal mandates via presidential decrees, and single-theme missions; the former did not. To the contrary, the unit's scope of activity was enormous, encompassing economic, social, *and* environmental policy. Its general tasks were to provide the analytic rigor SEDESOL required, translate its programs into "neoliberal language" easily intelligible to the president's economic cabinet (and hence, more likely to carry weight), devise the most economically efficient means to disburse PRONASOL moneys, and ensure SEDESOL's environmental policies complied with the new cost-benefit law.

From its general coordinator on down, Colosio staffed OESA with personnel a breed apart from those employed by the old SEDUE. In lieu of engineers and physicists, most of its thirty analysts were economists and many sported classic technocratic pedigrees.[57] In terms of analytic capacity the unit's department of environmental policy was particularly impressive. Led by Mexico's foremost *environmental* economist, Juan Carlos Beleaustegüigoitia,[58] and staffed by fourteen analysts (of whom twelve were economists), its mandate was to analyze Mexico's entire environmental regime and devise market incentives to achieve environmental goals. Despite its neoliberal bent, the department was more pragmatic than dogmatic with respect to environmental policy. Its basic philosophy reflected that of Beleaustegüigoitia, who was familiar with the limitations of *command and control,* but also understood this strategy's value and the limits of economic incentives.[59]

OESA's creation enhanced Colosio's presidential prospects considerably and appeared to bode well for environmental policy reform too. Its analytic endowments helped SEDESOL reclaim the authority over environmental policy formulation SEDUE had ceded to Finance, and provided a very practical justification to abort its task force project altogether: Why slog through the policy reform process with an interagency body when a unit with precisely this capacity already existed?

With respect to new policy initiatives OESA officials hoped to hit the ground running. Two factors, however, sharply reduced their prospects of success. First, in response to rising pollution levels and the political dynamics of presidential succession, *command and control* advocates at City Hall engineered new institutional arrangements that limited OESA's capacity to impose reforms on city officials. Second, the race for presidential succession heightened sensibilities to the costs of policy change, and any initiative that remotely threatened presidential hopefuls would face an uphill battle.

As noted, Mayor Manuel Camacho's prospects of receiving the PRI's nomination hinged, in part, on his environmental record and Camacho had placed his bets on the Comprehensive Program. But tackling the capital's mammoth pollution woes was no mean feat. Even with the PICCA, many residents saw little to applaud and especially during the city's long pollution season (November through March), print media carried stories peppered with public criticism. To cite just a few examples, Alfonso Cipres, president of the Mexican Ecology Movement, called the PICCA "an aspirin for a huge ecological problem," and Manuel Guerra, director of the Autonomous Institute for Environmental Research, opined that at best it was "a strategy to prevent catastrophe."[60] Homero Aridjis, meanwhile, leader of a high-profile environmental organization (the Group of 100), took aim at Mayor Camacho himself. Recalling Salinas's inaugural address, Aridjis claimed Camacho had failed to fulfill the president's environmental mandate: "[President Salinas] promised his government would give priority to fighting pollution. He also gave direct instructions to Camacho Solís to resolve the problem. But he hasn't done anything. Those instructions haven't been fulfilled; pollution has grown worse than ever. It's an urgent, grave health problem that can't be minimized or excused."[61]

Of course, such potshots would not determine Camacho's political fate (although they hardly helped). They did, however, give the mayor powerful incentives to produce results. As Camacho later explained, the public wanted "action"—i.e., plant closings, cleaner fuels, nonpolluting public buses, auto restrictions—all of which the Comprehensive Program was designed to achieve.[62] Unfortunately, he discovered the institutional context worked against quick results.

While the 1988 General Law of Ecological Equilibrium had given the DDF jurisdiction over many environmental matters in the capital, even this mandate was not enough to ensure the PICCA's smooth implementation. For example, none of the program's technical objectives (i.e., production of "cleaner" fuels and substitution of LP gas in thermoelectric plants) could be achieved in timely fashion absent close coordination among numerous agencies: the Energy Ministry, Petróleos Mexicanos (Pemex), the Mexican Petroleum Institute, and the Federal Electricity Commission. Similarly, effective enforcement of emissions standards hinged upon collaboration between the DDF, SEDUE, and the state of Mexico.

In short, the basic problem of interbureaucratic coordination remained, and in fact, was exacerbated by the multiple jurisdictions the law established. Under the law the DDF enforced emissions standards for vehicles and the commercial sector inside Mexico City, but not for industry (this was SEDUE's, and later, SEDESOL's responsibility). Nor could the city enforce standards in localities outside of the Federal District that comprised the greater Metropolitan Zone. Camacho's legal authority ended at the city limits and his regulatory reach was circumscribed even within city boundaries. While the DDF could encourage others to support the PICCA, it could not compel their participation. At best, these agencies related to the mayor as a peer; at worst, as a rival; but never as a superior. Table 5.3 illustrates the gaps between the jurisdictional scope of the environmental agencies in the Metropolitan Zone and the contaminating sectors in their jurisdiction.

To expedite implementation, Camacho determined to gain greater leverage over his bureaucratic peers by restructuring their basic institutional relationship. In late 1991 he made his case to President Salinas for a more hierarchical policy-making structure and on January 6, 1992, Salinas came through. The result was a presidential decree creating the Metropolitan Commission for the Prevention and Control of Environmental Pollution in the Metropolitan Area of the Valley of Mexico.[63] Among its permanent members were the mayor of Mexico City, the

Table 5.3   Overlapping Jurisdictions and Regulatory Gaps Established by the 1988 General Law

Entity	Jurisdiction			Sectors Subject to Regulation		
	Federal District	Metropolitan Zone	State of Mexico	Industrial Sector	Commercial Sector	Transport Vehicles
DDF	x				x	x
SEDUE/ SEDESOL	x	x	x	x		
St. of Mex.		x	x		x	x

governor of the state of Mexico, the director general of Pemex, and the ministers of Finance, Energy, Transportation, Health, and SEDUE (soon to be replaced by the new Social Development minister). The decree established both a commission president and technical secretary; the latter would run its day-to-day operations and both terms rotated biannually (thus, those who occupied the commission's top posts would retain office through the end of the Salinas administration). Not surprisingly, the commission's first president was the *Regente* of the Federal District, Manuel Camacho,[64] and at Camacho's behest, Salinas selected Fernando Menéndez Garza (director of the DDF's General Coordination on Environmental Projects) to serve as technical secretary.

The Metropolitan Commission was a classic example of effective institutional innovation. On the one hand, the post of commission *president* abolished the "horizontal equality" of its members (at least with respect to environmental responsibilities) and established vertical lines of authority between Camacho and his new subordinates; on the other hand, with city officials serving as both commission president and technical secretary, the DDF consolidated authority over environmental programs for the duration of Camacho's tenure. The result (illustrated in figure 5.1) was the fortification of *command and control* advocates at the expense

Figure 5.1   Mexico City's Evolving Environmental Policy-Making Structure, 1989–1992

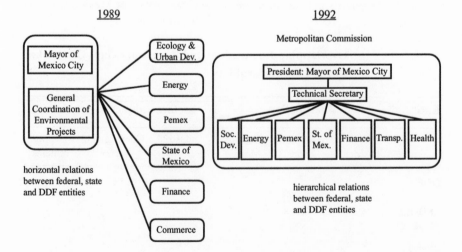

of any would-be reformers.[65] These institutional modifications—designed expressly to advance the PICCA—dimmed the prospects of swift policy change; yet possibilities still remained. Nine months later SEDESOL's Office of Economic and Social Analysis was up and running. But faced with stiff institutional constraints and intense jockeying of presidential aspirants, OESA's reform campaign quickly ran out of steam.

In October 1992 OESA's department of environmental policy began the drive to rationalize environmental policy and craft measures to achieve environmental objectives via economic incentives. Toward this end its first task was to assess how cost-effective Mexico's environmental policy regime really was. It quickly drew up plans to study every aspect of the regime including the PICCA—from regulations to enforcement, and from the federal level down to local governments, including parastatal entities. This massive top-to-bottom policy review and any subsequent reforms would "cost" its sponsor, OESA, nothing; they would, however, generate substantial political costs for Mayor Manuel Camacho and ironically, the minister of social development, Luis Donaldo Colosio.

Both Colosio and Camacho hoped to carry their party's banner into the 1994 presidential campaign. "By tradition," however, "those who aspire to the PRI's presidential nomination cannot openly campaign for it. . . . [although their supporters] work diligently behind the scenes to advance their man's prospects and to discredit other contenders."[66] In light of these unwritten rules OESA's policy review spelled trouble. There was little chance the final report would be released to the public, but its findings were bound to reverberate inside the corridors of power. They almost certainly would reflect poorly on the city government and embarrass Camacho in the process; yet this outcome would hardly advantage Colosio. To the contrary, it would likely be interpreted as part of his presidential strategy—a political attack against his rival. For Colosio this was a lose-lose scenario: the more he appeared to be campaigning for the nomination, the less likely he would receive it; and if Camacho eventually became the candidate Colosio's career was sure to suffer under a Camacho administration.

Either way the OESA project would generate enormous political costs for the social development minister that were virtually impossible to defray. Consequently, Colosio scuttled OESA's ambitious macro policy review before it began. This clipped OESA's wings, relegated it to a backbench role and ended any hope of significant policy reform for the duration of the Salinas *sexenio*.[67] Thereafter, OESA worked to conform SEDESOL's regulations to the new cost-benefit standard and conducted a series of feasibility studies that identified environmental issues most suitable for market-like remedies. The fact that none of these areas related to air pollution, however, underscored that the agency's days as an aggressive fast-track policy reformer were over.[68]

Explaining Outcomes:
Environmental versus Economic Policy Reform

Mexico's record on environmental policy reform contrasts sharply with its economic achievements. The attempts to combat air pollution in Mexico City by supplementing *command and control* with economic incentives were a logical extension of neoliberal philosophy. They were born of the realization that past efforts had not solved the pollution problem and that the current approach required enormous expenditures with little appreciable gain.[69] They also reflected the belief that effective pollution control measures, achieved in part via economic incentives, would complement economic reform by encouraging polluters (especially industry) to abandon inefficient, pollution-generating production practices. Under the highly technocratic Salinas administration the prospects of success appeared bright. Yet, five years of effort brought only meager results. Why?

One possibility, of course, is that the government simply lacked the interest required to achieve reform. This explanation, however, is unsatisfying. Even if we concede the administration's environmental rhetoric was partly a mask for symbolic politics, the $4.6 billion Comprehensive Program signaled a clear commitment to combat pollution, and as we have seen, the PICCA's economic inefficiencies gave some powerful actors ample incentives to push reform measures. It was not for lack of interest that these efforts failed.

A second approach might emphasize how the "lock-in" effects of past policy choice diminished any real chance of changing the multibillion dollar PICCA at all. Because the program's specifics (converting oil refineries and thermoelectric plants, retrofitting bus and taxi fleets, establishing effective administrative and enforcement mechanisms, etc.) shaped investment patterns among powerful state entities, they created a network of financial commitments that stretched far into the future. These sunk costs made scrapping the PICCA in toto a non-starter. Yet this position does not pass close scrutiny. Since few reform initiatives ever contemplated so dramatic an about-face, a lock-in argument cannot explain why more modest reform efforts failed to gain traction.

A third possibility is that the sheer complexity of Mexico City's air pollution problem and its multiple causes (demographics, transportation, industrialization, and geography) exceeded the government's capacity to craft and implement suitable policy reforms. Perhaps so. Yet, this position cannot account for why initiatives designed expressly to tackle complexity issues (i.e., the macro policy reviews contemplated by the interministerial task force and OESA) were aborted or never adopted. A more credible explanation is the absence of factors that proved crucial to successful economic reform: strong reform coalitions, effective institutional innovation by would-be reformers, and a willingness (or ability) to compensate "losers" for the costs of policy change.

Coalition Politics

As prior chapters indicate, coalitions are integral to successful reform. They provide the organizational strength needed to overcome resistance inside the state, control the policy agenda, and facilitate the cross-agency collaboration required to formulate, adopt, and implement new policy. They also expand the pool of resources from which reformers might compensate opponents to offset the costs of policy change. Perhaps the most striking contrast between Mexico's economic and environmental reform campaigns is the absence of dynamic coalition politics in the latter. Indeed, on this point both reform "waves" fell short.

During the first wave, the highly competitive political culture inside City Hall worked against interagency collaboration to the point reformers were hard put to perceive the benefits of joint action, or even their common interests in reforming the PICCA. To illustrate, when asked why its counterparts were not party to the General Direction of Pollution Prevention and Control's auto reconversion proposal, the agency's director replied: "They have their responsibilities, and I have mine; it's not necessary that we meet together or coordinate our activities."[70] While valid, this attitude also reflects a certain political immaturity: cosponsored proposals would almost certainly have carried more weight and been harder to ignore. Quick to protect their agencies' independence, would-be reformers squandered the potential to make real gains through aggressive collaboration.

But the failure to forge a dynamic coalition cannot be attributed solely to political culture or mere shortsightedness. Reformers at City Hall also lacked the close ideational proximity (i.e., policy preference) crucial to coalitional cohesion. As Robert Axelrod demonstrated thirty years back, ideological convergence (shared policy preference) is a major factor behind individual decisions to join a coalition,[71] and among city government reformers this quality was in short supply. The principal reformers inside City Hall—Gabriel Quadri, a trained economist, and Ramón Ojeda Mestre, an attorney—were hardly philosophical soulmates, and their divergent reform initiatives reflected as much. They both believed the PICCA should be modified, but never possessed the ideational singularity of Mexico's economic reformers. While it is difficult to ascertain the degree to which this inhibited collaboration between their agencies, it is not illogical to assume it played no role at all.

The potential for a strong reform coalition was greater during the second wave, especially with respect to the Finance/Budget Ministry task force project. But ultimately, that potential went unrealized. Both ministries shared a history of collaboration, common interests in minimizing the costs of pollution abatement, and an intellectual affinity for market-like prescriptions. They knew how to influence the policy agenda by exploiting their power of the purse, and clearly demonstrated this ability against SEDUE—a weak, underfunded agency in a state of perpetual crisis. The creation of SEDESOL changed everything, however. Its analytical capacity and strategic partisan activities, i.e., PRONASOL, provided the stature to counter Finance, plus the credibility and muscle to reassert independence from the interministerial task force. The peculiar politics of presidential succession, meanwhile, gave social development minister Colosio strong incentives *not* to share any credit for reform by collaborating with potential rivals, and in the end, to privilege political advancement over policy reform itself.

Institutional Innovation

Although various factors worked against coalition formation, the absence of strong, pro-reform coalitions was not the only obstacle to success. Reform advocates also fell victim to an inhospitable institutional context. In general, institutions that established actors' organizational positions and structured interagency relations offered reformers few initial advantages; even worse, in terms of institutional innovation, *command and control* proponents routinely beat reformers to the punch. Consider the early reform struggles inside the Department of the Federal District. Unlike the General Coordination for Environmental Projects, the positions would-be reformers occupied in the city bureaucracy afforded neither vertical nor horizontal influence over their peers, and hence, no real leverage over policy-making procedures. By contrast, the General Coordination moved quickly to exploit its organizational position, exert horizontal influence, and alter decision-making procedures to its advantage. In consolidating its power the agency seized control of the city's environmental programs and shunted its competitors to the periphery.

Terry Moe has argued that politically astute actors will "fashion structures to insulate their favored agencies and programs" from outside interference.[72] The GCEP exemplifies this dynamic nicely. There also is a "timing" aspect to Moe's insight, however, which warrants special attention. Simply put, *precedents matter,* and significant political advantages accrue to those who are "first out of the gate" at innovation. Those who set or rearrange the rules of the game not only determine the parameters in which others act, but can profoundly influence the value of any subsequent innovations that might be engineered. A striking example is the peculiar status of SEDESOL's Office of Economic and Social Analysis.

As noted, OESA was similar to, but fundamentally different than, the Offices of Deregulation and Privatization. The latter were typical of the instrument-creating behavior described in chapter 2. They were designed expressly to centralize policy authority inside insulated subunits. Their authority stemmed directly from presidential decrees that provided *legal mandates to undertake policy reform.* This allowed Mexico's deregulators, for example, to husband their resources and focus on a single policy objective. By contrast, OESA lacked a firm legal standing and single-theme mission: its operations encompassed various policy arenas (only one of which was environmental policy) and were based not on law, but solely on the minister of social development's authority.

The distinction was highly consequential. OESA neither centralized policy authority inside the unit nor provided would-be reformers appreciable autonomy to act. Perhaps most important, without the anchor of a legal mandate, OESA's environmental reform operations were subject to the discretion of the social development minister, and as we have seen, were easily curtailed. In part, the agency's unusual status reflected its creation as a vehicle to advance Donaldo Colosio's political prospects, not a specific set of environmental policy reforms. But presidential politics tell only part of the story. The *prior creation* of the Metropolitan Commission required OESA to function within the parameters it established. In terms of Mexico City's antipollution project those parameters subordinated SEDESOL (and therefore, OESA) to Mayor Camacho Solís and provided an explicit legal mandate to promote (not reform) the PICCA. Under these circumstances OESA's prospects of acquiring a legal mandate equivalent to its economic counterparts were remote at best.

In chapter 2 I argued that institutional variables were politically consequential; they structure political interaction in ways that limit what some actors can do, and enable others to do things they otherwise could not. Although the institutional context severely hampered would-be reformers, their ultimate failure was hardly inevitable (as we have seen, institutional dynamics also confounded *command and control* adherents). The outcome was determined as much by reformers' inability to advance their agenda via institutional innovation as by their protagonists' capacity to do so. The evidence presented reveals how consequential this was.

The Problem of Policy Costs

A third set of factors behind the reformers' poor showing centers on the issue of policy "costs." Because policy change is rarely pareto optimal it tends to generate winners and losers. A cardinal proposition in political science is that self-interested actors will support/promote policies that preserve or enhance their present status and vice versa.[73] As prior chapters indicate, conflict over policy costs is intrinsic to the reform process and displays distinct patterns as that process proceeds: conflict typically erupts between state actors over policy formulation and adoption, and again between state/societal actors during policy implementation. To advance reform, advocates must solve this dilemma by minimizing the costs of change or imposing them on potential losers. Because imposition strategies run the risk of political backlash, compensation is generally the tool of choice. Economic reformers, for example, eventually found it possible to minimize costs and achieve their goals partly by compensating potential losers as exemplified by Aeroméxico's pilots, Sicartsa's steelworkers, Cananea's miners, and even the Ministry of Transportation.

The fact that environmental reformers never perfected this tactic clearly worked against them. The one exception, of course, was the auto reconversion program which sought to upgrade Mexico City's vehicle fleet. To facilitate *implementation* this program promised to compensate auto dealers for low profit margins by creating a large, city-wide new car "market." This did nothing, however, to facilitate the policy's *adoption* (indeed, the General Coordination's refusal to support it, and other reform measures, was largely a product of the attendant costs). Absent any appreciable cost-offsetting measures, this reform initiative—and others—found little resonance among cost-bearers inside the state; it is not surprising that few were ever adopted.

Given the obvious impediment posed by policy costs, why were reformers slow to address this point? The answer is twofold. First, on the whole, environmental reformers exhibited less political sophistication than their economic counterparts, in part, due to a lack of experience (for example, save for the interministerial task force, would-be reformers were far less experienced at the politics of reform than those who engineered Mexico's massive divestment project). Second, reformers simply had little to offer potential losers. Change advocates at the DDF and OESA were in no position to help offset the monetary, political, or institutional costs their initiatives generated. For one thing, the absence of coalition partners invariably reduced the resources available to craft compensation packages. Equally important, as designed, the reform initiatives provided key cost-bearers (Camacho and Menéndez Garza at City Hall, and Donaldo Colosio at SEDESOL) no immediate gains to defray perceived costs. No doubt they would gladly have claimed credit for any environmental improvements achieved through economic incentives. But since such benefits would only materialize well down the line, this offered little incentive to shoulder heavy costs in the short term.

A close examination of Mexico's economic and environmental policy reform records highlights the pitfalls governments face in promoting neoliberal reforms. If any government seemed uniquely equipped to inject economic rationality into traditional *command and control* policies, it was the Salinas administration—staffed by savvy politicians, renowned for its technocratic expertise, and exemplary in its economic achievements. The failure to extend neoliberal principles into the environmental policy realm does not diminish Mexico's economic accomplishments, however. To the contrary, its record on economic reform remains impressive. Nevertheless, the sharp contrast in outcomes aptly illustrates the political minefield that awaits reform advocates and the difficulties of traversing it.

Despite repeated attempts to modify *command and control,* Mexico's environmental policy regime remained fundamentally unaltered from what it had been in 1988; indeed, the interests arrayed in support of *command and control* grew stronger. The evidence presented strongly suggests the paradigm's resilience turned on the very factors that brought economic reformers success—strong reform coalitions, effective institutional innovation, and a resolution to the problem of policy costs. As the record demonstrates, the presence or absence of these factors profoundly affects the prospects of successful policy change.

Notes

1. Detailed discussion of the historical record can be found in Ranier Godau Schücking, "La protección ambiental en México: sobre la conformación de una política pública," *Estudios Sociológicos* 3 (1985); and Jorge Legorreta and Ángeles Flores, "La contaminación atmosférica en el Valle de México," in *La Contaminación Atmosférica en México: Sus Causas y Efectos en Salud* (México, D.F.: Comisión Nacional de Derechos Humanos, 1992).

2. Even in Mexico's "limited pluralist" system, public agitation over environmental degradation grabbed policy makers' attention. Quadri provides a good, succinct review of Mexico's grassroots ecology movement in the 1980s. See Gabriel Quadri de la Torre, "Una breve crónica del ecologismo en México," *Ciencias* 4 (1990).

3. Author's interview. Mexico City, June 18, 1993.

4. Ozone is a "secondary" pollutant generated by the interaction of solar radiation, hydrocarbons, and nitrogen oxide. In 1990 ozone surpassed the government's maximum standard of 11 ppm/hr. on 86 percent of the days. *Informe de la situación general en materia de equilibrio y protección al ambiente, 1989-1990* (México, D.F.: Comisión Nacional de Ecología, 1991), 71, 76.

5. Richard A. Nuccio, "The Possibilities and Limits of Environmental Protection in Mexico," in Joseph S. Tulchin, ed., *Economic Development and Environmental Protection in Latin America* (Boulder, Colo.: Lynne Rienner, 1991), 112.

6. Martha Schteingart, "The Environmental Problems Associated with Urban Development in Mexico City," *Environment and Urbanization* 1, no. 1 (April 1989): 41.

7. See Gustavo Garza, "El Proceso de Industrialización de la Ciudad de México: 1845-2000," in *Lecturas del CEESTM*, 1, no. 3 (México, D.F.: Centro de Estudios Económicos y Sociales del Tercer Mundo, 1981); Gustavo Garza, "Hacia la superconcentración industrial en la Ciudad de México," *Atlas de la Ciudad de México* (México, D.F.: El Colegio de México y El Departamento del Distrito Federal, 1987); Nigel Harris and Sergio Puente, "Environmental Issues in the Cities of the Developing World: The Case of Mexico City," *Journal of International Development*, 2, no. 4 (1990): 506; and Robert. V. Kemper and Anyn P. Royce, "Mexican Urbanization since 1821: A Macro-Historical Approach," *Urban Anthropology* 8 (1979).

8. About 8.5 million people live in the city proper and 11 million more in its surrounding environs. See *Programa integral de lucha contra la contaminación en el Valle de México* (México, D.F.: Secretaría de Desarrollo Urbano y Ecología, Petróleos Mexicanos, Gobierno del Estado de México, Departamento del Distrito Federal, 1989), 3.

9. The higher figure is found in "La Ciudad de México Necesidad de una Descentralización," *Transformación* 2, no. 3 (March 1983). On the age of Mexico City's vehicle fleet see *Programa Integral*, 1.

10. Cradled in the Valley of Mexico, the Metropolitan Zone lies 7,000 feet above sea level and is ringed by mountains that soar another 9,000 to 16,000 feet. At this altitude the air is "thin" (e.g., 23 percent less oxygen than at sea level), fuel combustion incomplete, and solar radiation levels high. These circumstances facilitate the creation of ozone, which along with other pollutants, is trapped within the mountainous perimeter. See Fernando Menéndez Garza, "Mexico City's Program to Reduce Air Pollution," in Joseph S. Tulchin, ed., *Economic Development and Environmental Protection in Latin America* (Boulder, Colo.: Lynne Rienner, 1991); and Rodolfo Lacy, *La calidad del aire en el Valle de México* (México, D.F.: El Colegio de México, 1993). On the effects of altitude on combustion and ozone, see Jorge

Legorreta, *Transporte y contaminación en la Ciudad de México* (México, D.F.: Centro de Ecodesarrollo, 1989); on thermal inversions see *Desarrollo y medio ambiente en México. Diagnóstico, 1990* (México, D.F.: Fundación Universo Veintiuno, Fundación Friedrich Ebert Stiftung, 1990), 51-62; and Exequiel Ezcurra, "Las Inversiones Térmicas," *Ciencias* 22 (April 1991): 51-53.

11. See "Ley Federal para Prevenir y Controlar la Contaminación Ambiental," *Diario Oficial*, March 23, 1971; "Reglamento para la prevención y control de la contaminación atmosférica por la emisión de humos y polvos," *Diario Oficial*, September 17, 1971; and "Ley Federal de Protección al Ambiente," *Diario Oficial*, January 11, 1982. Centralization reflected more than the perceived advantages of maintaining federal jurisdiction over national environmental problems. As one high level official at the Ecology Ministry explained, the government's attitude bore the imprint of traditional elitism central authorities displayed toward the country's interior: "solo los chilangos saben lo que hacer"—or only the officials in Mexico City know best how to manage the problem. Author's interview. Mexico City, July 16, 1993.

12. One city agency that did display action was the General Direction of Urban Restructuring and Ecologic Protection. In the 1980s this agency developed several environmental protection projects, but lacked the financial, technical, and legal resources to tackle air pollution effectively. See *Memoria de gestión, General Dirección de Protección Ambiental 1982–1988* (México, D.F.: Departamento del Distrito Federal, 1988).

13. Author's interviews. Mexico City, June 22, 1992, and July 21, 1993. See also Raúl Monge, "Ní siquiera planes contra la contaminación existen, reconoce Sedue," *Proceso* 482 (January 27, 1986); and *Mexican Environmental Laws, Regulations, and Standards: Preliminary Report of EPA Findings* (Washington, D.C.: Environmental Protection Agency, May 3, 1991, revised June 27, 1991), 5.

14. See Enrique Velázquez, "Política Ecología Institucional: El Caso del Valle de México," *El Cotidiano* 47 (May 1990): 33; and Charles T. DuMars and Salvador Beltran del Río M., "A Survey of the Air and Water Quality Laws of Mexico," *Natural Resources Journal*, 28, no. 4 (Fall 1988): 808.

15. Indeed, the ministry's department chiefs could do little more than watch as highly trained technicians were lured away by more lucrative salaries in the public sector and elsewhere. Author's interview. Mexico City, May 21, 1992.

16. *Mexican Environmental Laws, Regulations, and Standards;* see also Ramón Ojeda Mestre, "Notas sobre Legislación Mexicana Referentes a la Contaminación," paper presented to the Standing Committee on Environmental Law of the American Bar Association and the Asociación Mexicana de Abogados, Mexico City, June 2-3, 1983.

17. Although specific data on SEDUE's earliest operations in Mexico City are unavailable, national figures suggest a pattern of weak inspection and lax enforcement. Between 1982 and 1984 SEDUE conducted 1,209 inspections nationwide, but issued *no* fines at all; between 1985 and 1988 the ministry conducted 5,405 inspections and issued only 179 fines. *Mexican Environmental Laws, Regulations, and Standards.* See also Linda Závala, "No Hay Reglamento Contra las Empresas que Contaminan: SEDUE," *El Universal*, November 28, 1984, 23.

18. Especially before mid-1986 (when a new minister took office) SEDUE officials seemed unwilling to admit the severity of Mexico City's pollution problem. For example, in January 1986 the subsecretary of ecology declared that despite soaring pollution levels there was "no reason for people to be alarmed." This stance severely undermined SEDUE's

credibility in the public eye. See Rosa Rojas, "No hay razón para la alarma, afirman Sedue y Salubridad," *La Jornada,* January 22, 1986, 1.

19. See *Informe General de Ecología,* 78; DuMars and Beltran del Río M., "A Survey of the Air and Water Quality Laws of Mexico," 807; and Luz Guerrero Cruz, "Birds Die in Winter Smog," *Voice of Mexico* 4 (June–August 1987): 49.

20. See Theodore Panayotou, "Economic Incentives in Environmental Management and Their Relevance to Developing Countries," in Denizham Eröcal, ed., *Environmental Management in Developing Countries* (Paris: Development Center of the Organization of Economic Cooperation and Development, 1991), 87.

21. The most notable "stopgap" initiatives were the 21 Emergency Measures promulgated by presidential decree in 1986, and the 100 Necessary Actions, adopted by SEDUE in 1987. The 21 Measures attacked pollution from state-owned enterprises. They required government thermoelectric plants to substitute natural gas for "dirty" sulfur-rich fuels, instructed the state-owned oil monopoly to produce low-led gasolines and low-sulfur diesel, and directed the city's public buses to install emission control devices. The 100 Necessary Actions drew up contingencies for environmental emergencies (i.e., extremely high pollution levels) that included forced school and plant closings; they also proposed verification programs for mobile and fixed emission sources. In devising these measures Mexican officials drew partly upon the regulatory experience in the United States, France, Germany, and Japan. See "21 acciones emergentes," *Diario Oficial,* February 14, 1986; and *Ecología: 100 acciones necesarias* (México, D.F.: Comisión Nacional de Ecología, SEDUE, January 1987). See also *Memoria del Primer Seminario Internacional Sobre Administración de la Calidad del Aire* (México, D.F.: Secretaría de Desarrollo Urbano y Ecología, 1987); and *Políticas y estratégias de abatimiento y control de la contaminación atmosférica en la zona metropolitana de la Ciudad de México, Memoria* (México, D.F.: Secretaría de Desarrollo Urbano y Ecología, 1988).

22. The PICCA's five main goals are to: (1) improve fuel mixtures; (2) expand public transportation, discourage private auto use, and control vehicle emissions via catalytic converters, tougher inspection programs, and cleaner fuels; (3) control emissions from industry, services, and thermoelectric plants; (4) reforest the Valley of Mexico; and (5) promote public environmental education campaigns. See *Programa integral contra la contaminación atmosférica en la zona metropolitana de la Ciudad de México: Avances a septiembre de 1991* (México, D.F.: Departamento del Distrito Federal, Gobierno del Estado de México, Instituto Mexicano del Petróleo, Petróleos Mexicanos, Secretaría de Desarrollo Urbano y Ecología, 1991).

23. On the cost of the Comprehensive Program, see *Energy and Environment Market Conditions in Mexico* (Washington, D.C.: U.S. Agency for International Development, n.d.).

24. See Bradley P. Miller, "Obedezco, Pero No Cumplo: Law, Transportation, Politics, and Pollution in Mexico City," *Stanford Journal of International Law* 28, no. 1 (Fall 1991): 235; see also Irene Gómez Baas, "Flagelo Para la Salud," *Tiempo,* November 16, 1989, 4–12.

25. See *Programa integral contra la contaminación atmosférica: Un compromiso común* (México, D.F.: Departamento del Distrito Federal, 1990), 48.

26. The law was published in the official register in January 1988 and took effect in March. See "Ley General del Equilibrio Ecológico y la Protección al Ambiente," *Diario Oficial,* January 28, 1988. For broader discussion of the General Law see Terzah N. Lewis, "Student Comment: Environmental Law in Mexico," *Denver Journal of International Law and Policy* 21, no. 1 (Fall 1992).

27. The General Assembly was created in 1988 to represent the citizenry; the first direct mayoral elections were held in 1997. For an in-depth analysis of Mexico City's political structure see Peter M. Ward, "Government without Democracy in Mexico City: Defending the High Ground," in Wayne A. Cornelius, Judith Gentleman, and Peter H. Smith, eds., *Mexico's Alternative Political Futures,* Monograph Series, 30 (La Jolla, Calif.: Center for U.S.-Mexican Studies, University of California, San Diego, 1989).

28. Carlos Salinas de Gortari, *Mensaje de Toma de Posesión* (México, D.F. Presidencia de la República, December 1, 1988), 18.

29. Author's interview. Mexico City, July 26, 1993.

30. See *Project 88—Round II: Incentives for Action: Designing Market-Based Environmental Strategies.* A Public Policy Study sponsored by Senator Timothy E. Wirth and Senator John Heinz (Washington, D.C.: n.p., May 1991), 5. For the classic argument of how government regulations can generate "social costs" that outweigh the original "damage" it was designed to correct, see Ronald H. Coase, "The Problem of Social Cost," *Journal of Law and Economics* 3 (October 1960).

31. For example, see Panayotou, "Economic Incentives in Environmental Management."

32. Panayotou, "Economic Incentives in Environmental Management," 89.

33. The one-time activists were Gabriel Quadri de la Torre and Ramón Ojeda Mestre—past leaders of the Pact of Ecologist Groups and the Mexican Academy of Ecologic Rights. The political protégés were Fernando Menéndez Garza and Jorge Gamboa de Buen.

34. Where other city environmental agencies were limited to a staff of four, the GCEP built its personnel levels up to thirty-six. Author's interviews. Mexico City, June 16 and 24, 1992.

35. In fact, the General Coordination even increased its analytic abilities at the expense of its competitors by recruiting its rivals' top analysts. Author's interview. Mexico City, July 16, 1992.

36. See Miller, "Obedezco, Pero No Cumplo," 190.

37. The author attended the meeting at which this plan was proposed to Mexico City auto dealers.

38. The "polluter pays principle" (PPP) stipulates that those who generate environmental externalities should assume the cost of subsequent government abatement measures. Polluters "pay" for abatement measures through such schemes as emissions charges, administrative charges (to cover costs of monitoring and regulation), or input taxes (i.e., on energy or chlorofluoro carbons). The PPP was developed by the Organization of Economic Cooperation and Development and is used most widely in OECD countries. See *The Polluter Pays Principle* (Paris: OECD, 1975); and *OECD and the Environment* (Paris: OECD, 1986).

39. See *Bases de gestión de la calidad del aire para la zona metropolitana de la Ciudad de México* (México, D.F.: Departamento del Distrito Federal, n.d.), 4.

40. Sheer politics, of course, also played a part: the fact that Menéndez's political rivals were the architects of the reform proposals hardly made them more palatable.

41. Ramón Ojeda Mestre, general director of pollution prevention, resigned on November 21, 1990, after publicly criticizing the DDF's overall air pollution program. Gabriel Quadri, director of ecological planning, retained his office, but lost his staff (to the General Coordination) and his influence on policy issues after going "public" with articles critical of the DDF's *command and control* approach. Author's interview. Mexico City, July 16, 1992. On Mestre's criticisms and resignation see Roberto Mena, "Business World," *News,*

June 15, 1990, 30; and Miller, "Obedezco, Pero No Cumplo," 174-175 and 188-189.

42. See *Programa nacional para la protección del medio ambiente 1990–1994* (México, D.F.: Secretaría de Desarrollo Urbano y Ecología, 1990), 40.

43. Figures on auto sales, registrations, and fuel consumption patterns are derived from an unpublished World Bank report. On the annual expense of *Hoy no Circula* see Lacy, *La Calidad del Aire en el Valle de México,* 59.

44. This was the Task Force to Modernize Environmental and Economic Policy. See *Mexico Environmental Project,* 25–27.

45. Examples of economic and self-financing instruments would include taxing older, polluting vehicles, levying surcharges on gasoline, and imposing fees to process environmental impact assessments, etc.

46. The World Bank experienced a sort of "green conversion" in the mid-1980s after being severely criticized for funding "environmentally insensitive" projects in Brazil, Indonesia, and India. Accordingly, the Bank created an Environment Department (staffed by 100 personnel), allocated funds specifically for "environmental projects," and altered its loan criteria to require environmental impact statements for all Bank-funded development projects. See "The U.S. Debate over the Environmental Performance of Four Multilateral Development Banks," *Ambio* 15, no. 5 (1986); Pat Aufderheid and Bruce Rich, "Environmental Reform and the Multilateral Banks," *World Policy Journal* 5 (Spring 1988); and *Environment and Development: Implementing the World Bank's New Policies* (Washington, D.C.: The World Bank, 1988).

47. See Jennifer Smith, "Salinas KOs Sedue; Chirinos to Veracruz," *News,* April 8, 1992, 1.

48. Author's interviews. Mexico City, July 22 and August 5, 1993.

49. For an exhaustive treatment of PRONASOL, see Wayne A. Cornelius, Ann L. Craig, and Jonathan Fox, eds., *Transforming State-Society Relations in Mexico: The National Solidarity Strategy* (La Jolla, Calif.: Center for U.S.-Mexican Studies, University of California, San Diego, 1994).

50. Critics claimed "Solidarity [was] openly pro-PRI . . . they go into communities where people need services and, at least at that moment, the people have to support the PRI. It is delivering services with the face of the PRI." See Marjorie Miller, "The Salinas Solution," *Los Angeles Times Magazine,* November 25, 1990, 14. Examples of scholarly work that arrived at basically the same conclusion include Alberto Aziz Nassif, "Las elecciones de la restauración en México," in Alberto Aziz Nassif and Jaqueline Preschard, eds., *Las elecciones federales de 1991* (México, D.F.: Miguel Ángel Porrúa/UNAM, 1992); and Denise Dresser, "Neopopulist Solutions to Neoliberal Problems: Mexico's National Solidarity Program," *Current Issue Brief Series* 3 (La Jolla, Calif.: Center for U.S.-Mexican Studies, University of California, San Diego, 1991).

51. Miguel Ángel Ramírez, "El Programa Nacional de Solidaridad se incorporaría al nuevo organismo; Secretaría de Desarrollo Social por Sedue; Colosio, al frente," *El Nacional,* April 8, 1992, 3.

52. Other technocrats like Jaime Serra (commerce minister) and José Córdoba Montoya (Office of the Presidency) were ineligible to serve as president due to foreign-born parents.

53. Colosio served as minister of ecology for the brief interim between the announcement of SEDESOL's creation and the Senate's ratification of changes to the Organic Law which abolished SEDUE and created the new Social Development Ministry.

54. In 1992 Colosio's political star was already on the rise: he had performed well as president of the PRI and under his leadership the party recovered from the near debacle of

the 1988 elections. Colosio also navigated the party through the treacherous waters of coalitional reconstruction churned up by Salinas's privatization and deregulation campaigns—both of which sharply attacked formerly privileged actors. Under Colosio the PRI regained private sector confidence and reconstituted a base of support among the beneficiaries of neoliberal reform.

55. Ironically, although the 1988 General Law gave the Department of the Federal District lead agency status in Mexico City's environmental problems, SEDUE often bore the brunt of public criticism, and its top officials suffered public ridicule. On those rare occasions when strong wind patterns "cleared" the air over the city skyscape, the running joke was that Mexicans owed their relief to the "Ministry of Wind." See Patricia Bush, "Pollution Plan Shines on a Clear Day in the City," *News,* February 2, 1992, 2. On the general state of "disrepair" at SEDUE, see Julia Carabia, "La Política Ecológica de la SEDUE," in Enrique Leff, ed., *Medio ambiente y desarrollo en México* (México, D.F.: Siglo XXI, 1990).

56. While the attorney general for environmental protection would enforce environmental law and prosecute violators, the National Ecology Institute would formulate the technical norms of environmental regulations.

57. Two prominent examples were OESA's general coordinator, Carlos Hurtado (Ph. D. economics, University of Chicago) and its director general of environmental policy, Juan Carlos Beleaustegüigoitia (Ph.D. economics, London School of Economics).

58. Environmental economics stress the role that markets or economic incentives play in sustainable development and pollution control. The recognition of Beleaustegüigoitia's preeminence in this field was shared by Mexican, World Bank, and U.S. EPA officials alike. Author's interviews. Mexico City, June 23, 1992; July 22 and 23, 1993.

59. Author's interview. Mexico City, July 23, 1993.

60. Quoted in Candace Siegle, "A City Drowning in Smog," *South,* February 1991, 18.

61. Quoted in Rodrigo Vera, "Manuel Camacho enfrenta la contaminación como un asunto de imagen," *Proceso* 738 (December 24, 1990): 6.

62. Author's interview. Mexico City, July 26, 1993.

63. See *Convenio de concertación para acelerar la lucha contra la contaminación ambiental en el Valle de México* (México, D.F.: Poder Ejecutivo, Presidencia de la República, 1992); see also *Diario Oficial,* January 8, 1992.

64. Subsequently, the commission presidency would shift to the governor of the state of Mexico, then minister of social development.

65. Besides additional authority, status quo advocates received a substantial upgrade in financial resources to boot. During its first year of operations the Metropolitan Commission's budget totaled $168 million—more than twice that commanded by SEDESOL's entire environmental program ($78 million). See Laurence Iliff, "Ecologists Hopeful Commission Can Clean up Mexico City," available from Lexis, Nexis Library, Wire Service Reports, UPI File, January 8, 1992.

66. See Wayne Cornelius, *Mexican Politics in Transition: The Breakdown of a One-Party-Dominant Regime* (La Jolla, Calif.: Center for U.S.-Mexican Studies, University of California, San Diego, 1996), 38.

67. Author's interview. Mexico City, June 22, 1993.

68. One of OESA's initiatives, for example, would create deposit schemes for discarded items that wrought environmental damage like used car batteries, oil, and tires.

69. Obviously, pollution levels would have been even higher without the Comprehensive Program, but for some reformers, this was really a question about the pace of deterioration, not of actual improvement.

70. Author's interview. Mexico City, June 6, 1990.

71. Robert Axelrod, "Conflict of Interest, an Axiomatic Approach," *Journal of Conflict Resolution* 11 (1967).

72. Terry M. Moe, "Political Institutions: The Neglected Side of the Story," *Journal of Law, Economics, and Organization* 6 (1990): 228.

73. The proposition forms the bedrock of the calculus Ames termed "political survival." See Barry Ames, *Political Survival: Politicians and Public Policy in Latin America* (Berkeley, Calif.: University of California Press, 1987).

Part III

Generalizing the Argument
and Conclusion

Chapter 6

Policy Reform in Comparative Perspective: Privatization in Argentina

Those years [of reform] were very stressful. We went into battle every week, every day.

—Domingo Cavallo

As Mexico's experience suggests, and reformers in the de la Madrid and Salinas governments can attest, the transition from statist to market policies is exceedingly difficult. I have argued that, ultimately, the reformers' success hinged upon coalitions, their institutional context, and the extent to which they solved the problem of policy costs. Because these dynamics proved critical across presidential administrations—and even policy realms—Mexico's experience affirms the basic propositions regarding policy reform set forth in chapter 1. To recap: To formulate and adopt coherent reform programs requires the development of a powerful coalition—one committed to policy change and insulated from countervailing forces in and outside the state. To implement reform successfully, this coalition must expand its membership to include at least some potential policy "losers."

To fully substantiate such claims, of course, these general propositions should be tested against a larger case selection outside the Mexican context. Although such an endeavor is beyond this project's scope, this chapter takes a first step toward broader comparative analysis by reviewing (briefly) the record of another Latin American reformer, Argentina. It lays particular stress on government efforts to privatize public sector corporations—focusing not on any one enterprise, but the process as a whole. The merits of this exercise are threefold.

First, like Mexico, the Argentine government pursued statist development for decades, following a similar policy trajectory that produced similar political constraints to reform (i.e., policy feedback and the reformer's dilemma). When reformers moved to divest public enterprises, therefore, they met stiff resistance

169

both in and outside the state. Second, despite these obstacles and significant set-backs, Argentina eventually established an impressive divestment record: among the nine major Latin American privatizers of the 1990s, it ranks second only to Mexico (see table 6.1). Understanding how the Argentines managed this achievement can help identify common determinants of success and strengthen the generalizability of our basic analytic framework.

Finally, the Argentine case offers unique comparative value. The privatization campaign began in 1985 under the government of Raúl Alfonsín, but with few exceptions it went nowhere. By 1989 the administration had managed to sell only four of 305 PEs, and the treasury had bagged only about $32 million in sales revenue (in an economy whose GNP was $70 billion).[1] By contrast, Alfonsín's successor, Carlos Saúl Menem, privatized more than 121 public firms between 1989 and 1994; many were among the largest, most politically important PEs in the government's portfolio. As in Mexico, the explanation for these dissimilar outcomes rests on the central political properties of successful reform (table 6.2 provides a quick summary of divestment outcomes mapped to explanatory variables).

Table 6.1   Major Divestment Programs in Latin American Countries, 1990–1995

	1990		1991		1992		1993		1994		1995		1990–1995	
	X	Y	X	Y	X	Y	X	Y	X	Y	X	Y	X	Y
Mexico	57	1.47	48	4.83	35	2.83	22	0.85	12	0.29	nd	nd	174	2.00
Argentina	11	1.94	10	0.93	39	2.23	37	1.75	24	0.30	2	0.46	123	1.21
Nicaragua	1	0.07	7	0.19	22	0.68	26	3.92	19	0.92	nd	nd	75	1.52
Peru	0	0	3	0.01	11	0.51	15	0.28	30	5.42	13	2.05	72	1.58
Brazil	1	0.01	5	0.33	16	0.48	8	0.48	14	0.28	1	0.06	45	0.27
Honduras	3	0.04	4	0.31	10	0.79	11	0.87	4	0.18	nd	nd	32	0.45
Venezuela	1	0.02	7	3.47	10	0.20	6	0.05	3	0.01	2	0.05	29	0.61
Bolivia	0	0	0	0	8	0.17	18	0.24	0	0	2	10.19	28	2.03
Colombia	0	0	5	0.30	4	0.01	4	0.61	3	0.24	nd	nd	16	0.24

X: The number of divestment transactions completed.
Y: Divestment revenues as a percentage of Gross Domestic Product.

Source: Inter-American Development Bank, *Progreso económico y social en America Latina: Cómo organizar con éxito los servicios sociales* (Washington, D.C.: Inter-American Development Bank, 1996).

Table 6.2   Argentina: A Comparison of Divestment Outcomes across Administrations

Determinant Factors	Alfonsín	Menem
Coalitions	no	yes
Effective Inst'l Innovation	no	yes
Policy Costs	unaddressed	addressed
Level of Success	low	moderate/high

In the end, the fate of both administrations' divestment programs turned largely upon reformers' capacity to forge strong coalitions, obtain leverage over policy through effective institutional innovation, and resolve the problem of policy costs via minimizing and imposition strategies.

Argentina: National Development and Institutional Context

Modern Argentina is the product of a unique political history characterized by massive immigration waves, deep social cleavages, and class animosities. Although these forces eventually produced a presidentialist system built upon highly competitive political parties (Peronism and Radicalism), the political system itself was far from stable. For most of the twentieth century a cycle of political turmoil gripped the nation as limited democratic, authoritarian, and military regimes came to power, fell, and then rose again. After its humiliating Falkland Islands defeat in 1982, the last military government ceded power to civilians and Raúl Alfonsín's middle-class Radical Party triumphed over the mass-based Peronists at the polls in 1983.[2]

Argentine Statism

During much of this century, Argentina, like Mexico, embraced a statist, import-substitution development model, initially as an ad hoc response to the economic distortions of the Great Depression. Beginning with Juan Perón (1946 to 1955), however, the government consciously pushed national development through public enterprise creation, low taxes, mass consumption, and protection/subsidies for domestic industry.[3] In the post-Perón era government intervention expanded categorically and by degree. Public sector growth was particularly significant: failing private firms were nationalized, new public enterprises (PEs) were created to fill production gaps and expand services, and new bureaucracies sprouted to manage resource and benefit allocations.[4] This process transformed the Argentine state into a major employer. Between 1955 and 1976, the number of public enterprise workers jumped from 148,000 to 431,000, while employment in the general government bureaucracy grew from 394,000 to 684,000.[5] By the late 1980s two million workers were employed directly by the government as a whole, and a million more indirectly via suppliers.[6]

Not surprisingly, state expansion spawned a host of vested interests. Organized labor, for example, captured the public sector, raising wages there significantly above those in many private firms. Private business interests, meanwhile, forged close ties to the state—as downstream consumers of cheap PE outputs, suppliers of PE production, or through various mechanisms as recipients of rents. And political incumbents of all stripes (Peronist, Radical, or military) stacked the bureaucracy with supporters, dispensing patronage to buy allies and reward friends, or withholding it to punish enemies. Such incentive structures gave statism a resilience that withstood multiple regime transitions of variable ideologies, and efforts by military regimes to reverse statist trends.[7] Consequently, notes Julio Cueto-Rua: "The tendency toward a large state role in the economy continued regardless of the nature of the government, military or civilian, Peronist or Radical. By the 1980s the statist economic regime had become so widespread that only a small group of conservative and provincial political parties actively opposed the state's quasi socialist economic policies."[8]

Yet Argentina's parastatals were anything but profitable. Between 1965 and 1987 the government pumped more than 2.5 times the subsidies into the public sector than it spent on defense, and more than six times the funds allocated to the social security system.[9] By 1988 state firms realized a combined loss equivalent to 5.5 percent of the gross national product, and cost the government $1.17 billion in subsidies to maintain their operations.[10] As in Mexico, many problems in the public sector stemmed from the inefficiencies generated in protected and monopoly markets, the perversion of the principal-agent relationship, featherbedding, excessive regulation, and rent-seeking. In addition, Argentine PEs had to comply with the Buy Argentine Law (Compre Argentino). Designed to promote private domestic business (PE suppliers), Compre Argentino required PEs to procure inputs domestically and allowed suppliers to sell to the state at above market prices.

Prior analysis of Mexico confirms that institutional factors play a major role in reformers' ability to effect significant policy change. Institutional relationships structure political interaction, shape patterns of governance (power centers, representation vehicles, contestation arenas, etc.), form the context for actors' strategic choice, and affect actors' capacities to influence the outcome of political/policy struggles. Because Argentina's institutional context was similar to Mexico's—yet different in crucial respects—the challenges, constraints, and opportunities to advance reform differed as well.[11]

The Institutional Context

Like Mexico, Argentina's formal institutions concentrated power and authority inside the executive branch to the point some have labeled the system "hyperpresidentialist."[12] Traditionally, the vast majority of legislative bills originated with the president, not Congress. Moreover, Argentine executives could appoint cabinet members without legislative confirmation, dismiss governors and other elected state officials, control central bank operations, and govern unilaterally by decree.[13] Compared to Mexico's "classic" model, however, the "strong" Argentine executive was relatively weak. Intense party competition, party factionalism and "loose corporatism" all tempered centralist tendencies, creating a moderate legislative balance to executive power and patterns of representation and contestation quite distinct from Mexico's.

For example, where the PRI provided Mexican presidents a rubber stamp legislative majority, the Argentine president and Congress did not automatically sing the same tune. During periods when both Radical and Peronist participation was allowed, legislators frequently sought partisan advantage—contesting the initiatives of presidents from opposing parties and eschewing bipartisanship "on principle." Party factionalism and indiscipline also diluted presidential power: in the 1970s and 1980s party factions effectively thwarted the stabilization policies of Peronist and Radical presidents alike.[14]

But it was Argentine corporatism that traditionally provided the strongest brake on presidential power, mainly by facilitating a highly aggressive and increasingly autonomous mode of representation that sharply reduced the autonomy of national leaders. Here, the contrast with Mexico was stark. Where Mexico's hegemonic PRI incorporated, "represented," and ultimately demobilized major social sectors (thus, insulating the policy elite and facilitating the adoption of reforms contrary to pressure group interests), the links between Argentina's parties and corporatist organs were never as tight. Instead, powerful corporatist bodies (comprising labor, landowners, and industrialists) typically functioned beyond the scope of party influence.[15] Even labor's affiliation with Peronism, some contend, was more shadow than substance. As James McGuire observed:

> Since its inception in the mid-1940s, Peronism has been strong as a collective identity, but weakly institutionalized as a party. Peronists have long regarded unions and plebiscitarian leaders, not party organizations, as the actors that really represent them. Restrictions on Peronist electoral participation from 1955 to 1972 reinforced the view that Perón and the unions embodied what mattered to the movement.[16]

Similarly, Argentina's major labor, industrial, and landowner corporatist entities routinely worked outside of political parties, growing more autonomous as the cycle of regime changes progressively "de-coupled" them from party politics and control.

Partisan/corporatist disarticulation had significant political and economic repercussions. In large measure corporatist organs overshadowed Congress and parties as preferred vehicles of political representation. Since Congress typically blocked or modified (but rarely initiated) legislation, they tended to bypass the legislature and direct their efforts toward capturing the president's attention.[17] The more prominent the state's economic role became, the stronger the incentives grew to pressure state leaders for economic advantages, and the more disruptive these groups' activities could be.[18] Through strikes and protests, capital flight, production slowdowns, or direct appeals to the president, labor and capitalist corporatist bodies pressed their demands, decreasing policy makers' degrees of freedom and forcing economic policy further away from "neutral" market principles. The upshot was twofold. Politically, "loose corporatism" produced a pattern of broad, vigorous contestation played out on multiple levels beyond the ballot box: in the executive (lobbying the president), the streets (labor protests), and the broader economy (production slowdowns, threatened layoffs).[19] Economically, it helped spawn a regime "in which the function of allocating resources and distributing income to production factors took place, not through market mechanisms . . . but through a system dominated by relentless, uncaring pressure groups."[20]

The era of reform saw a decline in corporatist bodies' utility as representation vehicles. Firms opposed to divestiture, for example, often pursued their own interests individually rather than rely solely on collective action; and in 1990 internal fissures split labor's principal peak organization into pro- and antireform factions. Nevertheless, the pattern of autonomous, party-decoupled interest articulation remained strong. These dynamics sharply reduced policy makers' autonomy and would greatly complicate efforts to reform public sector operations in the 1980s.

The Challenge of Policy Reform

While Argentines rejoiced at the transition to democracy in 1983, the disgraced military rulers left behind a record of economic mismanagement.[21] External debt, rampant inflation, trade imbalances, industrial bankruptcies, capital flight, and chronic fiscal deficits dominated the economic agenda of Argentina's new civilian president, Raúl Alfonsín. With respect to public enterprises, the situation was particularly grim. The public sector contained over three hundred enterprises, and was a dominant force in the aviation, transportation, energy, industrial, and service sectors. Some corporations fell under the direct competence of the federal ministries of Economy and Defense—others of state governments or decentralized administrative organizations. As table 6.3 suggests, many firms were highly inefficient, debt-ridden, and imposed significant stress on the Treasury (indeed, by the late 1980s the government's largest PEs accounted for roughly half the fiscal deficit).[22]

Table 6.3   Expenditure/Income Data of Ten Largest Argentine PEs: 1989 *(in millions of U.S. dollars, June 1989 value)*

Public Enterprise	Income	Expenditures	Loss
YPF (oil)	1,774	2,800	1,026
Ferrocarriles Argentinos (railroads)	150	650	500
SEGBA (electricity, Buenos Aires)	220	650	430
Gas del Estado	150	560	410
ENTel (telephone)	535	940	405
AyE (electricity, provinces)	270	600	330
Hidronor (water)	21	131	110
Encotel (post office)	121	198	77
YCF (coal)	28	55	27

Source: SIGEP (Argentine public enterprise auditor), derived from data published in *La Nación,* February 10, 1993.

Divestment under Alfonsín: Confusion, Delays, and Derailment

After traditional populist policies failed to revive the economy, the administration reluctantly adopted more painful stabilization measures in 1985,[23] and announced plans to privatize money-losing PEs. But institutional jealousies, organizational weakness, and a deficient legal framework impeded progress. To varying degrees four separate agencies pursued divestment between 1985 and 1989: the Commission 414, Ministry of Growth Promotion, Ministry of Public Works and Services, and its dependency, the Directorate of Public Enterprises (DEP).[24] Each had mandates besides privatization, and none made much headway on this front. With little legal leverage over PEs, the commission (composed of representatives from the state, banks, and ministries) occupied a peripheral position in the bureaucracy, far removed from public sector activities; the Ministry of Growth, meanwhile, drew cold shoulders from state agencies whose support was crucial to divestment. Perhaps most important, intense power struggles kept the Ministries of Growth, Public Works and Services, and the DEP at loggerheads.[25] As a result, would-be reformers never coalesced into a cohesive "change team" typical of successful reform projects, achieved the type of cross-agency collaboration required to execute wide-scale privatizations, nor managed to forge a community of interests (coalitions and allies) strong enough to advance reform inside the state.

Complicating matters further were the general legal framework and procedures governing divestment (or better, the lack thereof). Despite at least two attempts the Alfonsín government failed to pass legislation that specified such basic points as who could determine which corporations to divest (Congress? the president?), stipulated the alternatives to outright sales (mergers, liquidations, debt-equity swaps), or clarified sale procedures for firms operated by state governments.[26] Instead, privatization responsibilities remained decentralized, leaving the burden of divestment to the very ministries, state governments, or administrative organizations which supervised specific PEs. As in Mexico, this made privatization dependent on those least interested in seeing it occur (ministries and state managers). Combined with political infighting, these institutional arrangements impeded smooth policy formulation and adoption inside the state. But even when these hurdles were apparently surmounted the administration faced additional obstacles generated by policy feedback and the reformer's dilemma.

Like Mexico, efforts to divest Argentine state assets sparked intense opposition from status quo proponents—labor, state managers, the Congress, and even the private sector. Between 1983 and 1989 labor organized thirteen general strikes against the Radical government's overall economic policies, with some staged directly against divestment initiatives.[27] Union opposition stemmed from the syndicates' ideological affinity toward statism, plus fears that divestment would cost union jobs (ultimately, it did).[28] With careers on the line, state managers opposed divestment too, and as in Mexico, manipulated corporate information to stymie proposed sales.[29] In Congress, meanwhile, Peronist legislators stridently resisted divestiture and torpedoed plans to sell the national flagship carrier, Aerolíneas Argentinas, the telephone monopoly (ENTel), and parts of the oil sector.[30] Congressional opposition also cut across party lines (like Peronists, Radicals were strongly attached to statism and traditionally had used PEs to distribute patronage). Consequently, when Peronists won a majority in Congress in 1987—but before the new legislators had assumed office—Radical lawmakers passed legislation that specifically exempted the national petroleum company from privatization.[31]

If getting divestment past Congress, state managers, and labor was problematic, overcoming private sector resistance proved equally daunting. Among the more prominent opponents from this quarter were firms that derived rents from public sector operations or feared the loss of cheap outputs and established markets. To achieve their goals powerful corporate actors pulled out the stops. Some refused to buy PEs or tendered bids designed more to stall a sale than purchase the firm; others lobbied Congress and "bought" politicians; finally, some actively provoked labor unrest (or supported it) by threatening layoffs and subsidizing disruptive labor activities.[32]

Privatization also faced some opposition from the armed forces, which operated its own industrial complex (the General Directorate of Military Factories, or Fabricaciones Militares); such opposition was partly behind the failure to divest the SOMISA steelworks in 1986.[33] The military's reservations reflected a preoccupation with security and internal institutional interests. On the one hand, it considered most firms in Fabricaciones Militares "strategic," based on their contribution to military preparedness (besides SOMISA, for example, companies involved in chemicals, heavy engineering, shipyards, and military production all fell under the Ministry of Defense). On the other hand, the Defense Ministry routinely staffed its corporations with active or retired officers and servicemen. Alfonsín's insistence on prosecuting officers for human rights violations (a product of the general's "Dirty War") already had aggravated civil-military relations; and while Alfonsín managed to survive three coup attempts between 1987 and 1988, "the imperative of good relations with the Army, Navy, and Air Force" tempered the divestment drive against Fabricaciones Militares.[34]

Finally, in terms of political strategy the divestment program simply was ill conceived. Although data remain sketchy, there is no evidence the administration seriously tried to minimize the costs of reform for perceived policy losers;[35] without such palliatives strong opposition was virtually inevitable. The constellation of forces arrayed against divestiture magnified the opponents' potency, and absent tight corporatist controls, a pliable partisan majority in Congress, or private sector allies, their tactics proved highly effective. Plans to divest firms like ENTel, the National Reinsurance Institute, and Aerolíneas Argentinas were all challenged—and derailed—by some mix of labor, private business, and congressional resistance.[36] Consequently, "[m]ost of Alfonsín's privatization deals died in Congress, at the negotiation table, or in the streets."[37]

Divestiture's fate under Alfonsín was part of a broader pattern of economic policy failure. In 1988 hard times forced the government to suspend external debt payments, the central bank began selling off its foreign reserves to maintain the national currency's value, and the administration unveiled yet another stabilization plan (Plan Primavera), ultimately, to no avail. Throughout early 1989 inflation spiked sharply: 33 percent in April, 78.4 percent in May, etc. By election day (May 14) the severe economic downturn helped Carlos Menem capture the presidency—and Peronists the Senate. It also destroyed whatever credibility the Alfonsín government retained.

Convinced he could no longer govern effectively, the outgoing president asked Menem to form an interim National Unity Government until the official inauguration in December. Wanting no ties to the Radicals' misfortunes, Menem declined and the economic tailspin continued. In June inflation reached 114.5 percent. The rapid price changes ravaged personal spending power and made simple commercial transactions nearly impossible. They also sparked widespread looting and civil disobedience: that month desperate Argentines raided hundreds of stores in several cities and the state of siege which finally restored order left eleven persons dead and 2,000 more arrested. As Argentina's economic, social, and political situation crumbled around him, Alfonsín resigned in July and asked president-elect Menem to take power six months ahead of schedule. This time Menem agreed, but the Radicals paid a heavy price for his bailout. Since the Constitution would not permit new Peronist lawmakers to be seated until December, Menem conditioned the early takeover on a Radical pledge not to block his package of economic reform bills. Accepting this proviso opened the door to dramatic policy change.

Divestment under Menem: Toward a Winning Strategy

To the surprise of Argentines in general, and his own party in particular (the Partido Justicialista or PJ), Menem pursued an aggressive reform agenda in which divestment played an integral role.[38] Like its predecessor, it too encountered opposition and setbacks. But in the end, the administration managed to transfer nearly all the state's productive and service-providing entities into private hands—a remarkable record achieved in large part through institutional innovation, coalition politics, and a mix of minimizing/imposition strategies.

In terms of institutional innovation the administration pursued two tactics that dramatically strengthened its capacity to effect swift reform: it engineered a new legal framework to govern privatization and made crucial changes in divestment policy procedures. At Menem's behest the lame-duck Radical Congress quickly passed two major pieces of legislation relative to divestiture—the law of State Reform (Law 23.696 passed in August) and the Economic Emergency Law (Law 23.697 enacted in September). The former spelled out the firms subject to divestment, granted the president sweeping authority to restructure, merge, or privatize them, and authorized Congress to create a small, bicameral commission to monitor the process; the latter abolished the Buy Argentine Law, declared all government corporations to be in a state of emergency, and empowered the president to suspend their subsidization and restructure PE management teams. Together, they established a clear, one-year timetable to undertake the reforms (which was later extended to three years), and served as a type of omnibus privatization law. The authority to replace corporate management was particularly important. Like Mexican "resectorization" it struck directly at the problem of passive resistance by state managers. Once a PE was designated a divestment candidate (a determination Congress made *ex ante* via the State Reform Law) the president could replace its managers with pro-reform, interim "trustees," charged with overseeing the privatization process.[39] This gave reformers access to corporate information and the authority to restructure (i.e., dismiss) company personnel.

These legal refinements marked a considerable improvement over prior arrangements and helped spark a divestment upsurge during Menem's first two years. By the end of 1990 the state had sold off its two television channels, a railway line and petrochemical firms, the nation's largest winery, and most important, the telephone monopoly and national airlines, Aerolíneas Argentinas. It would be wrong, however, to credit these accomplishments solely to a better legal framework. The new laws did tilt agenda control decidedly in the president's favor, but they hardly guaranteed success: in the face of staunch labor opposition or a lack of private sector support, Menem would likely have fared no better than his predecessor. Equally important was that the administration addressed the reformer's dilemma in ways conducive to constructing a pro-reform coalition—something Alfonsín never managed to achieve.

Under Alfonsín, privatization had failed, in part, because policy "losers" (labor, state managers, the private sector) strongly resisted its attendant costs, and absent adequate compensation, had engaged in effective collective action against it.[40] The new legal framework effectively ended resistance from state managers, but the threat of labor and business opposition remained. As Javier González Fraga observed, opposition to privatization was "alive and well" in these quarters,[41] and in fact, helped delay the divestment of firms like Ferrocarriles Argentinos (railways), ENTel, Aerolíneas Argentinas, and the national highways.[42] From the outset of his administration, therefore, Menem worked to transform segments of these potential opponents into stakeholders in the reform program through a careful blend of minimizing/imposition strategies—an approach, notes Edward Gibson, that "involved the selection of winners and losers within both the business community and the labor movement."[43]

To preempt a united labor front, for example, the president exploited internal fissures inside its principal peak organization (the General Labor Confederation or CGT) where rival factions—the CGT-Azorpardo and CGT-San Martín—vied for supremacy. Neither was enamored with Menem's neoliberal agenda, but the latter was more amenable than the former, mainly because it represented many syndicates involved in the private, not public sector. After encouraging the division, Menem cut off (and greatly weakened) the Azorpardo faction by recognizing the CGT-San Martín as the confederation's only official representative with the state; thereafter, he cemented the relationship with higher wages for syndicates affiliated with CGT-San Martín.[44] Similar quid pro quos helped bring unions outside the confederation on board.[45] Finally, besides simple material compensation, Menem extended political benefits to cooperative union officials too. To facilitate ENTel's divestment, for example, the president appointed Julio Guillán, leader of the telephone union, as undersecretary of telecommunications (ultimately this tactic would fail; the rank-and-file voted Guillán out of office and the new leadership assumed a highly militant antidivestment stance).

But while supportive unions received various carrots, recalcitrants suffered the stick: in 1990 Menem brushed aside labor concerns over privatization, and to preempt effective antireform mobilization, outlawed strikes via decree in all public sector firms (the CGT-Azorpardo's stronghold). And when phone workers walked out to protest divestment-induced layoffs at ENTel, the president simply fired them. Given the robust nature of Argentine democracy—its competitive party system, the PJ's longtime trade union base, and upcoming midterm elections—Menem could ill afford to squander his political capital by alienating labor completely; hence, these imposition tactics were relatively mild by Mexican standards.[46] But they were enough. Although union opposition to reform policies did not evaporate after 1990, the possibility of a united front of labor opposition grew increasingly remote. By minimizing the costs of change for some labor unions and imposing them on others, divide and conquer tactics helped bring important segments of the labor movement into the reform camp.

Similarly, the administration also worked hard to convert business into a divestment supporter. Here, the tool of choice was compensation, packaged as extraordinary rent-seeking opportunities (debt write-offs, sheltered or monopoly markets, subsidies, etc.),[47] and offered primarily to those with access to large quantities of capital. To cite several prominent examples: in privatizing ENTel, the government, not the new proprietors, absorbed the firm's billion-plus dollar debt, and the owners were guaranteed annual profits of 16 percent of the value of assets they purchased; similarly, Aerolíneas Argentinas's new owners avoided most of the carrier's $46 million debt and received five- and ten-year monopolies on domestic and international flights respectively, to boot; for the new owners of Buenos Aires's metro system, meanwhile, the government provided special operational subsidies; but perhaps most striking was the ninety-five-year concession (or monopoly) granted to the new owners of SEGBA (electric power).[48] This pattern of compensation gave erstwhile opponents compelling incentives to support privatization: in exchange for traditional rents and subsidies, some of Argentina's largest entrepreneurs obtained proprietorship or management of former state monopolies with nearly risk-free rates of return.[49] The administration's willingness to [over]compensate business for the real and perceived costs of reform was critical to winning private sector support; this, plus new allies among labor, formed the basis of a state-societal coalition highly conducive to implementing divestment.[50]

Finally, Menem pursued three basic tactics to ensure military acquiescence (if not support) for privatization, and equally important, subordination to civilian control. First, he exempted the armed forces' various corporations from the initial round of divestments (the assault on Fabricaciones Militares would not come for two years). Second, unlike Alfonsín, who sought to bring the "Dirty War's" perpetrators to justice, Menem ended the military's nightmare of civilian retribution through presidential pardons, and demonstrated in very public, symbolic ways his support for the armed forces (military parades, naval tours, etc.). Finally, he made clear that economic revival took precedence over military interests and subordinated the armed forces to civilian authority through fiscal discipline and iron-clad budgetary procedures.[51] By the time divestment touched the military's crown jewels (1991), opposition to privatization was a nonfactor.

Still, this first round of privatizations was hardly problem free. Menem's early years were plagued by confusion, infighting, delays, and politically damaging scandals associated with divestiture. Four interrelated factors lay at the root of these problems. First, while the president took pains to construct a state-societal coalition, he displayed less interest in organizing a counterpart inside the state. To a large extent Menem pushed reform quickly—and unilaterally—running roughshod over real and perceived obstacles to change within the government. Second, this unilateralism strained executive/congressional relations, sparking a backlash from congressional Peronists that threatened gridlock and exposed conspicuous irregularities in the divestment process. The disclosure of irregularities, in turn, fueled corruption charges that tarnished the government's credibility and slowed the pace of divestment overall. Finally, each of the preceding factors was linked directly or indirectly to the omnibus laws at the heart of Menem's privatization program. Unlike Mexico's reformers, Menem initially pursued divestment without the benefit of a strong, cohesive reform coalition inside the state. The change of administrations in 1989 did bring fresh faces to the Ministries of Economy, Public Works, and the Directorate of Public Enterprises (the Ministry of Growth was abolished in 1987), and the old turf battles between these agencies receded somewhat. But ensuing interagency relations never jelled into the type of tight coalition that characterized Mexican privatization. For one thing, the Economy Ministry was bedeviled by discontinuities at the top (four ministers in three years),[52] which made smooth cross-agency relations hard to sustain. For another, not all the president's reform agents were classic neoliberals. For example, Public Works Minister José Roberto Dromi (whose agency held jurisdiction over many PEs) was an attorney, not an economic technocrat; in addition, many "trustee" managers that supervised specific divestments lacked technocratic credentials. Consequently, even when officials spoke in neoliberal terminology (i.e., "state reform") their interpretation of that terminology often differed. "Unity of views and continuity of personnel," notes Thomas Callaghy, "are central to the effective performance" of economic teams,[53] and in Menem's administration both were in short supply. As a result, actors at the epicenter of Argentina's divestment program tended to speak past each other, and because their ideas informed their actions, misunderstandings and conflict ensued.[54]

Equally important, there was no legal or institutional base on which to erect a powerful pro-reform coalition inside the state. The omnibus legislation gave the executive wide leeway to privatize, but did nothing to clarify overall responsibilities for divestment inside the executive branch itself. Moreover, the scramble to divest occurred so rapidly that the process lacked consistent norms and transparency (for example, tender rules sometimes changed in the midst of a PE auction and internal disputes over particular sales were resolved in nonstandardized fashions).[55] These factors impeded coalition building and policy formulation, plus discouraged cohesion among the economic team. Absent a clear privatization "czar," firm lines of authority, and consistent policy norms, internal squabbles divided the cabinet (infighting erupted "over who was in charge of what and how things were to be done"),[56] and the time, energy, and political capital expended on such turf battles did little to advance reform.

To keep divestiture on track, therefore, Menem relied increasingly on unilateral tactics—concentrating more power within the presidency and weakening other state entities that might conceivably obstruct the reforms.[57] To safeguard his initiatives from constitutional challenge, for example, the president persuaded Congress to enlarge the Supreme Court in 1990 (from five to nine justices), then "packed" it with sympathetic appointees; similarly, he also sacked four of the five members of the national Auditing Board—a type of fiscal tribunal which monitored irregularities in state accounts. The next year the purge continued, this time against the national attorney for administrative investigation (whose office prosecutes irregularities in public administration). When the agency's top official, Alberto González Arzac, challenged the legality of procedures related to the ENTel and Aerolíneas divestments, the president fired him via executive decree.[58]

In the short term removing opponents to strengthen vertical channels of authority helped steady the reform process by closing down avenues to debate or contest administration initiatives. But the leverage Menem gained over divestiture via unilateralism soon reached the point of diminishing returns. Tensions over privatization flared between the president and Congress, where Peronist lawmakers remained highly skeptical of Menem's very un-Peronist market philosophy.[59] Again, these tensions were partly a function of the omnibus divestment law. Enacted by a lame duck Radical Congress in the heat of the 1989 economic meltdown, the State Reform Law gave legislators *ex post* authority to monitor (but not veto) proposed transactions, yet empowered the president to initiate sales without congressional approval. By the time ENTel and Aerolíneas went to auction many legislators believed Congress had given away the store. To compensate, lawmakers subjected these early transactions to intense scrutiny. In some cases (like ENTel) they forced the administration to revise the terms of sale after the fact, and exposed financial improprieties many denounced as corruption.[60] In this instance, as with Aerolíneas (whose buyer, Iberia Airlines, reportedly was forced to pay $80 million in bribes to government officials), state agencies charged with auditing, prosecuting, and adjudicating cases of government financial irregularities proved unable (or unwilling) to fulfill these roles.[61]

The aura of corruption damaged the administration politically, and as executive/congressional relations deteriorated, the president increasingly bypassed Congress to push divestment (and other market reforms) via executive decrees.[62] This strategy, of course, helped maximize short-term gains, explained one official at the Economy Ministry, because it "obviated the need to go to Congress where special interests could kill or slow down" the reforms.[63] But in the long run, rule by decree was a poison pill. In the parlance of rational choice, the president's defection from cooperative interaction left lawmakers the "sucker's payoff," and the more vigorous his unilateralism, the more acrimonious and unproductive executive/congressional relations became (Peronist legislators were particularly peeved). By 1990 the relationship was abysmal. In the context of corruption, recession (late 1990), and the threat of hyperinflation (early 1991), the divestiture program became increasingly uncertain. Investors grew more wary of buying, some in Menem's inner court urged the reform program be abandoned altogether, and a backlog of proposed divestments remained in the pipeline (in steel, electricity, gas, and shipping)—hardly propitious circumstances in which to clinch quick deals.

After the January 1991 appointment of Domingo Cavallo as economy minister, however, the situation improved considerably. Cavallo (Ph.D. economics, Harvard) immediately recruited his own "change team" and packed his ministry with loyal, like-minded neoliberal enthusiasts.[64] He took steps to standardize divestment norms and procedures to bring more transparency into the process, com-

pleted the merger of the Ministry of Public Works and Services (which traditionally supervised PE operations) with his own agency, and created a special
privatization subunit inside the Economy Ministry.[65] This provided divestment an
institutional home (finally), streamlined the reform process, and concentrated authority directly under Cavallo's control. These innovations were enormously
consequential. They clarified lines of authority, minimized the infighting that characterized Menem's first two years, and greatly enhanced reformers' organizational
position inside the state. As Judith Teichman observed: "While formulation of
economic policy had always rested in the hands of the Minister of Economy, never
had it become so insulated . . . from societal forces [and] resistant to pressures
from other areas within the state."[66]

Cavallo quickly used his authority to revolutionize Argentina's monetary system, tame the inflation dragon, and stabilize the economy. At the heart of these
efforts was the April 1991 Convertibility Law. It fixed the peso's value to that of
the U.S. dollar, allowed full convertibility between the two currencies, and required the central bank to hold foreign reserves at least equal to the domestic money
supply (which essentially stopped the bank from printing money to finance deficit
spending). In economic terms the law proved a watershed. Between March and
December, monthly inflation rates dropped from 27 to 1 percent; capital repatria-
tion brought billions of dollars back into the country (boosting foreign reserves),
and the combination of an expanding money supply and low inflation caused domestic interest rates to tumble.

The Convertibility Law strengthened the credibility of Menem's market reform program, reduced economic uncertainty, and helped pave the way for further
privatizations. Despite its radical nature, it sailed through the Peronist-controlled
Congress largely because Cavallo abandoned Menem's unilateral reform strategy,
and instead, sought to erect a viable reform coalition inside the state. After an
early, well-publicized misstep,[67] the economy minister came to believe that pure
unilateralism had run its course, and now jeopardized both divestiture and other
market reforms. Accordingly, with congressional/executive relations in disrepair,
Cavallo devoted considerable effort to courting wayward lawmakers, sharing information and bringing them into the decision-making process. This strategy was
key to the Convertibility Law's swift passage and renewed progress on the
privatization front. Through painstaking negotiations Cavallo brokered a deal in
early 1991 that gave Congress the right to veto any subsequent divestment initiative.[68] He then nurtured that relationship, dispatching his closest advisors to con-
sult with Congress (and Peronist legislators) on specific privatization and other
reform proposals.[69] This shared decision-making arrangement did not eliminate
congressional opposition in toto; but as Corrales notes, it did give Congress (and
by extension, disgruntled Peronist legislators) a clear stake in the reform program,
and hence, the incentives to see it succeed.[70] Thereafter, divestment snowballed:
the sell-off targeted sectors ranging from oil and utilities, to agriculture and grain,
to steel, shipping, and railroads, to finance and social security.[71]

Explaining Outcomes

Evidence from the Argentine case supports two principal findings. First, the political outcomes of privatization projects differed markedly across administrations. Here, the contrast between Alfonsín's general failure and Menem's success is striking. Second, divestment under Menem demonstrated its own peculiar pattern: between 1989 and 1991 the government privatized about twenty-one PEs; but between 1992 and 1994 it managed to divest five times that number (table 6.1). This chapter has argued that the dissimilar outcomes across and within administrations turned strongly upon reformers' capacity to forge coalitions, gain leverage over policy via institutional innovation, and resolve the problem of policy costs. Nevertheless, it is possible that factors quite exogenous to this framework influenced outcomes significantly more than suggested. This position has strong intuitive appeal since policy in general responds to external stimuli (like domestic economic crises) and privatization programs remain sensitive to influences beyond policy makers' control. General market conditions, capital availability, pressure from international financial institutions, and even the broader political context can all help make or break divestment campaigns. To what extent, then, do such factors explain the outcomes observed?

Alternative Explanations

One line of thought found in the political economy literature would suggest that the economic crisis Menem faced was far graver than Alfonsín's, and that the greater urgency to solve that crisis explains why he accomplished more.[72] Part of the argument turns on the distinction some scholars draw between policies that are "crisis driven" and those which evolve from "politics as usual" (the former typically exhibit greater discontinuities than the latter).[73] Based purely on the numbers, at first blush this explanation seems promising. In 1989 Argentina's economic woes were probably worse than anytime in its history (per capita GDP of -7.5 percent, hyperinflation of nearly 5,000 percent, a $63 billion external debt, and a current-account deficit of $1.3 billion); by contrast, Alfonsín took power under what in hindsight appears "less severe" conditions (per capita GDP of -3.5 percent, hyperinflation of 433 percent, a $45 billion external debt, and a current-account deficit of $2.5 billion).[74] To the extent these conditions (and hyperinflation especially) induced greater receptivity to neoliberal prescriptions in the public and Congress, an economic crisis argument might explain a great deal about why Menem's reform efforts surpassed his predecessor's.

Nevertheless, in terms of analytic rigor this position does not pass close scrutiny. On the one hand, because a crisis's intensity is relative to what preceded it, the dependent variable is difficult to measure (to what depth must a crisis plunge before successful reform is guaranteed?); by default, this makes crisis arguments virtually unfalsifiable. On the other hand, even if some crises do generate greater urgency to reform, this only explains a state's motivations to pursue corrective policies, not its capacity to achieve them. Nor is there much support for more nuanced crises arguments. Some scholars, for example, suggest that crises bolster a state's capacity to implement reform mainly by discrediting/weakening the opposition. But as the record examined here illustrates, Argentina's two crises never weakened status quo proponents to the point they became nonfactors.[75]

A second possibility is that a dramatic improvement in market conditions (buyer demand for PEs in specific sectors, the availability of capital, etc.) explains the results of Argentina's divestment campaigns. But here too, the evidence is less than compelling. Consider those cases which marked Alfonsín's most dramatic privatization failure and Menem's most important early success: Aerolíneas Argentinas and ENTel. At roughly the same time the initial attempt to sell Aerolíneas fell flat (1988), governments across Latin America were selling their own national airlines—in Chile, Guatemala, and Mexico.[76] And while few governments had yet to divest their telecommunications firms (Chile's 1988 sale of Compañía de Teléfonos is an exception), several did so shortly thereafter: Mexico, Venezuela, and of course, Argentina. Although the market conditions Alfonsín faced were certainly not optimal, in both cases the government and bidders already had signed letters of intent, which ultimately died in Congress.[77] It was not for lack of buyers (or capital) that these early sales fell through. Moreover, Menem managed to divest large firms under market conditions just as bad (for example, there was only one bidder for Aerolíneas). Finally, while the success of Cavallo's Convertibility Law clearly brightened divestment prospects post-1991, this does not account for the government's earlier achievements.

A third possibility is that international financial institutions (IFIs) exerted greater pressure on Menem than Alfonsín, and hence, influenced divestment outcomes. This position finds support in cross-national studies linking debt relief and structural adjustment loans to IFI-prescribed adjustment policies (including privatization).[78] Throughout the 1980s Argentina's economic woes and increasing need of international credit exposed the government to this type of external pressure. Between 1985 and 1989, for example, Argentina and the International Monetary Fund engaged in near constant debt negotiations; also, during this time Argentina received several debt relief packages, plus three World Bank sectoral adjustment loans—aid packages linked to the adoption of measures like divestiture. And in 1990 the country's Central Bank president frankly conceded that divestments "represent a decisive element to unblock financial aid pending from the World Bank and the Inter-American Development Bank."[79] However, these facts do not adequately explain the issue at hand (successful divestment versus failure). Again, they speak more to the government's motives to reform than its capacity to do so.

A persuasive explanation must move beyond the arguments above. Both logic and the evidence suggest an approach based on coalitions, institutions, and cost calculations provides greater explanatory power. A systematic application of this framework, of course, would require—as with Mexico—detailed examinations of specific privatization episodes (i.e., ENTel, Aerolíneas). But even this brief overview demonstrates that Argentina's reform process displayed patterns consistent with these variables: under both administrations the absence or presence of coalitions and institutional innovation were critical to outcomes, and under Menem, the decisions central political actors made regarding the "costs" of policy change influenced implementation patterns. Given the relative inattention to coalition politics, costs, and institutional innovation under Alfonsín, the discussion below is confined to the Menem administration.

Coalitions, Institutions, and Policy Costs

Coalitions figure prominently in the literature on policy reform; indeed, in Haggard and Webb's view, successful reform "must be viewed as an exercise in coalition-building . . . [that creates] . . . a new base of political support among emerging winners."[80] On the whole, most authors stress the importance of state-societal coalitions in implementing or consolidating reforms, and Menem's first two years strongly support this proposition. At a time when confusion and internecine conflicts prevailed inside the administration, inducing segments of organized labor and business to support the government's program was critical to Menem's initial success. As I argued earlier, however, the scholarly focus on state-societal coalitions (while helpful) ignores the critical role coalitions play inside the state. And in Argentina the lack of such a coalition exerted appreciable drag on Menem's early divestment efforts. Despite the achievements, policy formulation suffered as officials locked horns over turf, cross-agency collaboration was less than smooth, and divestment criteria, norms, and procedures changed from case to case.

Among those factors that impeded coalition building was a subtle ideological dissonance between key officials, the absence of a cohesive "change team," and the president's penchant for going it alone. But the evidence also suggests that institutional factors played an important role. As I stressed earlier, institutional arrangements that structure relationships are politically consequential. They form the context for actors' strategic choice, and influence the relative autonomy decision makers have, plus the leverage actors can exert over the policy process. Both the absence of a strong coalition and the president's early anticoalition strategy can be traced, in part, to the incentives and constraints born of institutional dynamics.

Adam Przerworski has written that actors' capacity "to realize their interests is shaped by the specific institutional arrangements of a given system,"[81] and in

1989, president-elect Menem faced an institutional context hardly conducive to successful reform. It displayed multiple potential veto points (Congress, the judiciary, auditing agencies, corporatist organizations), provided insufficient autonomy against powerful vested interests, and left unclear some of the basic mechanics of divestiture. Knowing Alfonsín had fallen victim to these land mines, Menem determined to avoid them and his unilateralism reflected this determination. To gain leverage over the reform process he advanced innovations and formal rule changes that concentrated divestment authority within the executive branch (the omnibus law). This provided greater autonomy but left critical issues of role definition undetermined. The resulting paradox of centralized executive authority, but decentralized, ambiguous responsibilities within the executive branch itself, hindered coalition building because rather than facilitate cross-agency collaboration it bred conflict and confusion. Thus, while Menem's early divestment achievements were largely the product of concentrated authority coupled with a pro-reform state-societal coalition, ironically, so were many of his early problems.

The institutional innovations crafted under Domingo Cavallo were designed expressly to solve the problems Menem's measures created. Where the omnibus law actually structured conflict into the executive branch, Cavallo's initiatives sought to structure it out. The merger of the Economy and Public Works Ministries, for example, consolidated divestment authority under one roof, ending the tug-of-war between agency rivals. The establishment of a privatization subunit within the Economy Ministry streamlined the divestment process further. By strengthening reformers' organizational position inside the state these institutional changes (what I have called instrument-creating behavior) made a robust divestment campaign far more likely. They also created an institutional structure conducive to a tight-knit, effective technocratic team. This is no small point.

For the most part, competent highly trained officials managed Argentine economic matters before 1991, yet neither Menem nor Alfonsín achieved the type of coherent "change team" some deem essential to success.[82] Among the reasons is Williamson and Haggard's insight that "the competence" of economic officials alone "cannot compensate for a lack of authority."[83] That authority, in turn, derives from the influence inherent in one's official bureaucratic post, and of course, presidential support; but it can also derive from institutional changes. For good or ill, the internal organization of the policy-making apparatus plays a central role in reform outcomes, and institutional changes that clarify decision-making procedures restrict participation in the decision-making process, or otherwise shelter officials from countervailing pressures to enhance their probabilities of success. The institutional restructuring that accompanied Cavallo's arrival helped the change team he assembled realize its potential.

Finally, besides these structural refinements, the informal changes Cavallo made in privatization decision rules gave new life to the divestment project. Bringing Congress into the decision-making process proved a master stroke. On the one hand, it partially disarmed Peronist congressional critics (who opposed both the reforms and Menem's unilateralism); on the other hand, it converted an important opponent of change into a stakeholder in the reform program. These moves laid the foundations for collaborative action well suited to protect divestment from saboteurs inside the state.

One of the clearest distinctions, then, between divestment under the Menem and Alfonsín governments was the former's capacity to forge coalitions (in and outside the state) and make crucial institutional changes to advance reform. Absent these factors, divestiture of the magnitude Argentina achieved was highly unlikely. Nevertheless, success was no sure thing. Like its Mexican counterpart, the Argentine government confronted the legacies of past policy choices. Decades of statism had spawned dense linkages between PEs, state ministries, and various groups who strongly favored the status quo and aggressively opposed the costs of policy change. Potent lock-in effects ensued that enabled statism to withstand multiple regime changes and reform attempts well into the 1980s. Douglass North maintains that the effects of policy feedback constitute one of the major obstacles to effective privatization: confronted by "costly" policy change, North claims that tenacious status quo interests might not just survive reform efforts, but "attempt to 'sabotage' institutional transformation" (i.e., reform) itself.[84] Under Alfonsín public sector beneficiaries (labor, business, etc.) did exactly that.

Menem, of course, faced the same dilemma but on a grander scale. Because the dimensions of his divestment program reached further than his predecessor's, the costs it generated were steeper, and in some respects, more concentrated too. How actors responded to those costs affected government implementation strategies. Many affiliates of the CGT-Azorpardo, for example, held contracts in public enterprises and chose to defy the reform program. This resistance was integral to Menem's selective use of imposition strategies against the CGT-Azorpardo (mass firings at ENTel, banning strikes in public enterprises, etc.). By contrast, with less to lose from divestment the CGT-San Martín adopted a less implacable posture toward reform; to keep this faction loyal the government chose to minimize the costs of change via compensation. Similarly, where costs were high but the opponents' support was crucial to the program (i.e., private business) imposition strategies were a non-starter; consequently, the administration relied on extravagant compensation to offset the costs of reform. By resolving the reformer's dilemma in ways that encouraged coalition formation these minimizing/imposition strategies proved crucial to Menem's success.

Like Mexico, the Argentine government managed to implement policy change on an order of magnitude few anticipated. Despite problems and setbacks the Menem administration virtually emptied the government's portfolio of industrial, commercial, and service-providing entities. Yet Argentina's privatization process was more than Mexico's mirror image. A competitive party system, moderate congressional power, and vigorous, largely autonomous interest representation all posed unique challenges to divestiture. This institutional context—distinct from Mexico's—shaped the constraints and possibilities of success, as well as the strategies employed to achieve it. These dissimilarities notwithstanding, "any privatizing government," suggests Mary Shirley, "will need to overcome some of the same hurdles and address some of the same fundamental issues."[85] It is on this basis the theoretical merit of the Argentina/Mexico comparison rests. As the record indicates, Argentine leaders confronted some of the same basic challenges their Mexican counterparts did (policy feedback, the reformer's dilemma, distribution of costs), and in the end, they overcame them in the same ways too. In both countries coalition politics, institutional innovation, and attention to the issue of policy costs made the difference between divestment failures and success.

Notes

1. Of the four firms Alfonsín managed to privatize were Siam (an industrial conglomerate), the small domestic carrier Austral Airlines, plus two small firms, Lagos del sur (travel) and Opalinas Hurlingham (ceramics). See Javier A. González Fraga, "Argentine Privatization in Retrospect," in William Glade, ed., *Privatization of Public Enterprises in Latin America* (San Francisco: ICS Press, 1991), 80.

2. Argentina's dreary pattern of regime rotation can be summarized succinctly. Peronists assumed office in 1946, were purged by the military in 1955, and banned from political participation for the next two decades. The Radicals returned to power in 1958, suffered a military coup in 1962, and then governed between 1963 and 1966 before the military seized power again. In 1973 the Peronists returned, only to be crushed by a military coup in 1976. That dictatorship, in turn, lasted until democracy was restored in 1983. See Carlos Waisman, "Argentina: Autarkic Industrialization and Illegitimacy," in Larry Diamond, Juan Linz, and Seymour Martin Lipset, eds., *Democracy in Developing Countries: Latin America* (Boulder, Colo.: Lynne Rienner, 1989). For discussion of the transition to civilian rule see Aldo C. Vacs, "Authoritarian Breakdown and Redemocratization in Argentina," in James M. Malloy and Mitchell A. Seligson, eds., *Authoritarian and Democrats: Regime Transition in Latin America* (Pittsburgh, Penn.: University of Pittsburgh Press, 1987).

3. Through agricultural export taxes, Perón financed this scheme by redistributing landowner earnings to industrialists and workers. Small, medium, and large enterprises began to flourish and import-substitution became the prevailing development model. See Guido di Tella and Manuel Zymelman, *Las etapas del desarrollo económico argentino* (Buenos Aires: Editorial Universitaria de Buenos Aires, 1967), 235; and Eduardo F. Jorge, *Industria y Concentración Económica* (Buenos Aires: Siglo XXI Argentina Editores, S.A., 1971), 50, 176–177, 190–191.

4. See Felipe A. M. de la Balze, *Remaking the Argentine Economy* (New York: Council on Foreign Relations, 1995), 32; Paul H. Lewis, *The Crisis of Argentine Capitalism* (Chapel Hill, N.C.: University of North Carolina Press, 1990), chapter 11. See also Rosalía Cortés and Adriana Marshall, "State Social Intervention and Labour Regulation: The Case of the Argentine," *Cambridge Journal of Economics* 17 (1993).

5. Leslie Elliott Armijo, "Menem's Mania?: The Timing of Privatization in Argentina," *Southwestern Journal of Law and Trade in the Americas* 1, no. 1 (1994): 3.

6. Graciana del Castillo, "Privatization in Latin America: From Myth to Reality," *Serie Reformas de Política Pública* 32 (Santiago, Chile: ECLAC, 1995), 26.

7. Beginning in 1946 the initial Peronist governments wed ISI to political populism and established statism as official government policy. The Frondizi regime (1958-1962) pursued the developmentalist variant of ISI by courting foreign investment—a strategy the Illía administration continued through 1966. From 1966 to 1973 the Onganía military government tried but failed to break the statist model decisively—as did the later regime led by General Jorge Videla. For discussion see Monica Peralta-Ramos, *The Political Economy of Argentina: Power and Class since 1930* (Boulder, Colo.: Westview, 1992); and Kathryn Sikkink, *Ideas and Institutions: Developmentalism in Brazil and Argentina* (Ithaca, N.Y.: Cornell University Press, 1991), especially chapter three.

8. Julio C. Cueto-Rua, "Privatization in Argentina," *Southwestern Journal of Law and Trade in the Americas* 1, no. 1 (1994): 64.

9. "Deficit endemico en las empresas públicas," *La Nación* 8, November 13, 1988.

10. See Javier Corrales, "Coalitions and Corporate Choices in Argentina, 1976-1994: The Recent Private Sector Support of Privatization," *Studies in Comparative International Development* 32, no. 4 (Winter 1998): 27; and *Argentina: From Insolvency to Growth* (Washington, D.C.: The World Bank, 1993), 115.

11. Some of the basic attributes of the Argentine political system are remarkably similar to Mexico's (like accentuated presidentialism and corporatism); others, however, are quite different. For example, the party system is competitive, but parties themselves are weak, and historically, political decision rules like elections were less institutionalized in Argentina than Mexico. A good historical treatment of Argentina's peculiar political traits is found in Liliana de Riz and Catalina Smulovitz, "Instituciones y dinámica política: El presidencialismo argentino," in Dieter Nohlen and Liliana de Riz, eds., *Reforma institucional y cambio político* (Buenos Aires: Editorial Legasa, 1991).

12. On Argentine hyperpresidentialism see Carlos Santiago Nino, "Hyperpresidentialism and Constitutional Reform in Argentina," in Arend Lijphart and Carlos H. Waisman, eds., *Institutional Design in New Democracies: Eastern Europe and Latin America* (Boulder, Colo.: Westview, 1996).

13. Political reforms adopted in the early 1990s curtailed some of these traditional prerogatives. The president still appoints cabinet members, and more important, the "chief of the cabinet"—a powerful official analogous to a prime minister; but Congress can censure and remove the cabinet chief. Moreover, the president must now submit his "decrees of necessity and urgency" to Congress within ten days of issuing them. Finally, the Central Bank can no longer help presidents engage in deficit spending by printing money to finance state deficits. See Nino, "Hyperpresidentialism," 173; and Pamela K. Starr, "Government Coalitions and the Viability of Currency Boards: Argentina under the Cavallo Plan," *Journal of Interamerican Studies and World Affairs* 39, no. 2 (Summer 1992).

14. See Marcelo Cavarozzi, "Peronism and Radicalism: Argentina's Transitions in Perspective," in Paul W. Drake and Eduardo Silva, eds., *Elections and Democratization in Latin America, 1980–85* (La Jolla, Calif.: Center for U.S.-Mexican Studies, Center for Iberian and Latin American Studies, and Institute for the Americas, University of California, San Diego, 1986); and Peralta-Ramos, *The Political Economy of Argentina.*

15. Argentina's principal corporatist entities were the Argentine Rural Society (landowners), General Economic Confederation (domestic industrialists), Argentine Industrial Union (export-oriented domestic industrialists and multinationals), and General Labor Confederation (workers). See Davide G. Erro, *Resolving the Argentine Paradox: Politics and Development, 1966–1992* (Boulder, Colo.: Lynne Rienner Publishers, 1993).

16. See James W. McGuire, "Political Parties and Democracy in Argentina," in Scott Mainwaring and Timothy R. Scully, eds., *Building Democratic Institutions: Party Systems in Latin America* (Stanford, Calif.: Stanford University Press, 1995), 201. For a counterargument, see Steve Levitsky, "Crisis, Party Adaptation and Regime Stability in Argentina: The Case of Peronism, 1989–1995," *Party Politics* 4, no. 4 (October 1998).

17. For a good account of interest group pressure and "congressional bypass" see Luis Pássara, "El Rol del Parlamento: Argentina y Perú," *Desarrollo Económico* 32, no. 128 (January–March 1993).

18. Manzetti provides one of the richest accounts of the push-pull impact of these corporatist organizations. See Luigi Manzetti, *Institutions, Parties, and Coalitions in Argentine Politics* (Pittsburgh, Penn.: University of Pittsburgh Press, 1993).

19. On this pattern of contestation see Luigi Manzetti, "Institutional Decay and Distributional Coalitions in Developing Countries: The Argentine Riddle Reconsidered," *Studies in Comparative International Development* 29, no. 2 (Summer 1994).

20. De la Balze, *Remaking the Argentine Economy* 58.

21. By 1982 investment was down 25 percent, budget deficits were the highest ever recorded, the ratio of debt servicing to export earnings was 69 percent, and the foreign debt—$43.6 billion—equaled 70 percent of GNP. See Mario Damill and Roberto Frenkel, "Malos tiempos: la economía argentina en la década de los ochenta," in Roberto Frenkel, et al., *Argentina: evolución macroeconómica, financiación externa y cambio político en la década de los 80* (Madrid: CEDEAL, 1992), 26; Rudiger Dornbusch and Juan Carlos de Pablo, *Deuda externa e inestabilidad macroeconómica en la Argentina* (Buenos Aires: Editorial Sudamerica, 1988); and Gary W. Wynia, *Argentina: Illusions and Realities*, 2d ed. (New York: Holmes & Meier, 1992), 88–95.

22. *Argentina: Reforms for Price Stability and Growth* (Washington, D.C.: The World Bank, 1990), 76.

23. This was the celebrated Austral Plan (launched in 1985) and its successors. Although multifaceted, the plan essentially revolved around a combination of wage and price controls plus monetary reform. See Roberto Frenkel, "Heterodox Theory and Policy: The Plan Austral in Argentina," *Journal of Development Economics* 7, nos. 1-2 (October 1987); and Paolo Sylos Labini, *El plan austral y la política económica Argentina: algunos reflexiones* (Buenos Aires: Instituto Torcuato Di Tella, Centro de Investigaciones Económicas, 1987). See also Manuel Ángel Abdala, "The Regulation of Newly Privatized Firms: An Illustration from Argentina," in Werner Baer and Melissa H. Birch, eds., *Privatization in Latin America: New Roles for the Public and Private Sectors* (Westport, Conn.: Praeger, 1994), 53.

24. For a succinct review of the highs and lows of public enterprise reform under Alfonsín, see Aída Arango de Maglio, "Radicalismo y empresas públicas (1983/1989)," *Realidad Económica* 97 (1990); see also Alejandro E. Rausch, "Privatization in Argentina," in V. V. Ramanadham, ed., *Constraints and Impacts of Privatization* (New York: Routledge, 1993).

25. Fraga, "Argentine Privatization in Retrospect," 78.

26. Ibid., 88.

27. M. Victoria Murillo, "Union Politics, Market-Oriented Reforms, and the Reshaping of Argentine Corporatism," in Douglas A. Chalmers et al., eds., *The New Politics of Inequality in Latin America: Rethinking Participation and Representation* (New York: Oxford University Press, 1997), 82. See also Alan Riding, "Argentina's Privatization Battle," *New York Times,* November 28, 1988, D8.

28. Over the next few years labor's concerns would be realized: between 1990 and 1993 public enterprise payrolls plummeted from 222,000 to 42,000. *Argentina's Privatization Program: Experience, Issues, and Lessons* (Washington, D.C.: The World Bank, 1993), 14–15.

29. The steel firm SOMISA is a case in point. When the Alfonsín government announced plans to sell SOMISA in 1986, the company quickly released an "expert" audit that pegged its market value at $4 billion (four times what most observers believed appropriate). During a meeting with the president and his economic team SOMISA's CEO forcefully pressed his case, and the divestment initiative withered in the ensuing debates over asset valuation. See José Luis Machinea, *Stabilization under Alfonsín's Government: A Frustrated Attempt* (Buenos Aires: CEDES, 1990), 98–99.

30. Murillo, "Union Politics," 76; Gary Mead, "Mistrust Fans the Flames of Troubled Privatization," *Financial Times*, March 22, 1989, 6; Corrales, "Coalitions and Corporate Choices"; Robert Grosse, "A Privatization Nightmare: Aerolíneas Argentinas," in Ravi Ramamurti, ed., *Privatizing Monopolies: Lessons from the Telecommunications and Transport Sectors in Latin America* (Baltimore, Md.: Johns Hopkins University Press, 1996), 207; and Elenora Gosman, "Aerolineas Argentinas," in Arnaldo Bocco and Naum Minsburge, eds., *Privatizaciones: Reestructuración del estado y la sociedad* (del Plan Pinedo a los Alsogaray) (Argentina: Ediciones Letra Buena, 1991), 247.

31. Lewis, *The Crisis of Argentine Capitalism,* 492.

32. The ENTel divestment was a direct victim of "stealth bidding" by would-be buyers. See Alejandra Herrera, "The Privatization of the Argentine Telephone System," *CEPAL Review* 47 (August 1992): 152. On the general dynamics of private sector opposition see William Glade, "Privatization in Rent-Seeking Societies," *World Development* 17, no. 5 (1989); and Corrales, "Coalitions and Corporate Choices."

33. *Machinea, Stabilization under Alfonsín's Government: A Frustrated Attempt,* 98–99. For an overview of the corporations operated under the General Directorate of Military Factories see Anna S. de Kessler, "Privatization of the Enterprises of the Argentine Ministry of Defense," *Columbia Journal of World Business* 28, no. 1 (Spring 1993).

34. Armijo, "Menem's Mania?" 15.

35. Although Alfonsín worked hard to gain support for his economic policies from both labor and business, he focused his energies not on offsetting the "costs" of divestment, but mainly on bread and butter, bottom-line issues like general wages, salaries, prices, etc. See Edward C. Epstein, "Labor-State Conflict in the New Argentine Democracy: Parties, Union Factions, and Power Maximizing," in Edward C. Epstein, ed., *The New Argentine Democracy: The Search for a Successful Formula* (Westport, Conn.: Praeger, 1992).

36. Ibid. See also Henry Boneo, "Privatization: Ideology and Praxis," in William Glade, ed., *State Shrinking: A Comparative Inquiry into Privatization* (Austin, Tex.: Institute of Latin American Studies, University of Texas, Austin, 1986); and "Argentina: Reversing the Past Fifty Years," in *Privatization in Latin America: New Competitive Opportunities and Challenges* (New York: Business International Corporation, 1990), 85.

37. Corrales, "Coalitions and Corporate Choices," 36.

38. William C. Smith, "State, Market, and Neoliberalism in Post-Transition Argentina: The Menem Experiment," *Journal of Interamerican Studies and World Affairs* 33, no. 4 (Winter 1991); see also Enrique A. Bour, "El programa argentino de desregulación y privatización," in Felipe A. M. de la Balze, ed., *Reforma y convergencia: Ensayos sobre la transformación de la economía Argentina* (Buenos Aires: Ediciones Manantial, 1993).

39. *Argentina's Privatization Program: Experience, Issues, and Lessons,* 23.

40. On the dynamics of counterreform collective action, see Steve H. Hanke and Stephen J. K. Walter, "Privatization and Public Choice: Lessons for the LDCs," in Dennis J. Gayle and Jonathan N. Goodrich, eds., *Privatization and Deregulation in Global Perspective* (Westport, Conn.: Quorum Books, 1990).

41. Fraga, "Argentine Privatization in Retrospect," 93.

42. Ibid., 95; and Corrales, "Coalitions and Corporate Choices in Argentina."

43. Edward L. Gibson, "The Populist Road to Market Reform: Policy and Electoral Coalitions in Mexico and Argentina," *World Politics* 49 (April 1997): 358.

44. According to Erro, the government "implicitly assured higher wages to those unions willing to increase productivity and cut excess labor, as reflected in the push for a smaller but more efficient (productive) public sector. The CGT-San Martín was willing to take advantage of such a situation." See Erro, *Resolving the Argentine Paradox,* 213.

45. For example, in exchange for supporting divestment of the national steelworks, SOMISA, the administration approved wage hikes and additional healthcare funding for the powerful, non-CGT Metalworkers Unions. See Manzetti, *Institutions, Parties, and Coalitions,* 234.

46. For Menem, the political payoffs of this strategy came quickly. During midterm elections in 1991, 1993, and 1994, Argentine unions generally remained loyal to the PJ— not because labor had grown enamored with market reforms, but because absent any viable alternative for partisan representation, it simply had nowhere else to go. Thus, that faction the administration had treated "tenderly" remained in the president's fold (the pro-Menem CGT-San Martín); and after a season of discontent, in 1991 that faction the administration had "punished" returned too (the CGT-Azorpardo). For a general discussion of Menem's electoral strategies see Steven Levitsky and Lucan A. Way, "Between a Shock and a Hard Place: The Dynamics of Labor-Backed Adjustment in Poland and Argentina," *Comparative Politics* 30, no. 2 (1998).

47. In general, the government absorbed nearly all the debts of PEs it sent to auction. Corrales, "Coalitions and Corporate Choices in Argentina." See also, Manuel A. Solanet, "Privatization: The Long Road to Success in Argentina," *Business Forum* 19, nos. 1-2 (Winter–Spring 1994).

48. See, for example, Pablo Gerchunoff and Germán Colima, "Privatization in Argentina," in Manuel Sánchez and Rossana Corona, eds., *Privatization in Latin America* (Washington, D.C.: Inter-American Development Bank, 1993); Ben Petrazzini, "Telephone Privatization in a Hurry: Argentina," in Ravi Ramamurti, ed., *Privatizing Monopolies: Lessons from the Telecommunications and Transport Sectors in Latin America* (Baltimore, Md.: Johns Hopkins University Press, 1996); and Corrales, "Coalitions and Corporate Choices."

49. Some of these conglomerates included Pérez Companc, Acindar, Bridas, Garovaglio y Zorraquín, Techint, and Astra, etc.

50. A compelling assessment of Argentina's coalitional reconstruction under Menem is found in Gibson, "The Populist Road to Market Reform." See also Starr, "Government Coalitions and the Viability of Currency Boards."

51. On the relationship between Menem's budget procedures and military subordination see David Pion-Berlin, *Through Corridors of Power: Institutions and Civil-Military Relations in Argentina* (University Park, Penn: Pennsylvania State University Press, 1997), 122–133.

52. These were Miguel Roig (who died only a week into the new administration), Néstor Rapanelli, Antonio Erman González, and Domingo Cavallo.

53. Thomas M. Callaghy, "Political Passions and Economic Interests: Economic Reform and Political Structure in Africa," in Thomas M. Callaghy and John Ravenhill, eds., *Hemmed In: Responses to Africa's Economic Decline* (New York: Columbia University Press, 1993), 473.

54. The government's internal disputes over privatization were public knowledge. See, for example, the commentary "Un gobierno preocupado," *Somos,* August 1990, 116-117.

55. A prominent example in which tender rules were changed "mid-stream" was the privatization of ENTel. The administration denied one bidder (a consortium led by the U.S. firms Bell Atlantic and Manufacturers Hanover) an extension to acquire financing, but then provided another bidder group (TELECOM-STET, J.P. Morgan, Pérez) exactly the same type of extension. As to the tendency to resolve internal disputes in ad hoc fashion, Margheritis's observation is on the point: "[P]olicy content was defined along the way, through actors' interactions . . . the many conflicting situations that characterized the privatization process mostly resembled palace intrigues. The resolution of those disputes was linked, in terms of procedures, to no fixed rules, and, in terms of content, to personal discretion that was based on neither rational calculations nor economic efficiency rationale." See Roberto Pablo Saba and Luigi Manzetti, "Privatization in Argentina: The Implications for Corruption," *Crime, Law, and Social Change* 25 (1997); and Ana Margheritis, "Implementing Structural Adjustment in Argentina: The Politics of Privatization" (Ph.D. diss., University of Toronto, 1997), 172.

56. One example of such infighting erupted when Economy Minister Erman González and Minister of Public Works and Services José Roberto Dromi (whose agency supervised most PEs), clashed over how best to pursue ENTel's divestment. Eventually, the power struggle helped cost González his job and the Public Works Ministry its very existence (the ministry was abolished and its functions transferred to the Economy Ministry). Other disputes between the Economy Ministry and members of the economic team cast a shadow over Menem's neoliberal agenda, including divestment. In the early years especially, conflict erupted between the economy minister, secretary of the treasury, and president of the Central Bank. The resignations which followed these tussles, of course, undermined continuity. See Luigi Manzetti, "The Political Economy of Privatization through Divestiture in Lesser Developed Economies," *Comparative Politics* 25, no. 4 (July 1993): 441; see also Economist Intelligence Unit, *Argentina Country Report,* nos. 1, 4 (1990).

57. On the centralization of power under Menem see Christopher Larkins, "The Judiciary and Delegative Democracy in Argentina," *Comparative Politics* 30, no. 4 (July 1998); Charles H. Blake, "Economic Reform and Democratization in Argentina and Uruguay: The Tortoise and the Hare Revisited?" *Journal of Interamerican Studies and World Affairs* 40, no. 3 (Fall 1998); Saba and Manzetti, "Privatization in Argentina: The Implications for Corruption"; and Luigi Manzetti and Charles H. Blake, "Market Reforms and Corruption in Latin America: New Means for Old Ways," *Review of International Political Economy* 3, no. 4 (Winter 1996).

58. González's actions did not reflect an ideological aversion to divestment. Rather, he maintained the manner by which the firms' trustees were executing the sales violated the procedures explicitly established by the State Reform Law. In both cases the trustees intended to sell the corporations without conducting the required asset valuations. See Alberto R. González Arzac, "Aerolíneas, ENTel y la Inspección General de Justicia," *Realidad Económica* 97 (1990).

59. Although Radicals criticized Menem's reform approach, Peronists proved to be among the fiercest critics in Congress. After the collapse of both Alfonsín's government

and economic program, the Radicals were so discredited that opposing the Peronist president was simply counterproductive. As Rodolfo Terragno, ex-Radical minister of public works explained: "Today Radicalism cannot question the government without being asked, in turn, to report on what Radicalism has done. Menem's government is promoting massive and urgent privatizations, together with an abrupt deregulation and mutilation of the state. All this is being done in an effort to secure the dictatorship of the market. Before a model like this, no matter how we defend our record, we will always be vulnerable to the accusations: our state reform was, from today's perspective, timid, faithless, late, and ineffective." *Clarín,* August 28, 1990, 9.

60. The Congress deemed the administration's original ENTel offering as simply too generous: it guaranteed the new owners annual profits (via phone rates) of 16 percent on the firm's total net asset value, even though buyers would only purchase 60 percent of the company's equity. This arrangement would have provided annual profits of about $500 million—guaranteed by the government if the market "failed." Congress reduced the rate of return to reflect the portion of equity actually acquired (i.e., 60 percent). See "Argentina: Reversing the Past Fifty Years," 99. The corruption charges centered on the favoritism ENTel's trustee management showed in discharging the firm's outstanding debts to suppliers. Originally, part of the sales revenue was to be channeled into social welfare programs like education and health care, etc. But pressure from suppliers caused management trustees to shift priorities. In the end, two suppliers—Siemens de Argentina and FECOM-NEC— were paid $63 and $3 million respectively as part of the divestment transaction. The firm's many other creditors/suppliers received nothing. See Manzetti and Blake, "Market Reforms and Corruption in Latin America," 678.

61. Manzetti and Blake, "Market Reforms and Corruption in Latin America," 678.

62. Besides privatization, Menem also used decrees to advance market reforms relative to deregulation, taxes, salaries, debt, trade, and public administration reform. For a succinct summary see Delia Ferreira Rubio and Matteo Goretti, "Menem's Decretazo (1989-1998): The Inefficiency of the Constitutional Reform to Modify the Practice of the Executive Regarding Need and Urgency Decrees," paper presented at the 1998 meeting of the Latin American Studies Association, Chicago, Illinois, September 24–26, 1998.

63. Quoted in Saba and Manzetti, "Privatization in Argentina: The Implications for Corruption," 362.

64. In fact, Cavallo recruited several hundred technocratic-oriented officials—many from his research/consulting agency, the Fundación Mediterranánea. Some of the most prominent technocrats included Carlos Sánchez (vice-minister of economy), Edmundo Soria (secretary of transports), Luis Murina (undersecretary of administrative coordination), Juan Carlos Bongiovanni (undersecretary of trade), Ricardo Gutiérrez (secretary of finance), and Carlos Tacchi (secretary of public finances).

65. In October 1991 Cavallo designated Horacio Álvarez Rivero as undersecretary for privatizations. See "Impulso a la privatización," *Clarín,* October 18, 1991, 17.

66. Judith Teichman, "Mexico and Argentina: Economic Reform and Technocratic Decision Making," *Studies in Comparative International Development* 32, no. 1 (Spring 1997): 47.

67. This is the celebrated—and often cited—experience of Cavallo's first rocky face-to-face interchange with Congress. When lawmakers harshly criticized the economy minister's proposals, Cavallo's retort smacked of defiance: "If you don't like what I am doing, go to the President and ask him to appoint another Minister." *Review of the River Plate* (February 15, 1991), 70.

68. The terms of this informal pact are detailed in Javier Corrales, "Why Argentines Followed Cavallo: A Technopol between Democracy and Economic Reform," in Jorge I. Domínguez, ed., *Technopols: Freeing Politics and Markets in Latin America in the 1990s* (University Park, Penn.: Pennsylvania State University Press, 1997).

69. Margheritis, *Implementing Structural Adjustment in Argentina,* 176.

70. Corrales, "Coalitions and Corporate Choices in Argentina."

71. For review, see *Statistical Yearbook Republic of Argentina* (Buenos Aires: Instituto Nacional de Estadísticas y Censos, 1997).

72. For an example of such arguments see Mario Damill and Roberto Frenkel, "Restauración democrática y política económica: Argentina, 1984-1991," in Juan Antonio Morales and Gary McMahon, eds., *La política económica en la transición a la democracia: Lecciones de Argentina, Bolivia, Chile y Uruguay* (Santiago: CIEPLAN, 1993). For a nuanced argument that takes issue with the "crisis" account of successful reform, see Javier Corrales, "Do Economic Crises Contribute to Economic Reform? Argentina and Venezuela in the 1990s," *Political Science Quarterly* 112, no. 4 (1997-98).

73. For discussion of these policy types see Merilee S. Grindle and John W. Thomas, *Public Choices and Policy Change: The Political Economy of Reform in Developing Countries* (Baltimore, Md.: Johns Hopkins University Press, 1991), especially chapter 4.

74. The economic data relevant to both crises is derived from de la Balze, *Remaking the Argentine Economy.*

75. For discussion of these perspectives see Anne O. Krueger, "Virtuous and Vicious Circles in Economic Development," *American Economic Association Papers and Proceedings* 83 (May 1993); Kurt Weyland, "The Political Fate of Market Reform in Latin America, Africa, and Eastern Europe," *International Studies Quarterly* 42, no. 4 (December 1998); and Corrales, "Do Economic Crises Contribute to Economic Reform?"

76. In 1989 Chile privatized the LAN-Chile Airlines, Guatemala divested Aviateca, and Mexico sold off Mexicana Airlines (following Aeroméxico's 1988 divestment). See David L. Edgell Sr., and Wanda Barquin, "Privatization of Tourism and Air Transportation," in Paul H. Boeker, ed., *Latin America's Turnaround: Privatization, Foreign Investment and Growth* (San Francisco, Calif.: ICS Press, 1993), 171.

77. These bidders were the Scandinavian Airways System and Telefónica de España.

78. Barbara Stallings, "International Influence on Economic Policy: Debt, Stabilization, and Structural Reform," in Stephan Haggard and Robert R. Kaufman, *The Politics of Economic Adjustment* (Princeton, N.J.: Princeton University Press, 1992).

79. Quoted in *Ambito Financiero,* June 29, 1990.

80. Stephan Haggard and Steven B. Webb, "What Do We Know About the Political Economy of Economic Policy Reform?" *World Bank Research Observer* 8, no. 2 (July 1993): 158. A number of scholars frame at least part of their reform analysis around state-societal coalitions. For examples, see Starr, "Government Coalitions and the Viability of Currency Boards"; G. John Ikenberry, "The International Spread of Privatization Policies: Inducements, Learning, and 'Policy Bandwagoning,'" in Ezra N. Suleiman and John Waterbury, eds., *The Political Economy of Public Sector Reform and Privatization* (Boulder, Colo.: Westview, 1990), 94-95; John Waterbury, "The Political Management of Economic Adjustment and Reform," in Joan M. Nelson, ed., *Fragile Coalitions: The Politics of Economic Adjustment* (Washington, D.C.: Overseas Development Council, 1989); and Stephan Haggard and Joan Nelson, "Panel Discussion," in John Williamson, ed., *The Political Economy of Policy Reform* (Washington, D.C.: Institute for International Economics, 1994), 468, 473.

81. Adam Przeworski, "Some Problems in the Study of the Transition to Democracy," in Guillermo O'Donnell, Philippe C. Schmitter, and Laurence Whitehead, eds., *Transitions from Authoritarian Rule: Comparative Perspectives* (Baltimore, Md.: Johns Hopkins University Press, 1986), 58.

82. John Waterbury, "The Heart of the Matter? Public Enterprise and the Adjustment Process," in Stephan Haggard and Robert R. Kaufman, eds., *The Politics of Economic Adjustment* (Princeton, N.J.: Princeton University Press, 1992), 191.

83. Williamson and Haggard, *"The Political Conditions for Economic Reform,"* 579.

84. Douglass C. North, "Privatization, Incentives, and Economic Performance," in Terry L. Anderson and Peter J. Hill, eds., *The Privatization Process: A World Perspective* (Lanham, Md.: Rowman & Littlefield, 1996), 36.

85. Mary M. Shirley, "Privatization in Latin America: Lessons for Transitional Europe," *World Development* 2, no. 9 (1994): 1313.

Chapter 7

Rethinking the Politics of Reform: Retrospect and Legacies

The market model was very effective at destroying low-productivity jobs but totally incapable of generating new ones in significant quantities.
—Lorenzo Meyer

Like many developing countries Mexico entered the 1980s facing profound problems that challenged policy makers' skill, imagination, and political abilities. In many respects Mexican leaders rose to the task, and in some instances policy reformers achieved extraordinary success; in the economic sphere, for example, the outcome was no less than a complete transformation of Mexico's political economy. Yet the total reform record remains mixed. When reformers failed they did so wholesale: after five years of effort very little changed in Mexico's environmental policy regime.

The burden of this book has been to reexamine the politics of policy reform and explain the factors behind success or failure. The evidence presented demonstrates that coalition politics, effective institutional innovation, and the capacity to minimize or impose the costs of change on policy losers were integral to reform outcomes. When these factors were present success followed: reforms moved from the drawing table to adoption, and ultimately implementation. When they were absent, success proved elusive. This analytic approach helps clarify fundamental political forces that govern the process of policy reform, and ultimately shape political outcomes. Following a discussion of the contributions this framework makes to existing scholarship, this chapter concludes the study of Mexico's remarkable transition period by considering some of the central sociopolitical consequences Mexico's reform campaign ultimately produced, and in light of these consequences, how durable the reforms are likely to be.

Revisiting the Politics of Reform

Governments seeking to reverse long-standing statist policies face a daunting task. Beyond age-old issues of how to secure the general well-being by [re]allocating scarce resources and [re]structuring economic and political relations, neoliberal reformers also confront the consequences of policy feedback. Dense linkages that evolved between state agencies and social actors, the benefits some social groups derived from statist policies, plus the career and institutional concerns which developed inside the bureaucracy, all conspire to maintain the status quo. These forces create lock-in effects that raise the costs of change, making some policy alternatives extremely difficult to pursue. Moreover, as a consequence of prior statist policies the shift to neoliberalism triggers the reformer's dilemma—opposition from concentrated groups of losers whose antireform intensity is inversely proportional to their perceived costs. Surmounting these obstacles is by no means easy, and on the whole, by the early 1990s Latin America boasted only a limited number of successful, comprehensive reform campaigns. As Anne Krueger observed: "One of the most discouraging features of reform programs [in Latin America] has been the limited number of success stories."[1] Mexico's economic achievements, therefore, constitute a clear outlier in an otherwise sober regional picture, and its experience affords important insights into the politics of successful policy reform.

In chapter 1 I discussed several alternative explanations of successful policy transformation—adjustment arguments, autonomy arguments, and coalition arguments. Each set provides some purchase on why governments embraced market policies and/or why some might be able to transform their policies more successfully than others. But these arguments—either singularly or in combination—cannot fully explain Mexico's reform dynamics and mixed record of success. Adjustment arguments explain the *why* of reform, but not the *how.* Autonomy arguments of all stripes (systemic centralized power, the presence of insulated "change teams," and "embedded autonomy") tend to overpredict outcomes, underspecify the source and process of effective technocratic insulation, and/or offer no compelling account of successful policy implementation. Finally, conventional coalition arguments view coalitions as essential to policy *implementation* (or consolidation), but inconsequential to policy *formulation and adoption;* consequently, they emphasize alliances between state and nonstate actors but overlook the importance of reform coalitions inside the state. This limits the explanatory power of contemporary coalition analysis, as does the absence of a substantive theory as to what empowers a coalition to prevail in struggles over policy change.

These drawbacks notwithstanding, the literature on policy transformations has advanced our knowledge of reform considerably. This book owes a clear debt to preceding scholarship and draws heavily upon it. It also extends our understanding of successful reform dynamics. The argument presented stakes its claim on coalitions, both in and outside the state; it provides new insights into the role "change team" members can play, stressing their political as well as technical skills. Finally, it situates these factors within an institutional framework to assess how institutional arrangements influence policy struggles, and thereby, reform outcomes.

Perhaps the most striking paradox found in the general literature on policy reform in developing countries is the scant attention paid to coalitions inside the state. The paradox stems from one of the most consistent findings derived from multicountry studies of reform: in virtually no instance have domestic interest groups clamored for the type of comprehensive reform packages many governments pursued; instead of social pressures driving market reform efforts, and thereby explaining outcomes, policy change was instituted and advanced most often from the top down.[2] With little support for societal or group theory explanations of reform outcomes,[3] the search for causality shifted to the state.

Whether in a "limited pluralist" system like Mexico's, or more open ones, the state constitutes a realm of diverse interests, bureaucratic inertia, institutional jealousies, and differential power capacities—all of which greatly complicate the process of reform. Within this problematic milieu scholars identified a set of factors whose operation and interaction seemed most likely to determine success. Those closely correlated to successful policy formulation and adoption include: (1) the state's relative autonomy and degree of centralized authority within it, (2) the presence of an insulated, technocratic "change team" to whom policy formulation is delegated, and (3) the degree of presidential support these technocrats enjoy. The one factor most analysts conclude is critical to successful implementation is the development of a coalition between state reformers on the one hand, and societal actors that stand to benefit from the new policy direction on the other.[4]

For reasons discussed in chapter 2, reform accounts built around these factors offer compelling insights into the dynamics of successful policy change. However, notwithstanding the state's acknowledged prominence in reform and the diverse interests that flourish within it, the impact of coalition politics inside the state has gone largely unnoticed. By contrast, this book has stressed that reformers' capacity to coalesce, collaborate, and act jointly—both to formulate policy and marginalize opponents inside the government—is crucial to the success of large-scale reform projects, and is at least as important to outcomes as the state's degree of autonomy, the presence of a competent change team, and its level of presidential support. Evidence from Mexico's reform experience repeatedly bore this out: the Ministry Transportation, for example, resisted Aeroméxico's divestment and acquiesced only after budget-watching agencies moved jointly to seize control of the agenda and strip the carrier of subsidies; this same ministry bowed to transport deregulation only in the face of deregulators' persistence and an uncooperative Office of the Presidency; and Cananea's divestment—initially hobbled by political infighting and institutional jealousies—came to fruition only after more cooperative interactions emerged. That major reforms turned upon cooperation between actors (some of whom, like the OPR) were far removed from the actual formulation of specific initiatives) underscores the need to take intrastate coalitions seriously when assessing the dynamics of successful policy change.

Of course, the mere development of reform coalitions did not guarantee their success. As I have argued throughout, reformers operate within an institutional matrix whose constraints influence the leverage they can exert over the policy process and their probabilities of success. In Mexico, institutional arrangements provided reform advocates an initial endowment of power (e.g., influential bureaucratic positions), but they neither guaranteed reformers unquestioned advantage in policy struggles nor predetermined their outcomes. What mattered was how coalition members "played the game" inside the institutional context—one facet of which was the capacity to auger their organizational strength via institutional innovation.

"Surprisingly little systematic work," Haggard and Webb contend, "has been undertaken on how the organization of decisionmaking is likely to affect the success of adjustment efforts."[5] This study has devoted considerable time to this theme by tracing the evolution and reconstitution of institutional arrangements inside the Mexican government. In researching Mexico's policy transformations I was struck by how reformers gained control of the agenda by changing institutional variables, the frequency with which institutional innovation preceded reformers' success, and the diligence with which successful reformers pursued institutional change. The energy devoted to these activities is no mystery. To quote Terrance McDonald: "small changes in rules can bring about big changes in agendas";[6] to elaborate upon McDonald, institutional change helps coalition members alter their organizational position inside the government, and acquire greater authority, resources, and leverage over the policy process. The case studies illustrate just how consequential these endeavors can be, and the degree to which Mexican reformers engaged in them reflects an acute understanding of the *political*—not just technical—dimensions of reform. I will come back to this important, though undervalued aspect of reform shortly.

Institutional innovation is hardly a novel concept and political economists increasingly have recognized it as essential to providing "change teams" the insulation and leverage required to undertake and advance reform.[7] Indeed, some analysts contend the importance of innovation trumps that of policy change teams themselves. In reviewing thirteen separate market reform projects worldwide, Stephan Haggard, for example, suggests: "The critical question is not whether a technocratic team exists, but where it sits in the institutional matrix of decision making. It can be stated categorically that not a single reform effort in this group of [thirteen] cases was initiated and sustained without supportive changes in the institutional setting."[8]

Too often, however, previous work on neoliberal transitions has overlooked the pivotal role *individual* team members can play in the process of institutional change. Indeed, a good deal of scholarship puts the onus of such innovation—perhaps wrongly—on the national leadership. To cite several examples: Nelson has written that "In almost all cases of vigorous and sustained reform, political leaders concentrated authority for economic management in 'change teams' and protected those teams from political pressures both from outside and from within the government itself"; Callaghy opines that leaders "need to use, insulate and protect the technocratic staff" in order to succeed; Bates and Krueger, meanwhile, contend that "Economic technocrats become powerful ... because *politicians choose to make them so and organize the political process in a way that enables them to exploit the technocrats' informational advantages*" (emphasis mine).[9]

Mexico's experience, however, gives pause to accepting such broad, categorical propositions. Specifically, it suggests the links between presidential initiative, effective autonomous change teams, and the innovations conducive to reform are less straightforward than commonly believed. As preceding chapters illustrate, many of the organizational and procedural changes that sheltered reformers and turned the tide in their favor, were in fact initiated by team members themselves, then subsequently ratified by the president. Prominent examples include the offices of Deregulation and Privatization, "resectorization," and the deregulators' powerful bureaucratic veto. These dynamics suggest we may wish to revise our thinking regarding how change teams acquire autonomy, and expand our concept of the role team members play in facilitating reform beyond simply crafting appropriate policy. The case studies remind us that technocratic reformers can be more than potted plants, passively awaiting their anointment, protection, and autonomization by chief executives. The tendency to view them as such devalues the importance of individual agency on the one hand, and exaggerates executive influence on the other. This is no minor semantic quibble.

To be sure, presidents do initiate important innovations that contribute greatly to successful outcomes (by revising privatization criteria, for example, Carlos Salinas ensured that public enterprises previously deemed "priority" would not escape divestment).[10] And of course, their assent is required to give force and legitimacy to initiatives which percolate up from below. Analytically, however, prudence suggests we not press the case for executive initiative too far. Doing so implicitly invests "successful" reformist presidents with a type of farsighted leadership quality that few individuals facing imperfect information actually possess. Not only are presidents unable to superintend the entire bureaucracy, but often it is officials "on the ground," so to speak, who best understand the nature and location of potential policy veto points and how to eliminate them. Stated differently, the political skills policy reformers possess *matter,* and are as important to success as their technocratic ones. Knowing how and when to change the rules, manipulate institutional variables to their advantage, and seek additional allies outside the "change team" itself are potent political instruments in the reformers' toolbox and can be particularly effective in policy struggles inside the state. Although politically astute technocrats of the sort described here might be a rare breed, they do in fact exist. Their activities provide an additional lens through which to examine the process of institutional innovation and suggest that change team members can facilitate reform in ways few analysts have yet to fully appreciate.[11]

Mexico's record also suggests that successful reformers often deploy their political skills throughout the reform process, not just the early stages of policy formulation and adoption. Once new policy is adopted, the delicate task of implementing reforms outside the state begins. Yet, notes Omotunde Johnson: "It is one thing to design a program; it is another to implement it."[12] This observation applies with particular force to Mexico. As shown throughout this study, far from being a smooth, linear process, implementation is an inherently political and politically risky one. One of the chief difficulties, of course, is the reformer's dilemma: most reforms penalize status quo beneficiaries, and hence, spark opposition; implementing comprehensive projects in the face of sustained resistance risks depleting a government's political goodwill. That Mexico's informal political rules encouraged public contestation over policy implementation compounded the challenge by testing reformers' abilities to manage what some call the government's "stock" of political capital—i.e., the aggregate support and credibility governments enjoy at any given moment. This stock, Ardito-Barletta suggests, "can be maintained, spent, or increased during the life of that government," and in the course of reform, "[t]he government constantly needs to reevaluate how its policies and actions affect the stock of political capital, which it needs to govern effectively."[13]

Since most governments eventually see the folly of depleting their political capital by simply imposing the costs of policy change, successful implementation requires expanding the reform coalition outside the state in ways that incorporate at least some potential policy losers, and it is here that reformers' political skills assume greater importance. As we have seen, in Mexico coalitional expansion occurred through some variant or combination of the cost-minimizing strategies outlined in chapter 2 (compensation, persuasion, division). Thus, to varying degrees Mexican reformers complemented imposition strategies with minimizing ones, and at least in the realm of economic policy, employed them successfully to transform some opponents of change into stakeholders in the reform program. This helped produce a sea change in the government's historic economic role, a substantial revision in public-private sector relations, and a record of accomplishment few developing countries could match. We should expect policy change of this magnitude to create powerful ripple effects in society and the general polity. The next two sections, therefore, explore some of the broader repercussions of Mexico's economic reform campaign and their likely impact on the durability of reforms themselves.

Policy Reform and Sociopolitical Consequences

From the beginning of Mexico's postrevolutionary regime the state played an important role in national development, assuming new responsibilities as the need and means arose. The pursuit of import-substitution, public sector expansion, and full employment policies (through padding public enterprise payrolls) are just three examples. The long-run impact of statist policies was profound. They helped shape social classes (both labor and capitalists), the size of government bureaucracy, bureaucratic functions, and patterns of state-societal interaction; they linked social groups, economic interests, and government agencies in uniquely configured patterns. They also provided a stream of asymmetrical, often erratic benefits that gave important actors a stake in the prevailing development model. New market policies that restructured prior relationships and redirected benefit flows were bound to produce dramatic sociopolitical consequences.

Economic Reforms: The Social Impact

In ways large and small, positive and negative, a decade of reform touched millions of Mexicans' daily lives. But on balance, by the mid-1990s the aggregate social effect of the reforms was negative.[14] On the whole, living standards had dropped, job creation lagged, union strength declined, and income/wealth inequality widened dramatically. Table 7.1 depicts some of the major indicators of declining social welfare.

A principal factor behind this development was the tendency of some policies to cancel the benefits of others. Between 1983 and 1994, for example, fiscal discipline—and later wage/price controls—cut inflation significantly to the benefit of all Mexicans.[15] But for the poor and working class, austerity budgets and, deregulation offset this advantage by eliminating subsidies on a range of foodstuffs and, in some cases, restricting public service provision. Besides cross-cancellation, some market policies also concentrated benefits in select groups but failed to yield anticipated positive externalities beyond them. Trade is a case in point. In the early Salinas years trade liberalization sparked a non-oil export boom, especially in manufactured goods where exports soared between 1988 and 1994. Many analysts expected trade growth to bolster employment levels; but in the end, export expansion produced no appreciable upsurge in job creation. By March 1994 manufacturing employment had declined roughly 33 percent from 1980 levels,[16] as increasing competition forced private firms to produce more efficiently and take steps to lower labor costs.

Slack job growth in manufacturing, which reflects 22 percent of total employment, was symptomatic of a larger employment problem—one that government statistics tend to obscure.[17] Since the late 1980s over 1 million people entered the economically active population annually, but through the early 1990s the formal economy absorbed less than 30 percent of these new entrants (most turned to the informal economy). One keen Mexico watcher estimates that while the economy created 1.5 million new jobs between 1988 and 1993—far below the required annual target—it lost 500,000 in the corporate shakeout induced by Mexico's debt crisis.[18] Paradoxically, measures designed to resuscitate the economy weakened job prospects further: fiscal austerity and privatization helped fuel un- and underemployment by downsizing the public enterprise sector and general bureaucracy.[19] These trends, of course, affected organized labor in ways hardly benign, and labor's position continued to deteriorate as the reforms deepened.

Table 7.1   Mexico: Selected Economic and Social Indicators, Pre- and Post-Reform

	1980	1985	1988	1990	1992	1994	1995	1996	1997
Economic Indicators									
GDP growth	9.1	2.5	1.2	4.5	2.8	3.5	-6.9	5.1	-
GDP per capita growth	5.4	0.5	-.7	2.3	.6	-1.4 (1993)	-	-	-
CPI	-	63.8	51.7	29.9	11.9	7.1	52	27.7	-
Manuf. Exports (US $mil.)	1,786	6,377	8,546	10,658	32,054	45,786	59,131	-	-
Unemployment	4.5	4.4	3.5	2.7	2.8	3.7	6.2	5.5	-
Income distribution	.48 (1981)	50.58 (1984)	-	54.98 (1989)	50.31	-	53.7	-	3.9
Social Welfare Indicators									
Illiteracy rate	17	9.7	-	12.4	-	-	10.4	-	-
Infant mortality	60	53	41	-	36 (1993)	-	-	-	-
Population % with access to safe drinking water	-	82	69	79.5	83 (1993)	-	95	-	-
Average daily caloric intake	2,803 (1978–80)	2,925 (1984–86)	3,123 (1986–88)	3,062 (1988–90)	3,146	-	-	-	-
Physicians per 1,000	.9174	-	1.0352 (1989)	1.0799	1.1481	1.1933	1.2285	1.2285	-
Number of hospitals	59,983	59,250	-	63.122	71,700	65,953 (1993)	-	-	-
Expenditure on health care (as % of GDP)	.4	.3	.4	.3	-	-	-	-	-

Sources: GDP growth, *The Mexican Economy* (Banco de México, 1996, 1997): http://www.banxico.org.mx/public_html/doyai/mexecon96/at7.html; http://www.banxico.org.mx/public_html/doyai/mexecon97/at7.html; CPI; *The Mexican Economy* (Banco de México, 1996, 1997): http://www.banxico.org.mx/public_html/doyai/mexecon96/at24.html; http://www.banxico.org.mx/public_html/doyai/mexecon97/at15.html; GDP growth per capita, Latin America Network Information Center: http://lanic.utexas.edu/la/region/aid/aid94/Country/MEXCAR.html; and 1980 GDP per capita figures from Jaime Ros, "Mexico in the 1990s: A New Economic Miracle? Some Notes on the Economic and Policy Legacies of the 1980s," in Maria Lorena Cook, Kevin J. Middlebrook, and Juan Molinar Horcasitas, eds., *The Politics of Economic Restructuring: State-Society Relations and Regime Change in Mexico* (La Jolla, Calif.: Center for U.S.-Mexican Studies, University of California, San Diego, 1994); Export of Manufactures, unemployment, access to safe drinking water, physicians per 1,000 inhabitants, Inter-American Development Bank: http://database.iab.org/esdbweb/scripts/esdbweb.exc; income distribution, *Poverty Monitoring Database*, World Bank: http://wbln0018.worldbank.org/dg/povertys.nsf; and illiteracy rate, infant mortality, average daily caloric intake, number of hospitals, expenditure on health care, *Statistical Abstract of Latin America*, vol. 34 (Los Angeles: University of California Press, 1998).

Historically, the mix of economic statism and political corporatism had worked largely to labor's favor, providing unions periodic preferential treatment, political clout, and the chance to carve out increasingly lucrative enclaves inside public enterprises. But this arrangement suffered badly in the face of radical policy change; syndicates linked to the ruling party via corporatism bore heavy burdens under policy adjustment, and for the most part, reformers turned a deaf ear to union complaints as divestment erased labor's sheltered positions, diminished its political clout, and eliminated tens of thousands of union jobs. The upshot was a dramatic decline in union strength—materially, organizationally, and politically.[20]

The reforms also aggravated an already unequal distribution of income and wealth.[21] Not only did the richest 10 percent of Mexicans increase their share of national income, but while only one Mexican businessman ranked among *Forbes* magazine's billionaire list in 1988, Mexico sported twent-four billionaires just six years later—more than Britain, Italy, and France together, with a combined asset base representing 12 percent of Mexico's gross domestic product. One factor that helped concentrate wealth was the pattern of privatization. Whereas other divestment programs embraced the concept of "popular capitalism" by selling state assets on the capital market (e.g., Chile, Thatcher's Great Britain), the Salinas administration auctioned off most parastatals to large industrial groups and financial conglomerates—usually to those with prior experience in the firms' sectoral operations or related activities. The Cananea Copper Mine, for example, was sold to Grupo Minera, proprietor of Mexicana de Cobre; similarly, many of the eighteen commercial banks the government reprivatized went to financiers who controlled brokerage houses, prior owners, or industrial groups that had expanded into the financial sector during the 1980s.[22]

Salinas insisted this pattern of divestment would ensure newly privatized firms the capital needed to reinvest, modernize, and gain a stronger global competitive posture. There were substantial opportunity costs to this approach, however. By foregoing so-called popular capitalism the administration forfeited the chance to "share the wealth," enlarge the middle class, and give Mexicans outside the elite a greater stake in the new development model. Instead, Mexico's program allowed its largest financial interests to capture the economy's commanding heights.[23]

The Political Impact

These social developments contributed to one of the reforms' greatest political consequences, namely, the reconstitution of the PRI's historic governing coalition. In large measure, under Salinas Mexico's financial giants displaced popular sectors (organized labor, segments of the peasantry) as the cornerstone of regime support. This transition reflected the inevitable "winnowing effects" of dramatic policy reform, a distaste for neoliberal prescriptions among popular segments, and the government's need to shore up social support for policy change.

In the case of labor the combination of privatization and corporatism drove a wedge between the government and segments of the labor movement. Pursuant to aggressive divestment the administration moved against reform-hostile labor leaders, jailing some on corruption charges and forcing others to resign. Constrained by corporatist politics, many labor leaders placed the government's policy agenda (and their own positions) ahead of rank-and-file interests. Thus, the contract revisions that pared back worker benefits at Cananea and Sicartsa proceeded with the backing of local syndicates' national leadership,[24] and were but a microcosm of what occurred throughout the public sector labor movement. As a consequence, notes Judith Teichman, "The failure of union leaders to defend the interests of their rank and file . . . served to deteriorate the ties that have hitherto bound the rank and file of powerful elements of organized labor to the state."[25] Although union workers did not abandon the regime en masse, union leaders' capacity to deliver bloc votes for the ruling party (and hence, both labor's strategic value to the regime and the utility of political corporatism) declined markedly.

Nor were neoliberalism's corrosive effects confined solely to the old coalition's labor constituents. Segments of the PRI's peasant base took umbrage at reforms like the privatization of communal *ejido* lands and the North American Free Trade Agreement (NAFTA).[26] The former marked the end of Mexico's land reform program and dashed many peasants' hopes of receiving legal recognition of their land claims; the latter promised to expose small farmers to foreign competition. In Chiapas, peasants responded with the Zapatista National Liberation Army, Mexico's first guerrilla insurrection in two decades.[27] To the government's chagrin, the rebels quickly captured popular sympathies and upset the image Salinas had carefully crafted of a stable, progressive, and modernizing Mexico, enticing to foreign investment. The repercussions proved highly damaging: in a country whose leaders insisted that "first world status" was on the horizon, the Zapatistas' sudden appearance spooked many foreign investors and contributed to the December 1994 currency crisis that brought the economy (and nearly the government) to its knees.[28]

Mindful that radical policy adjustments would, most likely, transform former allies into antagonists, Salinas tried to compensate by actively courting Mexico's private sector, particularly large conglomerates and exporters. Like Argentina's Carlos Menem, he used pro-business reforms to build "a new strategic relationship with the most diversified, concentrated, and internationally competitive sectors of business."[29] As the reforms deepened the coalitional transition crystallized. Business conglomerates actively worked to secure the PRI financial donations, while the party aggressively milked its new cash cow: at a private 1993 dinner party presided over by President Salinas, PRI officials asked each of "Mexico's top business leaders, the beneficiaries of privatization," to cough up $25 million to fund the party's 1994 electoral campaigns.[30] Although news reports of the shakedown embarrassed the government, many entrepreneurs were happy to recompense the PRI handsomely for its pro-business performance, and through 1994 the PRI's new political coalition (plus the "political spending" of Salinas's highly touted

PRONASOL program) helped bring victory at the polls.

Yet partly as a consequence of sustained reform, the party saw its internal cohesion fracture and electoral fortunes wane. In 1987, Cuauhtémoc Cárdenas led antireform elements out of the PRI to run for president against Salinas. Besides producing the most controversial election in history, this development gave birth to a new political force, the left-of-center Party of the Democratic Revolution (PRD).[31] These and later defections, plus the fallout from the 1994 peso crash, cost Mexico's ruling party its vaunted internal discipline, reputation for economic competence, and ultimately much of its electoral appeal. In July 1997 the PRI lost control of the lower congressional house for the first time in nearly seventy years, was trounced in Mexico City's first ever mayoral election by the PRD, and lost gubernatorial races in Querétaro and Nuevo León to the center-right National Action Party (PAN). Finally, in July 2000, Mexicans ended the PRI's political dominance by electing the PAN's Vicente Fox their next president.

The Durability of Reforms

The dramatic sociopolitical developments discussed above raise questions regarding the durability of Mexico's market reforms. On the upside there is prima facie evidence to suggest the policy shifts will endure. To begin, Vicente Fox (a former Coca-Cola executive) favors the market; moreover, contemporary intellectual currents in Mexican policy circles pull strongly against a return to what many believe are the discredited concepts of statism. There are other impediments as well: the Mexican state remains deeply indebted and lacks both the financial resources to re-create a large public sector, or the stomach to face down likely pressures from international lenders to stay the course.

Besides these factors important institutional changes that accompanied new policies make a return to statism difficult. The North American Free Trade Agreement, for example, locks Mexico into a liberalized trade regime whose benefits—guaranteed access to the U.S. market, over $9 billion in foreign investment since 1994, and a 67 percent spike in trade with Canada and the United States—generate strong incentives not to pull out anytime soon.[32] It is notable that of Mexico's principal political parties, none have called for NAFTA's outright repeal. In addition, the Federal Law on Norms and Measures (engineered by the Office of Deregulation) wrought a sea change in Mexico's regulatory regimes.[33] It streamlined the stock of existing regulations and ensured that new ones were market-conforming, not market-resistant. Finally, the complementarity and interdependence of policies like divestment, deregulation, and trade liberalization create potent and mutually reinforcing incentives that most likely will steer policy along market paths for some time.

In short, a number of factors work against policy reversal. Nevertheless, Mexico's reforms are not completely set in stone. First, in actively courting various "winners" among private business, Mexico has followed the path of reform-consolidation prescribed in the scholarly literature, but whether the new market model can be sustained in the face of significant (and increasing) inequality is an open question. Much will depend upon expanding the pool of beneficiaries beyond what currently is a rather small "sacred circle."

Second, the PRI's stunning loss in the July 2000 presidential elections sparked a power struggle between old-line populists, pro-democratic reformers, and the party's technocratic wing. As of this writing it remains to be seen which faction will ultimately prevail (or even if the party can survive its abrupt de-coupling from the state's machinery and financial resources). But should the party endure, the outcome will shape the PRI's policy philosophy for years to come. According to Pedro Joaquín Coldwell, the party's former secretary-general, by converting the PRI into "a political instrument for the government's neoliberal project," the technocrats left the party's unreconstructed populists suffering "profound ideological confusion."[34] Old guard *priístas* not only loathe the technocrats' policy program but blame them for their party's electoral defeats. It is hard to imagine that an old guard-dominated PRI—returned to power in subsequent elections—would not seek to modify, if not reverse, Mexico's market model.

Finally, important changes among the patterns of governance detailed in chapter 2 also suggest the possibility of at least some policy "slippage." As noted, Mexico's "classic" political model concentrated power vertically at the federal level, and horizontally within the executive. While Salinas accelerated this trend,[35] his successor, Ernesto Zedillo, chose a very different path.[36] Strongly committed to both neoliberal and political reforms, Zedillo hoped to redefine the function of Mexico's presidency by limiting its discretional power. During the 1994 election campaign he pledged to govern by the rule of law (i.e., the Constitution) rather than traditional unwritten rules, abdicate the president's historic role as leader of the ruling party, relinquish the "right" to handpick his own successor, and encourage an independent judiciary and legislature. Despite occasional backsliding, once in office the president largely kept his promises.[37]

By limiting the presidency, however, Zedillo weakened a central component of Mexico's "classic" political system, thereby creating power vacuums and opportunities for new actors outside the executive to influence state policy. In the chaos and recriminations unleashed by the 1994 peso crisis, ruling party rank and file, Congress, and even strong-willed PRI governors rushed to fill the void.[38] In quick succession rank-and-file members took steps that made nearly all technocrats ineligible to be party candidates for high office; PRI congressional deputies demanded the government abandon neoliberalism altogether; and a number of PRI senators declared their independence from the president, vowing to vote *their constituents'* interests, rather than genuflect to the executive.[39] These developments marked a clear shift in the central axis of Mexican politics.[40] No longer was contestation over policy substance confined to select executive officials; instead, legislators displayed a new willingness to argue, debate, *and contest* policy issues, in lieu of rubber-stamping presidential initiatives. The showdown over Zedillo's 1997 budget drove this point home, as lawmakers sharply attacked the president's spending priorities and compelled his finance minister actually to *defend them* before a skeptical Congress.[41]

The retreat from *presidencialismo*, coupled with party turnover, increasing legislative autonomy, substantive policy contestation, and greater partisan competition, reflects significant changes in Mexico's traditional patterns of governance. Many voters have found a home outside the PRI, and lawmakers have found a voice. It is worth stressing that these developments constitute a political climate the opposite of which facilitated Mexico's rapid policy transformations. They bode well for the country's democratic transition, but conversely suggest maintaining strict fidelity to neoliberalism could prove a bumpy ride.

Although wholesale abandonment of neoliberalism seems unlikely in the short term, modifications to the existing development model do not. Despite its achievements, like many developing countries Mexico faces a backlog of pressing but unaddressed problems whose resolution will help promote economic prosperity and improve social well-being. Education, health care, housing, employment, poverty, and inequality all require substantial improvement to facilitate the accumulation of human capital increasingly recognized as central to long-term, equitable growth.[42] Early indications suggest a Fox administration will place more stress on these issues than its PRI predecessors, and because "free markets" alone are unlikely to resolve these problems, carefully crafted government action will be needed. This could well lead away from the minimalist government neoliberals typically prefer, and in Moisés Naim's words, force leaders to "rediscover the state," even as reformers rediscovered the market.[43] Ironically, the task of "humanizing" Mexico's market model while ensuring its continuity rests on the newly elected government of Vicente Fox, not on the party which orchestrated it.

Yet, the Fox administration also confronts a political climate in which the balance of power has changed markedly among central political actors, no party holds a majority of congressional seats, and lawmakers demand effective policy input. In this context constructing effective coalitions inside the state will help the new government advance its policy program; but executive-congressional and interparty negotiations will shape the course (and content) of policy far more than in the past.

Notes

1. Anne O. Krueger, *The Political Economy of Policy Reform in Developing Countries* (Cambridge, Mass.: MIT Press, 1993), 8.

2. On this point, Bates and Krueger's eight-country study typifies findings throughout the literature. "One of the most surprising findings," they note, "is the degree to which the intervention of interest groups fails to account for the initiation, or lack of initiation, of

policy reform." See Robert H. Bates and Anne O. Krueger, "Generalizations Arising from the Country Studies," in Robert H. Bates and Anne O. Krueger, eds., *Political and Economic Interactions in Economic Policy Reform: Evidence from Eight Countries* (Cambridge, Mass.: Blackwell, 1993), 455. A significant number of comparative studies reach similar conclusions. Some of the best include Stephan Haggard and Steven Webb, *Voting for Reform: Democracy, Political Liberalization, and Economic Adjustment* (New York: Oxford University Press, 1994); Joan M. Nelson, *Economic Crisis and Policy Choice: The Politics of Adjustment in the Third World* (Princeton, N.J.: Princeton University Press, 1990); John Williamson, ed., *The Political Economy of Policy Reform* (Washington, D.C.: Institute for International Economics, 1994); and Merilee S. Grindle and John W. Thomas, *Public Choices and Policy Change: The Political Economy of Reform in Developing Countries* (Baltimore, Md.: Johns Hopkins University Press, 1991).

3. The group theory approach is exemplified by Gourevitch, who saw policy change largely as a function of the "preferences of societal actors as shaped by their situation in the international and domestic economy." See Peter A. Gourevitch, *Politics in Hard Times: Comparative Responses to International Economic Crisis* (Ithaca, N.Y.: Cornell University Press, 1986), 54.

4. For a summary see Joan Nelson, "Conclusions," in Joan M. Nelson, *Economic Crisis and Policy Choice: The Politics of Adjustment in the Third World* (Princeton, N.J.: Princeton University Press, 1990), 347. On the importance of coalitions and implementation specifically, see John Waterbury, "The Political Management of Economic Adjustment and Reform," in Joan M. Nelson, ed., *Fragile Coalitions: The Politics of Economic Adjustment* (Washington, D.C.: Overseas Development Council, 1989).

5. Stephan Haggard and Steven B. Webb, "What Do We Know about the Political Economy of Economic Policy Reform?" *World Bank Research Observer* 8, no. 2 (July 1993): 162.

6. Terrance J. McDonald, "Institutionalism and Institutions in the Stream of History," *Polity* 28, no. 1 (Fall 1995): 131.

7. Shirley, for example, suggests that creating effective institutional entities with the technical capacity and motivation to privatize effectively is a "problem common to all privatizing countries," and lauds Mexico's Office of Privatization as a model response to the challenge. See Mary M. Shirley, "Privatization in Latin America: Lessons for Transitional Europe," *World Development* 22, no. 9 (1994): 1319.

8. The countries to which Haggard refers are Australia, Chile, Colombia, Indonesia, South Korea, Mexico, New Zealand, Peru, Poland, Portugal, Spain, and Turkey. Stephan Haggard, "Panel Discussion," in Williamson, *The Political Economy of Policy Reform*, 470.

9. Joan M. Nelson, "The Politics of Economic Transformation: Is Third World Experience Relevant in Eastern Europe?" *World Politics* 45 (April 1993): 436; Thomas Callaghy, "Lost between State and Market: The Politics of Economic Adjustment in Ghana, Zambia, and Nigeria," in Joan M. Nelson, *Economic Crisis and Policy Choice: The Politics of Adjustment in the Third World* (Princeton, N.J.: Princeton University Press, 1990), 263; and Bates and Krueger, "Generalizations Arising from the Country Studies," 463.

10. Similarly, by insisting on the passage of his omnibus reform law, Argentina's Carlos Menem bolstered his capacity to pursue reforms unilaterally.

11. A notable exception to this trend is the volume of essays contained in Jorge I. Domínguez, ed., *Technopols: Freeing Politics and Markets in Latin America in the 1990s* (University Park, Penn.: Pennsylvania State University Press, 1997); on the significance of politically oriented technical policy makers see especially chapter 1.

12. Omotunde E. G. Johnson, "Managing Adjustment Costs, Political Authority, and the Implementation of Adjustment Programs, with Special Reference to African Countries," *World Development* 22, no. 3 (1994): 401.

13. Nicolás Ardito-Barletta, "Panel Discussion," in Williamson, *The Political Economy of Policy Reform,* 460.

14. Guillermo Trejo and Claudio Jones, "Political Dilemmas of Welfare Reform: Poverty and Inequality in Mexico," in Susan Kaufman Purcell and Luis Rubio, eds., *Mexico under Zedillo* (Boulder, Colo.: Lynne Rienner, 1998), 69.

15. Wage and price controls were part of Mexico's overall stabilization program, embodied in the 1987 "Economic Solidarity Pact" and its subsequent revisions. See Laurence Whitehead, "Political Change and Economic Stabilization: The 'Economic Solidarity Pact,'" in Wayne A. Cornelius, Judith Gentleman, and Peter H. Smith, eds., *Mexico's Alternative Political Futures* (La Jolla, Calif.: Center for U.S.-Mexican Studies, University of California, San Diego, 1989).

16. See Manuel Pastor Jr. and Carol Wise, "Mexican-Style Neoliberalism, State Policy, and Distributional Stress," in Carol Wise, ed., *The Post-NAFTA Political Economy: Mexico and the Western Hemisphere* (University Park, Penn.: Pennsylvania State University Press, 1988), 51; and Diana Alarcón and Terry McKinley, "Increasing Wage Inequality and Trade Liberalization in Mexico," in Albert Berry, ed., *Poverty, Economic Reform, and Income Distribution in Latin America* (Boulder, Colo.: Lynne Rienner, 1998), 139.

17. Indeed, data in table 7.1 hardly capture the impact of either stagnant rural economies or the 1980s economic crisis, as workers struggled against waves of bankruptcies, public enterprise shutdowns, and layoffs in the Mexican bureaucracy. One reason for the discrepancy between these figures and reality is that the government only reports *urban* unemployment, ignoring the rural sector altogether. A 1991 study sponsored by the Mexican Labor Congress—which found a rural/urban open unemployment rate of 15 percent, and an underemployment rate of 41 percent—provides a far different picture. See Carlos Heredia and Mary Purcell, "Structural Adjustment in Mexico: The Root of the Crisis," (Washington, D.C.: The Development GAP, 1995); available from http://www.cs.unb.ca/~alopez-o/politics/structural.html.

18. See Wayne A. Cornelius, "Foreword," in Maria Lorena Cook, Kevin J. Middlebrook, and Juan Molinar Horcasitas, eds., *The Politics of Economic Restructuring: State-Society Relations and Regime Change in Mexico* (La Jolla, Calif.: Center for U.S.-Mexican Studies, University of California, San Diego, 1994), xii.

19. Enrique Dussel Peters, "Cambio estructural y potencialidades de crecimiento del sector manufacturero en México (1982–1991)," in Julio López, ed., *México: La nueva macroeconomía* (México, D.F.: Centro de Estudios para un Proyecto Nacional/Nuevo Horizonte Editores, 1994). In 1985 the de la Madrid administration furloughed roughly 51,000 government workers in various ministries and departments; in 1986 it discharged 10,000 more from the Fundidora de Monterrey steelworks. See Wayne A. Cornelius, "The Political Economy of Mexico under de la Madrid: The Crisis Deepens, 1985–1986," *Research Report Series* 43 (La Jolla, Calif.: Center for U.S.-Mexican Studies, University of California, San Diego, 1986); and Enrique Quintana López, "La bancarrota de Fundidora: Dimes y diretes financieros," *El Cotidiano* 3, no. 12 (1986).

20. See Kevin J. Middlebrook, *The Paradox of Revolution: Labor, the State, and Authoritarianism in Mexico* (Baltimore, Md.: Johns Hopkins University Press, 1995), 297.

21. See Pastor and Wise, "Mexican-Style Neoliberalism," 47; Carlos Marichal, "The Rapid Rise of the *Neobanqueros,* Mexico's New Financial Elite," *NACLA Report on the*

Americas 30, no. 6 (May–June 1997); Blanca Heredia, "State-Business Relations in Contemporary Mexico," in Mónica Serrano and Victor Bulmer-Thomas, eds., *Rebuilding the State: Mexico after Salinas* (London, England: Institute of Latin American Studies, University of London, 1996); Carlos Elizondo, "The Making of a New Alliance: The Privatization of the Banks in Mexico," *CIDE Documento de Trabajo* 5 (Mexico: CIDE, 1993); and Hector E. Schamis, "The Politics of Economic Reform: Distributional Coalitions and Policy Change in Latin America," *Working Paper* 250 (Notre Dame, Ind.: Helen Kellogg Institute for International Studies, University of Notre Dame, 1998), especially 20–25.

22. For example, multibillionaire Carlos Slim Helú (owner of the financial firm Carso-Inbursa and now-privatized phone company Telmex), purchased part of Banamex, Mexico's largest commercial bank; similarly, Eugenio Garza Laguera, who owned the financial firm Vamsa, took control of Mexico's second largest bank, Bancomer. See Marichal, "The Rapid Rise of the *Neobanqueros"*; see also Celso Garrido, "National Private Groups in Mexico, 1987–1993," *CEPAL Review* 53 (August 1994).

23. Ironically, the financial elite soon mismanaged their banks and when more than half defaulted between 1995 and 1996, the government was forced to absorb upwards to $40 billion of bad loans to keep them afloat.

24. A number of press reports cite the break between militant, antireform union locals and their more accommodating national leaders. See, for example, Salvador Corro, "Con su líder ausente, los mineros siguen rechazando las propuestas de la Compañía," *Proceso* 671 (September 11, 1989); Salvador Corro, "Por encima de sus lideres, los obreros de Sicartsa rechazan una modernización a costa de la mana de obra," *Proceso* 669 (August 28, 1989); Richard Johns, "Mexican Steelworkers Defy Union with Strike," *Financial Times,* August 23, 1989; see also Salvador Corro, "Con su líder ausente, los mineros siguen rechazando las propuestas de la compañía," *Proceso* 671 (September 11, 1989); and Herberto Castillo, "Ofensiva antisindical," *Proceso* 669 (August 28, 1989).

25. Judith Teichman, "Economic Restructuring, State-Labor Relations, and the Transformation of Mexican Corporatism," in Gerardo Otero, ed., *Neoliberalism Revisited: Economic Restructuring and Mexico's Political Future* (Boulder, Colo.: Westview, 1996), 162.

26. Merilee S. Grindle, "Reforming Land Tenure in Mexico: Peasants, the Market, and the State," in Riordan Roett, ed., *The Challenge of Institutional Reform* (Boulder, Colo.: Lynne Rienner, 1995).

27. To be fair, NAFTA was only one factor behind the Chiapas rebellion. Zapatistas also cited repression and corruption among their complaints. See Neil Harvey, "Rural Reforms and the Zapatista Rebellion: Chiapas, 1988-1995," in Gerardo Otero, ed., *Neoliberalism Revisited: Economic Restructuring and Mexico's Political Future* (Boulder, Colo.: Westview, 1996).

28. On Mexico's 1994 peso crisis see Maxwell A. Cameron and Vinod K. Aggarwal, "Mexican Meltdown: States, Markets and Post-NAFTA Financial Turmoil," *Third World Quarterly* 17, no. 5 (1996).

29. Edward Gibson, "The Populist Road to Market Reform: Policy and Electoral Coalitions in Mexico and Argentina," *World Politics* 49 (April 1997): 356. In privileging large conglomerates smaller firms were cut out of any benefits. Complaints over this situation brought little relief: to the end of the Salinas administration official policy consistently favored creating large conglomerates to help Mexico compete abroad. See *El Gobierno Mexicano,* no. 57 (México, D.F.: Presidencia de la República, 1993), 31. See also Manuel Pastor and Carol Wise, "The Origins and Sustainability of Mexico's Free Trade Policy," *International Organization* 48 no. 3 (1994): 459–489; Matilda Luna, "Entrepreneurial In-

terests and Political Action in Mexico: Facing the Demands of Economic Modernization," in Riordan Roett, ed., *The Challenge of Institutional Reform in Mexico* (Boulder, Colo.: Lynne Rienner, 1995); and Ben Ross Schneider, "Big Business and the Politics of Reform: Confidence and Concertation in Brazil and Mexico," in Sylvia Maxfield and Ben Ross Schneider, eds., *Business and the State in Developing Countries* (Ithaca, N.Y.: Cornell University Press, 1997).

30. Judith A. Teichman, *Privatization and Political Change in Mexico* (Pittsburgh. Penn.: University of Pittsburgh Press, 1996), 188.

31. Besides discontent over reform, these early dissidents also left the PRI over rules governing the party's internal operations and candidate selection (i.e., the imposition of candidates by the incumbent president, as opposed to their selection via democratic means). These political factors led other high-profile party members, like Manuel Camacho, to leave the PRI as well, and chart an independent political course. On the rise of the Party of the Democratic Revolution, see Kathleen Bruhn, *Taking on Goliath: The Emergence of a New Left Party and the Struggle for Democracy in Mexico* (University Park, Penn.: Pennsylvania State University Press, 1997).

32. Deborah L. Riner and John V. Sweeney, "The Effects of NAFTA on Mexico's Private Sector and Foreign Trade and Investment," in Riordan Roett, ed., *Mexico's Private Sector: Recent History, Future Challenges* (Boulder, Colo.: Lynne Rienner, 1998), 164.

33. See "Decreto que reforma la Ley Federal de Metrología y Normalización," *Diario Oficial,* January 7, 1992.

34. Leslie Crawford, "Zedillo under Fire As Peso Wobbles: Political Troubles Add to Problems Facing Mexico's President," *Financial Times,* August 31, 1995, 3.

35. Most scholars believe Carlos Salinas concentrated enormous power inside the presidency, and used that power more extensively (and effectively) than his predecessor, Miguel de la Madrid. He not only dominated the legislative agenda and handpicked his successor, but dismissed seventeen state governors and injected the presidency directly into electoral politics via the National Solidarity Program. See Miguel Ángel Centeno, *Democracy within Reason: Technocratic Revolution in Mexico* (University Park, Penn.: Pennsylvania State University Press, 1994); Wayne A. Cornelius, *Mexican Politics in Transition: The Breakdown of a One-Party-Dominant Regime* (La Jolla, Calif.: Center for U.S.-Mexican Studies, University of California, San Diego, 1996), 34, 36; and Roderic Camp, "Mexico's Legislature: Missing the Democratic Lockstep?" in David Close, ed., *Legislatures and the New Democracies in Latin America* (Boulder, Colo.: Lynne Rienner, 1995), 25.

36. Zedillo's presidential bid followed the March 1994 assassination of the PRI's first candidate, Luis Donaldo Colosio.

37. Luis Rubio, "Coping with Political Change," in Susan Kaufman Purcell and Luis Rubio, eds., *Mexico under Zedillo* (Boulder, Colo.: Lynne Rienner, 1998).

38. While the governors' rebellions centered mostly on political, not economic policy issues, their significance lies in the fact that declining presidential authority moved some old-line Mexican governors to assume an independent posture vis-à-vis Zedillo, and in states like Tabasco and Quintana Roo, demonstrate an independence from the president— and at times, outright defiance—that was unthinkable under Salinas. For discussion see Wayne A. Cornelius, "Subnational Politics and Democratization: Tensions between Center and Periphery in the Mexican Political System," in Wayne A. Cornelius, Todd A. Eisenstadt, and Jane Hindley, eds., *Subnational Politics and Democratization in Mexico* (La Jolla, Calif.: Center for U.S.-Mexican Studies, University of California, San Diego, 1999); and Denise Dresser, "Post-NAFTA Politics in Mexico: Uneasy, Uncertain, Unpredictable," in Carol

Wise, ed., *The Post-NAFTA Political Economy: Mexico and the Western Hemisphere* (University Park, Penn: Pennsylvania State University Press, 1998), 226–227.

39. The rank and file seized control of the PRI's 1996 17th General Assembly, and in a surprise move, overruled PRI leaders to require (for the first time) that every party candidate for the presidency, senate, or state governor to have been party members for at least ten years and have been elected to public office. These rule changes were aimed clearly at Mexico's now-disgraced, technocratic elite, many of whom—like Zedillo and his four predecessors—had never held elective office prior to winning the presidency. As one party delegate explained, "We have had to suffer the whims of powerful technocrats who send their buddies to be governors and senators, and they don't even know what our party stands for." See Julia Preston, "Rank-and-File Mount a Revolt in Mexico's Ruling Party," *New York Times,* September 23, 1996, A3; and "Mexican MPs Attack Free-Market Policies," *Independent* (London), January 13, 1996, 13; and Adolfo Garza, "PRI Senate Faction Breaks Tradition," *News,* September 22, 1997, 1.

40. As Dresser notes: "In the past, in order to decipher Mexico, analysts focused on the presidency and the PRI. After the 1997 election, the spotlight shifted to Congress." Dresser, "Post-NAFTA Politics in Mexico," 241.

41. In particular, legislators opposed Zedillo's social spending cutbacks and $26 billion commercial bank bailout. Julia Preston, "Opposition-Led Mexican House Greets Budget Angrily," *New York Times,* September 12, 1997, D4.

42. In Mexico, one in five primary schools has only a single teacher, and one in five fails to provide six complete grades of schooling; only 50 percent of students finish primary school, and of those that do (as of 1990–1991), 84 percent fail to meet the government's minimal academic requirements. Adequate health care is scarce in rural areas, and nationwide it is characterized by unequal access to service across class, ethnic, and geographic lines. Housing problems, meanwhile, are acute both in the shantytowns that ring major cities and in the countryside (according to 1990 census data, Mexico had a 4.6 million unit deficit in the stock of housing). See Trejo and Jones, "Political Dilemmas of Welfare Reform." For discussion of how governments might incorporate social policy goals into broader neoliberal frameworks see Nancy Birdsall, Carol Graham, and Richard H. Sabot, eds., *Beyond Trade-offs: Market Reform and Equitable Growth in Latin America* (Washington, D.C.: The Inter-American Development Bank, 1998).

43. See Moisés Naím, "Latin America's Journey to the Market: From Macroeconomic Shocks to Institutional Therapy," *ICEG Occasional Paper* 62, International Center for Economic Growth (San Francisco: ICS Press, 1995).

Appendix

Field Interviews, Mexico City

Federal Government

Luis Alberto Pérez Aceves — Former Director of Cananea Mining Company; Adjunct Director General, National Bank of Foreign Commerce.

Miguel Alemán — Senator, Veracruz; Chairman of Senate Ecology Commission.

René Altamirano — Director General of Control and Prevention of Environmental Contamination, Ministry of Urban Development and Ecology.

Cecelia Amero — Office of Privatization, Ministry of Finance.

Luz de Barrios — Office of Deregulation, Ministry of Commerce and Industrial Promotion.

Juan Carlos Beleaustegüigoitia — Adjunct General Director of the Office of Economic and Social Analysis, Ministry of Social Development.

Oscar de Buen — Coordinator of Advisors for Subsecretary of Infrastructure, Ministry of Communications and Transportation.

217

Juan Bueno Zirón	Foreign Trade Division, Ministry of Foreign Relations.
Alejandro Cano Ruiz	Advisor to the President, National Ecology Institute, Ministry of Social Development.
Alfredo Elias Ayub	Subsecretary of Energy, Ministry of Energy, Mines, and Parastatal Industries.
Arturo Fernández	Former Director General of the Office of Deregulation.
Rogelio Gasca Neri	Former General Director of Aeroméxico Airline.
Rogelio González	Director of Studies, Ministry of Urban Development and Ecology.
Victor Hugo Páramo	National Ecology Commission, Ministry of Urban Development and Ecology.
Carlos Hurtado	General Coordinator of Economic and Social Analysis, Office of Economic and Social Analysis, Ministry of Social Development.
Guillermo Ibarra	Juridical Director of Economic Deregulation, Office of Deregulation, Ministry of Commerce and Industrial Promotion.
Rossana Ingle	Director General of Operations and Corporate Control, Office of Privatization, Ministry of Commerce and Industrial Promotion.
Diana Lucer Ponce	National Ecology Commission, Ministry of Urban Development and Ecology.
Miguel de la Madrid	Former President of Mexico.
Emmanuel Mendez	Coordinator of Advisors, National Ecology Institute, Ministry of Social Development.

Gustavo Patiño	Subsecretary of Transportation, Ministry of Communications and Transportation.
Jesús Ponce	National Ecology Commission, Ministry of Urban Development and Ecology.
Alvaro Rebollo López	Public Accountant, Office of Privatization, Ministry of Finance.
Sergio Reyes Lujan	Subsecretary of Ecology, Ministry of Urban Development and Ecology; President of the National Institute of Ecology, Ministry of Social Development.
Evelyn Rodríguez	General Director of Economic Studies, Office of Deregulation, Ministry of Commerce and Industrial Promotion.
Carlos Sales	Advisor to the Minister of Finance, Ministry of Finance and Public Credit.
Gabriel Sod	Office of Deregulation, Ministry of Commerce and Industrial Promotion.
José Carlos Teñorio	Subdirector of the Program of International Cooperation for Ecology and the Environment, National Ecology Commission, Ministry of Urban Development and Ecology.

Mexico City Government

Manuel Camacho Solís	Mayor, Mexico City; former Minister of Ecology.
Juan Enriquez Cabot	Director of Metropolitan Services, Department of the Federal District.
Rodolfo Lacy	Director of Studies, General Coordination for Environmental Projects, Department of the Federal District.

Fernando Menéndez Garza	General Coordinator of Environmental Projects, Department of the Federal District; Technical Secretary for the Metropolitan Commission for Pollution Control.
Ramón Ojeda Mestre	General Coordinator of Pollution Prevention and Control, Department of the Federal District.
Gabriel Quadri de la Torre	General Coordinator of Environmental Planning, Department of the Federal District.
Sergio Sánchez Martinez	Director of Environmental Studies, Air Quality Management Group; Department of the Federal District.
Demitrio Sodi	President of the Ecology Commission, General Assembly, Mexico City.

General

Guillermo Becker	Former General Director, Sidermex.
Roberto Esquievel	Former Director of Operations, Altos Hornos.
Nícolas Gallegos	General Director, National Chamber of Freight Transport.
Napoleon Gómez Sada	President, Mining and Metallurgical Workers of the Mexican Republic (STMMRM).
Mariano Ladrón	Former Director of Maintenance and Operations, Aeroméxico Airline.
Emilio Ocampo	Former Director, Cananea Mining Company.
Gerardo Olvera	Director of Ecology, National Chamber of Manufacturing Industry (CANACINTRA).
Alvaro Zamúdio	Confederation of Chambers of Commerce (CONCAMIN).

International Financial Institutions

Joost Draaisma

Economist, The World Bank, Mexico City.

Jorge Martíns

Director, International Finance Corporation, Mexico City.

Researchers

Luis Aguilar

Center for International Studies, El Colegio de México.

Armando Baez

Institute of Geophysics, National Autonomous University of Mexico.

David Barkin

Department of Economics, Autonomous Metropolitan University, Xochimilco.

Miguel Basañez

President, Prospectiva Estratégica; Market Opinion Research International, Mexico City.

Carlos Bázdresch

President, Center for Research on Economic Instruction.

Humberto Bravo

Director, Institute of Geophysics, National Autonomous University of Mexico.

Jorge Castañeda

Political Science Department, National Autonomous University of Mexico.

Denise Dresser

Department of Political Science, Autonomous Technological Institute of Mexico.

Rafael Fernández de Castro

Department of International Studies, Autonomous Technological Institute of Mexico.

Enrique de la Garza Toledo

Coordinator of Master's Program in Sociology, Autonomous Metropolitan University, Iztapalapa.

Haynes Goddard	U.S. Environmental Protection Agency; Autonomous Technological Institute of Mexico.
Gonzalo Halffter	National Institute of Ecology; National Autonomous University of Mexico.
Blanca Heredia	Department of International Studies, Autonomous Technological Institute of Mexico.
Mario Huerta	Mexican Foundation for Ecologic Culture.
Victor Islas	Center for Urban Studies, El Colegio de México.
Bernardo Mabire	Political Science Department, El Colegio de México.
Luis Manuel Guerra	Director, Autonomous Institute of Ecologic Research, Mexico City.
Rogelio Ramírez de la O.	President, ECANAL, Mexico City.
Iván Restrepo	Director, Center for Ecodevelopment (1990).
Pedro Reyes	Director, Center for Ecodevelopment (1992).
Carlos Rico	Center for International Studies, El Colegio de México.
Luis Rubio	Director, Center for Research on Development.
Inder Ruprah	Department of Economics, University of the Americas, Mexico City.
Roberto Salinas	Director, Center for Research on Private Enterprise, Mexico City.
Manuel Sánchez	Director, Center of Analysis and Economic Research, Autonomous Technological Institute of Mexico.

Blanca Torres	Center for International Studies, El Colegio de México.
Gustavo Vega	Center for International Studies, El Colegio de México.
Humberto Oscar Vera Ferrar	Director, Center for Economic Studies on the Private Sector, Mexico City.
David Wilk	Research Fellow, Center for Research on Economic Instruction.
Francisco Zapata	Center of Sociological Studies, El Colegio de México.
Emilio Zebadua	Department of International Studies, Autonomous Technological Institute of Mexico.

Media

Miguel Basañez	*Este País,* Mexico City.
Claudia Fernández	*El Financiero,* Mexico City.
David Luhnow	*The News,* Mexico City.
Patricia Nelson	Editor, *The News,* Mexico City.
Patricia Paredes	*El Universal,* Mexico City.

Nongovernmental Organizations

Margot Aguilar	Group of Environmental Studies.
José Árias	Pact of Ecologist Groups.
Regina Barba	Pact of Ecologist Groups.
Feliciano Béjar	Group of 100.

Alfonso Cipres Villarreal   President, Mexican Environmental
                                   Movement.

Joel Cantú   World Environment Center, Mexico City.

Miguel Ángel García   Pact of Ecologist Groups.

Natalia Grieger   Alliance of Mexican Ecologists, Coordinator
                                   of the Mexican Green Party.

Enrique Mier   Mexican Ecologist Movement.

Federico Reyes   Group of 100.

Foreign Governments

Anne Alonso   Attaché, U.S. Environmental Protection
                                   Agency, U.S. Embassy, Mexico City.

Jerry Bowers   U.S. Agency for International Development,
                                   U.S. Embassy, Mexico City.

James Carrick   Consul, Canadian Embassy, Mexico City.

Francisco Cerón   U.S. Agency for International Development,
                                   U.S. Embassy, Mexico City.

Regina Degnan   U.S. Environmental Protection Agency, U.S.
                                   Embassy, Mexico City.

Debra Reiner   American Chamber of Commerce,
                                   Mexico City.

Paul St. Amour   Canadian Embassy, Mexico City.

Alice Tidball   Science Division, U.S. Embassy, Mexico City.

Bibliography

Abdala, Manuel Ángel. "The Regulation of Newly Privatized Firms: An Illustration from Argentina." In *Privatization in Latin America: New Roles for the Public and Private Sectors,* edited by Werner Baer and Melissa H. Birch, 45–70. Westport, Conn.: Praeger, 1994.

Acosta, Carlos. "Hasta marzo, la empresa decía que Cananea era ejemplar; en cinco meses se volvió un desastre." *Proceso* 669 (August 28, 1989).

Acosta, Carlos, and Carlos Puig. "En la oscuridad, a la sombra de Salinas, José Córdoba acumuló un poder inédito; ahora se hunde en el desprestigio, el vituperio y las sospechas." *Proceso* 961 (April 3, 1995).

Acosta, Carlos, and Ramón A. Sallard. "Corruptelas y maniobras convirtieron a Jorge Larrea en magnate mundial del cobre." *Proceso* 723 (September 10, 1990).

Adrian, Charles R., and Charles Press. "Decision Costs in Coalition Formation." *American Political Science Review* 62 (1968): 556–564.

Aharoni, Yair. "State-Owned Enterprise: An Agent without a Principal." In *Public Enterprise in Less-Developed Countries,* edited by Leroy P. Jones, 67–76. New York: Cambridge University Press, 1982.

Alarcón, Diana, and Terry McKinley. "Increasing Wage Inequality and Trade Liberalization in Mexico." In *Poverty, Economic Reform, and Income Distribution in Latin America,* edited by Albert Berry, 137–153. Boulder, Colo.: Lynne Rienner, 1998.

Aldrich, Howard E., and Sergio Mindlin. "Uncertainty and Dependence: Two Perspectives on the Environment." In *Organization and Environment: Theory, Issues, and Reality,* edited by Lucien Karpik, 149–170. London: Sage, 1978.

Alford, Robert. *Bureaucracy and Participation: Political Cultures in Four Wisconsin Cities.* Chicago: Rand McNally, 1969.

Allison, Graham T. *Essence of Decision: Explaining the Cuban Missile Crisis.* Boston, Mass.: Little, Brown, 1971.

Ambito Financiero, June 29, 1990.

Ames, Barry. *Political Survival: Politicians and Public Policy in Latin America.* Berkeley, Calif.: University of California Press, 1987.

Arango de Maglio, Aída. "Radicalismo y empresas públicas (1983/1989)." *Realidad Económica* 97 (1990): 29–54.

Ardito-Barletta, Nicolás. "Panel Discussion." In *The Political Economy of Policy Reform,* edited by John Williamson, 457–466. Washington, D.C.: Institute for International Economics, 1994.

Armijo, Leslie Elliott. "Menem's Mania?: The Timing of Privatization in Argentina." *Southwestern Journal of Law and Trade in the Americas* 1, no. 1 (1994): 1–28.

Aspe, Pedro. *Economic Transformation the Mexican Way.* Cambridge, Mass.: MIT Press, 1993.

Aufderheid, Pat, and Bruce Rich. "Environmental Reform and the Multilateral Banks." *World Policy Journal* 5 (Spring 1988): 301–321.

Axelrod, Robert. "Conflict of Interest, an Axiomatic Approach." *Journal of Conflict Resolution* 11 (1967): 86–99.

Aziz Nassif, Alberto. "Las elecciones de la restauración en México." In *Las elecciones federales de 1991,* edited by Alberto Aziz Nassif and Jaqueline Preschard. México, D.F.: Miguel Ángel Porrúa/UNAM, 1992.

Azpiazu, Daniel, and Adolfo Vispo. "Some Lessons of the Argentine Privatization Process." *CEPAL Review* 54 (December 1994): 129–147.

Babai, Don. "The World Bank and IMF: Backing the State versus Rolling It Back." In *The Promise of Privatization: A Challenge for U.S. Foreign Policy,* edited by Raymond Vernon, 23–56. New York: Council on Foreign Relations, 1988.

Bailey, John J. *Governing Mexico: The Statecraft of Crisis Management.* New York: St. Martin's Press, 1988.

Bailey, John, and Jennifer Boone. "National Solidarity: A Summary of Program Elements." In *Transforming State-Society Relations in Mexico: The National Solidarity Strategy,* edited by Wayne A. Cornelius, Ann L. Craig, and Jonathan Fox, 329–338. La Jolla, Calif.: The Center for U.S.–Mexican Studies, University of California, San Diego, 1994.

Banca Serfin, Banca Mercantil del Norte, and S. G. Warburg & Co., Inc. *Sidermex: Sidermex, S.A. de C.V., Private and Confidential Executive Summary,* company prospectus on file at the Office of Privatization, Ministry of Public Credit and Finance, Mexico City, n.d.

Banco de México. *The Mexican Economy.* México, D.F.: Banco de México, 1996.

———. *The Mexican Economy.* México, D.F.: Banco de México, 1990.

Bates, Robert H., and Ann O. Krueger, eds. *Political and Economic Interactions in Economic Policy Reform: Evidence from Eight Countries.* Cambridge, Mass.: Blackwell, 1993.

———. "Introduction." In *Political and Economic Interactions in Economic Policy Reform: Evidence from Eight Countries,* edited by Robert H. Bates and Anne O. Krueger, 1–26. Cambridge, Mass.: Blackwell, 1993.

———. "Generalizations Arising from the Country Studies." In *Political and Economic Interactions in Economic Policy Reform: Evidence from Eight Countries,* edited by Robert H. Bates and Anne O. Krueger, 444–472. Cambridge, Mass.: Blackwell, 1993.

Baumgartner, Frank R., and Bryan D. Jones. *Agendas and Instability in American Politics.* Chicago, Ill.: University of Chicago Press, 1993.

Bázdresch, Carlos, and Santiago Levy. "Populism and Economic Policy in Mexico, 1970–1982." In *The Macroeconomics of Populism in Latin America,* edited by Rudiger Dornbusch and Sebastian Edwards, 223–262. Chicago: University of Chicago Press, 1991.

Becker Arreola, Guillermo. "El fortalecimiento de la industria siderúrgica paraestatal." In *Sidermex: Ciclo "Rectoría del Estado,"* 49–61. México, D.F.: Instituto de Estudios Políticos, Económicos y Sociales, 1987.

Bennett, Douglas C., and Kenneth E. Sharpe. *Transnational Corporations versus the State: The Political Economy of the Mexican Auto Industry.* Princeton, N.J.: Princeton University Press, 1985.

Benveniste, Guy. *Bureaucracy and National Planning: A Sociological Case Study in Mexico.* New York: Praeger, 1970.

Biersteker, Thomas. "The 'Triumph' of Liberal Economic Ideas in the Developing World: Policy Convergence and the Bases of Governance in the International Economic Order." In *Governance without Government: Order and Change in World Politics,* edited by James N. Rosenau and Ernst-Otto Czempiel, 102–131. New York: Cambridge University Press, 1992.

Birdsall, Nancy, Carol Graham, and Richard H. Sabot, eds. *Beyond Trade-offs: Market Reform and Equitable Growth in Latin America.* Washington, D.C.: The Inter-American Development Bank, 1998.

Blake, Charles H. "Economic Reform and Democratization in Argentina and Uruguay: The Tortoise and the Hare Revisited?" *Journal of Interamerican Studies and World Affairs* 40, no. 3 (Fall 1998): 1–26.

Blau, Peter M., and Richard A. Schoenherr. *The Structure of Organizations.* New York: Basic Books, 1971.

Blaug, Mark. *Economic Theory in Retrospect,* 3d ed. New York: Cambridge University Press, 1979.

Boneo, Henry. "Privatization: Ideology and Praxis." In *State Shrinking: A Comparative Inquiry into Privatization,* edited by William Glade, 40–59. Austin, Tex.: Institute of Latin American Studies, University of Texas, Austin, 1986.

Borek, Theodore B. "Evaluating a Developing Institution: Mexicanization of Mining." *Arizona Law Review* 13, no. 3 (1971): 673–702.

Bour, Enrique A. "El programa argentino de desregulación y privatización." In *Reforma y convergencia: Ensayos sobre la transformación de la economía Argentina,* edited by Felipe A. M. de la Balze, 225–272. Buenos Aires: Ediciones Manantial, 1993.

Breyer, Stephen. *Regulation and Its Reform.* Cambridge, Mass.: Harvard University Press, 1982.

Bruhn, Kathleen. *Taking on Goliath: The Emergence of a New Left Party and the Struggle for Democracy in Mexico.* University Park, Penn.: Pennsylvania State University Press, 1997.

Business International Corporation. "Argentina: Reversing the Past Fifty Years." In *Privatization in Latin America: New Competitive Opportunities and Challenges,* 83–108. New York: Business International Corporation, 1990.

———. *Privatization in Latin America: New Competitive Opportunities and Challenges.* New York: Business International Corporation, 1990.

———. "Mexico: Privatization, Deregulation, and Liberalization." In *Privatization in Latin America: New Competitive Opportunities and Challenges,* 41–82. New York: Business International Corporation, 1990.

Callaghy, Thomas M. "Political Passions and Economic Interests: Economic Reform and Political Structure in Africa." In *Hemmed In: Responses to Africa's Economic Decline,* edited by Thomas M. Callaghy and John Ravenhill, 463–519. New York: Columbia University Press, 1993.

———. "Lost between State and Market: The Politics of Economic Adjustment in Ghana, Zambia, and Nigeria." In *Economic Crisis and Policy Choice: The Politics of Adjust-*

ment in the Third World, edited by Joan Nelson, 257–319. Princeton, N.J.: Princeton University Press, 1990.

———. "Toward State Capability and Embedded Liberalism in the Third World: Lessons for Adjustment." In *Fragile Coalitions: The Politics of Economic Adjustment,* edited by Joan Nelson, 115–138. New Brunswick, N.J.: Transaction Books, 1989.

Cameron, Maxwell A., and Vinod K. Aggarwal. "Mexican Meltdown: States, Markets and Post-NAFTA Financial Turmoil." *Third World Quarterly* 17, no. 5 (1996): 975–987.

Camp, Roderic Ai. *Politics in Mexico,* 2d ed. New York: Oxford University Press, 1996.

———. "Mexico's Legislature: Missing the Democratic Lockstep?" In *Legislatures and the New Democracies in Latin America,* edited by David Close, 17–36. Boulder, Colo.: Lynne Rienner, 1995.

———. *Politics in Mexico.* New York: Oxford University Press, 1993.

———. "Camarillas in Mexican Politics: The Case of the Salinas Cabinet." *Mexican Studies/Estudios Mexicanos* 6 (Winter 1990): 85–107.

Camposeco, Manuel. "Aeroméxico: el gatopardismo de la modernidad." In *Reconversión industrial y lucha sindical,* edited by Esthela Gutiérrez, 153–179. Caracas, Venezuela: Fundación Friedrich Ebert-México, Editorial Nueva Sociedad, 1989.

Cantú, Jesús. "Solidaridad, además de electorero, se manejó en Michoacán coercitivamente." *Proceso* 819 (July 13, 1992).

Carabia, Julia. "La Política Ecológica de la SEDUE." In *Medio ambiente y desarrollo en México,* edited by Enrique Leff. México, D.F.: Siglo XXI, 1990.

Cardoso, Fernando Henrique. "On the Characterization of Authoritarian Regimes in Latin America." In *The New Authoritarianism in Latin America,* edited by David Collier, 33–57. Princeton, N.J.: Princeton University Press, 1979.

Casanova, Pablo González. *Democracy in Mexico.* London, England: Oxford University Press, 1970.

Castillo, Alejandro. "La Difícil Desincorporación de SIDERMEX." *Expansión* (Mexico City), August 15, 1990.

Castillo, Herberto. "Ofensiva antisindical." *Proceso* 669 (August 28, 1989).

Cavarozzi, Marcelo. "Peronism and Radicalism: Argentina's Transitions in Perspective." In *Elections and Democratization in Latin America, 1980–85,* edited by Paul W. Drake and Eduardo Silva, 143–199. La Jolla, Calif.: Center for U.S.-Mexican Studies, Center for Iberian and Latin American Studies, and Institute for the Americas, University of California, San Diego, 1986.

Centeno, Miguel Ángel. *Democracy within Reason: Technocratic Revolution in Mexico.* University Park, Penn.: Pennsylvania State University Press, 1994.

Chertkoff, Jerome M. "Sociopsychological Theories and Research on Coalition Formation." In *The Study of Coalition Behavior: Theoretical Perspectives and Cases from Four Continents,* edited by Sven Groennings, E. W. Kelley, and Michael Leiserson, 297–322. New York: Holt, Rinehart and Winston, 1970.

Clarín (Buenos Aires), October 18, 1991.

———. August 28, 1990.

Cline, Howard F. *Mexico: Revolution to Evolution, 1940–1960.* New York: Oxford University Press, 1963.

Coase, Ronald H. "The Problem of Social Cost." *Journal of Law and Economics* 3, no. 1 (October 1960): 1–44.

———. "The Nature of the Firm." *Económica,* n.s., 4 (1937): 386–405.

Collier, Ruth Berins, and David Collier. "Inducements versus Constraints: Disaggregating Corporatism." *American Political Science Review* 73 (December 1979): 967–986.

Comisión Nacional de Ecología. *Informe de la situación general en materia de equilibrio y protección al ambiente, 1989–1990.* México, D.F.: Comisión Nacional de Ecología, 1991.

Comisión Nacional de Ecología, SEDUE. *Ecología: 100 acciones necesarias.* México, D.F.: Comisión Nacional de Ecología, SEDUE, January 1987.

Compañía Minera de Cananea: "¿Cobre por Libre?" *Expansión* (Mexico City), November 21, 1990.

Conesa R., Ana María, and Eduardo Larrañaga S. "Aeroméxico: El derecho de huelga en quiebra." *El Cotidiano* 25 (September–October 1988).

Contreras Montellan, Oscar F. *La Minería en Sonora: Modernización industrial y fuerza de trabajo.* Hermosillo, Sonora, México: El Colegio de Sonora, 1986.

Contreras, Oscar, and Miguel Ángel Ramírez. "Mercado de Trabajo y Relaciones Laborales en Cananea: La Disputa en Torno a la Flexibilidad." *Trabajo: Sociedad, Tecnología y Cultura* 8 (1992): 7–16.

———. "Novedades de la postguerra: fin del auge exportador y repliegue hacia el mercado interno." In *La nueva industrialización de Sonora: El caso de los sectores de alta tecnología,* edited by José Carlos Ramírez, 243–297. Hermosillo, Sonora, México: El Colegio de Sonora, 1988.

Cook, Maria Lorena, Kevin J. Middlebrook, and Juan Molinar Horcasitas. "The Politics of Economic Restructuring in Mexico: Actors, Sequencing, and Coalition Change." In *The Politics of Economic Restructuring: State-Society Relations and Regime Change in Mexico,* edited by Maria Lorena Cook, Kevin J. Middlebrook, and Juan Molinar Horcasitas, 3–52. La Jolla, Calif.: Center for U.S.-Mexican Studies, University of California, San Diego, 1994.

Cooley, Lawrence, et al. "Evaluation of UDAPE and the Policy Reform Project." Final Report, Implementing Policy Change Project. Washington, D.C.: U.S. Agency for International Development, May 1991.

Córdoba, José. "Mexico." In *The Political Economy of Policy Reform,* edited by John Williamson, 232–284. Washington, D.C.: Institute for International Economics, 1994.

Cornelius, Wayne A. "Subnational Politics and Democratization: Tensions between Center and Periphery in the Mexican Political System." In *Subnational Politics and Democratization in Mexico,* edited by Wayne A. Cornelius, Todd A. Eisenstadt, and Jane Hindley, 3–16. La Jolla, Calif.: Center for U.S.–Mexican Studies, University of California, San Diego, 1999.

———. *Mexican Politics in Transition: The Breakdown of a One-Party-Dominant Regime.* La Jolla, Calif.: Center for U.S.-Mexican Studies, University of California, San Diego, 1996.

———. "Foreword." In *The Politics of Economic Restructuring: State-Society Relations and Regime Change in Mexico,* edited by Maria Lorena Cook, Kevin J. Middlebrook, and Juan Molinar Horcasitas, xi–xx. La Jolla, Calif.: Center for U.S.-Mexican Studies, University of California, San Diego, 1994.

———. "The Political Economy of Mexico under de la Madrid: The Crisis Deepens, 1985–1986." *Research Report Series* 43. La Jolla, Calif.: Center for U.S.-Mexican Studies, University of California, San Diego, 1986.

Cornelius, Wayne A., and Ann L. Craig. "Politics in Mexico." In *Comparative Politics Today,* edited by Gabriel Almond and G. Bingham Powell, 425–484. Boston: Little,

Brown, 1988.

Cornelius, Wayne A., Ann L. Craig, and Jonathan Fox, eds. *Transforming State-Society Relations in Mexico: The National Solidarity Strategy.* La Jolla, Calif.: Center for U.S.-Mexican Studies, University of California, San Diego, 1994.

Corrales, Javier. "Coalitions and Corporate Choices in Argentina, 1976–1994: The Recent Private Sector Support of Privatization." *Studies in Comparative International Development* 32, no. 4 (Winter 1998): 25–51.

———. "Do Economic Crises Contribute to Economic Reform? Argentina and Venezuela in the 1990s." *Political Science Quarterly* 112, no. 4 (1997–98): 617–644.

———. "Why Argentines Followed Cavallo: A Technopol between Democracy and Economic Reform." In *Technopols: Freeing Politics and Markets in Latin America in the 1990s,* edited by Jorge I. Domínguez, 49–93. University Park, Penn.: Pennsylvania State University Press, 1997.

Corro, Salvador. "Los mineros de Cananea: de los golpes a los apachos verbales." *Proceso* 679 (November 6, 1989).

———. "Todo mundo sabía que la corrupción conducía a Cananea al desastre." *Proceso* 670 (September 4, 1989).

———. "Al contrario de Cananea, en Teléfonos el sindicato ni las manos metio," *Proceso* 673 (September 25, 1989).

———. "Por encima de sus lideres, los obreros de Sicartsa rechazan una modernización a costa de la mana de obra." *Proceso* 669 (August 28, 1989).

———. "Con su líder ausente, los mineros siguen rechazando las propuestas de la compañía." *Proceso* 671 (September 11, 1989).

———. "En diciembre Aeroméxico aún era viable; en enero se decidió ponerla en picada." *Proceso* 599 (April 25, 1988).

Cortés, Rosalía, and Adriana Marshall. "State Social Intervention and Labour Regulation: The Case of the Argentine." *Cambridge Journal of Economics* 17 (1993): 391–408.

Crosby, Benjamin L. "Policy Implementation: The Organizational Challenge." *World Development* 24 (1996): 1403–1415.

———. "Honduras's UDAPE: A Case Study," Implementing Policy Change Project. Washington, D.C.: U.S. Agency for International Development, 1996.

Cueto-Rua, Julio C. "Privatization in Argentina." *Southwestern Journal of Law and Trade in the Americas* 1, no. 1 (1994): 63–75.

Dahl, Robert. "Power." In *International Encyclopedia of the Social Sciences* 12, edited by David L. Sills, 405–415. New York: MacMillan and Free Press, 1968.

Dam, Kenneth W. *The Rules of the Game.* Chicago: University of Chicago Press, 1982.

Damill, Mario, and Roberto Frenkel. "Restauración democrática y política económica: Argentina, 1984–1991." In *La política económica en la transición a la democracia: Lecciones de Argentina, Bolivia, Chile y Uruguay,* edited by Juan Antonio Morales and Gary McMahon, 35–95. Santiago: CIEPLAN, 1993.

———. "Malos tiempos: la economía argentina en la década de los ochenta." In *Argentina: evolución macroeconómica, financiación externa y cambio político en la década de los 80,* edited by Roberto Frenkel, et al., 3–70. Madrid: CEDEAL, 1992.

Davies, R. E. G. *Airlines of Latin America since 1919.* Washington, D.C.: Smithsonian Institution Press, 1984.

Dávila, Alvaro. *El sistema de transporte de carga de México ante el Tratado de Libre Comercio,* Monograph. México, D.F.: Instituto Tecnológico Autónomo de México, n.d.

Dávila C., Enrique R. "La reglamentación del autotransporte de carga en México." In *El efecto de la regulación en algunos sectores de la economía mexicana,* edited by Francisco Gil Díaz and Arturo M. Fernández, 12–137. México, D.F.: Fondo de Cultura Económica, 1991.

Davis, Charles L., and Kenneth M. Coleman. "Neoliberal Economic Policies and the Potential for Electoral Change in Mexico." *Mexican Studies/Estudios Mexicanos* 10 (Summer 1994): 523–541.

De Buen, Oscar, and Juan Pablo Antún. "Reglamentación y prácticas comunes del transporte de carga en México." *Comercio Exterior* 39, no. 5 (May 1989): 392–403.

De Franco, Silvio, and Rafael Díaz. "PAPI Project Implementation Review," Final Report, Implementing Policy Change Project. Washington, D.C.: U.S. Agency for International Development, November 1994.

De Kessler, Anna S. "Privatization of the Enterprises of the Argentine Ministry of Defense." *Columbia Journal of World Business* 28, no. 1 (Spring 1993): 135–143.

de la Balze, Felipe A.M. *Remaking the Argentine Economy.* New York: Council on Foreign Relations, 1995.

De la Garza Toledo, Enrique. "¿Quién ganó en Telmex?" *El Cotidiano* 32 (1989).

de la Madrid, Miguel. *Quinto informe de gobierno.* México, D.F.: Presidencia de la República, 1987.

Del Castillo, Graciana. "Privatization in Latin America: From Myth to Reality." *Serie Reformas de Política Pública* 32. Santiago, Chile: ECLAC, 1995.

Departamento del Distrito Federal. *Programa integral contra la contaminación atmosférica: Un compromiso común.* México, D.F.: Departamento del Distrito Federal, 1990.

———. *Memoria de gestión, General Dirección de Protección Ambiental 1982–1988.* México, D.F.: Departamento del Distrito Federal, 1988.

———. *Bases de gestión de la calidad del aire para la zona metropolitana de la Ciudad de México.* México, D.F.: Departamento del Distrito Federal, n.d.

Departamento del Distrito Federal, Gobierno del Estado de México, Instituto Mexicano del Petróleo, Petróleos Mexicanos, Secretaría de Desarrollo Urbano y Ecología. *Programa integral contra la contaminación atmosférica en la zona metropolitana de la Ciudad de México: Avances a septiembre de 1991.* México, D.F.: Departamento del Distrito Federal, Gobierno del Estado de México, Instituto Mexicano del Petróleo, Petróleos Mexicanos, Secretaría de Desarrollo Urbano y Ecología, 1991.

De Riz, Liliana, and Catalina Smulovitz. "Instituciones y dinámica política: El presidencialismo argentino." In *Reforma institucional y cambio político,* edited by Dieter Nohlen and Liliana de Riz, 123–176. Buenos Aires: Editorial Legasa, 1991.

Derthick, Martha. *Policymaking for Social Security.* Washington, D.C.: Brookings, 1979.

Diario Oficial, January 7–8, 1992.

———. January 26, 1990.

———. February 5, 1989.

———. January 28, 1988.

———. February 14, 1986.

———. January 11, 1982.

———. September 17, 1971.

———. March 23, 1971.

Díaz Landero, Alejandro. "An Economic Appraisal of the Deregulation Process in the Mexican Transport Market." *Journal of Transportation Research Forum* 31, no. 1 (1990): 101–108.

232 _Bibliography_

Di Tella, Guido, and Manuel Zymelman. _Las etapas del desarrollo económico argentino._ Buenos Aires: Editorial Universitaria de Buenos Aires, 1967.

Domínguez, Jorge I. "Technopols: Ideas and Leaders in Freeing Politics and Markets in Latin America in the 1990s." In _Technopols: Freeing Politics and Markets in Latin America in the 1990s,_ edited by Jorge I. Domínguez, 1–48. University Park, Penn.: Pennsylvania State University Press, 1997.

———. ed. _Technopols: Freeing Politics and Markets in Latin America in the 1990s._ University Park, Penn.: Pennsylvania State University Press, 1997.

Domínguez, Jorge I., and James A. McCann. "Shaping Mexico's Electoral Arena: The Construction of Partisan Cleavages in the 1988 and 1991 National Elections." _American Political Science Review_ 89, no. 1 (March 1995): 35–48.

———. _Democratizing Mexico: Public Opinion and Electoral Choices._ Baltimore, Md.: Johns Hopkins University Press, 1996.

Dornbusch, Rudiger, and Juan Carlos de Pablo. _Deuda externa e inestabilidad macroeconómica en la Argentina._ Buenos Aires: Editorial Sudamerica, 1988.

Dresser, Denise. "Post-NAFTA Politics in Mexico: Uneasy, Uncertain, Unpredictable." In _The Post-NAFTA Political Economy: Mexico and the Western Hemisphere,_ edited by Carol Wise, 221–256. University Park, Penn.: Pennsylvania State University Press, 1998.

———. "Embellishment, Empowerment, or Euthanasia of the PRI? Neoliberalism and Party Reform in Mexico." In _The Politics of Economic Restructuring: State-Society Relations and Regime Change in Mexico,_ edited by Maria Lorena Cook, Kevin J. Middlebrook, and Juan Molinar Horcasitas, 125–147. La Jolla, Calif.: Center for U.S.-Mexican Studies, University of California, San Diego, 1994.

———. "Neopopulist Solutions to Neoliberal Problems: Mexico's National Solidarity Program." _Current Issue Brief Series_ 3. La Jolla, Calif.: Center for U.S.-Mexican Studies, University of California, San Diego, 1991.

DuMars, Charles T., and Salvador Beltran del Río M. "A Survey of the Air and Water Quality Laws of Mexico." _Natural Resources Journal_ 28, no. 4 (Fall 1988): 787–813.

Dussel Peters, Enrique. "Cambio estructural y potencialidades de crecimiento del sector manufacturero en México (1982–1991)." In _México: La nueva macroeconomia,_ edited by Julio López, 149–229. México, D.F.: Centro de Estudios para un Proyecto Nacional/Nuevo Horizonte Editores, 1994.

Economist Intelligence Unit. _Argentina Country Report,_ nos. 1, 4 (1990).

———. _Mexico Country Report,_ First Quarter (1991).

———. _Mexico Country Report,_ Fourth Quarter (1989).

Edgell, Sr., David L., and Wanda Barquin. "Privatization of Tourism and Air Transportation." In _Latin America's Turnaround: Privatization, Foreign Investment, and Growth,_ edited by Paul H. Boeker, 165–177. San Francisco: ICS Press, 1993.

Edwards, Sebastian. _Crisis and Reform in Latin America: From Despair to Hope._ New York: Oxford University Press, 1995.

Elder, Charles D., and Roger W. Cobb. "Agenda-Building and the Politics of Aging." _Policy Studies Journal_ 13, no. 1 (September 1984): 115–129.

El Diario Lázaro Cárdenas (Lázaro Cárdenas, Mexico), September 2, 1991.

El Financiero (Mexico City), March 8, 1990.

———. (Mexico City), August 21–23, 1989.

———. (Mexico City), May 17, 1988.

———. (Mexico City), April 8, 1992.

"El Gobierno Federal Desincorpora las Empresas AHMSA y Sicartsa." *El Mercado de Valores* 6 (March 15, 1990).

Elizondo, Carlos. "The Making of a New Alliance: The Privatization of the Banks in Mexico." *CIDE Documento de Trabajo* 5. Mexico: CIDE, 1993.

El Quijote (Lázaro Cárdenas, Mexico), August 27, 1991.

El Sonorense (Hermosillo, Mexico), August 24 and September 6, 1989.

El Universal (Mexico City), November 8, 1988.

———. (Mexico City), November 28, 1984.

Emerson, Richard M. "Social Exchange Theory." In *Annual Review of Sociology* 2, edited by Alex Inkeles, James Coleman, and Neil Smelser, 335–362. Palo Alto, Calif.: Annual Reviews Inc., 1976.

Epstein, Edward C. "Labor-State Conflict in the New Argentine Democracy: Parties, Union Factions, and Power Maximizing." In *The New Argentine Democracy: The Search for a Successful Formula,* edited by Edward C. Epstein, 124–155. Westport, Conn.: Praeger, 1992.

Erro, Davide G. *Resolving the Argentine Paradox: Politics and Development, 1966–1992.* Boulder, Colo.: Lynne Rienner, 1993.

Estudio del esquema rector del sistema nacional del transporte aérea. México, D.F.: Aconsa Consultores, S.A. de C.V., September 30, 1990.

Evans, Peter. *Embedded Autonomy: States and Industrial Transformation.* Princeton, N.J.: Princeton University Press, 1995.

———. "The State As Problem and Solution: Predation, Embedded Autonomy, and Structural Change." In *The Politics of Economic Adjustment,* edited by Stephan Haggard and Robert R. Kaufman, 139–181. Princeton, N.J.: Prince-ton University Press, 1992.

Excélsior (Mexico City), January 29, 1991.

———. (Mexico City), June 8, 1990.

———. (Mexico City), May 11, 1988.

Ezcurra, Exequiel. "Las Inversiones Térmicas." *Ciencias* 22 (April 1991): 51–53.

Fernández, Arturo M. "Deregulation As a Source of Growth in Mexico." In *Reform, Recovery, and Growth: Latin America and the Middle East,* edited by Rudiger Dornbusch and Sebastian Edwards, 311–339. Chicago: University of Chicago Press, 1995.

———. "Trucking Deregulation in Mexico." In *Regulatory Reform in Transport: Some Recent Experiences,* edited by José Carbajo, 101–105. Washington, D.C.: World Bank, 1993.

———. "Reformas al Marco Regulatorio de la Actividad Económica." *Opción,* no. 53 (December 1991): 7–12.

Fernández, Raquel, and Dani Rodrik. "Resistance to Reform: Status Quo Bias in the Presence of Individual-Specific Uncertainty." *American Economic Review* 81, no. 5 (1991): 1146–1155.

Fernández Moreno, Hector. "Origen y desarrollo del complejo de Siderúrgica Lázaro Cárdenas-Las Truchas." *Comercio Exterior* 25 (October 1975): 1127–1140.

Ferreira Rubio, Delia, and Matteo Goretti. "Menem's *Decretazo* (1989–1998): The Inefficiency of the Constitutional Reform to Modify the Practice of the Executive Regarding Need and Urgency Decrees." Paper presented at the 1998 meeting of the Latin American Studies Association, Chicago, Illinois, September 24–26, 1998.

Financial Times (London), August 31, 1995.

———. (London), November 6, 1991.

———. (London), October 12, 1989.

———. (London), August 22–23, 1989.

———. (London), March 22, 1989.

Financiera Nacional Azucarera. *Compañía Minera de Cananea: Reinicio de operaciones, relaciones con la comunidad, prestaciones especiales,* Internal Report. México, D.F.: Financiera Nacional Azucarera, n.d.

Fondo de Cultura Económica. *Reestructuración del sector paraestatal.* México, D.F.: Fondo de Cultura Económica, 1988.

Frenkel, Roberto. "Heterodox Theory and Policy: The Plan Austral in Argentina." *Journal of Development Economics* 7, nos. 1–2 (October 1987): 307–338.

Fundación Universo Veintiuno, Fundación Friedrich Ebert Stiftung. *Desarrollo y medio ambiente en México. Diagnóstico, 1990.* México, D.F.: Fundación Universo Veintiuno, Fundación Friedrich Ebert Stiftung, 1990.

Gamson, William A. "A Theory of Coalition Formation." *American Sociological Review* 26 (1961): 565–573.

Garrido, Celso. "National Private Groups in Mexico, 1987–1993." *CEPAL Review* 53 (August 1994): 159–175.

Garza, Gustavo. "Hacia la superconcentración industrial en la Ciudad de México." In *Atlas de la Ciudad de México,* 100–102. México, D.F.: El Colegio de México y El Departamento del Distrito Federal, 1987.

———. "Distribución de la industria en la Ciudad de México (1960–1980)." In *Atlas de la Ciudad de México,* 102–107. México, D.F.: El Colegio de México y El Departamento del Distrito Federal, 1986.

———. "El Proceso de Industrialización de la Ciudad de México: 1845–2000." In *Lecturas del CEESTM* 1, no. 3. México, D.F.: Centro de Estudios Económicos y Sociales del Tercer Mundo, 1981.

Gayle, Dennis J., and Jonathan N. Goodrich, "Exploring the Implications of Privatization and Deregulation." In *Privatization and Deregulation in Global Perspective,* edited by Dennis J. Gayle and Jonathan N. Goodrich, 1–23. Westport, Conn.: Quorum Books, 1990.

George, Alexander L. "Case Studies and Theory Development: The Method of Structured, Focused Comparison." In *Diplomacy: New Approaches in History, Theory, and Policy,* edited by Paul Lauren, 43–68. New York: Free Press, 1979.

Gerchunoff, Pablo, and Guillermo Cánovas. "Las Privatizaciones en la Argentina: Impactos Micro y macroeconómicos." *Serie Reformas de Política Pública* 21. Santiago: CEPAL, United Nations, 1994.

Gerchunoff, Pablo, and Germán Colima. "Privatization in Argentina." In *Privatization in Latin America,* edited by Manuel Sánchez and Rossana Corona, 251–299. Washington, D.C.: Inter-American Development Bank, 1993.

Gibson, Edward L. "The Populist Road to Market Reform: Policy and Electoral Coalitions in Mexico and Argentina." *World Politics* 49 (April 1997): 339–370.

Glade, William. "Toward Effective Privatization Strategies." In *Privatization of Public Enterprises in Latin America,* edited by William Glade, 117–130. San Francisco: ICS Press, 1991.

———. "Privatization in Rent-Seeking Societies." *World Development,* 17, no. 5 (1989): 673–682.

"Un gobierno preocupado." *Somos* (Buenos Aires), August 1990.

Godau Schücking, Ranier. "La protección ambiental en México: sobre la conformación de una política pública." *Estudios Sociológicos* 3 (1985): 47–84.

————. *Estado y acero: Historia política de Las Truchas.* México, D.F.: El Colegio de México, 1982.

Gómez Baas, Irene. "Flagelo Para la Salud." *Tiempo* (Mexico City), November 16, 1989.

González Arzac, Alberto R. "Aerolíneas, ENTel y la Inspección General de Justicia." *Realidad Económica* 97 (1990): 55–63.

González Fraga, Javier A. "Argentine Privatization in Retrospect." In *Privatization of Public Enterprises in Latin America,* edited by William Glade, 75–98. San Francisco: ICS Press, 1991.

Gosman, Elenora. "Aerolineas Argentinas." In *Privatizaciones: Reestructuración del estado y la sociedad (del Plan Pinedo a los Alsogaray),* edited by Arnaldo Bocco and Naum Minsburge, 245–258. Buenos Aires: Ediciones Letra Buena, 1991.

Gourevitch, Peter A. *Politics in Hard Times: Comparative Responses to International Economic Crisis.* Ithaca, N.Y.: Cornell University Press, 1986.

Graham, Carol. *Safety Nets, Politics, and the Poor: Transitions to Market Economies.* Washington, D.C.: Brookings Institution, 1993.

Grindle, Merilee S. *Challenging the State: Crisis and Innovation in Latin America and Africa.* New York: Cambridge University Press, 1996.

————. "Reforming Land Tenure in Mexico: Peasants, the Market, and the State." In *The Challenge of Institutional Reform in Mexico,* edited by Riordan Roett, 39–56. Boulder, Colo.: Lynne Rienner, 1995.

————. "Patrons and Clients in the Bureaucracy: Career Networks in Mexico." *Latin American Research Review* 12, no. 1 (1977): 37–77.

————. *Bureaucrats, Politicians, and Peasants in Mexico: A Case Study in Public Policy.* Berkeley: University of California Press, 1977.

Grindle, Merilee S., and John W. Thomas. *Public Choices and Policy Change: The Political Economy of Reform in Developing Countries.* Baltimore, Md.: Johns Hopkins University Press, 1991.

Grosse, Robert. "A Privatization Nightmare: Aerolíneas Argentinas." In *Privatizing Monopolies: Lessons from the Telecommunications and Transport Sectors in Latin America,* edited by Ravi Ramamurti, 203–220. Baltimore, Md.: Johns Hopkins University Press, 1996.

Guerrero Cruz, Luz. "Birds Die in Winter Smog." *Voice of Mexico* 4 (June–August 1987).

Guislain, Pierre. *The Privatization Challenge: A Strategic, Legal, and Institutional Analysis of International Experience.* Washington, D.C.: World Bank, 1997.

Gusfield, Joseph. *The Culture of Public Problems: Drinking-Driving and the Symbolic Order.* Chicago: University of Chicago Press, 1981.

Guzmán Chávez, Alenka. "Siderúrgica Lázaro Cárdenas-Las Truchas, 1977–1988." *El Cotidiano* 38 (November–December 1990).

Haggard, Stephan. "Panel Discussion." In *The Political Economy of Policy Reform,* edited by John Williamson, 467–471. Washington, D.C.: Institute for International Economics, 1994.

Haggard, Stephan, and Robert R. Kaufman. *The Political Economy of Democratic Transitions.* Princeton, N.J.: Princeton University Press, 1995.

————. "Institutions and Economic Adjustment." In *The Politics of Economic Adjustment: International Constraints, Distributive Conflicts, and the State,* edited by Stephan Haggard and Robert R. Kaufman, 3–37. Princeton, N.J.: Princeton University Press, 1992.

————. eds. *The Politics of Economic Adjustment: International Constraints, Distributive Conflicts, and the State.* Princeton: Princeton University Press, 1992.

Haggard, Stephan, and Steven B. Webb. *Voting for Reform: Democracy, Political Liberalization, and Economic Adjustment.* New York: Oxford University Press, 1994.

————. "Introduction." In *Voting for Reform: Democracy, Political Liberalization, and Economic Adjustment,* edited by Stephan Haggard and Steven B. Webb, 1–36. New York: Oxford University Press, 1994.

————. "What Do We Know about the Political Economy of Economic Policy Reform?" *World Bank Research Observer* 8, no. 2 (July 1993): 143–168.

Hall, Peter A. "Policy Paradigms, Social Learning, and the State: The Case of Economic Policymaking in Britain." *Comparative Politics* 25 (April 1993): 275–296.

————. "Conclusion: The Politics of Keynesian Ideas." In *The Political Power of Economic Ideas: Keynesianism across Nations,* edited by Peter A. Hall, 361–391. Princeton, N.J.: Princeton University Press, 1989.

————. *Governing the Economy: The Politics of State Intervention in Britain and France.* New York: Oxford University Press, 1986.

Hamilton, Scott. "Aeroméxico bankruptcy Unprecedented for State Airline." *Airfinance Journal,* no. 91 (June 1988): 36–37.

Hanke, Steve H., and Stephen J. K. Walter. "Privatization and Public Choice: Lessons for the LDCs." In *Privatization and Deregulation in Global Perspective,* edited by Dennis J. Gayle and Jonathan N. Goodrich, 97–108. Westport, Conn.: Quorum Books, 1990.

Hansen, Roger D. *The Politics of Mexican Development.* Baltimore, Md.: Johns Hopkins University Press, 1971.

Harris, Nigel, and Sergio Puente. "Environmental Issues in the Cities of the Developing World: The Case of Mexico City." *Journal of International Development* 2, no. 4 (1990): 500–532.

Harvey, Neil. "Rural Reforms and the Zapatista Rebellion: Chiapas, 1988–1995." In *Neoliberalism Revisited: Economic Restructuring and Mexico's Political Future,* edited by Gerardo Otero, 187–208. Boulder, Colo.: Westview, 1996.

Heredia, Blanca. "State-Business Relations in Contemporary Mexico." In *Rebuilding the State: Mexico after Salinas,* edited by Mónica Serrano and Victor Bulmer-Thomas, 131–150. London: Institute of Latin American Studies, University of London, 1996.

————. "Interview: Jesús Silva Herzog." *Journal of International Affairs* 43, no. 2 (Winter 1990): 327–342.

Heredia, Carlos, and Mary Purcell. "Structural Adjustment in Mexico: The Root of the Crisis." Washington, D.C.: Development GAP, 1995, < http://www.cs.unb.ca/~alopez-o/politics/structural.html>.

Herrera, Alejandra. "The Privatization of the Argentine Telephone System." *CEPAL Review* 47 (August 1992): 149–161.

Hickson, D. J., et al. "A Strategic Contingencies Theory of Interorganizational Power." *Administrative Science Quarterly* 15 (1971): 216–229.

Hindess, Barry. "Power, Interests and the Outcomes of Struggles." *Sociology* 16 (November 1982): 498–511.

Hirschman, Albert. "The Political Economy of Import-Substituting Industrialization in Latin America." *Quarterly Journal of Economics* 82, no. 1 (February 1968): 1–32.

Hogan, William T. *Global Steel in the 1990s.* Lexington, Mass.: Lexington Books, 1991.

Ibarra M., Jorge Luis, José Luis Moreno V., and Leopoldo Santos R., "Cananea: Resistencias regionales a la política de modernización." *Revista de El Colegio de Sonora* 2 (1990): 133–171.

Ikenberry, G. John. "The International Spread of Privatization Policies: Inducements, Learning, and 'Policy Bandwagoning.'" In *The Political Economy of Public Sector Reform and Privatization,* edited by Ezra N. Suleiman and John Waterbury, 88–110. Boulder, Colo.: Westview, 1990.

Iliff, Laurence. "Ecologists Hopeful Commission Can Clean up Mexico City." <Lexis/Nexis Library, UPI File, January 8, 1992>.

Immergut, Ellen M. "The Rules of the Game: The Logic of Health Policy-Making in France, Switzerland, and Sweden." In *Structuring Politics: Historical Institutionalism in Comparative Analysis,* edited by Sven Steinmo, Kathleen Thelen, and Frank Longstreth, 57–89. New York: Cambridge University Press, 1992.

Independent (London), January 13, 1996.

Instituto Nacional de Estadísticas y Censos. *Statistical Yearbook Republic of Argentina.* Buenos Aires: Instituto Nacional de Estadísticas y Censos, 1997.

Inter-American Development Bank. *Progreso económico y social en America Latina: Cómo organizar con éxito los servícios sociales.* Washington, D.C.: Inter-American Development Bank, 1996.

Johnson, Omotunde E. G. "Managing Adjustment Costs, Political Authority, and the Implementation of Adjustment Programs, with Special Reference to African Countries." *World Development* 22, no. 3 (1994): 399–411.

Jorge, Eduardo F. *Industria y Concentración Económica.* Buenos Aires: Siglo XXI Argentina Editores, S.A., 1971.

Journal of Commerce (London), November 2, 1989.

———. (London), June 24, 1988.

———. (London), April 19, 1988.

Kahn, Alfred E. *The Economics of Regulation: Principles and Institutions.* New York: Wiley, 1970.

Kaufman, Robert R. *The Politics of Debt in Argentina, Brazil, and Mexico: Economic Stabilization in the 1980s.* Berkeley: Institute of International Studies, University of California, Berkeley, 1988.

Kemper, Robert. V., and Anyn P. Royce. "Mexican Urbanization since 1821: A Macro-Historical Approach." *Urban Anthropology* 8 (1979): 267–289.

Krasner, Steven. "Sovereignty: An Institutional Perspective." In *The Elusive State: International and Comparative Perspectives,* edited by James A. Caporaso, 69–96. Newbury Park, Calif.: Sage, 1989.

———. *Defending the National Interest: Raw Materials Investments and U.S. Foreign Policy.* Princeton, N.J.: Princeton University Press, 1978.

Krueger, Anne O. "Virtuous and Vicious Circles in Economic Development." *American Economic Association Papers and Proceedings* 83 (May 1993): 351–355.

———. *The Political Economy of Policy Reform in Developing Countries.* Cambridge, Mass.: MIT Press, 1993.

Labini, Paolo Sylos. *El plan austral y la política económica Argentina: algunos reflexiones.* Buenos Aires: Instituto Torcuato Di Tella, Centro de Investigaciones Económicas, 1987.

"La Ciudad de México Necesidad de una Descentralización." *Transformación* 2, no. 3 (March 1983): 6–7.

Lacy, Rodolfo. *La calidad del aire en el Valle de México.* México, D.F.: El Colegio de México, 1993.

La Jornada (Mexico City), October 21, 1991.

―――. (Mexico City), December 4, 1990.

―――. (Mexico City), August 28, 1990.

―――. (Mexico City), March 8, 1990.

―――. (Mexico City), September 27, 1989.

―――. (Mexico City), August 23, 1989.

―――. (Mexico City), September 7, 1987.

―――. (Mexico City), January 22, 1986.

La Nación (Buenos Aires), February 10, 1993.

―――. (Buenos Aires), November 13, 1988.

Larkins, Christopher. "The Judiciary and Delegative Democracy in Argentina." *Comparative Politics* 30, no. 4 (July 1998): 423–441.

Larrañaga, Eduardo, et al., eds. *El derecho laboral en México: Realidad y encubrimiento.* México: Universidad Autónoma Metropolitana, Azcapotzalco, 1991.

Larrañaga, Eduardo, and Héctor Mercado. "Requisa e inexistencia de huelga en la CMA." *El Cotodiano* 21 (January–February 1988).

Latin American Weekly Report. "Cananea Is Finally Awarded to Mining Magnate Larrea." *Latin American Weekly Report* (September 20, 1990).

LatinFinance. "The 1991 Directory to Privatization in Latin America." *Privatization in Latin America, a LatinFinance Supplement* (March 1991).

Legorreta, Jorge. *Transporte y contaminación en la Ciudad de México.* México, D.F.: Centro de Ecodesarrollo, 1989.

Legorreta, Jorge, and Ángeles Flores. "La contaminación atmosférica en el Valle de México." In *La Contaminación Atmosférica en México: Sus Causas y Efectos en Salud,* 61–97. México, D.F.: Comisión Nacional de Derechos Humanos, 1992.

Levitsky, Steve. "Crisis, Party Adaptation, and Regime Stability in Argentina: The Case of Peronism, 1989–1995." *Party Politics* 4, no. 4 (October 1998): 445–470.

Levy, Brian. "The Design and Sequencing of Trade and Investment Policy Reform." *World Bank PRE Working Paper Series* 419 (May 1990).

Levy, Daniel C. "Mexico: Sustained Civilian Rule without Democracy." In *Democracy in Developing Countries: Latin America,* edited by Larry Diamond, Juan J. Linz, and Seymour Martin Lipset, 459–497. Boulder, Colo.: Lynne Rienner, 1989.

Lewis, Paul H. *The Crisis of Argentine Capitalism.* Chapel Hill: University of North Carolina Press, 1990.

Lewis, Terzah N. "Student Comment: Environmental Law in Mexico." *Denver Journal of International Law and Policy* 21, no. 1 (Fall 1992): 159–184.

Ley y códigos de México. México, D.F.: Porrua, 1983.

Looney, Robert E. *Mexico's Economy: A Policy Analysis with Forecasts to 1990.* Boulder, Colo.: Westview, 1978.

Los Angeles Times Magazine, November 25, 1990.

"Los 100 director generales de las empresas más importantes de México." *Expansión* (Mexico City), June 8, 1988.

Luna, Matilda. "Entrepreneurial Interests and Political Action in Mexico: Facing the Demands of Economic Modernization." In *The Challenge of Institutional Reform in Mexico,* edited by Riordan Roett, 77–94. Boulder, Colo.: Lynne Rienner, 1995.

Lustig, Nora. *Mexico: The Remaking of an Economy.* Washington, D.C.: Brookings Institution, 1992.

Machinea, José Luis. *Stabilization under Alfonsín's Government: A Frustrated Attempt.* Buenos Aires: CEDES, 1990.

Majone, Giandomenico. *Evidence, Argument, and Persuasion in the Policy Process.* New Haven, Conn.: Yale University Press, 1989.

Manzetti, Luigi. "Institutional Decay and Distributional Coalitions in Developing Countries: The Argentine Riddle Reconsidered." *Studies in Comparative International Development* 29, no. 2 (Summer 1994): 82–114.

——. "The Political Economy of Privatization through Divestiture in Lesser Developed Economies." *Comparative Politics* 25, no. 4 (July 1993): 429–454.

——. *Institutions, Parties, and Coalitions in Argentine Politics.* Pittsburgh: University of Pittsburgh Press, 1993.

Manzetti, Luigi, and Charles H. Blake. "Market Reforms and Corruption in Latin America: New Means for Old Ways." *Review of International Political Economy* 3, no. 4 (Winter 1996): 662–697.

March, James G., and Johan P. Olsen. *Rediscovering Institutions: The Organizational Basis of Politics.* New York: Free Press, 1989.

Mares, David. "Explaining Choice of Development Strategies: Suggestions from Mexico, 1970–1982." *International Organization* 39 (Autumn 1985): 667–697.

Margheritis, Ana. "Implementing Structural Adjustment in Argentina: The Politics of Privatization." Ph.D. diss., University of Toronto, 1997.

Marichal, Carlos. "The Rapid Rise of the *Neobanqueros,* Mexico's New Financial Elite." *NACLA Report on the Americas* 30, no. 6 (May–June 1997): 27–31.

Martínez, Gabriel, and Guillermo Fárber, eds. *Desregulación económica (1989–1993): Una visión de la modernización de México.* México, D.F.: Fondo de la Cultura Económica, 1994.

Martino, Orlando, Jerome Machamer, and Ivette Torres. *The Mineral Economy of Mexico.* Washington, D.C.: United States Department of the Interior, Bureau of Mines, 1992.

May, Judith V., and Aaron Wildavsky, eds. *The Policy Cycle.* Beverly Hills, Calif.: Sage, 1978.

McCoy, Terry L. "A Paradigmatic Analysis of Mexican Population Policy." In *The Dynamics of Population Policy in Latin America,* edited by Terry L. McCoy, 377–408. Cambridge, Mass.: Ballinger, 1974.

McDonald, Terrance J. "Institutionalism and Institutions in the Stream of History." *Polity* 28, no. 1 (Fall 1995): 129–133.

McGuire, James W. "Political Parties and Democracy in Argentina." In *Building Democratic Institutions: Party Systems in Latin America,* edited by Scott Mainwaring and Timothy R. Scully, 200–246. Stanford, Calif.: Stanford University Press, 1995.

Menéndez Garza, Fernando. "Mexico City's Program to Reduce Air Pollution." In *Economic Development and Environmental Protection in Latin America,* edited by Joseph S. Tulchin, 103–107. Boulder, Colo.: Lynne Rienner, 1991.

Middlebrook, Kevin J. *The Paradox of Revolution: Labor, the State, and Authoritarianism in Mexico.* Baltimore, Md.: Johns Hopkins University Press, 1995.

——. "State-Labor Relations in Mexico: The Changing Economic and Political Context." In *Unions, Workers, and the State in Mexico,* edited by Kevin J. Middlebrook, 1–25. La Jolla, Calif.: Center for U.S.-Mexican Studies, University of California, San Diego, 1991.

Miller, Bradley P. "*Obedezco, Pero No Cumplo:* Law, Transportation, Politics, and Pollution in Mexico City." *Stanford Journal of International Law* 28, no. 1 (Fall 1991): 173–246.

Moe, Terry M. "Political Institutions: The Neglected Side of the Story." *Journal of Law, Economics, and Organization* 6 (1990): 213–253.

———. "The Politics of Bureaucratic Structure." In *Can the Government Govern?* edited by John E. Chubb and Paul E. Peterson, 267–329. Washington, D.C.: Brookings Institution, 1989.

Monge, Raúl. "Ní siquiera planes contra la contaminación existen, reconoce Sedue." *Proceso* 482 (January 27, 1986).

Moore, Mick. "Leading the Left to the Right: Populist Coalitions and Economic Reform." *World Development* 25 (1997): 1009–1028.

Moorman, Robert W. "Privatization in Mexico Revisited." *Air Transport World* 28, no. 12 (1991): 94–95.

Moreno, José Luis. "Efectos laborales de la política de modernización en Cananea." In *Modernización legislación laboral en el noreste de México,* edited by Felipe Mora and Victor Manuel Reynosa, 268–295. Hermosillo, Sonora, México: El Colegio de Sonora, 1990.

Morris, Stephen D. *Political Reformism in Mexico: An Overview of Contemporary Mexican Politics.* Boulder, Colo.: Lynne Rienner, 1995.

Mumme, Stephen P. "The Cananea Copper Controversy: Lessons for Environmental Diplomacy." *Journal of Inter-American Economic Affairs* 38, no. 1 (Summer 1984): 3–22.

Mumme, Stephen, C. Richard Bath, and Valerie J. Assetto. "Political Development and Environmental Policy in Mexico." *Latin American Research Review* 23, no. 1 (1988): 7–34.

Murillo, M. Victoria. "Union Politics, Market-Oriented Reforms, and the Reshaping of Argentine Corporatism." In *The New Politics of Inequality in Latin America: Rethinking Participation and Representation,* edited by Douglas A. Chalmers, et al., 72–94. New York: Oxford University Press, 1997.

Naim, Moisés. "Latin America's Journey to the Market: From Macroeconomic Shocks to Institutional Therapy," *ICEG Occasional Paper* 62. International Center for Economic Growth. San Francisco: ICS Press, 1995.

———. *Paper Tigers and Minotaurs: The Politics of Venezuela's Economic Reforms.* Washington, D.C.: Carnegie Endowment for International Peace, 1993.

Nelson, Joan M. "The Politics of Economic Transformation: Is Third World Experience Relevant to Eastern Europe?" *World Politics* 45 (April 1993): 433–463.

———. "Poverty, Equity, and the Politics of Adjustment." In *The Politics of Economic Adjustment: International Constraints, Distributive Conflicts, and the State,* edited by Stephan Haggard and Robert R. Kaufman, 221–269. Prince-ton, N.J.: Princeton University Press, 1992.

———. "Introduction: The Politics of Economic Adjustment in Developing Nations." In *Economic Crisis and Policy Choice: The Politics of Adjustment in the Third World,* edited by Joan Nelson, 3–32. Princeton, N.J.: Princeton University Press, 1990.

———. "Conclusions." In *Economic Crisis and Policy Choice: The Politics of Adjustment in the Third World,* edited by Joan M. Nelson, 321–361. Prince-ton, N.J.: Princeton University Press, 1990.

———. ed. *Fragile Coalitions: The Politics of Economic Adjustment.* New Brunswick, N.J.: Transaction Books, 1989.

————. ed. *Economic Crisis and Policy Choice: The Politics of Adjustment in the Third World.* Princeton, N.J.: Princeton University Press, 1990.

News (Mexico City), September 22, 1997.

————. (Mexico City), April 8, 1992.

————. (Mexico City), February 2, 1992.

————. (Mexico City), June 15, 1990.

New York Times, September 12, 1997.

————. September 23, 1996.

————. November 28, 1988.

Nino, Carlos Santiago. "Hyperpresidentialism and Constitutional Reform in Argentina." In *Institutional Design in New Democracies: Eastern Europe and Latin America,* edited by Arend Lijphart and Carlos H. Waisman, 161–174. Boulder, Colo.: Westview, 1996.

North, Douglass C. "Privatization, Incentives, and Economic Performance." In *The Privatization Process: A World Perspective,* edited by Terry L. Anderson and Peter J. Hill, 25–37. Lanham, Md.: Rowman & Littlefield, 1996.

————. *Institutions, Institutional Change, and Economic Performance.* New York: Cambridge University Press, 1990.

Novedades (Mexico City), January 2, 1991.

————. (Mexico City), September 7, 1990.

————. (Mexico City), May 5, 1988.

Nuccio, Richard A. "The Possibilities and Limits of Environmental Protection in Mexico." In *Economic Development and Environmental Protection in Latin America,* edited by Joseph S. Tulchin, 109–122. Boulder, Colo.: Lynne Rienner, 1991.

Ocampo, Emilio. "Atmospheric Pollution from Transport Sources in Mexico City." In *Applying Economic Instruments to Environmental Policies in OECD and Dynamic Non-member Economies,* 231–250. Paris: OECD, 1994.

O'Donnell, Guillermo. "Corporatism and the Question of the State." In *Authoritarianism and Corporatism in Latin America,* edited by James M. Malloy, 47–87. Pittsburgh: University of Pittsburgh Press, 1977.

Ojeda Mestre, Ramón. "Notas sobre Legislación Mexicana Referentes a la Contaminación." Paper presented to the Standing Committee on Environmental Law of the American Bar Association and the Asociación Mexicana de Abogados, Mexico City, June 2–3, 1983.

Olson, Mancur. *The Logic of Collective Action: Public Goods and the Theory of Groups.* Cambridge, Mass.: Harvard University Press, 1965.

Önis, Ziya. "Privatization and the Logic of Coalition Building: A Comparative Analysis of State Divestiture in Turkey and the United Kingdom." *Comparative Political Studies* 24, no. 2 (July 1991): 231–253.

Organization of Economic Cooperation and Development. *OECD and the Environment.* Paris: OECD, 1986.

————. *The Polluter Pays Principle.* Paris: OECD, 1975.

Ortega Pizarro, Fernando. "Los soldados, para anunciar que Cananea había sido declarada en quiebra." *Proceso* 669 (August 28, 1989).

Pablo Saba, Roberto and Luigi Manzetti. "Privatization in Argentina: The Implications for corruption." *Crime, Law, and Social Change* 25 (1997): 353–369.

Panayotou, Theodore. "Economic Incentives in Environmental Management and Their Relevance to Developing Countries." In *Environmental Management in Developing Countries,* edited by Denizhan Eröcal, 83–123. Paris: OECD, 1991.

Pássara, Luis. "El Rol del Parlamento: Argentina y Perú." *Desarrollo Económico* 32, no. 128 (January–March 1993): 603–623.

Pastor, Jr., Manuel, and Carol Wise. "Mexican-Style Neoliberalism, State Policy and Distributional Stress." In *The Post-NAFTA Political Economy: Mexico and the Western Hemisphere,* edited by Carol Wise, 41–81. University Park, Penn.: Pennsylvania State University Press, 1998.

———. "The Origins and Sustainability of Mexico's Free Trade Policy." *International Organization* 48 no. 3 (1994): 459–489.

Patiño, Gustavo. "Evolución y Perspectivas del Transporte en México." Speech delivered at the Second Binational Transportation Conference, "United States-Mexico Transport '92." Acapulco, March 1992.

Peralta-Ramos, Monica. *The Political Economy of Argentina: Power and Class since 1930.* Boulder, Colo.: Westview, 1992.

Perrow, Charles. "Departmental Power and Perspective in Industrial Firms." In *Power in Organizations,* edited by Mayer Zald, 59–89. Nashville, Tenn.: Vanderbilt University Press, 1972.

Petrazzini, Ben. "Telephone Privatization in a Hurry: Argentina." In *Privatising Monopolies: Lessons from the Telecommunications and Transport Sectors in Latin America,* edited by Ravi Ramamurti, 108–145. Baltimore, Md.: Johns Hopkins University Press, 1996.

Petrocolla, Alberto, Alberto Porto, and Pablo Gerchunoff. "Privatization in Argentina." *Quarterly Review of Economics and Finance* 33 (1993): 67–93.

Pfeffer, Jeffery, and Gerald R. Salancik. *The External Control of Organizations.* New York: Harper & Row, 1978.

Pierson, Paul. *Dismantling the Welfare State? Reagan, Thatcher, and the Politics of Retrenchment.* New York: Cambridge University Press, 1994.

———. "When Effect Becomes Cause: Policy Feedback and Political Change." *World Politics* 45 (July 1993): 595–628.

Piñera, José. "Chile." In *The Political Economy of Policy Reform,* edited by John Williamson, 225–231. Washington, D.C.: Institute for International Economics, 1994.

Pion-Berlin, David. *Through Corridors of Power: Institutions and Civil-Military Relations in Argentina.* University Park, Penn.: Pennsylvania State University Press, 1997.

Poder Ejecutivo, Presidencia de la República. *Convenio de concertación para acelerar la lucha contra la contaminación ambiental en el Valle de México.* México, D.F.: Poder Ejecutivo, Presidencia de la República, 1992.

Poitras, Guy E. "Welfare Bureaucracy and Clientele Politics in Mexico," *Administrative Science Quarterly* 18 (March 1973): 18–26.

Polsby, Nelson. *Political Innovation in America: The Politics of Policy Initiation.* New Haven, Conn.: Yale University Press, 1984.

Presidencia de la República. *El Gobierno Mexicano,* no. 57. México, D.F.: Presidencia de la República, 1993.

———. *La preservación del medio ambiente: Una acción estratégica.* México, D.F.: Presidencia de la República, 1989.

———. *Las razones y las obras, gobierno de Miguel de la Madrid: Crónica del sexenio 1982–1988,* vol. 6. México, D.F.: Presidencia de la República, Fondo de Cultura Económica, 1988.

———. *The Mexican Agenda,* 13th ed. México, D.F.: Presidencia de la República, July 1992.

"Privatizaciones: Un Camino de Regreso," *Época* (Mexico City), November 18, 1991.

Project 88—Round II: Incentives for Action: Designing Market-Based Environmental Strategies. A Public Policy Study sponsored by Senator Timothy E. Wirth and Senator John Heinz. Washington, D.C.: n.p., May 1991.

Przeworski, Adam. "Some Problems in the Study of the Transition to Democracy." In *Transitions from Authoritarian Rule: Comparative Perspectives,* edited by Guillermo O'Donnell, Philippe C. Schmitter, and Laurence Whitehead, 47–63. Baltimore, Md.: Johns Hopkins University Press, 1986.

Purcell, John F. H., and Susan Kaufman Purcell. "Mexican Business and Public Policy." In *Authoritarianism and Corporatism in Latin America,* edited by James M. Malloy, 191–226. Pittsburgh, Penn.: University of Pittsburgh Press, 1977.

Purcell, Susan Kaufman. *The Mexican Profit-Sharing Decision: Politics in an Authoritarian Regime.* Berkeley, Calif.: University of California Press, 1975.

———. "Business-Government Relations in Mexico: The Case of the Sugar Industry," *Comparative Politics* 13 (1981): 211–231.

Quadri de la Torre, Gabriel. "Una breve crónica del ecologismo en México." *Ciencias* 4 (1990): 56–64.

Quintana López, Enrique. "La bancarrota de Fundidora: Dimes y diretes financieros." *El Cotidiano* 3 (1986).

Rausch, Alejandro E. "Privatization in Argentina." In *Constraints and Impacts of Privatization,* edited by V. V. Ramanadham, 166–196. New York: Routledge, 1993.

"Reestructuración Financiera de las Mineras Cananea y La Caridad." *Mercado de Valores* 13 (July 1, 1988): 10, 14.

Review of the River Plate (February 15, 1991).

Rey Romayo, Benito. *La ofensiva empresarial contra la intervención del estado,* Anexo Informativo. México, D.F.: Siglo Veintiuno Editores, 1984.

Rico Galeana, Oscar Armando. *Regulación y desregulación del servicio de autotransporte de carga.* Querétero, México: Instituto Mexicano del Transporte, 1992.

Riker, William H. *The Art of Political Manipulation.* New Haven, Conn.: Yale University Press, 1986.

———. *The Theory of Political Coalitions.* New Haven, Conn.: Yale University Press, 1962.

Riner, Deborah L., and John V. Sweeney. "The Effects of NAFTA on Mexico's Private Sector and Foreign Trade and Investment." In *Mexico's Private Sector: Recent History, Future Challenges,* edited by Riordan Roett, 161–187. Boulder, Colo.: Lynne Rienner, 1998.

Rodrik, Dani. "Understanding Economic Policy Reform." *Journal of Economic Literature* 34 (March 1996): 9–41.

Rogozinski, Jacques. *La privatización de empresas paraestatales.* México, D.F.: Fondo de Cultura Económica, 1993.

Ronfeldt, David. *Wither Elite Cohesion in Mexico: A Comment,* P-7509. Santa Monica: RAND Corporation, 1988.

Ros, Jaime. "Mexico in the 1990s: A New Economic Miracle? Some Notes on the Economic and Policy Legacies of the 1980s." In *The Politics of Economic Restructuring: State-Society Relations and Regime Change in Mexico,* edited by Maria Lorena Cook, Kevin J. Middlebrook, and Juan Molinar Horcasitas, 67–103. La Jolla, Calif.: Center for U.S.-Mexican Studies, University of California, San Diego, 1994.

Rubio, Luis. "Coping with Political Change." In *Mexico under Zedillo,* edited by Susan Kaufman Purcell and Luis Rubio, 5–36. Boulder, Colo.: Lynne Rienner, 1998.

Ruiz Harrel, Rafael. *Historia general de México*, vol. 2. México, D.F.: El Colegio de México, 1976.

Russell, Phillip. *Mexico in Transition*. Austin, Tex.: Colorado River Press, 1977.

Sachs, Jeffrey. "Life in the Economic Emergency Room." In *The Political Economy of Policy Reform*, edited by John Williamson, 501–523. Washington, D.C.: Institute for International Economics, 1994.

Salinas de Gortari, Carlos. *Quinto Informe de Gobierno*, Anexo. México, D.F.: Presidencia de la República, 1993.

———. *Segundo informe de Gobierno*, Anexo. México, D.F.: Presidencia de la República, 1990.

———. *The Mexico We Want by 1994*. México, D.F.: Presidencia de la República, 1989.

———. *Mensaje de Toma de Posesión*. México, D.F. Presidencia de la República, December 1, 1988.

———. *Reforming the State*. México, D.F.: Presidencia de la República, n.d.

"Salinas Strikes before the Miners Can." *Business Week*, September 4, 1989.

Samstad, James G., and Ruth Berins Collier. "Mexican Labor and Structural Reform under Salinas: New Unionism or Old Stalemate?" In *The Challenge of Institutional Reform in Mexico*, edited by Riordan Roett, 9–37. Boulder, Colo.: Lynne Rienner, 1995.

Sánchez, Manuel, et al. "The Privatization Process in Mexico: Five Case Studies." In *Privatization in Latin America*, edited by Manuel Sánchez and Rossana Corona, 101–199. Washington, D.C.: Inter-American Development Bank, 1993.

———. *El proceso de privatización en México: Un estudio de casos*. México, D.F.: Centro de Analisis e Investigación Económica, 1992.

Sariego, Juan Luis, et al. *El Estado y la minería mexicana: Política, trabajo y sociedad durante el siglo XX*. México, D.F.: Fondo de Cultura Económica, 1988.

Schamis, Hector E. "The Politics of Economic Reform: Distributional Coalitions and Policy Change in Latin America." *Working Paper* 250. Notre Dame, Ind.: Helen Kellogg Institute for International Studies, University of Notre Dame, 1998.

Schattschneider, E. E. *The Semisovereign People: A Realist's View of Democracy in America*. Hinsdale, Ill.: Dryden Press, 1960.

———. *Politics, Pressures, and the Tariff*. New York: Prentice Hall, 1935.

Schmitter, Philippe C. "Still the Century of Corporatism?" In *The New Corporatism: Social–Political Structures in the Iberian World*, edited by Fredrick B. Pike and Thomas Stritch, 85–131. Notre Dame, Ind.: University of Notre Dame Press, 1974.

Schneider, Ben Ross. "Big Business and the Politics of Reform: Confidence and Concertation in Brazil and Mexico." In *Business and the State in Developing Countries*, edited by Sylvia Maxfield and Ben Ross Schneider, 191–215. Ithaca, N.Y.: Cornell University Press, 1997.

Schteingart, Martha. "The Environmental Problems Associated with Urban Development in Mexico City." *Environment and Urbanization* 1, no. 1 (April 1989): 40–50.

Secretaría de Comunicaciones y Transportes. *Estadísticas Básicas del Auto-transporte Federal*. México, D.F.: Secretaría de Comunicaciones y Transportes, 1991.

———. *Convenio de concertación para la modernización del autotransporte federal de carga*. México, D.F.: Secretaría de Comunicaciones y Transportes, 1989.

———. *Programa para el autotransporte federal de carga*. México, D.F.: Secretaría de Comunicaciones y Transportes, May 1989.

———. *Desregulación del transporte*. México, D.F.: Secretaría de Comunicaciones y Transportes, n.d.

Secretaría de Desarrollo Urbano y Ecología. *Programa nacional para la protección del medio ambiente 1990–1994.* México, D.F.: Secretaría de Desarrollo Urbano y Ecología, 1990.

———. *Políticas y estratégias de abatimiento y control de la contaminación atmosférica en la zona metropolitana de la Ciudad de México, Memoria.* México, D.F.: Secretaría de Desarrollo Urbano y Ecología, 1988.

———. *Memoria del Primer Seminario Internacional Sobre Administración de la Calidad del Aire.* México, D.F.: Secretaría de Desarrollo Urbano y Ecología, 1987.

Secretaría de Desarrollo Urbano y Ecología, Petróleos Mexicanos, Gobierno del Estado de México, Departamento del Distrito Federal. *Programa integral de lucha contra la contaminación en el Valle de México.* México, D.F.: Secretaría de Desarrollo Urbano y Ecología, Petróleos Mexicanos, Gobierno del Estado de México, Departamento del Distrito Federal, 1989.

Secretaría de Energía, Minas e Industria Paraestatales. "La Semip ante la LII Legislatura." *Cuaderno de Divulgación* 24. México, D.F.: Secretaría de Energía, Minas e Industria Paraestatales, 1984.

Secretaría de Hacienda y Crédito Público. *El proceso de enajenación de entidades paraestatales.* México, D.F.: Secretaría de Hacienda y Crédito Público, 1992.

———. *The Divestiture Process in Mexico.* México, D.F.: Secretaría de Hacienda y Crédito Público, 1991.

———. *Reglamento interior de la Secretaría de Hacienda y Crédito Público.* México, D.F.: Secretaría de Hacienda y Crédito Público, 1990.

Secretaría de Programación y Presupuesto. *Plan Nacional de Desarrollo 1989–1994.* México, D.F.: Secretaría de Programación y Presupuesto, 1989.

———. *Plan Nacional de Desarrollo 1983–1988.* México, D.F.: Secretaría de Programación y Presupuesto, 1983.

Secretaría del Trabajo y Previsión Social. *Acuerdos para fijar las condiciones en que habrán de reanudarse las labores en la Compañía Minera de Cananea.* México, D.F.: Secretaría del Trabajo y Previsión Social, 1989.

Semo, Ilán. "The Mexican Political Pretransition in Comparative Perspective." In *Neoliberalism Revisited: Economic Restructuring and Mexico's Political Future,* edited by Gerardo Otero, 107–126. Boulder, Colo.: Westview, 1996.

Shepsle, Kenneth A. "Studying Institutions: Some Lessons from the Rational Choice Approach." *Journal of Theoretical Politics* 1, no. 2 (1989): 131–147.

Shirley, Mary M. "Privatization in Latin America: Lessons for Transitional Europe." *World Development* 22, no. 9 (1994): 1313–1323.

Siderúrgica Lázaro Cárdenas–Las Truchas. *Sicartsa, Crisol de México.* Lázaro Cárdenas, Michoacán, México: Siderúrgica Lázaro Cárdenas-Las Truchas, S.A., 1986.

Siegle, Candace. "A City Drowning in Smog." *South,* February 1991.

Sikkink, Kathryn. *Ideas and Institutions: Developmentalism in Brazil and Argentina.* Ithaca, N.Y.: Cornell University Press, 1991.

Simon, Herbert A. *Administrative Behavior,* 2d ed. New York: Free Press, 1957.

Skocpol, Theda. "Bringing the State Back In: Strategies of Analysis in Current Research." In *Bringing the State Back In,* edited by Peter Evans, Dietrich Rueschemeyer, and Theda Skocpol, 3–37. New York: Cambridge University Press, 1985.

Skocpol, Theda, and Kenneth Finegold. "State Capacity and Economic Intervention in the Early New Deal." *Political Science Quarterly* 97 (1983): 256–278.

Skowronek, Stephen. *Building a New American State: The Expansion of National Administrative Capacities, 1877–1920.* New York: Cambridge University Press, 1982.

Smith, Peter H. *Labyrinths of Power: Political Recruitment in Twentieth-Century Mexico.* Princeton, N.J.: Princeton University Press, 1979.

———. "Does Mexico Have a Power Elite?" In *Authoritarianism in Mexico,* edited by José Luis Reyna and Richard S. Weinert, 129–151. Philadelphia, Penn.: Institute for the Study of Human Issues, 1977.

Smith, William C. "State, Market, and Neoliberalism in Post-Transition Argentina: The Menem Experiment." *Journal of Interamerican Studies and World Affairs* 33, no. 4 (Winter 1991): 45–82.

Solanet, Manuel A. "Privatization: The Long Road to Success in Argentina." *Business Forum* 19, nos. 1-2 (Winter–Spring 1994): 28–31.

Sonnichsen, C. L. *Colonel Greene and the Copper Skyrocket.* Tucson, Ariz.: University of Arizona Press, 1974.

Spalding, Rose. "The Mexican Variant of Corporatism." *Comparative Political Studies* 14 (July 1981): 139–161.

Stallings, Barbara. "International Influence on Economic Policy: Debt, Stabilization, and Structural Reform." In *The Politics of Economic Adjustment,* edited by Stephan Haggard and Robert R. Kaufman, 41–82. Princeton, N.J.: Princeton University Press, 1992.

Starr, Pamela K. "Government Coalitions and the Viability of Currency Boards: Argentina under the Cavallo Plan." *Journal of Interamerican Studies and World Affairs* 39, no. 2 (Summer 1992): 83–133.

Steinmo, Sven. "Political Institutions and Tax Policy in the United States, Sweden, and Britain." *World Politics* 41 (July 1989): 500–535.

Steinmo, Sven, Kathleen Thelen, and Frank Longstreth, eds. *Structuring Politics: Historical Institutionalism in Comparative Analysis.* New York: Cambridge University Press, 1992.

Stevens, Evelyn P. "Mexico's PRI: The Institutionalization of Corporatism?" In *Authoritarianism and Corporatism in Latin America,* edited by James M. Malloy, 227–258. Pittsburgh, Penn.: University of Pittsburgh Press, 1977.

Stigler, George J. "The Theory of Economic Regulation." *Bell Journal of Economics and Management Science* 2, no. 1 (Spring 1971): 3–21.

Stinchcombe, Arthur L. *Constructing Social Theories.* Chicago: University of Chicago Press, 1968.

Story, Dale. *The Mexican Ruling Party: Stability and Authority.* Stanford, Calif.: Hoover Institution, 1986.

Suleiman, Ezra N., and John Waterbury. "Introduction: Analyzing Privatization in Industrial and Developing Countries." In *The Political Economy of Public Sector Reform and Privatization,* edited by Ezra N. Suleiman and John Waterbury, 1–21. Boulder, Colo.: Westview, 1990.

Tandon, Pankaj. *Welfare Consequences of Selling Public Enterprises, Case Studies from Chile, Malaysia, Mexico and the U.K., Mexico: Aeroméxico, Mexicana,* 2. Washington, D.C.: The World Bank, 1992.

Teichman, Judith A. "Mexico and Argentina: Economic Reform and Technocratic Decision Making." *Studies in Comparative International Development* 32, no. 1 (Spring 1997): 31–55.

———. "Economic Restructuring, State-Labor Relations, and the Transformation of Mexican Corporatism." In *Neoliberalism Revisited: Economic Restructuring and Mexico's*

Political Future, edited by Gerardo Otero, 149–166. Boulder, Colo.: Westview, 1996.

————. *Privatization and Political Change in Mexico.* Pittsburgh, Penn.: University of Pittsburgh Press, 1995.

Texas-Mexico Multimodal Transportation, A Report by the Policy Research Project on Texas/ Northern Mexico Infrastructure and Free Trade. Austin, Tex.: Lyndon B. Johnson School of Public Affairs, University of Texas at Austin, 1993.

Texas-Mexico Transborder Transportation System: Regulatory and Infrastructure Obstacles To Free Trade. Austin, Tex.: Lyndon B. Johnson School of Public Affairs, University of Texas at Austin, 1991.

Thompson, James D. *Organizations in Action.* New York: McGraw-Hill, 1967.

Thorp, Rosemary. *Progress, Poverty, and Exclusion: An Economic History of Latin America in the Twentieth Century.* Washington, D.C.: Inter-American Development Bank, 1998.

Thwaites Rey, Mabel, José Castillo, and Andrea López. "La regulación de los servicios públicos privatizados." *Realidad Económica* 129 (January–February 1995): 63–84.

Tichy, Noel M., and Charles Fombrun. "Network Analysis in Organizational Settings." *Human Relations* 32, no. 11 (1979): 923–965.

"Transferencia de Empresas con Participación Accionaria de Nacional Financiera." *Mercado de Valores* 3 (February 1988).

Trejo, Guillermo, and Claudio Jones. "Political Dilemmas of Welfare Reform: Poverty and Inequality in Mexico." In *Mexico under Zedillo,* edited by Susan Kaufman Purcell and Luis Rubio, 67–99. Boulder, Colo.: Lynne Rienner, 1998.

United Nations. *Population Growth and Policies in Mega-Cities: Mexico City.* New York: United Nations, 1991.

United States Agency for International Development. *Energy and Environment Market Conditions in Mexico.* Washington, D.C.: U.S. Agency for International Development, n.d.

United States Environmental Protection Agency. *Mexican Environmental Laws, Regulations, and Standards: Preliminary Report of EPA Findings.* Washington, D.C.: Environmental Protection Agency, May 3, 1991, revised June 27, 1991.

United States International Trade Commission. *Review of Trade and Investment Liberalization Measures by Mexico and Prospects for Future United States-Mexican Relations,* Investigation No. 332–282, U.S.I.T.C. Publication 2275. Washington, D.C.: United States International Trade Commission, 1991.

Uno Mas Uno (Mexico City), September 7, 1990.

Urrutia, Miguel. "Colombia." In *The Political Economy of Policy Reform,* edited by John Williamson, 285–315. Washington, D.C.: Institute for International Economics, 1994.

"The U.S. Debate over the Environmental Performance of Four Multilateral Development Banks." *Ambio* 15, no. 5 (1986): 291–295.

Vacs, Aldo C. "Authoritarian Breakdown and Redemocratization in Argentina." In *Authoritarians and Democrats: Regime Transition in Latin America,* edited by James M. Malloy and Mitchell A. Seligson, 15–42. Pittsburgh, Penn.: University of Pittsburgh Press, 1987.

Van de Walle, Nicolas. "Privatization in Developing Countries: A Review of the Issues." *World Development* 17, no. 5 (1989): 601–615.

Van Meter, D., and C. Van Horn. "The Policy Implementation Process: A Conceptual Framework." *Administration and Society* 6 (1975): 445–488.

Vázquez Rubio, Pilar. "El plan de mejoramiento del servicio en Aeroméxico." *El Cotidiano* 21 (January–February 1988).

Vázquez Talavera, César. *La reconversión industrial en la aviación comercial.* México, D.F.: Universidad Autónomo Metropolitano, Xtapalapa, 1992.

———. "La aviación: una reconversión en los aires." *El Cotidiano* 46 (March–April 1992).

Velázquez, Enrique. "Política Ecología Institucional: El Caso del Valle de México." *El Cotidiano* 47 (May 1990).

Vera, Rodrigo. "Manuel Camacho enfrenta la contaminación como un asunto de imagen." *Proceso* 738 (December 24, 1990).

Vera Ferrer, Oscar Humberto. "The Political Economy of Privatization in Mexico." In *Privatization of Public Enterprises in Latin America,* edited by William Glade, 35–57. San Francisco: ICS Press, 1991.

Villarreal, René. *Mitos y realidades de la empresa pública. ¿Racionalización o privatización?* México, D.F.: Editorial Diana, 1991.

———. "Industrial Restructuring of the Public Steel Industry: The Mexican Case." *Public Enterprise* 10, no. 3 (September–December 1990): 257–278.

Villegas, Daniel Cosio, ed. *Historia moderna de México: La vida económica.* México, D.F.: Editorial Hermes, 1965.

Voljc, Marko, and Joost Draaisma. "Privatization and Economic Stabilization in Mexico." *Columbia Journal of World Business* 28, no. 1 (March 1993): 123–133.

Voz de Michoacán (Lázaro Cárdenas, Mexico), September 7, 1991.

———. (Lázaro Cárdenas, Mexico), September 6, 1991.

———. (Lázaro Cárdenas, Mexico), August 31, 1991.

Vuylsteke, Charles. *Techniques of Privatization of State-Owned Enterprises,* vol. 1, *Methods and Implementation.* Washington, D.C.: The World Bank, 1988.

Waisman, Carlos. "Argentina: Autarkic Industrialization and Illegitimacy." In *Democracy in Developing Countries: Latin America,* edited by Larry Diamond, Juan Linz, and Seymour Martin Lipset, 59–109. Boulder, Colo.: Lynne Rienner, 1989.

Ward, Peter M. "Government without Democracy in Mexico City: Defending the High Ground." In *Mexico's Alternative Political Futures,* edited by Wayne A. Cornelius, Judith Gentleman, and Peter H. Smith, 307–323. La Jolla, Calif.: Center for U.S.-Mexican Studies, University of California, San Diego, 1989.

———. "The Politics of Planning in Mexico," *Third World Planning Review* 8 (August 1986): 219–235.

Waterbury, John. *Exposed to Innumerable Delusions: Public Enterprise and State Power in Egypt, India, Mexico, and Turkey.* New York: Cambridge University Press, 1993.

———. "The Heart of the Matter? Public Enterprise and the Adjustment Process." In *The Politics of Economic Adjustment,* edited by Stephan Haggard and Robert R. Kaufman, 182–217. Princeton, N.J.: Princeton University Press, 1992.

———. "The Political Context of Public Sector Reform and Privatization in Egypt, India, Mexico, and Turkey." In *The Political Economy of Public Sector Reform and Privatization,* edited by Ezra N. Suleiman and John Waterbury, 293–318. Boulder, Colo.: Westview Press 1990.

———. "The Political Management of Economic Adjustment and Reform." In *Fragile Coalitions: The Politics of Economic Adjustment,* edited by Joan M. Nelson, 39–56. Washington, D.C.: Overseas Development Council, 1989.

Weber, Max. *Economy and Society,* vol. 1. New York: Bedminster Press, 1968.

Weir, Margaret, Ann Shola Orloff, and Theda Skocpol. "Introduction: Understanding American Social Politics." In *The Politics of Social Policy in the United States,* edited by

Margaret Weir, Ann Shola Orloff, and Theda Skocpol, 3–35. Princeton, N.J.: Princeton University Press, 1988.

Weldon, Jeffrey. "The Political Sources of Presidencialismo in Mexico." In *Presidentialism and Democracy in Latin America,* edited by Scott Mainwaring and Matthew Soberg Shugart, 225–258. New York: Cambridge University Press, 1997.

Weyland, Kurt. "The Political Fate of Market Reform in Latin America, Africa, and Eastern Europe." *International Studies Quarterly* 42, no. 4 (December 1998): 645–674.

Whitehead, Laurence. "Political Change and Economic Stabilization: The 'Economic Solidarity Pact.'" In *Mexico's Alternative Political Futures,* edited by Wayne A. Cornelius, Judith Gentleman, and Peter H. Smith, 181–213. La Jolla, Calif.: Center for U.S.-Mexican Studies, University of California, San Diego, 1989.

Williamson, John, ed. *The Political Economy of Policy Reform.* Washington, D.C.: Institute for International Economics, 1994.

Williamson, John, and Stephan Haggard. "The Political Conditions for Economic Reform." In *The Political Economy of Policy Reform,* edited by John Williamson, 527–596. Washington, D.C.: Institute for International Economics, 1994.

Wilson, James Q. "The Rise of the Bureaucratic State." In *The American Commonwealth,* edited by Nathan Glazer and Irving Kristol, 77–103. New York: Basic Books, 1976.

World Bank. *World Data.* Washington, D.C.: World Bank, 1995.

———. *Argentina's Privatization Program: Experience, Issues, and Lessons.* Washington, D.C.: World Bank, 1993.

———. *Argentina: From Insolvency to Growth.* Washington, D.C.: World Bank, 1993.

———. *Argentina: Reforms for Price Stability and Growth.* Washington, D.C.: World Bank, 1990.

———. *Environment and Development: Implementing the World Bank's New Policies.* Washington, D.C.: World Bank, 1988.

Wynia, Gary W. *Argentina: Illusions and Realities,* 2d ed. New York: Holmes & Meier, 1992.

Index

adjustment arguments, 11–12, 200
Aerolineas Argentina, 176–78, 180, 182, 185
Aeroméxico Airline, 29, 60–63, 66–74, 77–78, 85; bankruptcy of, 71–73; and labor, 62, 67, 79–73; nationalization of, 67; privatization of, 68–73
AHMSA. *See* Altos Hornos de México
air pollution: causes of, 134–37, 142; and command and control policy, 139; and the Comprehensive Program against Air Pollution, 139–40; and environmental legislation, 137, 140; and policy reform, 143–44, 146–47, 153
Aldrich, Howard, 40
Alemán, Miguel, 84
Alfonsín, Raúl, 174, 177–78, 184; and civil–military relations, 177; privatization efforts of, 170, 175–78, 184–85, 187
Alford, Robert, 46
Altos Hornos de México (AHMSA), 84
Anaconda Copper, 75, 78
Ardito–Barletta, Nicolás, 204
Argentina: and civil–military relations, 177, 180; and corruption of privatization process, 180, 182; and economic crisis, 174–75, 177, 184; and political development of, 171; and transition to democracy, 171, 174
Aridjis, Homero, 150

ASPA. *See* Association of Aviator Pilots
Aspe, Pedro, 59, 70, 71n47, 73, 87, 89–92, 95, 148
ASSA. *See* Association of Aviation Flight Attendants
Association of Aviation Flight Attendants (ASSA), 70–73
Association of Aviator Pilots (ASPA), 70–72
Atlantic Richfield, 75
Autonomous Institute for Environmental Research, 150
autonomy arguments, 12–15, 200
Axelrod, Robert, 155

bankruptcy (quiebra): of Aeroméxico, 71–73; of Cananea, 80–83; as a privatization strategy, 73
Bates, Robert H., 10, 203
Belaustegüigoitia, Juan Carlos, 149–50
Bethlehem Steel, 84
bureaucratic politics, 10, 111, 116–17
bureaucratic veto: and deregulation, 119, 127, 203; and environmental policy, 144–45
Buy Argentine Law (Compre Argentino), 172, 178

Callaghy, Thomas, 181, 203
Camacho Solís, Manuel, 140–41, 146, 148, 150–53, 157–58

251

About the Author

A former National Science Foundation and Ford fellow, **Mark Williams** is associate professor of political science at Middlebury College, in Middlebury, Vermont.